Pioneers and Makers of Arkansas

By Josiah H. Shinn, A. M.

Member Imperial Russian Geographical Society, St. Petersburg; Member Imperial Russian Historical Society, St. Petersburg; Honorary Member of Pennsylvania and West Virginia Historical Societies; State Superintendent of Public Instruction, Arkansas, two terms; Chief Clerk, Office Secretary of State, three terms; President Southern Educational Association, two terms; Vice President National Educational Association; President Arkansas Educational Association; Judge Liberal Arts Department, World's Columbia Exposition, Chicago, Ill.; Accountant in Indian Office, Washington, D.C., and Chicago, Ill., three years; Founder of Southern School Journal; Author of "History of the American People," "History of Arkansas," "History of Education in Arkansas," published by the U. S. Government; "History of the Shinn Family in Europe and America," "U. S. Land Surveys," "History of Russia," "Russia at the World's Fair," published in English and Russian; "The Public School and the College," "The South in Public Education," "Vassar College," "Life and Public Services of Brigadier General Lewis G. Arnold;" Correspondent for many Societies and Publications, and founder of The Washington Literary Bureau

JANAWAY PUBLISHING, INC.
Santa Maria, California

Notice

In many older books, foxing (or discoloration) occurs and, in some instances, print lightens with wear and age. Reprinted books, such as this, often duplicate these flaws, notwithstanding efforts to reduce or eliminate them. The pages of this reprint have been digitally enhanced and, where possible, the flaws eliminated in order to provide clarity of content and a pleasant reading experience.

Copyright © 1908, M. C. Shinn

Originally published
Little Rock, Arkansas:
1908

Reprinted by:

Janaway Publishing, Inc.
732 Kelsey Ct.
Santa Maria, California 93454
(805) 925-1038
www.janawaygenealogy.com

2014

ISBN: 978-1-59641-316-0

Made in the United States of America

PREFACE

This modest volume does not deal with downfalls either of Roman or any other vaunted civilization or empire; it has nothing whatever to do with submergences, whether the thing overwhelmed be kingdom, satrapy or monarchy, Persian, Assyrian or Egyptian; it makes no vain appeals to the lessons of history and depends in no sense on industrial conformity to an organizing authority.

It will deal less with the permanency of our institutions than with the institutions themselves; less with methods than matter; less with evolution and law than with humanity. The modern scientific spirit with its crucifixon of thought and interest will be entirely and exclusively ignored.

This book will be devoted to the people, who fashioned and builded a State, and it makes not a raps difference to the author whether these people had Bagehot's conception, or Lubbock's conception of progress or not. It is enough for him to know that they were human beings,—that they lived and acted their parts,—and that all that they did contributed to everything that now prevails. They were here first and did their work as human beings unmanacled by science and formality and therefore interestingly. As men and women, they performed a life's work, died and were buried. They cleared farms, made roads and enacted laws—all for their own comfort and well-being—the highest end and aim of life. They seemed to know that by the sweat of their brows they should eat and that he who provided not for his own had denied the faith and was worse than an infidel. They sought to better their condition and laid by for a rainy day. They were your fathers and mine.

The aim of this book will be as Macaulay expressed it—"to make the past present, to bring the present near, to invest with the reality of human flesh and blood beings whom we are too much inclined to consider as personified qualities," rather than to rob history of its human element by a cataloguing of facts without effort to read their meaning. With Lord Acton, the sanest historic authority, we believe that "History is the conscience of mankind," and have therefore set out thousands of facts as a potent influence in showing what the pioneers really did—their modus operandi—their hopes, joys and sorrows, as parts of an experience we are interested to know and from which we may one and all draw general lessons of moral and political wisdom.

The book was made while busily engaged upon other matters—in fact, is the outgrowth of more pretentious historic study—but will not lose interest or value by reason thereof. It is the outgrowth of years of grubbing in old newspapers, old letters, old legal tomes, and documents, and of contact with graveyards, tombstones and death registers.

It is sent to the world with some misgivings but with a larger hopefulness. Scribbling in magazines run riot in misstatement, over-statement and folderol about the difference between the way we do things and the way in which our grandfathers did them. We are glibly told that a cabinet officer today does not only twice as much work as did his predecessor fifty years ago but that he does it twice as well. Our government officials are said to conduct the affairs of the people with a keener, greater business energy than they did in days of old, and we are expected to believe it. Our cabinet officers are globe trotters and runabouts—on exhibition everywhere under the ostensible plea of getting into closer touch with the bigger things of today. They splurge more but work and think less than did their predecessors—men who worked out the rules and regulations by which the real business of government is done at this good hour. The experience of one hundred years, crystallized into rules unequalled elsewhere in the world, is treated to the Don Quixotean lances of a Keep Comimssion or some other commission of fledgelings, whose only recommendation is noise. We are told that they are doing things and when the noise dies and cold reason returns, we find that they have simply brought a lot of changes without a single iota of improvement. Experience is more and more derided, and change is more and more taken for real evolution. We have a new Indian policy—a new land policy—a new fiscal policy, with every change in our cabinet officers and we are asked to believe that each of these new polices is an improvement on the old, simply because it comes heralded as a modern improvement, forgetting that every real improvement must come through the throes of a biting experience, and not through a mere political change of officers.

We undoubtedly do many things differently and better than did our fathers. We travel differently and better; we have a different and better physical light; we have different and better facilities of many kinds, but with all these differences and betterments, we are not doing more proportionately than did our grandfathers—and in many cases we are doing proportionately less. We have possibly more knowledge and it is intimated that we certainly have less wisdom; we have more preaching and less morality; more of the spectacular and less real productivity; more brag and less accomplishment. We have more goober grabblers on the surface but not an equal number of profound thinkers; more tinkerers but no greater number of real workers; more shouters but no greater number of real converts. We have more money and less conscience; more wealth and less restraint; more ease and less happiness. Our Bible is the same old book our fathers read but we have learned to skip the difficult lines. Our Cæsar is the same old story about Gaul but we have destroyed its hard places. Morality today is just what it always was but we have decked it with strange clothes. We have changed the material world and have improved it by the change, and with impious hands have claimed a like right to change the moral and spiritual world—to alter the unchangeable and limit the infinite.

We have done really great and wonderful things but in claiming credit for them we have slandered the dead and run rough shod over past greatness and goodness, without adding a particle to our real greatness or a single iota to our real goodness. We are really doing things—great and imperishable things—but we are the heirs of the ages—the recipients of centuries of experience, and should gratefully acknowledge our indebtedness.

All that is old is not good and all that is new is not bad. The fathers worked for better things and made material progress; we started where they left off but have by no means reached the goal. We are and ought to be proud of our age but this should not lead us to flippantly decry the majestic work of our fathers. I would have no man look backward for the mere glory of ancestral worship, nor pause a single instant in the real work of developing the world. I would only look back to catch the rays of the world's great lamp of experience, for without a genuine, real and hard experience there can be no lasting, permanent and general improvement. There is no sound method of judging the future but by the past, and with this thought as a basis, I launch my "Pioneers and Makers of Arkansas" with the hope that it may give courage to thinkers and workers everywhere and nerve them for a greater and more successful work.

JOSIAH H. SHINN.

Washington, D. C.,
October 1, 1908.

CONTENTS

Chapter 1.—The Formation of Arkansas Territory—The Foundation of the Arkansas Gazette—The Leading Men at Arkansas Post.... 9

Chapter 2.—Woodruff's Power at the Post—Early Post-Offices—The Original Spelling of the Word Arkansas...................... 15

Chapter 3.—Who's Who of Old Arkansas Post—French and American Settlers... 23

Chapter 4.—First Officers of the Territory—All Non-Residents....... 29

Chapter 5.—General Miller, Our First Territorial Governor—His Opinion of Early Little Rock—General Jackson's Opinion of General Miller 34

Chapter 6.—Early Settlers on the Rivers of Eastern Arkansas and on the Arkansas River.. 40

Chapter 7.—The Settlement of Crystal Hill—Pyeatts, Carnahans—Grays 45

Chapter 8.—Alexander S. Walker, Soldier, Lawyer and Legislator... 51

Chapter 9.—Robert Crittenden—William O. Allen—The First Duel in Arkansas 58

Chapter 10.—Samuel Mosely—Francis Notrebe—Terrance Farrelly.. 66

Chapter 11.—Pringles—Harringtons—Morrisons and Dardennes—List of Revolutionary Patriots.. 72

Chapter 12.—Samuel Calhoun Roane................................ 80

Chapter 13.—Shirt Sleeved Millionaires............................ 93

Chapter 14.—The Coming of the Covered Wagons.................. 102

Chapter 15.—Distribution of Settlements in 1820................... 109

Chapter 16—Benjamin Fooy and Fooy's Point—W. B. R. Horner—St. Francis and Helena.. 117

Chapter 17.—Great Cherokee Indian Agents—Matthew Lyon, Edward W. DuVal and David Brearly................................... 131

Chapter 18.—First Authentic Maps of the Territory showing Roads, Towns, County Lines and Streams.............................. 144

Chapter 19.—Longevity of the Pioneers—Some Old Marriages and Marriage Customs 157

Chapter 20.—Early Election Practises............................. 166

Chapter 21.—Governor George Izard.............................. 172

Chapter 22.—Robert Crittenden 179

Chapter 23.—Chester Ashley—Thomas Willoughby Newton......... 185

CONTENTS—Cont.

Chapter 24.—The Superior Court of Arkansas—Andrew Scott—Benjamin Johnson.. 195

Chapter 25.—Ambrose H. Sevier—William S. Fulton—Pre-emption.. 206

Chapter 26.—Joab Hardin—The Bentleys—Major Welborn—Abner Harold—Colonel Thomas Mathers—The Arkansas Traveler...... 217

Chapter 27—Rev. Cephas Washburn............................. 222

Chapter 28.—Major Isaac Watkins................................ 228

Chapter 29.—Slaveholders of 1830............................... 235

Chapter 30.—The Fletchers...................................... 240

Chapter 31.—Edmund Hogan.................................... 250

Chapter 32.—The Two P Architecture—The Martins............... 255

Chapter 33.—Henry L. Biscoe................................... 264

Chapter 34.—Caleb Lindsey—Other Lindsey Families.............. 269

Chapter 35.—The Brilhart and Davis Families—Marriages and Deaths 280

Chapter 36.—The Lafferty Family................................ 290

Chapter 37.—The Kaufmans, Coffmans and Cuffmans.............. 300

Chapter 38.—Augustus Hill Garland............................. 307

Chapter 39—The Deshas.. 331

Chapter 40.—Abraham Ruddell.................................. 338

Chapter 41.—The Wilson Family................................. 348

Chapter 42.—The Rector Family................................. 370

Pioneers and Makers of Arkansas

CHAPTER I.

THE FORMATION OF ARKANSAS TERRITORY—THE FOUNDATION OF THE ARKANSAS GAZETTE.—THE LEADING MEN AT ARKANSAS POST.

March 2, 1819, is a notable date for Arkansas, as on that day the president approved the bill which created the territory of Arkansas. The debate, which led up to the final vote in Congress, was more than usually dramatic and was participated in by Taylor of New York, Clay of Kentucky, Walter of North Carolina and McLane of Delaware. In Committee of the Whole House, Representative Taylor offered an amendment containing two divergent propositions;—one prohibited the further introduction of slavery into the territory, and the other provided for the emancipation of all negroes born in the territory after the expiration of twenty-five years. The speeches on one side bristled with arguments and fancies concerning free labor, its dignity and worth; the evils of slavery, its wastefulness, its slovenliness, and, greatest of all, its antagonism to pure reason and its incompatibility with free institutions.

On the other hand were arrayed arguments and fancies, showing the constitutional rights of slaveholders to travel at will carrying their chattels, the improved condition of the African in slavery as compared with his free condition in Africa, and brilliant exaggerations of plantation life.

CLOSE SHAVE FOR ADVOCATES OF SLAVERY.

The House of Representatives was about equally divided in sentiment. The amendment was divided and its first clause failed by a vote of seventy ayes to seventy-one noes; the second clause carried by a vote of seventy-five ayes to seventy-three noes. Thus the further introduction of slavery was permitted, but a gradual emancipation provided. This did not suit the framers of the bill and when it was reported to the house it was moved to refer it to a special committee with instructions to strike out the second clause. On this vote the ayes numbered eighty-eight and the noes numbered the same. The tie was broken by the vote of the speaker in the affirmative. When the special committee reported back, the vote upon concurrence stood eighty-nine ayes to eighty-seven noes. It was a close shave, but the advocates of slavery won. Suppose the vote had been registered the other way on one or both these propositions, what would have been the result upon Arkansas affairs? Who can answer the question with any assurance of accuracy? Missouri would have been admitted as a free State beyond all question and the line between the free and slave territories in the West would have been drawn much farther to the South. But what of its influence on after Arkansas history? Would the hands of the Arkansas development clock have gone forward or backward? There are two sides to the question, but it is not outside the realm of sound prediction to say that the victory of the South in Congress in 1819 was a stumbling block to the rapid development of the territory.

This congressional debate presaged the dawn of limitations upon the slave power, which found legal status when Missouri was admitted as a State, and sounded the eventual death knell of slavery throughout the country.

The discussion showed that little or nothing was known about the population of the State, or its resources. The committee which reported the bill ignored these questions and the disputants were without facts. Some one from Missouri suggested that there might be fourteen thousand people in the proposed territory and the speakers adopted this unit of measurement, and it has ever since remained unquestioned. The real population was nearer ten thousand than fourteen thousand, as we shall show in another chapter upon the census of 1820, the first enrollment of the pioneers as Arkansans.

BIRTH OF ARKANSAS TERRITORY.

July 4, 1819, was another notable date for Arkansas, as on that day, under the provisions of the act of March 2, 1819,

Arkansas territory was legally born, with its capital at Arkansas, as the Post of Arkansas was called.

October 30, 1819, was another notable date, indicating the arrival of William E. Woodruff at Arkansas with his printing press.

BIRTH OF THE GAZETTE.

The greatest date for Arkansas history, however, is November 20, 1819, the date when the first issue of the Arkansas Gazette made its appearance at Arkansas.

Other events have had a more or less marked influence on Arkansas men and affairs, and their dates have become monumental landmarks signaling the student to corner-stones of political growth,—bases from which new bearings are to be made. But towering over all these, in both absolute and relative importance, must be rated the first issue of the Arkansas Gazette, the initial beacon of a greater intelligence, the first headlight of a greater progress, and the commanding index to the march of improvement and power.

William E. Woodruff lacked the higher forms of education, was not blessed or burdened with wealth, but was the happy possessor of a trade. He had something which he could do, and he had that something well in hand. Opportunity in 1819 seemed to have her habitat in the West and the sons of the East were seduced by her call. It has been said that the energetic sons of the East went West at that time, while the drones remained at home. This is a superficial showing, however, as a very slight acquaintance with affairs will demonstrate that these stay-at-home drones had energy enough to take care of the East and place mortgages on the seemingly greater energies of the West.

WHEN OPPORTUNITY WHISPERED.

Woodruff had a trade, but no location. He might have worked at the cases in New York and made a competence. Opportunity whispered that the West was a better field and Woodruff inclined his ear. He found nothing that promised at Wheeling, at Louisville, at Russellville, or at Nashville. It seemed that he had been beguiled by a siren voice and that the West was not what it had been painted. Panegyric has lauded his rowing a boat from Wheeling to Louisville, and his walking from Louisville to Nashville. This is superficial also, as the common heritage of men at that time was to row or walk. All pioneers could do either, and it was a poor specimen of manhood that would hitch up a team to go ten miles. Walking was in vogue and its devotees numbered all the able-bodied populace. The caravans of covered wagons that moved from the Atlantic States in early days carried the household goods, the aged and the infirm. The men and women walked with the horses from the Fords of the Dan, to the Fords of the White, and were all the better for it. Woodruff could row a boat, and walk four hundred miles, two things which proclaimed his title to ordinary American manhood as measured by the standards of his day, standards which Americans might adopt today without any loss of prestige, strength or power.

But although he had not found a mecca, he still had hopes. There was St. Louis on the borders of civilization and Arkansas Post far beyond its confines. Should he take St. Louis, or should he take Arkansas Post? St. Louis already had a newspaper and the competition there would be great indeed. Arkansas Post was the capital of a new territory, had no paper, and with a true Macedonian cry was shouting, "Come over and help us." It is said that he tossed up a dollar and that the decree of chance favored Arkansas. There is nothing in the after life of William E. Woodruff that points to the habit of settling momentous questions by an appeal to chance. His life seemed to be made up of balances in which reason was the umpire. Reason pointed to Arkansas Post with unerring finger and William E. Woodruff crossed the Rubicon and entered Arkansas. The issue of his after life demonstrated the wisdom of his choice.

He landed at Arkansas with his printing press on October 30, 1819, and on November 20 of that year, just twenty-one days after his arrival, issued the first copy of the Arkansas Gazette, and continued to issue it at the same stand, without the loss of a single issue, and without a tardy issue, on every Saturday, to December 29, 1821, the date of the first issue at the City of Little Rock.

THE GAZETTE IN TWO LANGUAGES.

Arkansas Post at this time was one hundred and thirty-three years old, and was largely populated by people of French descent. So large was the proportion of French speaking people in Arkansas Post and in the territory at large, that Woodruff printed his announcements for office in English and French. The whole population at the post could not have numbered more than two hundred, and most probably not more than one hundred and fifty. There were thirty dwelling houses built in the French style, besides several stores, a mill and a hotel. The two principal streets were Front street and Main street. The principal business was the buying of peltries and cotton. The French hunters and trappers lived on almost every stream in eastern Arkansas and bartered their wares at Arkansas Post or New Madrid. The cotton plantations were around Arkansas Post, but did not yield the quantum of goods or money that followed the trade in furs and skins. The mercantile business of the post was considered large for the times.

BUSINESS MEN OF 1819.

James Scull ran a mill which did a large business. The principal cotton factor was William Drope of New Orleans, and Frederick Notrebe acted as his agent at the post. Drope ran this business in conjunction with a store which carried everything from sugar to sawmills. Samuel Mosely kept another large general store on Main street, and for ten years had been the principal competitor of Notrebe. Mosely died before Woodruff reached the place, and his widow in January, 1820, married Terrence Farrelly of the firm of Farrelly & Curran. This firm opened up at the post in December, 1819, having come from Pittsburg with a large stock of all kinds and sorts of goods, plenty of energy and a determination to win. They occupied the house formerly occupied by Captain Allen, and reached out with claw hammer hands for cotton and peltries. Eli J. Lewis was postmaster, clerk of the Circuit Court, tanner and storekeeper, and the boomer of the town.

BIG ADVENTURES OF THE EARLY DAY.

Lewis & Thomas kept the largest general store down on Front street, carried dry goods, groceries, hardware, queensware, boots and shoes, hats, caps, books and stationery. In the first issue of the Gazette they took a double column three quarter page advertisement and kept it going all the time. They offered eighty barrels of good whisky, one barrel of peach brandy and one barrel of fourth proof whisky, among an array of other articles that would have done credit to Marshall Field, or any other kind of department store. Pryor & Richards had been doing a good business, but closed out about the time of Woodruff's arrival. Farrelly & Curran were passably good advertisers; Notrebe touched it gingerly but Lewis & Thomas had the modern idea and took printer's ink in preference to anything else as a means to an end. It is possible that Woodruff would have starved before getting a sound start had it not been for the generous help of this firm. Woodruff's rates were one dollar for each fifteen lines and fifty cents for the same space for each subsequent insertion. Lewis & Thomas carried a standing advertisement of about two hundred lines, which warmed Woodruff's heart all through the winter of 1819-20, when he found it most difficult to make both ends meet.

THERE WERE DELINQUENTS THEN ALSO.

The subscription price of the paper was three dollars a year if paid in advance and four dollars a year if paid at the end of a year. The frequent calls in the paper for advance subscriptions during the first year justify the conclusion that a very large number of his subscribers preferred to pay thirty-three and one-third per cent. more and wait till the end of the year for a receipted bill; and the most urgent plea at the end of the year to call and settle, showed that there were quite a large number of subscribers who still owed the printer, and who were not anxious about the receipt. Human nature has not changed much since Adam and Eve started the race of mankind. If a higher and a lower price is set out in a paper every day, and the subscriber knows that he has violated every condition upon which the lower price rests, he will still demand the lower price when he comes to settle. Nearly all of Woodruff's subscribers who settled at the end of the year demanded the three-dollar rate, although every issue of the paper informed them that this was an advance rate. When all other sins are old avarice is yet young; it is never satisfied; it blinds our eyes, disposes men to fraud, increases with wealth, is both knave and fool, is insatiable. And Old Billy Woodruff met this sin in 1819-20, as every editor of the country meets it to-day.

CHAPTER II.

WOODRUFF'S POWER AT THE POST—EARLY POST OFFICES—THE ORIGINAL SPELLING OF THE WORD, "ARKANSAS."

He is half done who has made a good beginning. William E. Woodruff landed at Arkansas Post on Saturday, October 30, 1819, without friends, money or renown. He had youth, energy and a printing press to his credit and with these he began his work. The coming of a printing press to any town is an event of note; what must it have been to the inhabitants of that isolated town, the post of Arkansas.

A man with a bell could run all through it in thirty minutes calling its people to arms or to events of pleasure. The whole town was soon down on Front street gazing at the young easterner, Woodruff, with earnestness, and with rapt wonder at the strange machine, the printing press.

ARKANSAS POST'S GREATEST HONOR.

Arkansas had long been a post under both French and Spanish rule. Its people were not unacquainted with the politer forms of life as expressed in the higher walks of life at Paris and Madrid. Arkansas was continued as a post under American rule and hither had come many of the officers of the American army. Arkansas had been honored signally by Congress in being selected as the capital of the territory. True, there was no other town in the territory, but that did not detract from the honor rightly ascribable to a town already there,—and a town that had lived longer than several of the colonial governments.

But the greatest honor the town ever had was the honor conferred on it by the unknown printer, William E. Woodruff.

Robert Crittenden on October 30, 1819, was not as big a man as Woodruff in the eyes of the inhabitants of Arkansas, nor was the governor, James Miller, who arrived a short time afterward. Crittenden and Miller could run the territory, but it took Woodruff to show it off.

There was only one road, the one running from Davidsonville in Lawrence county, to Ouachita in Louisiana, and over this road, once a month, the mail was carried on horseback. Sometimes during 1819 and 1820 that mail rider did not show up, for two whole months, and frequently his pouches did not contain a single letter or package for Arkansas. The people of the town wanted more of the limelight. They desired to have some sort of recognition in the great outside world. They wanted more mails, more roads, more opportunities. Woodruff's printing press was the means to the end, and Billy Woodruff was the man of the hour. The fullblood Quapaws from the Southwest looked on with grunts, long and deep; the halfbreeds disclosed their French or Spanish antecedents by long and suspicious scrutiny; while the Americans whispered, "Now watch the town grow."

Nor were these people very far wrong in their estimates of men. Crittenden and Miller were greater in a special sense, but not equal to Woodruff in the permanency of influences set to work by him and them. Crittenden and Miller fixed certain forms and blazed the way for rising political institutions. Woodruff fixed forms of thought and prepared men for conduct under any and all institutional forms. Crittenden and Miller were evanescent. Woodruff was permanent and far more influential.

THE GAZETTE BROUGHT RESULTS.

But aside from generalities, Woodruff filled the bill as outlined by the populace. He had not been there four months before he got mails once every two weeks, and the promise from the postmaster general of a weekly mail. A road was cut to Cadron, and another to Montgomery's Landing. People began to migrate to the territory, and hardly an issue of the paper came out that did not tell of these waves of people pushing over the country. More letters came in the mail pouches, and, greatest of all, the Arkansas Gazette every week carried the happenings of the world to the firesides of the people. The printer was the greatest man in town, as he ought to be in every town.

Woodruff had no subscribers when he landed, nor did he waste any time in getting them. The people took the job off his hands. He asked no man to take the Gazette, but old citizens of the town took his lists and drummed the town and country.

Woodruff unloaded his press and moved it into an old house off Front street which belonged to Richmond Peeler and set it up ready for operation. This house had no value before Woodruff occupied it, but by January 20, 1820, it had so increased its worth as to be sold in an action for debt by Joseph Stillwell and was bought in by Woodruff.

Woodruff was the "whole push." He had no helper but himself, and not only had to prepare all the matter, but set it up and run the press. The editorial matter of the paper cost nothing for the reason that there was no editorial matter in the paper. One column was given to local reporting and all the rest of the paper to advertisements and general reading matter clipped from Eastern and foreign papers. The reading matter occupied about seventy-five per cent of the paper and the advertising about twenty-five per cent.

The paper was printed on sheets eleven inches wide by eighteen inches long, and had four pages of four columns each. It was uniformly of this size while printed at the post.

There was no special delivery of the paper in town and each subscriber was requested to call for his paper. The subscribers did this with alacrity, as they all wanted the news, besides never tiring of seeing Billy Woodruff work. I have never passed Hearst's newspaper office in Chicago without seeing from twenty to fifty men and women standing there gazing at the wonderful machines. One would think that the interest would wear out in time, but it does not. No thorough going man can pass a great newspaper press without complimenting it by a look. So much the more was the feeling at Arkansas Post.

CELEBRATION IN HONOR OF THE GAZETTE.

The machine talked faster than the men could talk, and ever so much better. In twenty-one days Woodruff ran off his first edition a bright, well printed, newsy document. It set the post on fire and cost Lewis & Thomas a barrel of whisky in celebration.

Woodruff wrote a sensible salutatory, one line of which is worth a quotation, and then worth remembrance. He said: "It is the duty of every man to be useful in whatever situation he may be placed, in life," and then proved his right to say it by keeping the Gazette going as a headlight for the State's progress to power.

AN EARLY ORACLE.

One anonymous writer in the first issue stated what the town needed and what it could well do without. He said, first, that the town and territory had a sufficient number of lawyers —more than were then making a living by their practice.

The outlook then was about the same as it is today so far as the law is concerned. It is a great profession, but it is overcrowded from Bangor, Maine, to Pasadena, California.

The writer said, second, that probably enough physicians were on hand to meet every demand, and that unless things got very much worse, no more doctors were needed.

But the thing wanted and wanted bad was an influx of farmers, or a lot of men to work the farms. These pictures of the pen show the condition of things better than any words of ours and lead to the conclusion that things have not changed materially in eighty-seven years.

The first issue of the paper had five marriage notices and one obituary, which was a good beginning and a fair omen. Fifty-one letters were advertised and the names on the list belong to men who in other parts of the territory and State acquired celebrity.

There were two tailors in town and they both advertised the latest cuts and fashions. The day of "Hand-me-downs" had not come and all people dressed more decently and adorably.

Mr. Craig kept a tavern where men of fashion congregated, to discuss the news and show their clothes. Stokeley H. Coulter, a fine old-fashioned tailor from North Carolina, kept all the latest plates, beneath which ran the legend, "Clothes make the man and I make the clothes." Out on Main street J. B. Burt kept another shop with the motto, "Eat to please yourself, but dress to please others." In 1820 a third tailor shop was opened by John B. O. Ragan, who took for his trademark the words: "The tailor makes the man, and that suit is best that fits best."

Shoemakers were flush with money at the place, as $2.50 pegged shoes were unknown. A tailor-made man had fine sewed boots, which cost from $10 to $15 a pair. And the father of the writer of this article made fine beaver hats which proclaimed their wearers as finished productions.

These advertisements are indices to the town. They show a degree of wealth and thrift not found in ledger footings and balances. They also show a high degree of refinement and social standing. In this atmosphere the Gazette began its career and in this community for two years it sustained itself with credit.

EARLY ARKANSAS POSTOFFICES.

When the paper started there were but two postoffices in the territory, Arkansas Post and Davidsonville. In less than six months there were six with the following postmasters:

Arkansas Post, Eli J. Lewis.
Davidsonville, Richard Searcy.
Cadron, Thomas H. Tindell.
Clark Court House, Jacob Barkman.
Hempstead Court House, John English.
White River Postoffice, Peyton Tucker.

In the original records of postoffices at Washington, D. C., the postoffice at Arkansas Post is listed under the spelling, "Arkansa," a form retained on the record for seven years, when it gave place to the form "Arkansas."

WOODRUFF'S INFLUENCE ON SPELLING.

The act creating Arkansaw territory contained the word Arkansas eight times, and each time it was spelled with a final w, and not a final s. President Roosevelt has just given official notice to the world that he proposes to change the recognized spelling of about three hundred words. Spelling by law will never prove profitable for the reason that lawmakers and executors are not specialists in orthography, and Roosevelt's mandate will likewise fail.

John Scott, delegate to Congress from Missouri in 1819, is said to have drawn the bill which cut off Arkansas from Missouri, and he is responsible for the act which legalized "The Territory of Arkansaw," with its capital, "Post of Arkansaw" on the "Arkansaw" river.

Two other laws were passed by Congress prior to 1819, which applied to Arkansas County in Missouri territory, both drawn by Missouri men and both times using the form "Arkansaw."

So far as Missouri could do it she attempted to fasten on the people of Arkansas forever the spelling, Arkansaw, and it will be interesting to note the failure of this spelling and the causes which led to its downfall.

A general article is far too short for a complete explication of a series of beautiful Indian words, but not too short for an enumeration or an induction, whose force may be grasped by all who read.

The following is an array of strangely resonant Indian words in the singular number:

Chippewa, Omaha, Altamaha, Chocta, Chickasa, Tensa, Moapa, Nebraska, Kansa, Arkansa, Quapa, Arickasa, Sagina, Oklahoma, Maricofa, Alabama, Apalachicola, Pensacola, Tampa, Ponca, Nemaha, Umatilla, Arizona, Taya, Kiowa, Oneida, Yakima, Ka, Jacarilla, Pima, Dakota, Yuta.

Nearly all of these retain this singular form today and only take a final s when pluralized. The words Chocta, Chickasa, Quapa, Sagina, and Ka for many years were pluralized by adding an s, but after awhile were changed in the singular so as to end in w. These five words are universally spelled in the singular with a final w. An attempt was at one time made to change Chippewa to Chippeway, but failed. The change from Yuta to Utah was successful. The four words, Tensa, Kansa, Arkansa, and Taya, at a very early date took on a final s to denote a singular, and Taya changed to Texas. Prior to 1819 the universally proper way to spell these words, was Kansas, Arkansas, Tensas, and Texas, and it was also universally recognized that these forms were in the singular number. It is idle to speculate upon the causes for this change, as they are beyond the analysis of the human mind.

But from 1812 to 1819 efforts were made to change Arkansas from its plural form to the real singular Arkansaw, and to place it in the Choctaw category. This might have succeeded but for the pertinacity of William E. Woodruff, Sr.

He published the act creating the territory in the first issue of his paper and changed the eight spellings of the law, "Arkansaw," to the recognized form, "Arkansas." He headed his paper "The Arkansas Gazette," and on the publication line placed the words "Arkansas, Arkansas Territory." He kept this up until he moved to Little Rock, when he changed the publication line to "Little Rock, Arkansas Territory." In all the thousands of times that he used the word in the paper he spelled it "Arkansas." The people of Arkansas never saw any other form in the Gazette, their leading paper, and they very rarely saw any other form in any other paper. William E. Woodruff more than any other man, yea, more than all men combined, taught the people to love the form "Arkansas," and it is safe to say that this form will never be changed.

But there was a time when it might have been changed easily and that time was in 1819-20. William E. Woodruff could have followed the form used in the law and thus taught the people to love and revere that form. He could have printed the name of his paper "The Arkansaw Gazette" and other papers would have gradually fallen into line.

The newspapers hesitated for a long time and for about a year spelled the word "Arkansaw," but when they saw Woodruff's paper clinging so persistently to the older form they went back to "Arkansas."

The Washington Intelligencer printed the law and used the Arkansaw spelling. The same paper followed the final w form for two years. The two St. Louis papers of 1819 refused to make the change and always spelled the word "Arkansas." Niles' Register took up "Arkansaw" for a while, but abandoned it.

When the annals of Congress were printed in 1853 the original act was printed with the word "Arkansas" and not "Arkansaw," which seemed to imply that the word had never been spelled with a "w." But the session laws of 1819, printed at the same time, show the eight recurrences of the word with the form, "saw."

Peter's Digest of the United States statutes in 1854 reproduced the original act and used the "w," but in all the notes used an "s."

Nuttal, the only scientific man who has ever written a great deal about the State, and who visited it in 1818, persistently used the form, "Arkansa," a triumph for all who advocate the original spelling of this beautiful word.

Another man of science, Featherstonaugh, visited the State in 1835, and left two forms of spelling. Whenever he referred to the State he wrote "Arkansas," but whenever he referred to the river he used "Arkansa." Frederick Gerstaecker, the German hunter, who tramped all over the State from 1839 to 1842, always spelled the word "Arkansas."

William E. Woodruff may have never known that the legal spelling was "Arkansaw." If so, he triumphed through ignorance. The probabilities are, however, that he did know, but refused to follow the law, so far as its barbarous spelling was concerned. It was about this time that the following verses appeared in many papers creating no end of merriment from Maine to Missouri:

"I love the girl from Arkansaw
Who can saw more wood than her maw can saw
And can saw much more than her paw can saw
In the grand new State of Arkansaw.

> "Then sing and saw
> For maw and paw,
> For that old saw
> Of Arkansaw.

"See saw the girl from Arkansaw,
Whose saw outsaws her maw's best saw,
And saws a saw her paw can't saw,
The oldest saw of Arkansaw.

> "Her maw can saw,
> Her paw can saw,
> And she can saw,
> In Arkansaw."

CHAPTER III.

"Who's Who" of Old Arkansas Post—French and American Settlers.

To the solemn tread of the tune "Old Hundred" we approach the "Old Timers" who are in the strictest sense the "First Families of Arkansas."

The glory of ancestry sheds a halo around their posterity; birth is nothing without it. The deeds of the Old French settlers at Arkansas Post have for the most part been obliterated. The French were attracted in the earliest times to the post by reason of the superior prowess of the Quapaw Indians who inhabited Arkansas. They were the dominant tribe of the South Mississippi Valley and the French were eager to cultivate amicable relations with them. This resulted in the maintenance of an army post on the Arkansas and in intermarriages between the French and the Quapaws.

Much criticism has been wasted upon "Alice of Old Vincennes." All of the descriptions of the book are historically true, and every character in it might have been found in the personages who lived at Arkansas Post from 1718 to 1800.

SOCIETY AT ARKANSAS POST.

The Catholic church, with its priests and their civilizing and refining influence, was there from the very beginning. The law of France and Spain had been well represented by soldiers, officers and men, who had won distinction on European ground, and who carried with them the social atmosphere of a distant world. The French immigrants to Louisiana had come from all grades of French life except the highest nobility. Under the rule of the United States the post was still maintained and the presence of officers like Colonel J. B. Many, Colonel Armistead and Major Bradford, with garrisons of from fifty to one hundred men, assured some degree of social advantage and brought in great floods of light from the outer world.

True the community declined. On the whole it was a degenerate community. It retained godliness and gentleness, but it lost energy, virile power and industry. The common outdoor dress was the Canadian overall and blouse, unchanged and unchangeable, and the highest aspiration seemed to end in being either a noted trapper or a first rate hunter. Despite all this there were brilliant exceptions and to these we now turn in order to introduce you to the "Who's Who," the real old First Families of the State.

THE VAUGINES.

We have the authority of Nuttal for saying that Lewismore Vaugine was a superior man. This testimonial is still further reinforced by the voluntary testimony of Colonel Preston, a representative of the United States land office from Washington, who visited this community a few years after Nuttal. One of Vaugine's ancestors belonged to the nobility of France, as Nuttal says, and was sent over by the king as commandant of the Post of Arkansas. He acquired large interests and remained. Susette Vaugine, his sister, a winsome, piquant and attractive blossom of the forest, attracted the affections of the soldier, Chalmette, the commandant in 1780. A daughter of Lewismore Vaugine captivated Don Joseph Valliere, the commandant from 1786 to 1790. The birth and position of the Vaugines was of the best, and these two marriages simply increased their prestige and power. Francis Vaugine, born 1793, brought this family far into the last century and into closer contact with real American life. Francis Valliere was connected by blood with the Vaugine name.

THE BOGIES.

Lewis Bogy, or as Nuttal spells it, Bogie, was not a native of Arkansas, but was, nevertheless, one of its most prominent men. Nuttal brought a letter of introduction to him from learned men of the East, and his own testimony is enough to give Louis Bogy a place quite apart from the other residents of the place. That he could follow Nuttal in his scientific and botanical disquisitions and be interested therein, attests his mental parts. He was born in Canada, but came to the post in 1790, where he remained until he died. Ignace Bogy was another prominent member of this line.

THE VARSIERS.

Francis Varsier was born at the post and christened by the Catholic fathers in 1793. His father and mother were both natives of this region, from forbears that came from the south of France.

FRANCIS D'ARMAND.

This Frenchman did not live at the Post, but was so well known there as to make it proper to consider him at this point. Distinguished in France, he decided to improve his fortune in "La Louisiane," He came in 1766 and selected a site near the mouth of the White, put up a huge chateau and engaged in trade. His fortunes grew apace as did the reputation of his noted home. His houses were to be seen as late as 1833, and William Montgomery, who purchased the place, made it one of the most noted landings on the Mississippi river. It was the Monte Carlo of the Mississippi Valley.

Other Frenchmen who were here more than one hundred years ago are Francois Imbeau, Baptiste Imbeau, Joseph De Chassein, Antoine de Chassein, Baptiste Socie, Joseph Bonne, Baptiste Bonne, Louis Bartelmi, Francois Coupot, Joseph Valliere, the Closseins, Antoine Barraque, Eteinne Vaugine, Pierre La Farve, John Larquer, and Pierre Michel. It would be interesting to know how many of these are represented in Arkansas by name and blood today.

SYLVANUS PHILLIPS.

Phillips county carries this man's name and is his monument. Born in the United States, he was in early life attracted to the West and in 1797 built a log cabin near the mouth of the St. Francis river in Arkansas, and was, as he said, the only settler for miles around. His nearest neighbors were Antoine Tessier and Joseph De Plasse, who lived at the mouth of the Cache. Beyond their residences there were no other settlements in that direction. In 1798 he explored the Arkansas river for some distance above Arkansas Post, but found no settlement in that direction. In 1799 the commandant of the post, fearing an uprising of the natives, warned Phillips to remove to the post. He did so and remained there for many years, and was joined by J. B. Mooney and the Pattersons, all related by marriage, and who with him made extensive explorations for mineral and timber wealth. He gained in this way a great knowledge of the territory, a knowledge which Sam C. Roane, in later years, was enabled to use as an effective club in breaking up the gigantic land frauds which threatened to despoil the State of hundreds of thousands of acres of land.

CHRISTIAN PRINGLE.

This man was born in Hagerstown, Maryland, in 1760. In his twentieth year he took his gun and, accompanied by his dog, started into the wilderness of the West. For two years he rambled over West Virginia, Kentucky and Tennessee, equally at home in one place as in another. In 1782 he reached Arkansas Post, where he spent the remainder of his life. He was universally respected and died in January, 1820. He seems to have been an unmarried man, but this is not clear.

THE WINTERS AND STILWELLS.

Sometime between 1790 and 1798 Elisha Winter and Gabriel Winter went to New Orleans and began the manufacture of cotton rope. They were Kentuckians and their free handed, open hearted ways soon gained them the friendship of people in power. As recompense for introducing a manufacture into the province, it is said that the commandant granted them one million arpens of land on the Arkansas river. In 1798 these men, accompanied by Joseph Stilwell, who had acquired an interest in the grant, arrived at Arkansas Post and began a so-called survey of their lands. This Winter-Stilwell grant extended from the Post along the Arkansas river on its northern side to Argenta, and proved a great impediment in after years to the newcomers seeking for homes. In 1819, a man seeking lands had no chance between Arkansas Post and Little Rock. The Quapaws owned all on the south side and the Winters and Stilwells claimed to own all on the north side. The Quapaws could not sell, and while the Winters and Stilwells were eager to sell, no one would buy for fear that the grantors had no legal title. The Winters erected houses on their land, sub-let in many cases, made a stubborn fight in Congress, but were finally ousted by the United States and their claims disallowed.

Joseph Stilwell was a man of varied parts, could speak Spanish, French, English and Quapaw and was most highly respected. He was a member of the first territorial legislature, being elected to fill a vacancy, and made his announcement when seeking the place in both English and French, which proves the existence of a French speaking voting population in other parts of the territory. Harold Stilwell was another prominent member of this family.

It will be a matter of greater interest, however, to say, that Joseph Stilwell was a revolutionary soldier. He was born in 1752 in Monmouth county, New Jersey, and enlisted as ensign in the first regiment of New Jersey troops, and was soon promoted to the captaincy, and was in command in the affair at Sandy Hook in June, 1776. He was then made captain in Col. Forman's battalion on July 18, 1776, in detached militia service. He was in the battle of Monmouth and suffered all the hardships of the many campaigns in New Jersey. In Monmouth, Somerset and Gloucester counties, New Jersey, there were twenty-two men of the name Stilwell, three of them being brothers of Joseph and all related by blood lines.

After the war the Stilwells, in common with hundreds of other Jersey families, were without homes and the day of pensions had not arrived. The West was open to them and there they went in companies of from ten to fifty.

Joseph Stilwell drifted into Kentucky, where he met the Winter family, and from there he migrated to Arkansas Post, where he spent the last twenty-two years of his life. He died at the post on September 10, 1822, leaving an aged wife, a number of children and troops of grandchildren.

HEWES SCULL.

This gentleman came from Philadelphia to Arkansas Post in 1802. His ancestors were from Salem and Gloucester counties, New Jersey, and were brave and public spirited men. Eight men of that name were in the Continental line from South Jersey. On one occasion a noted Philadelphian was excoriating New Jersey for leaning too much toward Toryism. One of the Sculls happened to hear him and remarked: "Shut up, you old fool. You don't know whereof you speak. Every Scull in New Jersey was in Washington's Army." This play upon the word "skull" made New Jersey appear very patriotic.

Hewes Scull, like many an other Jerseyman, was attracted to the West by the stupendous effort made by the land speculators of Southwestern Ohio to people Symmes' Purchase, the region around Cincinnati. Scratch a grave in the Cincinnati cemeteries dug before 1810 and you will in all probability discover a Jersey man's bones. But Hewes Scull did not leave his body at that place. He heard of Arkansas Post through some French traders and made his way to that point. He was a merchant and trader and amassed some wealth. He was honored by the people of Arkansas county with many positions of honor and trust and was in every sense a splendid type of the early pioneer. James Scull has his name perpetuated in the treaty made with the Quapaws in 1824, and by this document it is certain that he was as that time worth $7,500, owed to him by the Quapaws, and which the government agreed either to pay in money or by the grant of two sections of land in the old reservation. The government let him take the land.

There may be a few more names in this locality, or in some other, that represent families who have been on Arkansas soil continuously for one hundred years; if so, their owners can easily attach themselves to this list of the noble clan of old families and be entitled to all the privileges of the order. It is surprising, however, how few there are who are thus to the manor born.

If there is a divine right for the existence of the noble order of the "Colonial Dames," or the "Society of May-flower Descendants" or "The Settlers of America," there is an equal right and chance for the "Who's Who of Arkansas," the descendants of ancestors who were in Arkansas one hundred years ago. And if it be an honor to descend from one whose feet first touched American soil at Plymouth Rock, it can be made an equal honor to descend from ancestors who lived on any particular soil, but best of all, on Arkansas soil, one hundred years ago. If all that is ancient is beautiful the sons and daughters of the ancient may be pardoned for their desire to perpetuate the memory of their ancestors.

The second death of oblivion must never come to the few names that connect Arkansas in the eighteenth with Arkansas in the nineteenth century. Horace Greely said that the only certainty which follows us is oblivion, but he might have softened it by saying, "He who saves a life from oblivion adds to the reminiscences of eternity."

CHAPTER IV.

First Officers of the Territory—All Non-Residents.

The territory of Arkansaw was created on March 2; its governor and secretary were appointed by President Monroe on March 3, and the announcement thereof printed in the Washington Intelligencer, the congressional record of that day, on March 4, 1819. That closed the Washington end of the affair and the new territory was not again mentioned in any print at Washington until the following December.

Four lines were used by the Washington Intelligencer in announcing the appointment of James Miller of New Hampshire as governor, and Robert Crittenden of Kentucky as secretary. So far as Washington people were concerned they were not interested in the territory nor in the men who were to govern it. Some few knew that James Miller had gained a glorious reputation at Lundy's Lane by saying "I'll try, sir," but that day was over. Why revive its memory at this time? A lesser number had heard of Robert Crittenden and even these could not tell what he had done to deserve the honor. Why should the appointing power at Washington in choosing men to govern a territory always select them from men living outside its boundaries and to the least extent interested in its affairs? Is it because there are no qualified men in the territories? Not at all. In the case of Arkansas it was certainly not the case.

Major Vaugine would have made every whit as good a governor as James Miller did. Sylvanus Phillips would have filled the bill, as would Richard Searcy. Hewes Scull would have made equally as good a secretary of the commonwealth as did Robert Crittenden. In the first place there was very little for either officer to do and that little required nothing more than firmness, honesty and a small modicum of business ability. Talent was of far less use than tact, and the home product was more likely to possess this than any foreign importation.

It is a beautiful fiction of our politicians and lawyers that ours is a government resting on the consent of the governed. No consent whatever was given by the inhabitants of Arkansas to the Act Creating the Territory of Arkansaw. They were never consulted. What consent was given by the people of Arkansas to the appointment of the executive and judicial officers from 1819 to 1836? The law was made without consulting the people, and the officers who were chosen were for the most part appointed by a power outside the boundaries of the territory.

Politics is a game of·favors. The aid extended in one field must be repaid by favors in another. The president of the United States is supposed to select the wisest and best men, but it is somewhat strange that in territorial matters he never finds wisdom or goodness within the territory.

All that can be said in favor of the current method of appointment is that it introduces, or may introduce, new blood into the body politic, and may possibly induce a desirable class of citizens to become permanent residents.

CRITTENDEN WAS A YOUNG-LAWYER.

Robert Crittenden was a young lawyer from Kentucky, a scion of a family that afterwards became somewhat distinguished in that State and in the nation. There were too many Crittendens for Kentucky's omnivorous office-seeking propensities, and her friends were always most gracious in their desire to lend a few of them to other States and territories. In this way Kentucky lent a great many of her men to Arkansas and Missouri.

So far as Arkansas is concerned she has never had any reason to be ashamed of her Kentucky settlers, and least of all of Robert Crittenden. True, Arkansas had men within her borders thoroughly competent to do the work as well as Crittenden did it, but they were not competent, it may be, to become what Crittenden became. Crittenden made a good secretary of the territory, but his fame does not rest upon this, nor did his management thereof reflect any transcendent ability. The office was a minor one, and the fact that a man of superior ability filled it did not make the office an iota greater.

Crittenden had a shorter distance to travel than Miller and got to Arkansas Post nearly six months before Miller. Crittenden received $1,000 a year and the governor $2,000. A man who gets twice the salary is supposed to have twice the dignity, and may be permitted to travel more at will. Crittenden was on time, but Miller was about six months off the date, the salary running on nevertheless. The government was to begin on July 4, 1819, with a governor, a secretary, a council, and a court. The council, to save money, was to consist of the three members of the court, all of whom were non-indigenous productions. One of the judges, Judge Andrew Scott, hailed from Potosi, Missouri, and got to Arkansas Post before any of the others. There he began to make those friends who ever afterward made his life enjoyable and who never relaxed their affectionate regard.

Robert Crittenden and Robert P. Letcher came in next, and came in together, as Letcher was also a Kentucky production. Charles Jouett, the third member of the court, appointed from Michigan, soon followed and the machinery of government was ready for operation. True, the governor was not there, but by the double action of the law, Crittenden could act as governor while commissioned as secretary.

MILLER MAKES LEISURELY TRIP.

James Miller, the governor, was signaled at Pittsburg late in September and seventy-five days after that his high and mighty ship, the Arkansaw, landed at the wharf at Arkansas Post. What marvelous speed! What a wonderful junket! Just a trifle more or less than ten miles a day. Billy Woodruff could have walked the whole distance in half the time and would have done it for half the money. If a chip had been thrown on the Ohio when the gallant craft, the Arkansaw, left Pittsburg, it would have reached the mouth of the Arkansas or the mouth of the White more than thirty-five days earlier than did the governor. The chip would have attended to the business of floating and would have reached there in good time. Miller had other fish to fry. He was the hero of Lundy's Lane and heroes in the United States can't travel like chips. They must slow up at all the landings and let the populace see what a real hero looks like. He must get off the boat at certain places and let the people touch his clothes for some virtue to soak through them to the devotee.

I have seen a bewildering mass of people stand around William Jennings Bryan waiting to grasp his hand. I have seen hundreds, who finding their time would never come, push through and touch his coat. I asked Bryan, at my table the same day, after he had helped himself the third time to the choice chicken my Kentucky wife had prepared for her kingliest of men, just how he felt when men pushed through to touch the hem of his garments like they did in the days of Christ.

Said Bryan: "Well, you have a Blue Grass wife who will appreciate my answer whether you do or not. How do I feel? Why, sir, I feel like a prize steer at a Kentucky fair."

So it is with every hero. So it was with James Miller. At Cincinnati there were a great many heroes of the war of 1812 and they all wanted to see the author of the memorable words "I'll try, sir." All the old citizens were down on Rat Row, as the insignificant wharf of the time was called. This was before the advent of the Storers, the Tafts and the Longworths, the men who now confer honor by inheritance on Losantiville, the old name of Cincinnati, the Queen City of the West.

The men who waited on Miller were original heroes of two wars, the War of Independence, and that other war which rubbed our independence in. These men were not the sons or grandsons of great men, but were great themselves. Miller had to stop and he had to stay. He was taken up to that old magnificent hotel which in early days faced Front street and was there dined and wined until further trial was out of the question. He swept everything before him at Lundy's Lane, but was signally conquered at Losantiville. Not satisfied with one great feast, they laid out another for the night in order that the women of Cincinnati might grasp his hand.

Out on the streets if you met a man and said "Will you have one on me?" his answer came pat, "I'll try, sir." And when after awhile you said, "Turn about is fair play. Will you have another?" The answer was the same old saw, "I'll try, sir."

It was a trying time for Cincinnati. Everybody seemed to be impressed with the idea that this was the exact time to try and keep on trying. The whole town was on the ragged edge of an incipient drinking festival and most thoroughly committed to the New Hampshire logic, "I'll try, sir."

It was the same way at Louisville, at Paducah, at Cairo and at every one horse landing along the route. The only wonder is that the hero of Lundy's Lane got to Arkansas Post at all.

He arrived, however, in the middle of December and Billy Woodruff noted the event in twelve short lines. He was sworn in and for four years made a good governor of the territory.

CHAPTER V

GENERAL MILLER, OUR FIRST TERRITORIAL GOVERNOR—HIS OPINION OF EARLY LITTLE ROCK NOT FAVORABLE—GENERAL JACKSON'S OPINION OF GENERAL MILLER.

There is so much in the life and character of James Miller that is worthy of study, that we are warranted in giving a fuller exposition than we have already given.

He was born in the fastnesses of the mountains in the Granite State, a poor boy, and was singularly fortunate in not having a superabundance of opportunities. Bacon has said, "A wise man will create opportunities," and it is far better to be endowed with common sense, the basis of wisdom, than to be born with a silver spoon. The silver spoon will come to every one who has sense and courage to master his own mind and use his own hands.

Nor will a wise man waste time in a useless discussion of the equality of opportunity. Equality of opportunity is far more prevalent in the United States than equality of wisdom.

MILLER'S HONORABLE CAREER.

James Miller had an abundance of that old-fashioned common sense which was the almost universal heritage of Americans one hundred years ago. He entered the army and was a good soldier. In 1808 he had risen to the rank of major in the Fourth United States Infantry, and in two years more had become the lieutenant colonel of the Fifth; he was transferred to the Sixth in 1812 and was made colonel of the Twenty-first in 1814. He won the honor of a brevet colonelcy in 1812 for distinguished service at Brownstown, Canada, and was promoted to the rank of brigadier general in July, 1814, for distinguished services at Niagara Falls.

Congress on November 3, 1814, by unanimous resolution presented him with a gold medal as a testimonial of the high sense entertained by Congress of his gallantry and good conduct in the several conflicts of Chippewa, Niagara and Ft. Erie. He resigned his position as general in the United States army on more into the interior than all the other territorial governors combined. He and Major Bradford were almost all the time from 1820 to 1824 busy with Indian disputes and Indian outrages. They attempted pacifications that promised much, but were thwarted, not only by the Indians, but by the rapacious whites. The latter class wanted all the land lying inside the boundaries despite the fact that the Indians had a legal right to more than one-third of it.

WHITE MAN'S RULE IN ARKANSAS.

Miller was respected by the Indians, but soon decided that the two peoples could not live in harmony and prosperity inside the same boundary, and advised the general government that it would be wise to begin the removal of the Indians. His advice was taken, and in a short time after he left the State there was but one government in the territory, and that was the white man's rule. His advice to the successive legislatures was sound and resulted in laws that brought a fair degree of prosperity. He had an able supporter in young Robert Crittenden, but it is very unfair to say that Miller was not himself the active spirit from 1819 to 1825. It would be easy to prove that he did more real work than any territorial governor who succeeded him.

EARLY LITTLE ROCK A BAD TOWN.

He did not like Little Rock as a location for either the county seat of Pulaski county or the capital of the territory, and for this he is not to be blamed. One who reads all that has been printed of Little Rock from 1821 to 1825, and even for many years thereafter, can not but conclude that this town during these years was not a heavenly resort, nor a summer resort, nor any very desirable resort for the best people.

It had good people but it unfortunately had too great a number of very bad people, and these were always on parade. That Little Rock triumphed over her surroundings and evolved into a model city is a strong argument for the survival of the fittest and a proof that we grow better as we grow older. But in 1820 Little Rock hadn't enough people of any kind to make it an attraction for the capital. Nuttal in 1819 found a settlement at Cadron that surprised him. He said no settlement in the State except Arkansas Post could compare with it in numbers. By a little patience I think I could count up as great a number having Cadron for a center as could have been counted at the Post in 1819. Little Rock in 1819 could not muster a corporal's guard. A writer in the Gazette after it had been removed to Little Rock, after the Gazette had been there a year, in January, 1823, summed up the Little Rock houses for the years 1821 and 1822. In the first year there was one hotel, one boarding house and seven private houses; in 1822 there was one hotel, one boarding house and one private residence. The writer was evidently correct, for Mr. Woodruff made no comment. Two speculative factions were at work trying to strangle each other, and thus kept dwelling house people away. The speculators herded at the hotel and the boarding house.

Governor Miller preferred the "up river" country. He and the one hundred and fifty others who lived up there, staunch Kentuckians and Tennesseeans, tried to have the county seat removed to Cadron in 1820. The bill was introduced in the council by Thos. H. Tyndall, of Cadron, and had a close shave. Four members voted for it and four voted against it. The chairman of the Committee of the Whole House, W. B. R. Horner, of St. Francis township, Arkansas county, dissolved the tie by voting no, which killed it for that session, or part of a session. The matter came up again in October of the same year and Cadron was successful.

But as the capital had been moved to Little Rock, the county seat question had to be threshed out again, and this time Little Rock won. Had the matter been left to the vote of Pulaski county, in 1822, both as to capital and county seat, the Cadronites would doubtless have won.

Dr. Menifee was somewhat of a power in those days, and Tyndall, McIlmurrey and Kuykendall were able supporters. Events have proved that Little Rock was the proper place for both the county seat and the capital, and the State is to be congratulated that the change to Cadron was not made. But it was most difficult in 1820 for any one to see in the cocoon, Arkopolis, the brilliant butterfly, Little Rock of today.

MORE HONORS FOR MILLER.

In 1824, President Monroe appointed Governor Miller collector of the Port of Salem, which terminated his career in Arkansas. Prior to this appointment, the people of the First congressional district of New Hampshire had elected him as their representative to Congress, so that he was at once governor of Arkansas territory, Congressman from New Hampshire and collector of the port at Salem. The old general resigned his position as governor, and then did what no one had ever done before, resigned his place in Congress, and settled down as collector.

JACKSON'S COMPLIMENT TO MILLER.

In the race between Adams and Jackson in 1828, Miller supported John Quincy Adams, but Jackson won out, and after his inaugural began to enforce the sound doctrine "To the victors belong the spoils." Civil service has flung round this truth the mantle of hypocrisy, but the doctrine still works, and works forcefully, in every department at Washington. The most violent partisans that have ever held cabinet positions are working full time on political manipulations in Washington today.

Jackson chopped off official heads on all sides, and Miller, soldier as he was, asked no quarter and prepared to go. His friends, however, went to Jackson and made a special plea in Miller's behalf. Jackson listened to them in grim silence until they were through. He then said: "You tell General Miller that so long as Andrew Jackson is president of the United States, the hero of Lundy's Lane will remain collector at the Port of Salem."

Andrew Jackson was a virile, strenuous president and not a mere imitation. He recognized the transcendent valor of Miller, and at the same time recognized his right to support Adams, not only actively, but with what would now be termed a most pernicious activity. Miller held the post assured to him by Jackson through several successive administrations and died in 1849.

CHAPTER VI.

EARLY SETTLERS ON THE RIVERS OF EASTERN ARKANSAS AND ON THE ARKANSAS RIVER.

When we consider that but four hundred years have elapsed since the first white people came to the Western world, and that during the next year the United States will celebrate the tercentennial of the oldest English settlement in America, we begin to appreciate how really modern all things are on the Western continent, and what may be really accomplished in one hundred years.

Virginians have always invested the settlers of the Tidewater section of their State, the part settled during the first century of her existence, with something akin to veneration. They were not invested with the title, "First Families of Virginia" for the reason that these settlers were noblemen or men of exalted rank. The fact is that they were not. The Washingtons, the Jeffersons, the Peytons, the Balls, the Slaughters and other noted families were from the great middle rank in England. The fewest number were from the major nobility, and a larger, but by no means the greater, number were from the minor nobility. The majority were representatives of the great families of English yeomen, sturdy, energetic and brave. They were the first to people Virginia; the first to battle against forest and swamp; the first to have chances at the resources of the commonwealth, and thereby obtaining wealth and refinement for themselves and for their children. They were actually the first families to settle the country, and as the centuries rolled on they became a class by themselves, the F. F. V.'s.

In time the families of Arkansas will divide into the newer and the older, and to rescue from oblivion those who were in Arkansas one hundred years ago was the purpose of a previous chapter, and is the purpose of the one we now write.

EARLY LAND GRANTS.

The United States began the investigation of land grants in Missouri, Louisiana and Arkansas soon after the purchase of that region in 1803. Exhaustive examinations were made as to the dates of settlements, the length of their existence and the nature of the claims. Thousands of claims were rejected, but several hundred were confirmed and deeds given to the claimants. The following list shows when the various settlements in what is now Arkansas were begun as sworn to by clouds of witnesses, and shows an additional number of people that were here one hundred years ago, together with their seating places in the wilderness.

BENJAMIN FOOY.

The Fooy family in Arkansas sprang from Benjamin Fooy, a native of Holland, born in 1759. He tried to better his condition in many parts of the world and in 1794 found himself opposite the present city of Memphis in Spanish territory at the village of Hopefield, or as it was called then, Camp Esperanza. The Commandant Augustine Le Grande granted him a concession of land, upon which he settled and upon which he died thirty years afterward, on December 27, 1823.

Thirty years in the forests of Arkansas, thirty years on the banks of the mighty Mississippi. Honored was he by the Spaniards while in control; honored again while the territory was known as Louisiana; honored still more in the days of the territory of Missouri, and most of all under the territorial laws of Arkansas. He was a justice of the peace for years and under the last control a judge of the Court of Common Pleas. His character was above reproach, and his philanthropy and hospitality were only bounded by his means. He left an aged wife, a large number of children, and a still larger number of grandchildren, whose descendants still ramify eastern Arkansas. Lands were confirmed to him at Hopefield and Wappenocke as having been settled prior to 1799, and to Isaac Fooy at Hopefield under a settlement of 1801.

Other Hopefield and Wappenocke settlers were Montford Perryman, Wappenocke, 1801, and William Grace of the same place, 1802.

ALLIGATOR LAKE.

This region is now Crittenden county and the confirmed concessions recorded in 1811 and 1813 upon which patents were issued were as follows:

Antoine Pena, Augustine Gonzales, John Francis Almendras, John Dominiques, John Andre Escriveve, Francis Groson, Jasto Martin, John Rodrigues and Elizabeth Jones, whose settlements were made between 1798 and 1802. Elizabeth Jones was also confirmed in her right to a farm on Elk Lake opened in 1801.

On Copperas creek of the St. Francis the earliest settler in that region was John Hogan, in 1800, who was joined in 1803 by John Taylor. They and their families were not disturbed by other additions to their neighborhood until some time in 1810.

ST. FRANCIS RIVER SETTLEMENT.

In addition to those named in the previous chapter there were the following: John McLean and Jesse Stephens settled on the St. Francis near the mouth of the Eel river in 1803; a little higher up was William Gregory of 1802; along its banks somewhere was the farm of Mary Edwards, whose husband located there in 1803. In the same year Charles Stenson settled at the mouth of the river, and three miles above him was the home of Edward Proctor, who had lived there since 1800. On the waters of the St. Francis Moses Burnett and Joseph Sevier had homes, the former coming in 1797 and the latter in 1800. John Grace settled on the low ground above Big island in, 1800 and Caty Gallowhorn on an island in the Mississippi river in 1801. Enos Chartruce also made a home on the St. Francis in 1800. Joseph Stilwell also had a concession on the St. Francis from 1799.

ON THE MISSISSIPPI RIVER.

Besides Fooy, Phillips, Mooney and D'Armand, there were the following settlers, widely separated from each other and almost cut off from the world: In 1803 Ebenezer Fulsome took up ground on the Mississippi about three miles above the mouth of the St. Francis. In the same year Moses Perry settled between the White and St. Francis, and William Bailey south of the St. Francis on Caney creek. Along the banks were Abraham Ramer, a settler of 1802; Joseph Gazzia, of 1798; Sylvanus Phillips of 1797; Pat Cassidy, adjoining Phillips and Patterson, 1803; William Patterson, 1797, all near where Helena now stands, and William McKinney, seven miles below Hopefield, 1802, with George Roebuck, a near neighbor. John Le Fevre had a landing seven miles below the mouth of the St. Francis and settled there in 1802.

William H. Glass and John Dill were between him and the mouth of the river and moved there in 1802. Daniel Mooney had a home between the St. Francis and the Mississippi, the date of which ran back to 1797. In the neighborhood of Benjamin Fooy were John Henry Fooy, William Porter and William Riggs, dating from 1799 to 1802.

WHITE RIVER.

At Belle Point on the White river Augustin John Friend had a home dating back to 1793, and his neighbor, Charles Furnish, from 1801. Below these lived Joseph Michel and Alexander Bridoute, John Fayac had for years prior to 1800 lived at the fort on White river, while Joseph Michel had another clearing at the Bay of White river dating from 1801. Away up the White river, above Poke bayou, lived B. H. McFarlane, who claimed a residence from 1804. In 1803 Archibald Fallen drove his stakes on Lock creek, and Moses Price made a home on the bay in 1803. As early as 1789, Francis Francure had a home on the White twelve miles below Red river.

CACHE RIVER.

Elijah McKinney settled on the Cache in 1803; Samuel Treat, in 1801; Peter Le Fevre, in 1800; Francis Michel and Louis Gossiat had a home on Big lake before the opening of the nineteenth century and died where they lived.

Abraham Hickland came to Pleasant lake in 1803 and James Patterson in 1802; Thos. Williams to Cypress bayou in 1803; Joseph Calais to Prairie Catocke in 1800, and John Diana to Turk's Prairie in 1799. Over on Black river near Clover Bend,

Anthony, Nicholas and John B. Janis had a concession of 1801 which was confirmed in 1813, while that of Joseph Gingnolet about seven miles from them had the same age. In 1791 Peter Burrell and John B. De Plaice had cabins on the Cache.

THE ARKANSAS RIVER.

Besides those heretofore named there were the following: Charles Refeld and Albert Berdu, of 1800, two miles from the Post; Athenas Racine, of 1801, on the prairie six miles above; John Bartran on the bayou near Vaugines; Samuel Treat, in 1802, two miles from the Post; Michael Petersel, 1800, on the river; Michael Wolff, 1801, on Bayou Hunt; Joseph Greenwald, 1793, five miles away; William Bassett, 1799, at the Post; Andrew Fagot, 1798, at same place; Jean Baptiste Dernissee, on the river from 1800; Jacob Bright, Martin Serrano and Peter Jordalles all had possessions near the Post dating back to 1795, while John Lavergne, one mile north, antedated them two years. In the same category were Jean Lavale, Pierre Pertuis, Alexis and Jean Jardales. About two miles from the Post on farms antedating 1800 lived Christian Pringle, Francis Gimblet, John Hadsell and George Leard. John B. Cathoit moved to the neighborhood six miles northeast in 1803 and in the same year John B. Minard settled on the bay below the village. George Kepler on the lake, with Christopher Coffman above and Lavergne below him; in 1803 Pierre Perti lived three miles east and in the same year Charles Bogy on River Grues. In 1802 John B. Dardenne was found on the river above the Post; Madame Francis Valliere had a farm in 1802 and two miles below the Post lived Etienne Vasseau, in the same vicinity as lived Baptiste Placide. Near the Post Mary Dernisseau had possession in 1802, and contemporary with her was Christopher Kaufman on Kaufman's bayou. (The spelling is Coffman at one place, and Kaufman at another.) Of about the same time was John Languies, while in the year before James Davis, Samuel Brown and George Duval settled on Crow Creek. Raphael Brinsbeck had lived two miles east of the Post since 1793, while Francis Vasseau for the same time had lived on the river.

Four miles below, Jacob Goris, 1793; five miles out, Elisha Winter, 1799; and Anthony Wolfe, 1796; six miles out, Michael LaCourse, 1796; four miles below, Joseph Bogy, 1792, and Elizabeth Pertuis, 1792. Fifty miles up the river lived Michael Bonne, from 1801, and fifty leagues above was the home of Louis P. Levy, 1801; thirty miles above lived Peter Dervsier, 1800.

EARLY SETTLERS IN LITTLE ROCK.

In 1763 John B. Imbau settled at Little Rock and in the same year Joseph Bartholomew located about forty miles above the Post. In 1801 Leon Perry was on Kaufman's bayou and C. Kepler on the west side of the Big Prairie. Dating back into the eighteenth century were the settlements of Francis de Vaugine, Petro Pertuis, Joseph Trudeau and F. Imbau on the Arkansas river.

Above Cadron at Casatete (Cassitot) lived Benjamin Stanley from 1777 to 1780, and John and William Stanley from 1779 to 1782. The Stanleys failed to have their claims confirmed for lack of a ten years' settlement, but they antedated all other Anglo-Americans in western Arkansas.

CHAPTER VII.

THE SETTLEMENT OF CRYSTAL HILL—PYEATTS, CARNAHANS, GRAYS.

Of the settlers who came into Arkansas when it was a part of Louisiana Territory (1803-1812) little has ever been written, because very little is known. Less than five hundred souls inhabited the District of Arkansas in 1803, and the census of 1819 gave the district a population of ten hundred and twenty-six. Unfortunately the rolls of that census are lost, so far as they pertain to the Territory of Louisiana, which in 1810, included all that is now known as Missouri and Arkansas. The rolls for the Territory of Orleans, now the State of Louisiana, for 1810 are intact, and disclose a number of names that in 1820 were in the Territory of Arkansas.

In 1810 the northern boundary of Arkansas was much farther to the north than the present State line, the line surveyed by the Missourian, Brown, in 1823-4. The hideous jog in the northeast corner of the State was enumerated in 1810 in the District of Arkansas by the United States marshals who took the census, so that the number ten hundred and twenty-six included settlers in territory now forming a part of Missouri.

It may be safely said that the population of Arkansas increased from 1803 to 1810 not more than four hundred souls, and very probably not more than three hundred. Where did these three hundred settle? Who were they? Were they your ancestors? Was your grandsire or granddame one of these? To help to an answer to these questions is the object of this work.

THE PYEATTS OF CRYSTAL HILL AND CADRON.

The very foremost of the Americans to enter Arkansas between 1803 and 1810 was a band of North Carolinians, who, in 1806, brought their families to the high lands above Crystal Hill, on the south side of the Arkansas river. The chief spirit of the party was John Gozel, but seven other heads of families united with him to form the settlement.

One year later Major John Pyeatt and his brother, Jacob, with their families, settled at Crystal Hill. It has been said that they were from Georgia, but I am inclined to believe they were from North Carolina. These two settlements were about a mile apart and existed, it seems, without any kind of communication with the outside world. In 1815 Major Gibson of the United States army went up the Arkansas and stopped at Major Pyeatt's. To his amazement Major Pyeatt had not heard of the war of 1812, nor of the many events that had transpired in the world since 1807.

To live eight years in the heart of a wildnerness, cut off from all communication with old associations or the world's progress, seems very much like being buried alive. If, as Gibbon says, solitude is the school of genius, Major Pyeatt must have been genius personified. Some other eminent man has said: "Solitude is the audience chamber of God;" but this is hardly applicable to Crystal Hill. It is certain that these settlers were isolated and that they suffered many privations, but it is only along lines like these that civilization proceeds.

Near Major Pyeatt there lived a Frenchman, Louis Brangiere, who, mistaking the rock crystals and talc in the bluff, about one mile below White Oak bayou, for silver, became a prospector and developer of mines. He opened a mine and spent considerable money upon it, but without striking pay dirt. Nuttal found the old implements and pans in 1819. John Trammel in 1815 also found this mine and took specimens to Arkansas Post, where Francis Notrebe, a new comer from France, and a clerk in a commission house decided they contained gold. Notrebe afterward found gold in Arkansas, but not through mining channels. For years after this, and even down to this good hour the whole region from Crystal Hill on one side to the mouth of the Cadron on the other was, and is believed by many, to be rich in mineral, but no one has ever made it pay.

The fake mine of Brangiere is the only reason for Brangiere's importance in history, unless his remarkable talent for developing pre-emption claims be considered. He tried to blanket the whole region around Crystal Hill in a great blanket claim in 1820, and enlisted Colonel Alexander S. Walker as his attorney in working the claim. The colonel believed in "bluffing," and at once published a notice in the Gazette, warning all persons, as they valued their peace on earth or their happiness hereafter not to trespass by so much as a hair on Brangiere's vested and inalienable rights. General Hogan knew Brangiere and he knew Colonel Walker. Hogan lived on the interdicted ground, and when he read Walker's bluff he published a card telling Brangiere and Walker to go to Hades and be quick about it. Hogan held his ground and Walker went to the legislature. Brangiere got lost in the shuffle.

CRYSTAL HILL MARRIAGES AND DEATHS.

Major John Pyeatt died in 1826, and his wife, Betsy, and his son, Peter, were appointed by the Pulaski Court as administrators. This son was not the recluse his father had been. He had a good horse and saddle and he took long rides to the northward on Saturday night, returning late Monday morning. Away up on Poke Bayou, near where Batesville now stands there came in 1814 a band of Peels and Millers from Kentucky. Young Peter Pyeatt discovered that James Miller of Poke Bayou had a daughter most fair to look upon, and this explains his mysterious pilgrimages. Mary Miller said "Yes," and in December, 1822, Rev. John Carnahan united them in holy wedlock and Crystal Hill gained another family. From this Poke Bayou family of Millers came in time a second governor for Arkansas named Miller and he was born at Batesville in less than a year after the Pyeatt-Miller marriage.

Jacob Pyeatt, after living several years at Crystal Hill, moved to Cadron and founded a new settlement in the year 1815. His wife, Margaret, died at Cadron in 1822. Nuttal found "J. Piatt" at Cadron in 1819. His spelling of the word is not the result of ignorance, but simply shows the tendency of the human mind to travel along the easiest line. Not only this. In New Jersey, a State very near to Philadelphia, there lived a distinguished family of Piatts, from whom the noted Don Piatt descended. Nuttal confused the spelling of a family name that he knew with another that sounded just like it.

It has been said that John Pyeatt was a major in the revolutionary army, and this is doubtless true, as the claim was made at a time when its falsity could have been easily disproved. I have revolutionary services not recorded, and many recorded services have been lost. Pyeatt township will forever commemorate this family, a far greater monument than most of us get.

REV. JOHN CARNAHAN.

Between 1810 and 1815 this minister of the gospel settled at the upper end of Crystal Hill, adjoining the Pyeatt's, William Lockwood and Jonathan Pharr. Mr. Carnahan preached sermons at Arkansas Post in 1811, and was doubtless the first protestant preacher to make a permanent residence in Arkansas. William Patterson, the father-in-law of Daniel Mooney and Sylvanus Philipps, is traditionally assigned to the ministry of the Methodist church, and if he really was a preacher the credit of living first in Arkansas belongs to him, and goes back to 1803.

John Carnahan had a daughter, who, on February 10, 1820,

was married to Henry P. Pyeatt at Big Rock. Near the residence of James Pyeatt, another son of Major John Pyeatt was located and opened the first religious camp ground in Arkansas on May 24, 1822. At that time a five days' meeting was held under the auspices of Rev. John Carnahan, with reported good results for the cause of Christianity, as represented by the Cumberland Presbyterian church. This camp meeting was held two years before the formation of the Baptist church at Little Rock. In 1825 another great camp meeting was held by Mr. Carnahan at Cadron, and in 1826 a still greater one at Crawford court house. At this meeting denominational lines were broken down, and the Baptists, Methodists and Presbyterians united in a great season of love. The testimony of John Carnahan to the zeal and good offices of these kindred Christian bodies on that occasion is one of the sweetest records of these early days. On May 15, 1825, John Carnahan and Rev. Robert Sloane held another camp meeting at Crystal Hill, which seems to have been blessed by the Lord. Just what family this old backwoods preacher had I do not know, but I do know that in 1826 Mrs. James Carnahan was buried, and that in the same year Samuel Carnahan was appointed as her administrator. Away up in Washington and Benton counties are Carnahans of Crystal Hill, and Peels of Greenbrier and Poke Bayou. The Cumberland Presbyterian church at Little Rock has honored itself by framing into its structure a memorial window in memory of this first —this pioneer Protestant preacher.

THE GRAYS.

Joseph Gray, Jacob Gray and Shared Gray migrated to Arkansas in 1818 and settled in what is now Pulaski county. They migrated from East Tennessee. Joseph Gray died in 1821 and Wright Daniel administered upon his estate. Jacob and Shared lived for many years after this, gathering wealth and honors. On the United States pension rolls the fact appears that both Jacob and Shared Gray were placed on the rolls in 1834 with pensions beginning from 1831.

Jacob was recorded as a revolutionary soldier of the South Carolina militia and Shared as a soldier of the North Carolina militia. Jacob at that time (1834) was seventy-one years of age and Shared seventy-seven. Both were then living in Pulaski county. Thinking that Shared was a missprint for Sampson I looked up the original record, but found that Shared was right. Sampson Gray was in Pulaski county in 1818, and was a son of one of the immigrants; he was a popular and noted man. These men also have a township in Pulaski county standing to their everlasting credit.

JAMES VANN.

In 1809 this pioneer entered the Territory of Louisiana and settled in that part of the District of Arkansas now known as Randolph county. He, too, was a revolutionary soldier of the continental line of North Carolina. In 1811 the McKnights and Richardsons settled in Lawrence county, and it is a tradition of the family that they felt the earthquake shocks of that year.

SHERIFF DANIEL MOONEY.

Daniel Mooney was appointed sheriff in 1810 under the old Louisiana law and was continued from 1812 to 1815 under the Missouri law, when he resigned and was succeeded by Hewes Scull, who held the office until 1819. Daniel Mooney had the whole of the present State of Arkansas as his bailiwick, and when he arrested a man for a capital offense he was forced under the law to take him clear to Washington, Missouri, for trial. How would the present sheriffs of Arkansas like his job? Joseph Stilwell was made auditor of accounts in 1810 and held the place until 1815. His duties called him to all parts of the State, and it is said that he and Mooney knew every Indian trail and every hog track in the State.

A STRANGE COINCIDENCE.

One night last week I sent one of the clerks of the congressional library for the session laws of the Territory of Missouri. Six volumes were brought me fresh from the bindery. Upon opening them I found the paper as old and musty as I found the paper to be in the old session laws I used to ponder over while in the office of secretary of State at Little Rock. The books were very old, but had been rebound. On the flyleaf of every volume I found the name "John Scott" in bold, clear letters. I had before me the books that once belonged to John Scott, the Missouri delegate, who drew the law that made Arkansas a territory.

Venerable books! The signature was that of the brother of Judge Andrew Scott, the first judge of Arkansas Territory, and the first county judge of the county in which I was born. My mind went back, there under the dome of the nation's greatest library, to John R. Homer Scott, my friend, and the nephew of the man who once owned the books I held in my hands. I cried inaudibly: "Truly, I am growing old." John Scott is gone. Andrew Scott is gone. John R. Homer Scott is no more. John Scott's books were before me and will be before archaeologists and students for five hundred years to come. Under the six little volumes before me were four giant volumes of the Arkansas Gazette. William E. Woodruff, Sr., has gone, too, but he has left his mark in these books, which ages will not be able to destroy. They bristle with the life of other days and carry that life forward into immortality.

CHAPTER VIII.

ALEXANDER S. WALKER, SOLDIER, LAWYER AND LEGISLATOR.

Colonel Alexander S. Walker was a Virginian of the Tidewater region, born about the year 1786, of parents whose ancestors ran far back into Colonial days. Little is known of his early life. On July 1, 1808, he enrolled his name on the lists of the new regiment, the First regiment of United States riflemen, under Colonel Alexander Smythe, a Virginian, born on Irish soil.

The United States at that time was in a flurry. England was suspicious, Spain was objecting and France was in arms. No one knew where the blow would fall, but every indication pointed to New Orleans. Five regiments of infantry were hurried into the Territory of Mississippi and several vessels of the

Marine Corps to the mouth of the Mississippi. The riflemen were all picked men, men whose aim was sure and their nerves of iron. This regiment, the First Rifles, was ordered to Fort Adams, in Mississippi territory. Alexander S. Walker was rapidly advanced and in three short months held the grade of captain. The regiment was quartered in the swamps and in less than a year lost one hundred and three men by sickness and death and fifty-three by desertion. Sickness was on all sides and was undermining the morale of the army. In July, 1809, the government was four months in arrears with the soldiers' pay and this added another element of discontent.

Captain Walker objected to the location of the camp and circulated a petition for a change, which he presented in person to General Wilkinson. The general answered with an oath that he could make no change, that the localities had been selected by the secretary of war, and that in locating the camps he had simply obeyed orders. Captain Walker forgot himself and said, "Damn such orders." That night he took a little more whisky than the malaria demanded as an antidote for his anger. This loosened his tongue and he went so far as to say that he didn't blame the men for deserting; that no government had the right to order men to any death save death at the cannon's mouth, and that the camps had been pitched in the worst spots imaginable. A second lieutenant, Matthew Cannan, of the same regiment, was equally outspoken.

When all this reached headquarters the devil was to pay and no pitch hot. Walker and Cannan were arrested. A court-martial was convened at Arkansas Post and a trial had. Walker expressed no contrition, nor did Cannan. In December, 1809, they were both adjudged "guilty," and on January 1, 1810, they were dishonorably discharged from the United States army.

THE COURAGE OF WALKER.

Walker was down and out. But what of that? Shall the soul refuse to aspire because for a reputed sin a stigma has been put upon it? Alexander S. Walker had sinned against every rule of war and by a war court was humiliated. Was that to end his career? Was there to be no further room for ultimate success? Why are we so eager to cast a stone at a humiliated soul? Is it because we have no sin, or is it because our sin has not gone to the proper court-martial? Has the muck-raker a patent on sinlessness? Is Collier and all that conceited, aimless, money-grabbing crowd, the index finger of a stainless life? Nay, verily.

On the other hand, of what stern stuff must a man be made who deliberately communes with himself and says: "I, myself, am down; terribly but not irremediably down; despite the blow I will arise." Alexander S. Walker felt keenly the humiliation to which he had been subjected, but neither fretted nor repined. He had been stricken by a power he could not resist—censured, as Jackson was censured a few years later, but he did not whine nor hide.

Within the very theater where had been enacted his undoing he began the work of his restoration. A restoration, not to the military rank he had forfeited, but to a place in the broad and generous confidence of his fellow-men. Courts-martial may esteem this or that point of law or evidence at a little less or a little more than its legitimate content, but the silent judgment of mankind is a far more accurate balance.

WALKER AS A CIVILIAN.

Within sight of the Post where he had been cashiered he began the battle of civil life. Upon that ground, or in its immediate neighborhood, he spent more than thirty years of his after life. He flaunted, silently, his growth in the esteem of his fellows, in the very faces of those who would have made him a pariah. He had a good education and a very stubborn will. He dug a living out of the ground through the years 1811 and 1812. In his cabin he read law and studied the game of politics. He had friends in the district of Arkansas when the territory of Missouri was created, and these friends sent him in 1815 to the House of Representatives at St. Louis, and Henry Cassidy to the council. In 1816 he was sent to the Assembly from Lawrence county along with Joseph Hardin, while Edmund Hogan was sent from Arkansas; in the council James Cummins represented Arkansas and Richard Murphy Lawrence. In 1818 Lawrence was represented by Perry Magness, Joseph Hardin and John Davidson, while Arkansas sent Edmund Hogan. The long horseback rides from the Arkansas to the mouth of the Missouri only made him grimmer and sterner. The stigma of cashierdom was more than offset by these signal marks of honor. In the heat of passion and debate men hurled his former degradation into his teeth, but he, although passionate, somewhat overbearing and brave to a fault, answered never a word. What could he answer? He had been disgraced in the days agone, but not so signally as to take offense when anger forced an antagonist to forget his nobler part. He was not disgracing his position now, and that position was slowly sponging out the old account.

WALKER IN HEMPSTEAD COUNTY.

In 1819, when Arkansas became a territory, he was appointed sheriff of Hempstead county, which indicates a residence there at the time, although there is no other record of the fact. In November of the same year the first territorial election for delegate to Congress took place, and there were six candidates for the place, viz: Alexander S. Walker, Henry Cassidy, James Woodson Bates, Perley Wallis, R. F. Slaughter and Stephen Austin. Hempstead in his excellent history of Arkansas names but five and states that there were but one hundred and two votes cast. In this he was misled. He took his returns wrong. Arkansas township in Arkansas county cast one hundred and two votes and voted for only five men. There were twelve hundred and seventy-two votes cast in the territory for six candidates. James Woodson Bates had been a resident of the territory for a year, having come in in 1818, just before the creation of the territory. He had been there a little longer than Andrew Scott and still a little longer than Robert Crittenden. Bates always claimed that he came to Arkansas on his own motion, while Scott and Crittenden were there on salary and by appointment. Young Robert C. Oden had another way of expressing it. He said that he came because he wanted to, but that Scott and Crittenden had to be hired. He afterward used this logic against Henry W. Conway. Bates wanted a salary and announced for Congress, pointing to his long twelve months' residence as a partial reason. Perley Wallis was a lawyer and had been in Arkansas about four years. R. F. Slaughter could not boast of so long a residence as Bates, but he used the residence racket for all it was worth. Henry Cassidy and Alexander S. Walker could boast of a residence of about nine years each, and were the only real old residents in the race. Stephen F. Austin did not reside in the territory at all. The people knew his father and thought that a son of Moses Austin would make them a good representative. They ran him without consulting him and came very nearly electing him. Bates got four hundred and one votes; Austin, three hundred and forty-three; Walker, two hundred and twenty-six; Cassidy, one hundred and fifty-six; Slaughter, one hundred and thirty-eight, and Wallis, eight. Bates had a plurality of fifty-eight votes over Austin, his closest competitor, and one hundred and seventy-five over Walker. Austin, the future founder of Texas, almost became the delegate to Congress from Arkansas. His name was not announced anywhere until eleven days before the election, and did not get on any ticket in Arkansas county, nor on the tickets of two townships in Lawrence county. But for this slight circumstance the whole history of Arkansas and Texas would probably have been very different. Had Austin's name gotten on these other tickets there would have been no Conway-Crittenden feud—the glories of the Alamo would not have transpired. The vote cast indicates a population for the territory at that time of but a little more than ten thousand, rather than the usual estimate of fourteen thousand. The census authorities inform me that eight to a voter, including slaves, is the highest ratio of voters to population. This would make the population in November, 1819, about ten thousand one hundred and eighty-four.

Austin was so flattered by this vote from a constituency he never saw that he decided to run down that way. He entered Arkansas in May, 1820, and "lit a running." Governor Miller was so charmed with him that he, on July 15, 1820, appointed him judge of the First Circuit Court, which position he held but a few months, when he resigned to become "the founder of Texas."

Shortly before his appointment two army officers, Colonel Wm. McCray and Major S. B. Archer, visited the territory, arriving at the Post in January, 1820, with the announced possibility of remaining. To clinch the decision favorably, Governor Miller appointed Major S. B. Archer to the same judgeship he afterward offered Austin. Major Archer held the matter under advisement until July 1, 1820, when he declined the appointment, preferring to retain a place whose duties he knew to accepting a place for which he had had no antecedent training. Hempstead notes the appointment of Archer, but intimates that this was probably a mistake of the copyist, and that the record should be S. F. Austin and not S. B. Archer. The record is right, as the Gazette of that date notes Archer's arrival, his appointment to the judgeship, his declination and the subsequent appointment of Austin.

Alexander S. Walker's vote came from the following places: Arkansas county, forty-nine; Lawrence county, two; Clark county, seventy-three, and Hempstead county, one hundred and two. In other words, he got the greatest number of votes in the county of which he was then sheriff and the next greatest number in Clark. He surely had a residence of some kind at Arkansas Post in the early part of 1819, but the largest part of his Arkansas county vote came from Point Chicot township. He surely had a residence in Pulaski county in 1820 and for many years thereafter. In 1819 he had twenty-seven thousand five hundred acres of unconfirmed land on White river and about an equal amount of confirmed land scattered through the five counties of the State. He may have had five residences for all the record shows. I have found no record of his marriage, but he was a married man and reared a family. In June, 1820, he took hold of Brangiere's claims upon the Crystal Hill country, and although foiled as to General Hogan, was successful as to many other persons more easily convinced. But practicing law and running plantations had fewer charms for Walker than the game of politics. In 1825 the people of Pulaski county elected him to the legislative council. This was a most exciting race and showed the old man's game spirit.

EARLY BALLOT BOX IRREGULARITIES.

When the returns were all in Walker was ahead, defeating Hogan about twenty votes. The Revising Board, composed of Thomas W. Newton, Sr., Matthew Cunningham and another, found certain irregularities in the returns of two townships and threw them out. This made the vote a tie and a new election was ordered. Walker came out in a card appealing to the people to stand for their rights and "not to let a stripling hardly acclimated cheat them out of their votes."

Thomas W. Newton answered that he had no desire to defraud, but that a stripling was every whit as good as a cashiered officer. In the second race Walker was elected by thirteen votes. In 1827 Hogan beat Walker by about the same majority and in 1829 Wharton Rector and Walker were elected to the House of Representatives from Pulaski county. In 1831 Walker was elected sheriff of the county to fill out the unexpired term of S. M. Rutherford. While he was sheriff of the county David Rorer was the county judge. Professor Reynolds in his admirable little story book tells the ox-yoke story as related by Judge Pope in his Early Days. Reynolds has a picture showing Walker dressed as an old-time planter carrying a gun, with Rorer dressed as a field hand carrying an ox-yoke. This picture is utterly incongruous and is not fair to Judge Rorer. Prof. Reynolds describes Rorer as one of that shiftless, harmless, easy-going class of people always to be found on the borderland of civilization. There is no evidence whatever to support the description. Rorer was elected by the people as their county judge. He was repeatedly appointed administrator for people dying intestate, some leaving good estates, but the most of them very little property. Rorer owned the ferry at Little Rock and kept a good house of entertainment on the north side. He entertained Governor Pope, and his whole life merits a better description than the one alluded to. He had to carry the ox-yoke because Walker had a gun. The duel between Walker and Colonel Francis Notrebe in 1816 has already been told by Judge Pope. In 1819, when Governor Miller appointed W. O. Allen, brigadier general of the Arkansas militia, Allen appointed Alexander S. Walker colonel of the First regiment. In this position Walker trained the men who afterward became the leaders of Arkansas. In his regiment were men who in after years were the ornament of both civil and military life.

Such was the life work of a peculiarly eccentric man. He had grave faults, but with them he had transcendent virtues. He began life with a load, but he carried it so nobly as to win the esteem of all his fellows. The lesson of his life is refreshing to the soul. He was afterwards appointed by President Jackson Indian Agent for the Senecas and died near Fort Gibson in 1837 or 1838.

CHAPTER IX.

ROBERT CRITTENDEN—WILLIAM O. ALLEN—THE FIRST DUEL IN ARKANSAS.

Gregory, in his description of Thornton, the home of the Brontes, has said of its people: "Dwelling in the seclusion of a village, at that time much cut off from the centers of population, they nursed their piety and their prejudices." The village of Arkansas Post was much cut off from the centers of population, and its inhabitants certainly nursed their prejudices, but it can not be said that they gave much attention to their piety. All through the Gazette's life of two years at the Post there is no record of a resident preacher, and few references to a traveling minister. The residents of this isolated village nursed their politics and their prejudices. Politics throughout all territorial days had nothing whatever to do with parties, but was a purely personal affair, the aggrandizement of self with a perennial prejudice against all others having the same propensities.

ROBERT CRITTENDEN A CARDINAL WOLSEY.

Young Robert Crittenden, as secretary of the territory, had little to do under the score of official duties. There were only five counties, with about fifteen county officials and about a dozen justices of the peace to commission. I have issued a thousand commissions a day in the after-life of Arkansas and could have performed all of Crittenden's legitimate duties in a day without breaking the sacred surroundings of the eight-hour law.

For the first six months of the first year Crittenden was also loaded down with the dread weight of the governor's office, which possibly took a solid week of his time. Official duties being few, there was plenty of time for nursing prejudice and coddling politics. Crittenden was a past master in both these arts, but he still had plenty of time to practice law and deal in real estate. In fact, these last comprised his business and the others were his pastime.

He and Bates began the practice of law in 1819 as partners, with Bates as the head of the partnership. When Bates went to the bench the same year Crittenden tried it alone, but before the year expired Bates went to Congress, and the partnership was revived, to remain in full force for three years, until politics and prejudice arrayed these men against each other with a fervor that never abated.

Bates said that Crittenden desired to run the politics of the State, manage the governor and direct the delegate; that when Miller showed spirit and independence he was called "an old fool," and when he (Bates) proposed to do his own thinking as a delegate, Crittenden wanted to turn him out. Crittenden was called "Cardinal Wolsey" on account of his supposed influence with the governors, an influence that never counted in fact, but which made a good supposititious asset.

Crittenden had a partnership with Elijah Morton, another Kentuckian, in the real estate business, and they were together interested in many real estate deals. Bates said that Crittenden carried his pockets full of blank justice of the peace commissions, which, by judicious distribution, laid the foundation for the Crittenden machine which began to grind in 1823. Politics and prejudice controlled at Arkansas Post in 1819 and 1820, but not exclusively. There were some not wedded to these gods, who seem to have taken a loftier ideal and to have gauged their actions by a better standard.

GENERAL WILLIAM O. ALLEN.

It is now about eighty-seven years since William O. Allen went down to an untimely death at Arkansas Post. The more one studies the fragments of his speeches, and the more one investigates his life and character, the more one is convinced that he was the ablest man in the territory of Arkansas in 1819 and 1820. Intellectually, he was the superior of Crittenden or Bates, the two most luminous characters of those years. And while Bates far transcended Crittenden in mental vigor and logical power, Allen not only transcended Bates in these, but was his superior in self-discipline and independence.

Like Bates, he was born and educated in Virginia. His family was of equal respectability and his training similar in kind. Each had the American reverence for the profession of law, and each spent the heyday of young manhood in dreams of future conquests at the bar. Each migrated to the territory of Louisiana, Allen being there while it yet had that name and Bates reaching it after it bore the name Territory of Missouri. Allen was in St. Louis when the tocsin of war was sounded in 1812, and the spirit of his ancestors became reanimate in him, impelling him to offer his services for the common good. Crittenden at that time was but a sixteen-year-old boy in central Kentucky, but when the Second Rifles was formed in 1814 he became its ensign and went to the front. Bates had no military spirit, although equipped with a full amount of soldierly courage.

ALLEN'S SIX YEARS IN THE ARMY.

Allen enlisted in the Twenty-fourth Infantry on January 1, 1812, and on April 14 of that year was advanced to the captaincy of a company. On June 15, 1814, he was transferred to the Thirty-fifth Infantry, and on May 17, 1815, to the Artillery Corps, holding his rank. He resigned from the service at Arkansas Post on March 18, 1818. During these long years he served in many parts of the United States and made the acquaintance of the leading military spirits of the age. In 1812 his regiment was with the army in Ohio and Michigan, but was never under fire. On August 2, 1813, it had its baptism in blood at Fort Stephenson, Ohio. On December 19, 1813, it was present at the action at Lewiston Heights and the surrender of Fort Niagara. On March 14, 1814, it took part in the action at Longwood, Upper Canada. During the remainder of the war the regiment remained on duty in Upper Canada. As a member of the Corps of Artillery his lot was cast in the Southern Military Division, in turn being stationed at Fort Barrancas, at New Orleans and at Arkansas Post and Fort Smith. This corps was made up of the chociest spirits of the war. Its colonel was the famous Moses Porter, and its lieutenant colonels, all in commission from 1815 to 1821, were: Constant Freeman, James House, F. K. Huger, William Lindsey and William McRae, each at one time or another on duty at the Post. Its majors during this period were: Forney, Nye, Armistead, Many, Hindman, Bankhead and Walbach.

COLONEL GEO. B. ARMISTEAD AT THE POST.

Allen was a close friend of Colonel George Armistead during all the years of his residence at the Post, and, like Armistead, had become the owner of property in that old Arkansas town. When the fortunes of war carried Armistead to other fields, Allen became the manager of his property, and after the death of Allen, this trust was confided to William E. Woodruff, Sr. until Armistead's death.

There must have been attractions in a business way at Arkansas Post in 1816, 1817 and 1818 that we at this distance of time can not estimate or appreciate. Allen resigned his place in the army, gave up a career among distinguished associates to enter civil life, and chose Arkansas Post as the place for a beginning. All through 1818 and 1819 he was quietly engaged at building up his old business, the law. When bluff old General Miller reached the Post he was gratified to find Allen there, and at once appointed him brigadier general of the Arkansas militia. The necessity for a defense of the settlements against Indian outrages necessitated immediate action. A brigade was formed by Allen, one regiment of which was placed under the command of Colonel Alexander S. Walker.

ALLEN'S RAPID PROMOTION.

Life moves with resistless energy for those capacitated to stem its currents. Allen was elected to the first legislature, in the fall of 1819, by the people of Arkansas county. This body met in February, 1820 and was in session but for a few short weeks. Few speeches of that legislature have come down to us, but singularly enough the greater number of these are those of Allen. Upon these speeches and the narration I have just concluded, the judgment is predicated that Allen was the ablest man at the Post. His greatest speech was upon the removal of the county seat from Little Rock to Cadron.

Tyndall, the Cadron member, was all fire and seemed likely to have everything his own way. Allen rose above place and circumstance. He stood for the dignity of a legislative body, and urged that the only function of legislation was to deal with general principles and not local affairs. That it was the duty of the body to pass a general law covering the modus operandi of locating county seats and for their removal. That it was no part of a legislator's duty to choose between rival county towns, or to locate a county seat for the people of Pulaski county. It was a long speech, well delivered and logical.

Tyndall had but one answer, and that was, "We were sent here to legislate, and if we can't locate a little county seat at Cadron, we had better go home." Hardin, another bluff old soldier, agreed with Tyndall, and said: "We are here to make laws and if we want to make a law carrying the county seat to Cadron we have the right to do so." Allen won the fight by a close shave, the vote being five for non-consideration and four for. During the next week, Allen discussed the militia situation so forcefully, so intelligently and so logically as to carry his propositions overwhelmingly. He had made an indelible mark on the people and on his companions in legislation. No one doubted his future career of usefulness.

ALLEN'S UNTIMELY DEATH.

But who can read the future? Before that body adjourned William O. Allen was a corpse. In March, 1820, he challenged

Robert C. Oden to mortal combat, which challenge was accepted, the seconds being George W. Scott and Elijah Morton. The duel occurred on an island in the Arkansas river on March 10, 1820. Allen fired first and his bullet went true to its aim, struck a button over Oden's heart, glanced aside and inflicted a severe but not a mortal wound. The impact of the ball knocked Oden down, and as he fell he fired a random shot, which struck Allen in the head, killing him instantly. Oden was accidentally saved and Allen was accidentally killed. The accident of a button and the accident of a random shot changed the issues of the combat. Such is dueling.

GAZETTE'S COMMENT ON DUEL.

The cause of the duel may never be known. The Gazette of the following week noted the death of Allen, and said: "We sincerely regret to see a practice still continue which has been universally condemned by every philanthropic mind."

But there was not one syllable about the reasons leading to the fight. Captain John R. Homer Scott, born in Missouri a few years before the duel, in his later years gave Judge Pope a version from memory as told him by his father, Judge Andrew Scott, which, to my mind, is unsatisfactory. He said that Allen and Oden were at dinner and that Oden finished first. Seeing Allen's cane near, he picked it up and began twirling it. Allen finished, and, being lame, reached toward Oden for the cane. Oden, in playfulness, retreated, Allen pursuing as best he could. This was kept up until Allen became angry, limped to his room and wrote the challenge.

ANOTHER VERSION OF THE AFFAIR.

In 1885 the writer was on Grand Prairie, between DeWitt and Stuttgart. He traveled off the main road and approached a large frame house for information, and was invited to remain for dinner. At table was an old man, a relative of some sort of the owner of the house. The conversation reverted to the Post and the duels fought there. The old man gave this version of the Allen-Oden duel: Allen and Oden were at table when a discussion began between them over Allen's speech in the legislature. Allen was about forty-five years of age and Oden about twenty. Oden was passionate and very sensitive. As the argument grew warmer, Oden accused Allen of disputing his word, seized Allen's cane and struck Allen a smart blow. The blow resulted in the challenge. Up to this time both men had been friends, and Allen had formed a great liking for Oden. Years after this conversation I jotted down its substance, but could not recall the name of the narrator. The version of Mr. Scott, a man of remarkable memory as well as of absolute veracity, may be the correct one. The old man's story seems, however, to furnish a better motive.

THE LAW REGARDING DUELING.

In what follows we have the printed report of the Gazette and it is collated and reproduced here to show the iron-clad sentiment which prevailed at that time with reference to dueling. In 1820 the Grand Jury of Arkansas county indicted Robert E. Oden for receiving a challenge, and George W. Scott and Elijah Morton for officiating as seconds. It was not murder nor manslaughter to kill in a duel, and the only offense was sending or receiving a challenge, or officiating as seconds. At the trial the prosecution offered to put Scott and Morton on the stand to prove the reception of the challenge. The court held that this could not be done until it was proven that the challenge itself was lost. This foiled the prosecution and the jury was forced to find a verdict "Not guilty."

On the next day the trial of Scott and Morton began, and, although they made no denial whatever, the case against them was not proved. The defense moved to quash, on the ground of variance—the indictment being laid at the Post and the evidence showing that the duel occurred on an island in the river. The court held that the words "Arkansas Post" were descriptive merely and that the indictment was good. The jury, however, brought in the verdict "Not guilty under the indictment."

The Gazette made but few remarks regarding the result of the trials, but advised the people to repeal the laws they had and let those who wanted to kill each other do as they pleased. An anonymous writer noted the mistrial in both cases and advised the enactment of a new law, permitting the seconds to testify as to the challenge and making the offense murder.

William Montgomery, the foreman of the juries, answered this writer, denying that the verdict was "not guilty," but "not guilty under the indictment," and in a very pompous manner said no writer, "whether he be vagrant or gentleman, should malign a jury of which he was a part."

PUTS AN END TO DUELING.

At the next session of that legislature an iron-clad law against dueling was passed. Death resulting from a duel fought on Arkansas soil was declared to be murder. Seconds were authorized to testify, and the courts required to take their testimony, immunity for the testifying witness being provided for. This law was passed in October, 1820, and it has had a good effect. No duel has been fought in the State or territory since its enactment, although it has been easy at all times to evade it.

William O. Allen was an unmarried man, and no wife nor child was brought to grief by his death. He left an estate, upon which Eli J. Lewis and Daniel Mooney administered. The advertised list of property filled nearly a column of the Gazette. In the list was a library of books, legal, historical, mathematical and astronomical, which had no equal in Arkansas then, and which doubtless entered into the family collections of other men and became the basis of the educational development of many of the sons and daughters of Arkansas. Is it possible to trace that library? Will those who have very old books look in them to see whether the name of William O. Allen appears therein? Many of them ought to be in existence today.

In April, 1820, the Comet arrived at Arkansas Post, being the first steamboat to travel up the Arkansas. Her captain was named Byrne, and he brought his wife, the sister of William O. Allen, to the Post to investigate his death and to settle his estate. Thus the law of sequence comes to the forefront of affairs. A duel results in a death. A steamboat owner, driven by love, forces his vessel along paths heretofore considered impassable and navigation of a great river ensues.

CHAPTER X.

SAMUEL MOSELEY—FRANCIS NOTREBE—TERRENCE FARRELLY.

In the lives of Samuel Mosely, Francis Notrebe and Terrence Farrelly, all born on foreign soil, but who acquired wealth and honor at Arkansas Post, there is much to inspire every human being—much to show that life is not the victim of luck, fate or chance.

The Scotch are noted for thrift, the Irish for wit and the French for versatility. Neither of these men could claim to have been knighted by the king's own hand, but each of them sprang from a line of knights famous in Scotland, Ireland and France. When knighthood was in flower these ancestors enjoyed its fruits, but their remote descendants, the men of whom we write, had neither fruit nor flower. They were of poor parents and inherited nothing but the disposition to have something and an opportunity to attain their aims. It has been said that a Scotchman needs no open door of opportunity—that he can make his opportunity at will. From the Gazette we ascertain that Samuel Mosely was born in Aberdeen, Scotland, about 1784. The story of how he spent his younger life and of how he found his way to Arkansas Post may never be known. He was found at the Post in 1812, and drops out of sight completely until the month of November, 1818, when the St. Louis Republican announced the marriage of Samuel Mosely to Mary King at Arkansas Post, on October 22, 1818. The family of the bride is not known, but as Wigton King had been a resident at the Post since 1814, and was a justice of the peace from that time until the creation of the Territory of Arkansas, and for many years thereafter, it is supposed that she was his daughter.

NUTTAL'S REFERENCE TO OPPORTUNITY.

The next historic reference to Mosely is found in the quaint old diary of Nuttal, containing his experiences in Arkansas in 1819-1820. He notes the residence of Mosely in the Arkansas river, and states that he had lately died, after many years of residence at the Post, and further that he died at the age of thirty-five. He then called attention to the fact that in the few years that Mosely had resided at the Post he had gathered quite a fortune, dying with an estate of $20,000. Forgetting his scientific mission for awhile, Nuttal turns aside to comment upon the opportunities of a region that in so short a time could give one man so great a fortune. Mosely died the richest man in Arkansas county, Nuttal says, and his fortune was certainly a great one in that day. His death is noted in the Gazette months after it occurred as having happened on September 19, 1819. He had been married not quite a year, but his death notice contains no reference to children, nor do the after references to his estate disclose any, but there may have been a child. In December, 1819, Eli J. Lewis and Daniel Mooney gave notice in the Gazette that, as administrators, they had the settlement of the estate in hand and would proceed with their work as the statutes required.

The widow did not remain a widow long, for on January 22, 1820, she was wedded to Terrence Farrelly, of the firm of Farrelly & Curran, the Irishman of our present article. The life of Samuel Mosely is best interpreted by his achievements. He came to the Post poor and died the richest man there. The long years of hard work, the intensity of his struggle may only be estimated; he left no record disclosing the stages of his efforts or the sacrifices he must have made. He came unheralded and unknown, and died the richest, and very probably, the best-known man at the Post. It has been said that five things are necessary to success—ability, integrity, dispatch, patience and industry—and, judged by his success, Mosely must have had all these abstract substances in the highest degree.

COLONEL FRANCIS NOTREBE.

Francis Notrebe was not only a native of France, but a soldier of France, under that master of war, the great Napoleon, but he did not win his title of colonel in the French army. History is silent as to the place of his birth, his early education and the causes that led to his enlistment as a French soldier. He has told his Arkansas friends the reasons for his abandonment of France, and they are alike creditable to his patriotism and his will. As a common soldier he risked his life to give France a republic, and was an enthusiastic follower of Napoleon so long as that genius kept his eye single to the freedom of France.

When ambition led the general to overthrow the republic and to set up an empire on its ruins Notrebe would not go with him. He was proud of Napoleon but placed France and its interests above his affections for the man. He could not fight for an empire, and after great difficulty succeeded in separating himself from the army and in reaching the United States. After years of rambling life he found himself, in 1813, at Arkansas Post. Here he found congenial French people, and after awhile a congenial business. He was essentially a merchant, and as a clerk in the great trading houses at the Post he soon found the natural trend of his mind. Barham & Drope, Prior & Lewis and Louis Bogy were great traders and maintained great warehouses far up the Arkansas, in what is now Indian Territory and Kansas. At these places and at the Post they carried on a large trade with the Indian tribes.

In a small way Notrebe began business for himself at the Post in 1819. His advertisements in the Gazette show that he was just embarking and that fortune had not begun to smile.

EARLY LITTLE ROCK MERCHANTS.

In 1820 the sheriff of Pulaski county published a list of men who had taken out licenses as merchants or grocery keepers for that year at Little Rock. At the head of the list was Chester Ashley, then a young unmarried man, and a briefless lawyer. While Sam C. Roane pieced out an income by acting as pressman for Woodruff, the future great senator of Arkansas attained the same end by keeping a small grocery. When Woodruff moved to Little Rock two years later his paper did not give him a support and he began the sale as sole agent for an Eastern house of a line of patent medicines. The other names on the list were George W. Brand, William Drope, Thomas W. Johnson and Francis Vaugine. In 1821, when the second list was published, the name of Francis Notrebe appeared and was retained there for several years. Notrebe was thus connected as a merchant with Arkansas Post and Little Rock, but his principal business as well as his affections were centered at Arkansas Post. Between 1822 and 1825 he extended his business relations to the upper Arkansas, and at his death, several years later, was the richest man in the territory. When Governor

Pope entered the territory, in 1829, he made the acquaintance of Notrebe, and in 1832 was his guest at Arkansas Post. The display of silver and cut glass, as well as the retinue of servants maintained by Notrebe, excited the governor's surprise, as he did not expect such service in the wilds of the West.

Judge Pope has left an interesting description of Colonel Notrebe as he was in the days subsequent to 1832. He was a man of commanding appearance, very black hair and a dark complexion. He possessed large but regular features and in his youth was doubtless a handsome man. He was said to have all the refinement and elegance of the French race. He was a married man and reared a family of children, but I have not been fortunate enough to find the family name of his wife nor the date of his marriage, which probably took place before he reached Arkansas.

CUMMINS-NOTREBE WEDDING.

Kentucky sent several young lawyers into Arkansas between 1819 and 1830, but in all probability no one of them was better equipped than William Cummins of Louisville. Tradition gives him high rank among the lawyers of the territory and State from 1830 to 1840, but of the years before 1830 little is said. He began a suit at Arkansas Post before that august and pretty judge, the daughter of the rich Frenchman, Colonel Notrebe, and managed it so well as not only to win it, but to marry the judge. As Mrs. William Cummins, the daughter of Notrebe presided over a hospitable and elegant home in Little Rock for many years, and died, leaving children.

Colonel Francis Notrebe was connected with the Missouri militia prior to 1819, and was continued in that service under Arkansas law, and in this service won his military title. In 1820 when the Court of Common Pleas was instituted at the Post, Colonel Francis Notrebe, James Hamilton and Joseph Stilwell were appointed judges of the court, which position they held until the court was abolished. In 1821, when the new town of Arkansas Post was laid off, James Hamilton, Francis Notrebe, Doctor Robert McKay, Colonel David Brearly and John Maxwell were made its first trustees.

It has been said that every man has in himself a continent of undiscovered character, and in this sense, Notrebe was most happy in becoming the Columbus of his own soul.

GENERAL TERRENCE FARRELLY.

Terrence Farrelly was born in County Tyrone, Ireland, about 1795, but was brought to Meadville, Pennsylvania, by his parents about the year 1800. What educational opportunities were afforded him is not known, but it is supposed that they were somewhat above the average. I have not been fortunate enough to find an authoritative reference to his father, but am inclined to believe that he was a son of Patrick Farrelly of Meadville, born in Ireland in 1760, a lawyer, and a member of the Seventeenth Congress (1821-23). He was re-elected to the Eighteenth and Nineteenth Congresses and died at Meadville, January 12, 1826, while serving his third term. He was elected as a Democrat and was a strict constructionist. The few speeches that remain proclaim him a man of extensive parts, and he voted for Henry W. Conway's improvement schemes in Arkansas in 1825, although violating his principles in so doing. Henry W. Conway was more of Whig than anything else and was warmly supported in all his territorial measures by Henry Clay, and opposed by the old line strict constructionists. From the fact that Patrick Farrelly voted for Arkansas improvements, I infer a close relationship between Patrick and Terrence, and an appeal from Terrence which effected this result. Patrick Farrelly had another son, John W. Farrelly, born at Meadville, July 7, 1809, who became a prominent man. He was a member of the Pennsylvania Senate in 1828, where he remained for many years. He served one term in the Thirtieth Congress as a Whig, and was appointed by Taylor sixth auditor of the treasury. He died at Washington.

Terrence began his life as a merchant in Meadville, but in 1817 removed to Pittsburg. There he became acquainted with another young Irishman, Thomas Curran, and with him formed a partnership for a hardware establishment at Arkansas Post. They arrived at the Post in November, 1819, and rented a store of General William O. Allen, where they carried on business until the latter part of 1820, when Curran removed to Davidsonville, Lawrence county, where, on February 18, 1821, he married Mrs. Jane Dodge. This firm gave William E. Woodruff, Sr., a good advertisement for the first issue of his paper and kept it up until the firm dissolved. Terrence had not been at his new home long before he became acquainted with the rich young widow, Mrs. Mary Mosely, and with true Hibernian directness, made a short wooing and won the prize. He was married on January 22, 1820, and in a short time Lewis and Mooney, Samuel Mosely's administrators, notified all interested parties to settle with Terrence Farrelly, who now had charge of the Mosely estate. Thus, while others waited for fortune's favors, Farrelly captured them by love and wit. He was now an American landlord and at once set about to be an American leader of affairs.

FARRELLY AS A LEGISLATOR.

And why shouldn't he be a leader? He was blessed with every element that a leader should have. Do you ask for wit? He was born in Ireland and blessed with the fullest amount of Irish wit. Do you ask for wealth and power to please? He had just married the richest woman in Arkansas and has been given full control of her estate. Do you demand business ability? He was in the Arkansas territorial legislature from 1821 to 1836, a longer period than any other man ever served, before or since, and was at all times either on the Committee on Banking or on the Committee on Auditor's and Treasurer's Books. Do you ask for a sound judgment and a good knowledge of law? For fifteen years he was on the Judiciary Committee of the Arkansas legislature, and did more toward fashioning Arkansas law in his day than any twenty men that can be named. Do you want honesty and faithfulness? Then reread what I have written and add that he was the first county judge of Arkansas County from 1830 to 1832, and could have had the place ever afterward but that he positively refused to serve. Is courage what you seek? He was adjutant-general of the Arkansas militia under Generals W. O. Allen, Edmund Hogan and William Bradford. More than that, he was the chief adviser of Maj. Bradford, and to this advice the territory was indebted for the nine regiments of splendid troops the territory afforded in 1825. We have had adjutant generals since Farrelly's day, but none that could muster an army like he had under his charge. The regiments were real live flesh and blood soldiers, commanded by the following colonels: First Regiment, Jack Wells; Second Regiment, James Lemons; Third, Joseph Hardin; Fourth, James Scull; Fifth, Thomas Dooley; Sixth, Pearson Brierly; Seventh, Hartwell Boswell; Eighth, Daniel Mooney; Ninth, Jacob Pennington. General Terrence Farrelly was not afraid of any of these colonels, nor of all of them combined. He could make and unmake them at pleasure. And after all of this category of public services, when Statehood came, Arkansas county sent him to the Constitutional Convention, and no man in the body equalled him in influence and worth. Do you ask for an organizer—a boss? Terrence Farrelly bossed the politics of Arkansas county and had no rival. For sixteen years he carried the county in his pocket, and so gentle was his rule, so wise, so patriotic as never to create a schism or revolt. Outside of Arkansas county, he was looked upon as a sound and safe man, worthy of any and every trust, and honored throughout the State. He had talents and he used them to improve, exalt and gladden life. He was just, and thereby ennobled his own character. His wit made him the god of moments, and in later times, his genius would have made him god of the ages. No man of the period extracted as much sweet out of life as did he, and in that he proclaimed his wisdom. There was no pleasanter character in territorial days than Terrence Farrelly, the Irish-American.

CHAPTER XI.

PRINGLES—HARRINGTONS—MORRISONS AND DARDENNES—LIST OF REVOLUTIONARY PATRIOTS.

In speaking of that old Marylander, Christian Pringle, who died in 1820, after a residence in the neighborhood covering forty years, a doubt was left as to his marriage. He left a wife, who in 1823 re-entered the connubial State by marrying James Young at Arkansas Post. Christian Pringle left a son and a daughter, that are of record, and possibly other children. John

Pringle was born at the Post about 1804 and on July 15, 1824, married Mary Jones at the same place. This is the first mention of the Jones family and her father's name is not known. The daughter of Christian Pringle was also born in Arkansas about 1806, and on January 26, 1825, married John, a son of the pioneer soldier, Joseph Stilwell.

MAJOR JOHN HARRINGTON AND DESCENDANTS.

John Harrington was a New Englander, whose father was born in Ireland and a soldier of the American revolution. John, born in Massachusetts in 1769, served in the Indian wars of 1793, and in the second war with Great Britain in 1812, in which he won several promotions in rank, terminating with major. When he was mustered out of the service he was induced to go to Arkansas, where in 1814 he purchased a plantation and settled down to a peaceful and contented life.

He lived about twenty miles above Samuel Moseley's immense plantation on the Arkansas, and had for his neighbors, Mr. William Morrison, Mr. Mason, Madame Embree, whose daughter afterward married Judge Sam C. Roane, and Major Vaugine, in a region that was afterward named, Richland, and from which the township was called.

Nuttal had the happy faculty of "sensing" strong characters and of honoring all such with a short note. He said of Major Harrington, "He was a farmer in comfortable circumstances." The major owned property at the Post and was a favorite with Governor Miller. The old man died on his farm on August 29, 1829, in his sixtieth year. He had a son, Bartley, who was a man of parts, and who exercised a great local influence. The treaty between the United States and the Quapaw Indians was negotiated at the house of his father, although at that time under the control of the son. Both father and son were well known to the Indians, and the Harrington house was selected, not alone on the ground of its contiguity, but for the sounder reason, that the Indians held Major Harrington in high esteem. This treaty was negotiated on the part of the United States by Robert Crittenden as special commissioner, and was witnessed by Thomas W. Newton, Robert C. Oden, Terrence Farrelly, Bartley Harrington, D. Barbin, special Indian agent, Gordon

Neil, Edmund Hogan, brigadier general of the Arkansas militia, Thomas W. Johnson, Antoine Barraque, Etienne Vaugine and Joseph De Chassin. Hogan was dressed in his valiant military suit, as was Farrelly, his adjutant-general, and Oden, the lieutant-colonel of the Second regiment. Thomas W. Newton was aide-de-camp to the governor, and, altogether, this display of epaulettes was supposed to be the right thing for the Indians.

CRITTENDEN DEALS WITH INDIANS.

Robert Crittenden made one of those strictly American farce talks, in which he assumed the role of "The Great Father," and bunkoed the Indians in the American fashion of that day. They sold as fair a piece of God's heritage as was ever seen for a mess of pottage. The government had sent down about seven thousand dollars as expense money, and it was the handling of this money that brought Henry W. Conway and Robert Crittenden face to face in mortal combat, in which Conway went to an untimely death. There were two things that counted with the Indians far more than the epaulettes and the jangling swords. One of these was their faith in Major John Harrington, and he hesitated to advise. The other was the jingle of the ducats that Crittenden offered. In this way "Harrington's" had become one of the mile posts of Arkansas growth, the removal of the Quapaws. Harringtons is settled firmly in the archives of the government, to remain there forever, as a place where something of importance happened, and out of which other important happenings were evolved. What happened at Harringtons may have been a crime against a race, but as old Major Harrington told them: "Better this than worse." The Indians did not get full value, nor anything like it; but they got more than they could use, and a home for all future time. Civilization gained by the purchase and Arkansas development was thereby assured.

CANDIDATES IN FIRST LEGISLATURE.

Bartley Harrington was a candidate for a position in the first legislature, but was defeated by General W. O. Allen. He represented the county in the council of the fourth legislature. He died in September, 1835, on the river returning from New Orleans. Alfred Harrington, another son, was married to Polly

Mason of Pulaski County on March 2, 1820, at the house of the bride's father, Ephraim C. Davidson officiating. On August 19, 1821, at the house of the major, Archibald Taylor was married to Mary Harrington, Esquire Wigton King performing the ceremony. At the same place on November 28, 1819, Benjamin Kuykendall was married to Eliza Harrington. Four years later, on January 29, 1823, Dempsey Kuykendall, a brother of Benjamin, died in Vaugine township at the age of thirty, leaving a wife, and five children, who have doubtless carried the name down to the present. On February 14, 1830, Allen Harrington was married in Richland township to Clarissa McKenzie, but whether he was a son or grandson of Major Harrington, I can not say.

The blood of Major Harrington is carried by many brave men and fair women of Arkansas today. They have always been sturdy Americans and have contributed their full share to the greatness, the wealth and refinement of Arkansas.

WILLIAM MORRISON.

Concerning this pioneer I have not been as successful as with Major Harrington. I am satisfied that he was a little older than Major Harrington, from the fact that his wife died on April 27, 1827, at the age of sixty years. The major died two years later at the same age. The death of William Morrison is not noted, nor the birth of his children, although I am satisfied that he left children, who have filled honorable stations in Arkansas county. He lived about six miles above the cut-off and had for his nearest neighbor Joseph Kirkland, of whom I have found no further record. Near them lived the old French settler, John B. Dardenne, who gave the government considerable trouble in later years. Under the Spanish regime he was granted about six hundred acres on the north side of the Arkansas river at Chactas Prairie, near where the town of Russellville now stands. This title was regularly confirmed by the government, but no patent issued. In 1817, the government negotiated a treaty with the Cherokees, by whose terms the Cherokees were to surrender lands in Tennessee and Georgia for lands in Arkansas. The lands in Arkansas were north of the Arkansas river and west of a line drawn from Point Remu (Remove) to the White River above Batesville. The government was to remove all settlers from this vast tract, excepting John P. Lovely. Now John B. Dardenne did not live within limits and was not removed. He owned land within it, however, but because of the non-issuance of the patent, there was no record of title, and therefore no exception in the treaty. The Cherokees owned his lands and there was no relief save by an act of Congress. The Committee on Public Lands in their report said that Dardenne was entitled to relief, and that he was willing to take satisfaction in one of three ways: (1) To be given his identical lands in the Cherokee reservation: (2) To be given $10,000 in money: (3) To be permitted to take up an equal quantity of unoccupied land anywhere in Lawrence land district. The committee reported in favor of the latter proposition. Dardenne's name is perpetuated in Dardanelle Rock, and his descendants are in many parts of Arkansas, in Indian Territory and in Kansas. One wing of the family of the writer, by marriage, carries this old French name and blood. The first marriage of a Dardenne to a Dardenne occurred on December 8, 1822, when Abraham married Harriet at Arkansas Post.

MARRIAGES IN ARKANSAS IN 1819 AND 1820.

The following marriages, not elsewhere noted, were celebrated in Arkansas in 1819. At Arkansas Post:—in November Francois La Fargue to Agnes Pinneaux; in August, David Walter to Millet Michel; in September, Francois Duval to Catherine Dudley; in October, Michael Cotoner to Elizabeth Kepler, and Brenhard Raphael to Catherine Gossien. In 1820: —At Strawberry in Lawrence County, January 24, Napoleon B. Ferguson to Elizabeth Allen, and on February 1 George Bradley to Eleanor Bayliss. At Utica on the St. Francis by Daniel Mooney Judge William Reece to Sarah Dukes in October; by Judge W. B. R. Hornor on May 29, at same place, J. Clark Dunn to Clarissa Murch, and Ichabod Dunn to Margaret, daughter of Gabriel Latimer, one of the most noted men of the St. Francis and Mississippi river settlements. On September 29, 1821, Margaret Dunn died and on the same day her infant son passed away. At Blakeley town, Clark County, July 4, Thomas Fish to Emily Hemphill, late of South Carolina. At Arkansas Post on

July 29, Antoine Bonneau to Adele Godin; at Little Rock on September 16, Mr. Martin to Miss Daniel, the daughter of Wright Daniel. Their given names are not preserved, but their descendants of Little Rock will doubtless be in position to complete the omission. At the University of Virginia, in October, Joseph Selden, Judge of the Superior Court of the Territory of Arkansas to Harriet Gray of Albemarle County, Virginia. At Arkansas Post on December 30, Eli J. Lewis to Polly, daughter of Joseph Stilwell.

"GET THERE ELI."

Lewis was a hustler in business and politics, as will be shown hereafter in a sketch of his remarkable career, the one man for whom the phrase "Get there Eli" was coined, and what follows will show that he believed marriage to be a success. When he married Polly Stilwell he was a widower, his wife Sally having died on January 1, 1820. Polly died within four years, on April 21, 1824, when he made a third venture, marrying the belle of the Mississippi river, the daughter of Sylvanus Phillips at Helena, in August, 1825. At Mound Prairie on November 24, William Trimble, U. S. District Attorney, to Lounetta, daughter of Colonel Abraham Stuart; at Utica on January 11, Charles Ewell, of Kentucky, to Barradel Latimer, daughter of Griswold. These became the forbears of thousands of descendants through the eighty-five years that have elapsed since William E. Woodruff first heralded these marriages to the world.

REVOLUTIONARY SOLDIERS AS SHOWN BY THE PENSION ROLLS.

This roll of heroes is a government record and is the highest form of evidence. It is the pension roll of the revolutionary soldiers alive in Arkansas in the counties named in 1833 and 1834, and will serve as an index to all descendants, who may desire to take membership in any of the patriotic orders. The publication of this list must not be taken as an exhaustive presentation of all soldiers in the revolution in Arkansas. There were others, as will be shown from time to time, but they were not on this roll.

Revolutionary pension roll for the State of Arkansas with ages of the pensioners:

Crawford County: Isaiah Mobley, aged seventy-nine years; Clement Mobley, sixty-seven, both of the South Carolina militia.

Hempstead County: Benjamin Clark, Sr., seventy-six, North Carolina militia; William Conway, seventy-six, South Carolina militia; Morgan Cryer, Sr., seventy-eight, South Carolina militia; Morgan Cryer died in Clark county in November, 1833; John Holman, ninety-seven, Virginia Continental Line.

Independence County: Lawrence Angel, seventy-one, North Carolina Continental Line; John Carothers, eighty-eight, South Carolina militia; Benjamin Hardin, sixty-nine, North Carolina militia; David Vance, seventy-five, Virginia Continental Line; John Weldon, seventy-five, South Carolina Continental Line, John Welden died in April, 1835.

Lawrence County: James Ferguson, eighty-two, State not given; James Van Zant, seventy-eight, Pennsylvania Continental Line.

Jackson County: John Robinson, seventy-seven, Pennsylvania militia.

Pulaski County: Jacob Gray, seventy-one, South Carolina Militia; Shared Gray, seventy-seven, North Carolina militia; Asher Bagley and Benjamin Bagley, ages not given, both of the First regiment of the New Jersey Continental Line.

Washington County: James Leiper, seventy-seven, North Carolina militia; Arthur Murphy, seventy-two, North Carolina Continental Line, and Warren Philpot, seventy-seven, of the North Carolina militia.

THE FRENCH HERO, MONSIEUR LE NOIR DE SERVILLE.

This gentleman, who died on Arkansas soil December 30, 1828, was of the flower of France and one of the foreign contingent that lent its assistance to the cause of American Independence. He came to the United States as a French marine with the fleet commanded by Count de Grasse, and was wounded at Yorktown in attacking and carrying one of the British redoubts on the evening of October 14, 1781. Being honorably discharged he returned to France, but in after years came back to the United States and in time found a home in Arkansas near the plantation of Monsieur A. Barraque in Richland township. He was accidently killed by the falling of a tree and was buried with all the honors of war. It was a grand sight to see the blending of nationalities at this military interment of a foreign hero.

Adjutant General Terrence Farrelly, Colonels A. S. Walker, Francis Notrebe, and several companies of the First and Second regiments, Acting-Governor Robert Crittenden and his dashing aide-de-camp, Colonel Yell, made up the military cortege, while the French families from far and near and the American contingent of wealth, prowess and achievement made the occasion a memorable one in early days. I do not know whether this grave is in Richland, or in Barraque township of Jefferson County, nor do I know whether it carries a mark by which it may be identified. It was all in Richland township, Arkansas county, in 1828, but I am inclined to believe that the grave is at what is now Redfield. It would be a graceful thing for the citizens of Jefferson County, if they have not already done so, to erect a modest monument over the remains of the foreign soldier Le Noir de Serville, who died a stranger in a land for which he fought; and if the spot of interment can not be found, to place a memorial at the intersection of two of the most prominent streets of the beautiful bluff city. There is enough distinguished French blood in Jefferson County carrying American names to do this graceful thing without sacrifice or pain, and it would honor them while commemorating the life and services of the gallant man.

DON CARLOS DE VILLEMONT.

This Spaniard was commander of the Spanish garrison at the post for many years prior to 1803, and maintained his residence there and at Point Chicot after the cession of the country to the United States. He took a wife in this region about the year 1800, and died at the Post at the age of fifty-six, on August 9, 1823, leaving his wife and a large family of children. No one was better known at that place than this old Spanish grandee, and no one there was as much respected. He united an almost princely suavity of manners with a character that was without blemish. He was absolutely upright, most charmingly sociable and as cheerful as sunlight. His death was regretted by every man, woman and child at the Post, and elsewhere where he was known. With all this, he had a charming family to whom he was devoted, being the kindest of husbands and the most affectionate of fathers. The Gazette leaded its columns as a memorial to the man. One of his daughters, Matilda, was on August 9, 1826, married to Doctor John Gibson of Point Chicot, by Judge Eskridge of the Superior court. Another died at Point Chicot in 1835, a single woman of unblemished character and most charming manners. The blood of this gentle Spanish ancestor still flows in the veins of Arkansas men and women.

CHAPTER XII.

SAMUEL CALHOUN ROANE.

Arkansas Post, as has been shown, was a magnet of remarkably attractive power for men of parts from 1812 to 1819. It is our purpose now to deal with a man who, without any injustice to others, may be denominated the greatest jurist of territorial days. The life of Samuel Calhoun Roane was in many respects the most remarkable of the State's history. It was a record of privation, of struggle and of triumph. It was interesting, because for the most part it was spent on Arkansas soil, with all its intensest energies given to the elucidation of those great questions which in their ultimate effects fixed limiting forms upon the mechanisms of territory and State. It was important because Sam C. Roane became one of our own people and in the totality of his living represented the highest, cleanest and best type of Arkansas manhood.

THE ROANE FAMILY.

Some families exist for a century; others maintain their vigor for a much longer time. Some men, like Napoleon, become the Hapsburgs of a new line; others simply become greater Hapsburgs in an existing line. The Bachs triumphed over centuries and are still a great family. Heredity has stamped itself on the Adams, the Breckinridges, the Marshalls of our own country and on the Rose family of Arkansas. It is true of some people who boast of their ancestry that, like the potato, their best part is under the ground. But, like all other flippancies, this saying proves nothing, and is not exactly true. Pride in an unsullied ancestry is the logical outgrowth of the morality which enjoins a clean life. We are to honor our fathers and mothers, and this logically leads to pride in ancestry. Strength of mind is a rock for reverential regard and it is a poor tribute to mental strength to limit it to a life in being. The common history of every-day people proves the doctrine of inherited power far better than the exceptional records of the great men of the world. Sturdiness, manliness and vigor have passed down the centuries from father to son, making the world's mass of sturdy, manly and vigorous men today, its safety valve and governing power.

The Roanes were a sturdy, manly, vigorous family in the old colonies of Virginia and North Carolina, and one does not read far before finding this stock doing yeoman service for home and country on fields of battle and in heroic private lives. When the great West was opened up we find the Roanes in the van making greater names in the new world, Kentucky, Illinois and Tennessee.

THE TENNESSEE ROANES.

Samuel Calhoun Roane sprang immediately from the Tennessee branch of the family. Three brothers of this surname were born in Virginia in the eighteenth century. One of them remained on the ancestral estate and in time became governor of the Old Dominion. Another, Archibald Roane, migrated to Wilson county, Tennessee, and in due time became governor of the State, with a county named in his honor. The third brother, Hugh, also migrated to Wilson County and although not credited with the political ability of his brothers, became the father of three sons, two of whom became men of prominence one becoming a great lawyer in Arkansas and another its governor. The Roane family has given a governor to Virginia, another to Tennessee and another to Arkansas, but the three governors combined lacked the mental vigor and polish of the Arkansas jurist, Sam C. Roane, the subject of our sketch. The great William Wirt at one time thought Sam C. Roane overmatched by the combined talent of the Little Rock bar, while remaining the equal of any part of it standing alone. Later on in his association with Roane he decided that Roane was more than equal to the entire bar of Arkansas, and the equal of any lawyer in the country. What shall we say of heredity in the face of a family record like this? Was there no antecedent crucible for the preparation of a matrix of this kind? If chance can account for the Roane family on scientific principles, then moral injunctions and godly lives are not worth the price we pay for them. Back of the stature of the Roanes was the frugal, temperate, sacrificing lives of their fathers and grand-fathers, as back of all worth is to be found these habits and qualities in the profoundest degree.

THE ARKANSAS ROANES.

In the year 1818 the discussion began concerning the making of the State, Missouri, and the creation of the territory, Arkansas. Before either of these acts was consummated, Samuel Calhoun Roane, a poor but a well-equipped young lawyer, passed through the opening territorial gate and pitched his tent at Arkansas Post. Henry Clay in the halls of Congress in 1824, in that masterful answer to the sneers of John Randolph, said: "I was born to no proud patrimonial estate; from my father I inherited only infancy, ignorance and indigence. I feel my defects, but so far as my situation in early life is concerned, I may without presumption say that they are more my misfortune than my fault." Clay in this splendid exaggeration omitted entirely his inheritance of intellect, as logically traceable to his father, as were the inheritances of infancy, ignorance and indigence.

Samuel Calhoun Roane inherited indigence, infancy and intellect, but his education was not neglected. He outgrew the infancy by regular stages, and came to Arkansas to beat down the indigence by the use of intellect. Like Woodruff, he came into the territory without much money, but ready to do something; unlike Woodruff, he had a profession and not a trade. No lawyer can beckon clients at will, and all through the years 1818 and 1819 Roane had difficulty in making buckle and tongue meet. Other lawyers were at the Post, not his equal in power, who were doing better than Roane, not in practicing law, but in making money in other lines. Joshua Norvelle was the district attorney under Missouri law and had a salary. James Woodson Bates had a real estate agency, but soon gave this up for a salary. Robert Crittenden had a salary as secretary of the commonwealth, but made more money as a real estate agent. Roane had too much of a legal mind to make a successful real estate vendor. In early 1819 he formed a law partnership with Joshua Norvelle. The town of Rome was laid out in April, 1819, and the troubles growing out of the titles to its lots brought the firm of Roane & Norvelle some little money, but not enough to give either of the partners a good suit of clothes. Then, as now, good young lawyers were classified by the seediness of their clothes. A tailor-made suit every six months indicated ten years of privation and the beginning of power. A tailor-made suit every year indicated eight years' privation mitigated by gains made in other lines. A tailormade suit every two years was a sign of brains and purpose, while a suit that lasted three years was indicative of great will power and superior legal attainments.

THE TOWN OF ROME.

Rome, the imperial city, has gone; so has Rome of Arkansas county. It was once entitled to a place on the maps, but unfortunately while it existed no maps were made in Arkansas. Rome was about five miles out of Arkansas Post and was designed to be rat proof. The overflow of the Arkansas drove the rats to higher ground and Arkansas Post was a "ratty" town. Rome was to be on still higher ground and offered great inducements. Its principal street was called Don Carlos, and the grandees reserved this for themselves. Crittenden and Morton were largely interested in its development and in the sale of lots. William Craig, another quaint character of that day, was also a vigorous promoter. Unfortunately the title to the original grant was in dispute and this created trouble and finally destroyed the town. It began in 1819 and lasted about ten years. In 1822 it had the following residents: Edward Brown, W. B. R. Horner, Robert Johnson, William B. Locke, Elijah Morton, George Sampson, John Taylor, Sr., and William Trimble. Everybody around the Post owned one or more lots, which they looked upon as a bonanza.

JOSHUA NORVELLE.

The partnership of Roane & Norvelle did not last long. Norvelle was a good young lawyer in a Missouri town, but afflicted with salaryomania. In 1815, just about the time when fees were beginning to grow, he was offered the prosecuting attorney's place at Arkansas Post.

Joshua Norvelle accepted the place because of the salary and with his wife moved to the Post. He held the office and the salary until July, 1819, when he was out of a job. He and Roane then joined forces, but the salary phantom was so imbedded in Norvelle's constitution as to unfit him for the slow work of an office lawyer. His Missouri friends prevailed on President Monroe to give him a place somewhere, and he was sent to St. Bartholomew's Island as consul. He was credited with being a good officer while there. He left his wife at Arkansas Post and then forgot to maintain her.

On July 11, 1821, Maria Norvelle, wife of Joshua Norvelle, filed a suit at Arkansas Post for a divorce on the ground of desertion and non-support. Before the case came on for trial Joshua Norvelle died. He passed away at St. Bartholomew on August 12, 1821, and I have not found any further history of his wife.

OTHER MEN WHO BECAME PROMINENT.

Sam C. Roane stuck to his office. He did odd jobs on the outside in order to make a living, but he never lost faith in the law. Judge Witter was at Arkansas Post in December, 1819, and met William E. Woodruff and was shown through the Gazette establishment. Woodruff had one helper, and that only on press days. Witter was there on press day and was introduced to the pressman, Sam C. Roane. Witter's description of Roane is laughable. He said in effect that Roane was as far from the dainty, well-dressed man he afterward became as Arkansas Post was from the New Jerusalem. Roane kept books for Pryor & Richards at night, earning a few extra dollars, and drinking in the weird and wonderful experiences of Pryor, one of the greatest travelers that Arkansas has ever known. When the first legislature convened in February, 1820, Roane was made engrossing clerk and he honored the place. But Sam C. Roane's law office was always open. Dinsmoor & Spaulding kept their office open also, as did Crittenden & Bates. The difference was that Roane kept a law office, pure and simple, while these others kept a real estate office with a law attachment.

These men advertised, giving one line to the law and thirteen lines to real estate. Ashley at Little Rock stuck to the law, but put up a grocery next door to his office as a mainstay.

Neither Roane, Crittenden, Ashley, Morton nor Newton were married men. Young Newton carried the mail from Arkansas Post to Little Rock in 1820 and 1821, and then became deputy clerk at Little Rock, while studying for the bar. While Spaulding was the first man admitted to the bar, Newton was the first one to prepare himself for the bar in an Arkansas office. When these men were ready to marry they all took different directions. Ashley went to Missouri, while Crittenden, Oden, Morton and Newton went to Kentucky for wives. Chester Ashley was the first, marrying Mary W. Elliott at Potosi, Missouri, on July 2, 1821. Robert Crittenden went next, being married at Frankfort, Kentucky, on October 1, 1822, to Ann Morris. Elijah Morton took the Kentucky fever also and on September 20, 1821, married Nancy W. Stewart at Russellville, Kentucky. Oden and Newton waited longer, but in May, 1829, they both went back to Kentucky and married. Oden was married on May 1 at Bardstown to Frances Crozier, while Newton was married on the 15th to Mary K. daughter of Colonel John Allen, at Shelbyville, Kentucky. I can't blame these gentlemen for their predilection for Kentucky women, for the reason that I have lived with a Kentucky wife for thirty-two years, and if I desired to throw rocks she stands in the way, dominating as is her right and duty.

In the eyes of the larger world it would seem, however, that these gentlemen exercised a sound and most excellent judgment, but as the boys around the State house used to say, their course did not indicate good political sagacity. Ashley triumphed over his Missouri environment and reached the United States Senate. A Missouri wife, therefore, is not impedimenta in Arkansas politics. The men who went to Kentucky, however, for wives, leaving the Arkansas girls alone and forlorn, seem to have been marked men politically ever afterward. Morton never tried for political place, but Crittenden failed most egregiously to elect himself and destroyed the chances of every man he favored. Newton broke the rule once for a single term in Congress, but could never break the "hoodoo" again. Oden ought to have succeeded, but fate was against him.

THE EMBREES OF ARKANSAS COUNTY.

This family came into the territory about 1815 from Virginia, and was located on the Arkansas river between Mason's and Colonel Vaugine's in 1819, when Nuttal made his trip up the river. Mr. Embree was then dead and Mrs. Embree was running the plantation. She had a large family of children, the most prominent sons being Jordan and Benjamin, well known in later days. Colonel Embry of Atkins was a cousin of the husband of Mrs. Embree, although he spelled his name in a different way, and a more barbarous way, to my mind, as the word Embree has much to commend itself to every one. But Mrs. Embree had a daughter, Maria, and this daughter captivated Sam C. Roane. She was of an excellent family and would own in her own right a splendid farm on the Arkansas. She had varied charms and Roane fell in love. In the language of that day he loved the ground she walked on and idolized the house she lived in. On February 20, 1825, he married her in Vaugine township, Arkansas County. He did not marry in haste, nor did he marry before he could support his wife creditably. His tide turned between 1820 and 1825.

THE TURN OF THE TIDE.

In August, 1820, he was appointed United States district attorney for Arkansas and was reappointed on May 19, 1821. The salary for the first four years was two hundred and fifty dollars per annum, with a per diem of five dollars a day, while the Superior Court was in session, an average of about three days a month. He was reappointed in 1825, and again in 1829, serving thirteen years in all. The salary improved from 1825 to 1829, but was never what it should have been. Holding a government office was no bar to holding a State office in those days, nor was residence of any very fixed character demanded. In 1821 the people of Clark County elected him to the Legislative Council by a majority of six votes over Eli Langford and the council elected him president. He served the citizens of

Clark County four years in this capacity, when his work at Little Rock became too onerous for further political engagements.

Governor Miller appointed him, Robert Bean and James Billingsly commissioners to locate the site for a court house in Pulaski. Roane and Bean agreed upon Little Rock and the Circuit Court confirmed the selection. On March 12, 1822, Henry Armstrong, Archibald McHenry and Wright Daniel were appointed commissioners to let out the contract and put up the building. That ended the Pulaski contest and gave Little Rock security and a chance to grow. In 1823 he digested the laws of the territory, which added to his fortunes and fame. In 1822 Roane became the leading council for the plaintiff in *Riley* v. *Bradford*, with Sevier, Crittenden and Ashley as associates, while Major Bradford was represented by Trimble, Quarles and Oden. This was a noted cause, involving a forced enlistment of a man in the United States army at Fort Smith from 1817 to 1821. The jury gave a verdict for the plaintiff for fourteen hundred and fifty dollars.

In 1822 General Edmund Hogan of Crystal Hill sued William Russell of St. Louis and Little Rock for libel, and retained Sam C. Roane, Chester Ashley and Neill McLane as his attorneys. Russell was represented by Trimble and Sevier. The jury gave a verdict for Hogan for twenty-four hundred dollars. Nor did Roane neglect his federal business. In 1821 he gave notice to wood and timber thieves along the Mississippi that they might expect an enforcement of the law, and for four years he so followed them that they gave up the business and became law-abiding men.

GREAT WORK IN THE LAND FRAUD CASES.

In the sale of the Louisiana territory to the United States in 1803 provision was made for the protection of all settlers then on any part of this vast area. In 1806 the government of the United States began an investigation to ascertain who was entitled to preference in land claims and kept the investigation on foot for many years. It is safe to say that every honest Spanish claim growing out of antecedent settlement, that is, a settlement made prior to 1803, was presented to these investigating boards before they passed out of existence, and that almost every honest claim had been confirmed before 1820. From 1820 to 1824 Congress was overrun with claimants, who averred that they had been overlooked and thereby wronged. On May 26, 1824, Congress authorized the Superior Courts of the territories to try these new claims. In 1825 and in 1826 all was quiet in Arkansas. In the latter part of 1827, however, the Superior Court at Little Rock was confronted by one hundred and twenty-six cases demanding confirmation, and demanding it vigorously. Every claim was a Louisiana claim sold by John J. or James Bowie, or some other speculator, to men who lived in Arkansas. These purchasers were all honest and ignorant of the origin of the claims they were pressing to judgment.

In looking over these claims one is surprised to find that men. like Major Bradford, Robert Crittenden and A. H. Sevier were so deceived by them as to invest in them. All the best element of the Arkansas population seemed to have been deluded into buying, and as a consequence every reputable lawyer in the territory, except Richard Searcy, was on one side of the case, and Sam C. Roane alone upon the other. He retained Searcy as a helper and these two started in to beat the entire bar of Arkansas. The odds were fearful, and when it was ascertained that the court had a leaning the wrong way the case seemed hopeless. The trials began in December, 1827, with a written motion by Roane to postpone until he could learn a little more about the Spanish language and law, but more particularly that he might have time to go down into Louisiana and hunt up evidence. The court, composed of Johnson and Eskridge, overruled the motion. The trial was forced to an issue and Roane did the best he could with the evidence at hand and interposed the case of Soulard v. The United States, a case decided by Judge Peck of the United States Supreme Court, which was a bar to the actions in hand, but all to no purpose. Between December 19 and December 24, 1827, the court confirmed one hundred and seventeen of these claims, and the lawyers of the Little Rock bar were in a frenzy of delight. Roane took his exceptions and his medicine. He was not only a good lawyer, but something of a wit. Shortly after the trial Judge Ben Johnson said to Roane: "I suppose you wanted a good long adjournment in order to learn a little Spanish law." Roane drawlingly answered, "Yes, that was partly my object; but my greatest reason was that the court might have time to acquaint itself with American law." The judge said: "Well, the court seems to have been satisfied with the knowledge it had." "True," said Roane, "but the medicine has not had time to work yet. When the court really studies the law its satisfaction will turn to confusion."

ROANE'S TUSSLE WITH WILLIAM WIRT.

But Roane's confusion did not end with the loss of the cases at Little Rock. When the news got to the office of William Wirt, the attorney general of the United States, it created a sensation. Wirt at once jumped to the conclusion that Roane had been over-powered by the Little Rock bar and had mismanaged the cases. He wrote Roane an interminably long and terribly dry letter. He could not conceive how such a thing could happen. You, Mr. Roane, were on the ground and you were supposed to know Spanish law. More than that, you were supposed to know the case of Soulard v. The United States, the very mention of which would have apprised the court that a higher power had already passed upon these very questions, and saved the country this erroneous ruling. Roane could take a great deal, but he could not take this veiled lecture from William Wirt. He answered Wirt most vigorously and most effectively. The attorney general was informed that every principle of the Spanish law known to him or to Richard Searcy was given to the court; that efforts had been made to secure a postponement in order to learn more of these principles and to get relevant evidence. That the case of Soulard v. The United States was thrown at the court time and time again, but that the court had always dodged the blow. He informed Mr. Wirt that his salary was two hundred and fifty dollars a year and that he had spent one hundred dollars of that for evidence, and that this, like the case, had faded away. Then with a master hand he said that future action was worth far more than criticism of the past. You have let two years pass in correspondence and the time for a bill of review has nearly elapsed. I have found evidence in Louisiana that will reverse these cases, and if you will send Isaac Preston of New Orleans to testify as an expert it is very probable that other conclusions will be reached.

The motions for the bills of review were fought by the Arkansas bar to the last minute. The court found itself in a dilemma, but there was no way out of it than by a reversal. William E. Woodruff printed fifteen or sixteen pages of cleancut extra matter in every issue for a month, notifying man after man to come in and show cause why a bill of review should not issue. The original papers were spirited away by interested parties in order that they might not be used in criminal actions. Roane won out and won so thoroughly and so completely as to place himself at the very head of the Arkansas bar. When Johnson met Roane after his great victory he said: "Well, Roane, I see that you have learned a little more Spanish." "Yes, your honor," said Roane, "and the court has learned a little more law." Johnson and Roane were friends and each appreciated the good points of the other.

Governor Pope was charged with saying that Roane had not used proper diligence in the original trial of the cases, but denied this in a full-page letter to the people. He said he thought that Roane had been over-powered by the tremendous number of lawyers arrayed against him, but that he never charged him with any delinquency. When an attempt was made to oust Roane Pope asked, "Who is there to take his place, since all the reputable lawyers are on the other side?" Pope also gave out the information that while in Washington he had heard from Graham and Wirt, and that these gentlemen said that all any lawyer could do was done by Roane in 1827; that he was not overpowered by the Little Rock bar, but slaughtered by the Little Rock court, in its effort to override a decision of the United States court. That ended the influx of fraudulent and forged claims, and gave Roane that prominence at the bar which led to wealth and affluence. The character of the Superior Court, however, suffered a severe blow, from the effects of which it never recovered, and when it passed out of existence in 1836 the people did not grieve.

The original decisions of 1827 seemed to make all these Spanish claims good, and the traffic in them increased so alarmingly that Graham, the land commissioner, held up the registry and appealed to Congress. When the court reversed itself in 1831 the people were disgusted. Could there have been an election for Superior Court judges, there is little doubt but that Eskridge, Trimble, Bates and Johnson would have gone down under an overwhelming vote of popular disfavor. General Arbuckle and others went to Congress for relief, claiming that they bought under the decision of the Arkansas court, and that as the court had gone wrong they should not be made to lose thereby. When catechized more closely by congressmen, Arbuckle was forced to admit that Roane's position and the cases cited by him had created a doubt in his mind, and in the minds of Arkansas generally, as to the soundness of the court's decisions, and that although he had bought twenty-four hundred dollars worth of these claims since the decisions, he never felt that he had an absolutely valid title. Congress refused the relief.

ROANE'S FURTHER HONORS.

From 1831 to 1836 he was judge of the First Territorial Circuit Court, and in 1836 was chosen by Jefferson County as her representative in the constitutional convention. From 1836 to 1837 he served Jefferson County as State Senator, and was the first president of the Arkansas Senate under the State regime.

While President of the Senate, Roane frequently acted as Governor of Arkansas, during the frequent absences of Governor Conway. The columns of the Gazette from 1837 to 1840 contain numerous proclamations signed "Sam. C. Roane, Acting Governor."

SAM C. ROANE AS ACTING GOVERNOR.

Speaking of Sam. C. Roane recalls the fact that he is the only acting governor of Arkansas not recorded by the Secretary of State in his list of governors and acting governors of Arkansas. All the rest are duly credited, but Sam C. Roane's name is remarkable for its absence. This is a great injustice to a worthy man, and to the facts of history. Lists of this kind have a great historic value, and they should be absolutely authentic. Why Jacob Frolich, the compiler of the original list, omitted Roane, I am not able to say. Certainly not intentionally, for Jake Frolich was an absolutely fair man. In compiling this old record, he laid the State under perpetual obligation to him, and certainly left a monument to his own painstaking care and personal zeal. He left out Roane, however, and no secretary since his day has noted the omission. For five years I had the preparation of this report in hand, and made many corrections, but failed to discover the error I am adverting to now, and possibly would not have discovered it but for the series of articles I am now writing. In the columns of the Gazette for 1837 and 1838 there are many proclamations signed by Sam C. Roane as acting governor of the State of Arkansas, being the first acting governor the State ever had. It is also true that he acted more frequently, and for a longer period, in that capacity than any other man since his day, except the present officer. Roane as acting governor in 1837 organized the militia of Arkansas, commissioned its officers and sent them to Fort Towson to operate against the Indians.

MANY ERRORS IN OFFICIAL LISTS.

I have in my after researches found quite a large number of errors in the early Arkansas official lists as published, and have also found many of the officers who are recorded in blank in the published lists. The State should provide for the revision of these old lists, so that they may import absolute verity and certainty. An appropriation of two hundred and fifty dollars would pay for the whole research, and the truths of history seem to demand the investment.

THE WIT OF ROANE.

Upon reading of the duel between Isaac Knott and Alex Shott, Judge Roane remarked: "Knott was shot and Shott was not," a conclusion reached by George D. Prentice on independent lines. At a dinner table in one of the old Arkansas taverns, Judge Roane noticed that the butter contained many flies. Calling the landlord to one side, he said: "I see you mix your flies with the butter. Would it not be better to place all the flies on one plate and the butter on another, leaving it for the guests to mix them according to their own tastes? I merely suggest this for your own reflection."

Roane was an Arkansan to the core, and with any sort of a reckoning must be classed as one of the really great men of the State. Sam C. Roane had a brother, James, prominent in Eastern Arkansas, but not connected with political affairs. His brother-in-law, Jordan Embree, represented Jefferson County in the legislature of 1844. The brother John Selden Roane, was prominent in Jefferson County politics and in 1849 was elected governor of the State.

Sam C. Roane left nine children: one son Andrew, died in infancy; two other sons, John Jordan and Samuel Calhoun, grew to manhood. The six daughters married as follows: Juliet to Colonel M. L. Bell, Fannie to Flowers McGregor, Hennie to L. H. Oliver, Mary to Mr. Dorris, Johanna to Captain Chalmers, and Ida to Captain John S. Bell.

CHAPTER XIII.

SHIRT-SLEEVED MILLIONAIRES.

It has been said of Pittsburg that it has more than one hundred shirt-sleeve millionaires and but very few of the silk hat variety. It is meant by this that the rich men of today were the poor boys of yesterday. The contrast may be greater in Pittsburg, going to the extreme of extremes, or as my wife pithily expressed it after returning from a visit to her millionaire kin in the Iron City, "Pittsburg is the Eden of dirt and diamonds,"—yet it is nevertheless true that the entire West notes its rich of today as the poor of yesterday.

Nowhere in the Mississippi valley is the generality of this truth better attested than in the history of Arkansas. Mosely, Farrelly, Notrebe, Ashley, Roane, Barkman, Horner and hundreds of others came in as poor men, without illustrious ancestry or great friends. Crittenden in an open attack upon Judge Eskridge, who came poor and made money quickly, disclosed the fact that Judge Trimble, who came in 1820 clad in homespun and dreams, had retired from the State within ten years with $20,000 in gold honestly made, something better than any lawyer in the Mississippi valley had been able to do up to that time. In the furious fight between William Strong of St. Francis and W. D. Ferguson of Crittenden, in the thirties, it developed that Ferguson came to the State in 1824 without bag or baggage and in fifteen years, as Strong said, had made his "Golcondry" besides "holding down an office every day of the time and sometimes two."

HENRY W. CONWAY'S WEALTH.

Ambrose H. Sevier in 1825 told the people of Pulaski in an appeal for votes that "he came among them an orphan, without wealth, without relatives and without friends." Henry W. Conway in 1823 in his first race for delegate to Congress told the people that "he had tried Tennessee, Illinois and Missouri before coming to Arkansas, but without success; that he had not made anything in those States and had been in Arkansas since 1821 without the trappings of wealth or the aid of influential friends." Conway exaggerated at this time for he had influential friends, who gained for him an office in 1821, receiver of public moneys at Little Rock, and another in 1823, that of postmaster, the two not being incompatible as things were then. Nor is it exactly square to say that the public conscience is more acute today than then. A more exact expression would be, there are more guests at the table today, and the pie must be cut into smaller pieces. Conway on his own account started a town in 1819, in Southern Illinois, called "America," which has long since changed its name. In May of the same year he, and his uncles, William and Thomas Rector, laid off the town of Osage, Missouri. When he died in 1827, after six years of Arkansas atmosphere, he was "not so ailing as he was in 1823." It took nearly a column of the Gazette to display his holdings. In Little Rock he owned a six-room frame house, each room 16x20, with a fire place in each room. The house had an upper and lower gallery, eight feet wide, with a passage way above and below stairs, with a brick kitchen and smoke house detached. This house was not on any submerged tenth, but stood out "commanding like" on the bluff in front of the ferry on a lot three hundred feet long and one hundred and forty-five feet deep with a splendid frontage on three streets. When erudition lends itself to an investigation of really historic homes it will not start with the "Crittenden mansion" of 1830, but will go back into real history and dig up this best house in Little Rock, in 1823. There were better and more noted houses in other parts of the State at that time, but historians have made their starting point so far down the line of years as to exclude these old historic landmarks. Conway also owned forty lots in Little Rock, one hundred and seventy acres of the best bottom land within three miles of Little Rock, and lands all over the territory and in the States of Illinois and Missouri. He was a good type of the shirt sleeve Crœsus at home, although wearing a silk hat at the capital of the country.

CAPTAIN NATHANIEL PRYOR.

Captain Nathaniel Pryor led a life of wonderful adventure before settling at Arkansas Post in 1814. Prior to 1804 it was said that he had been in every Eastern State, never satisfied, always eager to move on. When the Lewis and Clark expedition was formed by President Jefferson, Nathaniel Pryor was one of the thirty-two selected spirits who were to make the trip. This was a memorable trip to the Pacific, the first ever made by Anglo-Americans, and the names of the members of the party, Pryor's among the rest, still distinguish rivers and mountains along the path of the great march. For years afterward he traded up the Missouri and in 1814 began his operations on the Arkansas. Nuttal traveled with him up the river in 1819, and has left us an interesting account of his manner of trading. He was, in river parlance, half horse and half alligator, a shirt sleeve explorer and trader and a silk hat merchant prince in St. Louis and New Orleans before Pittsburg began to call the roll of its shirt sleeve millionaires.

THE UNKNIGHTED PIONEERS.

These men had no pedigree that they were familiar with and wanted none. A coat of arms would have been looked upon as an anamoly, but real arms were somewhat of a necessity, if not a delight. They could shoot bears with deadly precision and with equal skill could bring down an Indian or desperado.

The moral tone of each neighborhood was higher than it is today, being protected and upheld by fathers and brothers, always at hand and always loaded for bear, while now we must ride six miles for a constable or a policeman, who is often not on his beat when wanted, and not equal to the occasion when found. These old-time shirt sleeved gentry did each year as a simple matter of course and without claiming any kind of credit for its deeds what in a kingly country would have brought a coat of arms. Thus when, in 1260, William De Gylpin killed a wild boar in the wilds of Westmoreland, King John knighted him and gave him a crest, which was afterward elaborated into a coat of arms. The crest was nothing more than the picture of a wild boar, but the descendants of William Gylpin through six centuries have prized the crest more than gold and have fought for its honor on every English battlefield. The old Arkansas pioneers turned a wilderness into an Eden, drove the snakes out of its borders, left their descendants silk hats and a good name. They had buckskin breeches, wool hats of a most uncertain age, but of no particular shape, good pruning hooks and shooting irons, but, best of all, unsullied names. They were all on the democratic level, with the postmaster and storekeeper as a sort of oracle. Well-to-do farmers were, of course, a little better than the ne'er-do-wells, and a man with a thousand acres cut a wider swath than one with a quarter section. They all came in on the level of equal opportunity and of almost equal poverty. Every fellow from anywhere had a chance, and what was in him had a chance to come out. Very soon after the flood of migration began to rise men began to be measured by the ice they had cut. A man with one hundred cattle and twenty negroes became a neighborhood nabob, and was called Colonel to distinguish him from the man who had no land, but hired himself to others. A man with a half dozen pretty girls and a good farm was called Judge, and insensibly the orderly laws of caste were evolved from the chaos of democratic opportunity. The sons came to wear silk hats, and the grandsons, if they had nothing else, could boast of the most pleasing memories. The shirt-sleeve brigade always makes the fortunes for its silk-hat descendants; but the silk-hat brigade has never been able to make an invention that would preserve and make everlasting the good solid chunks of wealth rolled up by its shirt-sleeve ancestry.

SOME OF THE EARLIEST OFFICERS.

Captain James B. Many, with a body of United States soldiers, came to Arkansas Post in 1804 to take charge of the country under the new regime. The Spanish commandant, with all the pride of his nation, fired a salute to the Spanish flag as it ran down the galliards for the last time, and with equal courtesy fired a salute as the Stars and Stripes took its place. Captain Many remained at the Post for some time, and in 1816 made an affidavit before the Spanish Claims Commission which fixed the settlement of Joseph Mason on Plum Bayou as older than the American occupancy. Colonel Francis Vaugine, Joseph Bogy, Andre Fagot, Jean Lavale, Pierre Pertuis, Alexis Jardeles and Jean Jardeles made separate affidavits before Judge George Bullitt at the Post in October, 1816, that Joseph Mason came in 1798 during the time of Don Carlos de Villemont's occupancy. Henry Cassidy also made oath that he surveyed for Winters in 1802 and found Mason there. Nuttal notes his residence on Plum Bayou in 1819, which proves a long and continuous residence. He was a Kentuckian and introduced into the region many of the farming customs that still prevail. I have no proof that the family was perpetuated on Arkansas soil, but I believe that it was. Polly Mason, who married Alfred Harrington on May 2, 1820, was probably a daughter, as the marriage was in Joseph Mason's township, and the Harringtons near neighbors. The ceremony was performed by Ephraim C. Davidson, a justice of the peace, who came in in 1819. James W. Mason opened an office at the Post as a physician on April 7, 1821, and may have been a son of the old pioneer.

Chevalier Pierre Pertuis, named above, died at the Post December 2, 1821, at the age of sixty-five having lived in this region all his life. His daughter, Nina Pertuis, married Victor Vasseur at the Post in June, 1822, the ceremony being performed by Judge Andrew Scott. I think the name Pertuis is nearly extinct in Arkansas, but the blood of the old chevalier is still perpetuated. At his funeral were two older men than he—

Joseph Dardene, born 1748, who died at the Post in 1837 in his eighty-ninth year, and Francis Varsier, born 1756, and died at the Post in January, 1836, in his eightieth year. Longevity seems to have marked these old Frenchmen for her own.

EARLY SETTLEMENT ON POKE BAYOU.

The examination cited above disclosed the fact that B. H. McFarlane had made a settlement on the south side of White river above the mouth of Poke bayou in 1804 and that he had lived there continuously for ten years. His right to a square mile of land was confirmed in 1813. Nicholas Trammel had a square mile in Independence, confirmed in 1817, based on a ten years' continuous residence, which he sold in 1821 to Morgan Magness, a Tennesseean. The occupancy was proved by Charles Kelley, one of the oldest settlers of Independence County.

In one of Captain Many's reports the interesting information was given that the winter's rations for the garrison had been laid in, consisting of twenty-five buffaloes and five thousand bushels of corn. Hewes Scull had a mill at which this corn was ground and the toll yielded a good income. The soldiers quartered there were generally artillerymen, and in the days of the first occupancy made long trips to the West in search of buffaloes, but in later times the meat was brought down on boats.

FIRST CIVIL COURT.

Soon after Captain Many took possession, Stephen Warrell, a lieutenant of the artillery and a native of Pennsylvania, was made deputy governor, and resigned his army position to take up his new duties. He organized the first civil government under the United States for the regulation of property transfers, marriages and the like. Another lieutenant under Many, Robert Weir Osborne, also a native of Pennsylvania, was made clerk of the court in October, 1806. Whether Warrell died or resigned is not clear, but in 1808 Osborne was made deputy governor and Richard W. Honey, clerk, a position he held until the territory of Missouri was formed, in 1813. Honey was not an army man and his records still remain to gladden the heart of the antiquarian and to enlighten all interested parties upon the court proceedings of that time. When the territory of Missouri was created, George Bullitt of Missouri was appointed judge and moved his family to the Post, where he remained until 1819, the leading citizen of the town. He was a man of parts and impressed upon the District of Arkansas and upon the counties of Arkansas, Lawrence, Pulaski, Clark and Hempstead their organic form under Missouri law, which form was perpetuated by the act creating the territory of Arkansas. Judge Bullitt organized these five counties and enforced the laws of Missouri and was a factor in early territorial life for six long years.

BULLITT ORGANIZED TERRITORY.

Crittenden is given an absolutely unwarranted credit for organizing the new territory of Arkansas. It was organized by Bullitt, and Congress, in making Arkansas Territory, continued the organic divisions and the laws then existing, and so specifically stated in the organic act. The so-called first legislature of the territory, wherein Crittenden, Scott, Jouett and Letcher spread Missouri law over the territory, was supererogation, pure and simple. Congress had already done this and Congress was the only power that could do it. An examination of the other work done by this so-called first legislature shows that there was much fuss over very few feathers.

It is time that the hoary chestnut about Crittenden's arduous task in organizing a new territory be relegated to the junk department, and that George Bullitt be given the credit he deserves. Five counties, with fourteen thousand people, were under law and progressing finely when Crittenden went to Arkansas. Not a thing was changed, except to substitute the word "Arkansas" for the word "Missouri," and put in five new officers, a governor, secretary of State, and three new judges, to do what George Bullitt had been doing for six years single-handed and alone. When Bullitt left Arkansas Post for his new home at Cape Girardeau his departure was universally regretted, and in his new home he gained an enviable reputation. John Dodge was his clerk at Arkansas Post, and in after years was a leading citizen of the new commonwealth.

In 1819 the Superior Court was established, with Andrew Scott, Charles Jouett and Robert Letcher as judges. David E. McKinney was clerk of this court for many years and became a landmark in early judicial affairs. Jouett and Letcher were quitters, and in 1820 Benjamin Johnson succeeded one, and in 1821 Robert Selden succeeded the other.

EARLY COUNTY ADMINISTRATIONS.

The old county officers, three from each county, clerk, sheriff and coroner, appointed in 1818, continued to administer county affairs under the new territory and all of these came into the territory during the years 1816 or 1817. Eli J. Lewis, Hewes Scull and Oliver H. Thomas were, respectively, clerk, sheriff and coroner of Arkansas County from 1817 to 1821. Thomas was a young merchant from Baltimore, Maryland, very enterprising and popular. He was connected with the early militia organizations at the Post and, like his partner, Lewis was a big man at every feast. He committed suicide in 1822. W. P. L. Blair was clerk of Clark County in 1818; resigned in September, 1819, and was succeeded by H. L. Biscoe from Richmond, Virginia; Moses Graham, a citizen of Clark for many years, was sheriff in 1818 and died in September, 1819, when S. M. Rutherford, a clerk for many years under Pryor & Richards, was appointed in his stead.

NON-RESIDENT OFFICEHOLDERS.

It will be seen that a man could reside at Arkansas Post and still be sheriff of Clark County, as Rutherford did not actually move from the Post for several years. Mathew Logan was coroner of Clark County from 1818 to 1821. W. P. L. Blair was also one of the promoters of the town of Rome, in Arkansas County, and in some way, not explainable at this distance of time, a large number of Clark County people lived at the Post. Jacob Barkman's wife died at her residence, five miles from the Post, in August, 1821, when at the same time her husband was postmaster at a crossroads in Clark County. When Blair resigned as clerk, Sam C. Roane of Arkansas Post was made clerk pro tem.; Roane was prosecuting attorney in Clark in 1820, still residing at the Post, and represented Clark County without ever living in it; Blair was a thorough going man and along with the old Frenchman, Peter Jardelow, made a lot of money. Other old residents of Clark County, Zachariah Davis, Samuel Parker, Adam Stroud and Abner Hignite, had residences in 1817 and 1818 at the Post, and their connection with Clark County at that time was principally that of hunters and trappers. There were courts in Clark County before the Common Pleas Courts were established in 1819, and Blair, Graham and Logan were county officials one year before these courts sprang into existence.

EARLY SETTLERS IN CLARK COUNTY.

In 1822 the town of Crittenden was laid off by Adam Stroud, Wm. Kelley and John Bull and advertised in the Gazette as the county seat of Clark. Stephen Clanton of Pulaski County was one of the first Common Pleas judges of Clark County, and died in 1821. The Fish family, the Fentors, the Scarboroughs and the Deans entered Clark in 1818 or 1819. Thomas Fish was the most prominent of early Clark County men and died February 4, 1823. Patrick Cassidy was perhaps, with one exception, the first Anglo-American to settle in Clark County, his claim going back to 1800. The exception is the claim of Archibald Price and Louis Cavet on the Ouachita many years before this. At all events, Cassidy resided there in 1800 on a twelve hundred-acre tract, purchased by him of Price and Cavet. Cassidy had large holdings on the Mississippi and was one of the candidates in 1819 for delegate to Congress.

In Hempstead County Colonel J. M. Stewart was clerk from 1818 to 1823, and Benjamin Clark coroner for the same period. They entered Hempstead County in 1815, and Colonel Stewart was for years Hempstead's leading citizen. He was a major in a Tennessee regiment in the War of 1812, and died at Washington on February 24, 1825. Benjamin Clark, the coroner, was a wealthy planter, as things were counted then, and, with the exception of Stewart and John Wilson, was the most prominent man in the county.

COLONEL ALEXANDER S. WALKER.

Colonel Alexander S. Walker was sheriff from 1818 to 1823, though living all the time at Arkansas Post. Since writing the sketch of his life I have ascertained that after serving Pulaski County as sheriff from 1830 to 1831, he again ran for the legislature, but was beaten by Allen Martin. In 1835 the Democrats of the legislature nominated him for auditor of State, but the Whigs swept everything before them and he was beaten. Then Old Hickory, President Andrew Jackson, took up the old wheel horse and made him agent for the Seneca Indians. President Madison dismissed him from the United States service in 1810, and President Jackson reinstated him to an arm of the civil service in 1835. He died in 1837 at Fort Gibson with his name on Uncle Sam's pay rolls. This rounds out the career of one of the most remarkable men ever connected with Arkansas affairs.

In Lawrence County, Richard Searcy was clerk from 1817 to 1821; Joseph Hardin, sheriff from 1817 to 1825, and Robert Blane, coroner from 1817 to 1821. In Pulaski County, R. C. Oden was clerk from 1819 to 1821; Lemuel R. Curran, sheriff from 1818 to 1821, and Jacob Pyeatt, coroner for the same period. Lemuel R. Curran was one of the leading spirits of Cadron, and died there on March 8, 1821.

Thus the counties were organized when Crittenden and his associates entered the State, and the matter of organization was a matter of the supremest indifference and moment. Had the new officers never come it would have made no difference whatever. The shirt-sleeve pioneers were organized for work, were doing excellent work in a lawful way, and were piling up that wealth which supports their silk-hat descendants of today.

CHAPTER XIV.

The Coming of the Covered Wagons.

The scarcest commodity in the territory from 1819 to 1825 was money. In fact it was not needed to any great extent and when circulated was in the main Spanish silver. The finding of Spanish coins in odd places of the State is no evidence of Spanish occupancy, for American settlers used this coin for more than two decades. Between 1819 and 1825 the territory issued scrip which from the start never had a general value of more than fifty cents on the dollar of Spanish money. Sam C. Roane conceived the idea of utilizing this scrip for fees and in 1820 advertised that he would take it at par in payment of fees. As he was single and always lived within his means, there is little doubt but that he made considerable by holding the scrip for the golden moments when he could use it to advantage. There is no proof, however, that his cash charges were not materially less than his scrip charges. William E. Woodruff would never take it for more than seventy-five cents on the dollar, but preferred cash. The merchants took it at fifty and sixty cents on the dollar, and passed it out at par to the unsuspecting customers who sold them cotton and peltries, but, if required, were ready to pay silver. These merchants did not wait for cotton and peltries to come to them, but ran pole boats up the river stopping at every settlement to points far up in Kansas. Every farmer had a heavy two-horse wagon and kept a number of horses, as the only method of travel in the interior was by wagon or on horseback. The horse trails were far more numerous than wagon roads, and horseback riding very popular.

THE BARBECUE AND BERGU.

The barbecue was a feature of early territorial life, and the pioneers could smell a feast of this kind for fifty miles. The bergu was another great feast and consisted of five hundred squirrels properly cleaned and boiled to the consistency of soup in a twenty gallon iron caldron. A barbecue or a bergu was the social occasion of the period, but politicians soon turned it into a machine for vote getting and for sampling bad whisky and worse oratory. When camp meetings began in 1823, another social outlet was created and it was no uncommon thing to see three hundred horses hitched to swinging limbs of trees in the forest, whose riders, male and female, had traveled from forty to fifty miles. When preaching was over and the basket dinner eaten, the men parceled themselves off in squads to attend to more important matters, swap horses, trade land and do the other fellow up before he had time to get in his work on him. One eye was always towards the horns of the altar, while the other sought for soft snaps and easy mutton. Thus they prayed and preyed until four o'clock, when they struck the trail for a long ride home.

THE IMMIGRATION OF 1815-1830.

The greater part of the immigration of this period was by wagon. When Uncle Sam counted the people in 1820-21, he found fourteen thousand two hundred and seventy six, which had grown in 1830 to something more than thirty thousand. The great line of march after 1817 was the Great National Road from Missouri to Davidsonville. In 1820 this was extended to Cadron through Batesville, and in 1821 down to Red river through Clark and Hempstead counties. Branches from this road went east and west, but they were tough propositions, and like Jordan, "hard roads to travel." The St. Louis Republican in 1819 stated that one hundred persons a day passed through St. Charles, one-third of whom passed Southward, distributing themselves as they were suited clear down to Red river. Some bands of immigrants carried one hundred head of cattle, each one of them making music with a bell. Every party had from three to twenty slaves. The ferries on the Mississippi took over from three hundred to five hundred persons a day, and from thirty to fifty wagons. Missouri got the most of this migration from 1819 to 1830, but from 1830 to 1850 the larger part of it entered Arkansas. In 1819 we found the State inhabited by people who came by water and who lived on the rivers of Eastern Arkansas. In 1815 the method of transportation began to change and the covered wagon and the national road began to get in their superior work. In the census of January, 1821, Lawrence County had five thousand six hundred and five people, practically all of whom came in from Missouri after 1816. They settled first on Strawberry river, then spread to the Current and Black, always taking the best lands. Some of these reached Poke Bayou as early as 1814, but the very largest part did not arrive until after 1818. Hempstead County, in 1821, had two thousand two hundred and forty-eight people, one-third of whom were there in 1817 and 1818. They settled on Mount Prairie and spread, like a great setting hen, clear to Red river.

WHEN PULASKI EXTENDED TO FT. SMITH.

The third county in size was Pulaski, with nineteen hundred and twenty-three people, and settlements at Cadron, Crystal Hill, Pecannerie, Little Rock, Crawford Court House, and on the Saline near Benton. There were but nine counties in 1821, and Pulaski extended clear up to Ft. Smith. The fourth county was Arkansas, with twelve hundred and sixty-one people. Phillips came next with twelve hundred and one, the larger part coming directly across the river from distributing points on the National road from Nashville to Natchez, while a great number came by boat from Southern Indiana and Ohio, and from river points in Kentucky and Pennsylvania. The next county was Clark, with eleven hundred and forty people, the larger part coming by way of the National road, while the smaller part came by way of the Post. Miller County came next with nine hundred and ninety-nine people, nearly all of whom came the Missouri route, with a very small number coming up from Louisiana. The smallest county was Crawford, with five hundred and forty-seven souls, included in the Pulaski County enumeration. Lawrence and Independence County were listed together in this census, although separate counties, and together had more than one-third the population of the whole territory. This shows how much more important the wagon was in determining population and its location than the boat. Far-away Hempstead had more than one-seventh of the population, and although for the most part from Georgia, North Carolina, Virginia and Kentucky they came in from Missouri in wagons guided by the National road.

This distribution of population is always a fascinating study. The greatest factor in the immigration from 1812 to 1817 was cheap and good lands. Under the influence of this law a great number of clean, honest, yet poor people came into the territory from every Eastern State. Davidsonville in 1817 had merchants from rockbound Vermont, and Mount Prairie had merchants from Maine. The major part of the population, however, was from the older Southern States.

MILITARY OFFICERS WERE NABOBS.

The factor most largely entering into the immigration from 1817 to 1825 was the soldiers' land bounties. Congress gave its soldiers of the Revolution and the war of 1812 a preference in free lands. This brought another mass of clean, honest, brave, and somewhat richer men. A colonel received one thousand acres, and when a colonel moved to the territory he came in state, bringing cattle and slaves and cutting a very wide swath. Before leaving his Eastern home, he had probably bought all the land warrants he could find, with the hope of becoming rich. Thousands of American soldiers in the East were satisfied to remain there, and in many cases generously gave their warrants to their poorer neighbors, while others sold them to speculators, who thrive in every country, and who, like the poor, are always with us.

THE PROLIFIC RECTOR FAMILY.

In 1817, Arkansas, Missouri and Illinois formed one land district, with General William Rector as surveyor general. This man had a host of kinsmen by the name of Rector, another host by the name of Conway, and still another host by the name of Sevier, three names written large upon the early annals of the territory and State. General William Rector had more power, so far as determining the location of certain families was concerned, than the president of the United States. He was one of nature's noblemen, but undoubtedly had more kin-people than any man since Adam, and by a strangely fortuitous chain of circumstances, which will be treated hereafter, they nearly all fell into Arkansas, and for thirty years dominated it as clansmen of the older order.

THE GREAT RECTOR SURVEY.

In 1818, General Rector received instructions to survey sixty townships, or about one million, three hundred and eighty-two thousand acres of land for soldiers' bounties. Complying, he surveyed the most of it on the St. Francis and White rivers, and on February 17, 1818, land offices were opened at Davidsonville, called the Lawrence Landoffice, and at Arkansas Post.

Within two years these offices were removed to Batesville and Little Rock. Surveys were extended to the Cadron, to Poke Bayou, to the Strawberry, to Mount Prairie and to Red river. Notwithstanding the fact that these were soldiers' lands, many, who were not soldiers, obtained titles to them. Rector finished the survey in 1819, and then began a series of surveys for preemption lands and for sale. The records of the land offices for 1819, 1820, and 1821 show that the very least quantity was sold; that a very little larger quantity went to pre-emptioners or Spanish land claimants, while the very largest part of the surveyed lands was given away as soldiers' bounties.

The greatest money-making business at that time outside of speculation was surveying, and General William Rector could place the contracts where he pleased. His surveyors came to know the best lands, and had opportunities for buying claims that even speculators did not have, and many of them became rich men. William Russell of St. Louis was probably the greatest speculator in Arkansas lands from 1816 to 1830, and there is hardly a county in Arkansas east of a line through Pt. Remove north and south that will not show his name in many places on the first deed records. Not only did these surveyors become rich, but they also became men of influence and character, and had much to do with the early development and growth of the territory. But no speculator, nor any surveyor, could keep a soldier, or his assignee, from placing his warrants where he pleased on unoccupied lands.

This accounts for the rush to Arkansas and Missouri from 1818 to 1830, and warrants the conclusion that the general character of the immigration was as good as any that ever entered any country. The very largest part of it was the citizens soldiery of the republic, not afraid to fight and not afraid to work. Along with it came a certain proportion of floaters, and a few genuine birds of prey. Where the carcass lies there will always be found the buzzards, and where the saints pitch their tents there the devil will open a saloon. These classes, however, were few in number, although they made considerable noise and kicked up a moral stench which seemed to come from a larger crowd. The Mississippi river towns were the greatest "hell holes," as they were called at that time, with Arkansas river towns a close second. The rest of the State was practically immune.

FIRST ANTI-GAMBLING ASSOCIATION.

In 1830, the town of Helena organized an Anti-Gambling Association, with Judge W. B. R. Horner at its head. This association gave notice to all gamblers, thieves and thugs to get out "within twenty-four hours," and signed the notices as our forbears signed the Declaration of Independence. When the disreputable class read the notices, they stopped not to argue or bluff, but like the Arab pulled up their stakes and ingloriously ran away. The list of names forming this early Helena Association contains the very names that have given Phillips County its character and reputation. I shall give them the honor that is justly due them in proper season, for, like the band of Bozzaris, "Such men were not born to die."

At Washington, in Hempstead County, a kindred society was formed at an earlier date, and the men behind it were Hempstead's most solid citizens. Little Rock began the work in 1825, but being the capital, it failed to be as effective as the other towns. Many of the early legislators were born gamblers, while a few of them were professional gamblers. When lawmakers do privately what they condemn publicly, it is hard to regulate the town in which they meet. The mouth of the White river, afterward called Napoleon, was the worst place in the territory, and owing to its inaccessibility flaunted its gambling into the teeth of the law longer than any other place.

GAMBLERS DRIVEN FROM LITTLE ROCK.

The Little Rock Times in 1835, under the fearless management of Andrew Jackson Hunt, a young man from Zanesville, Ohio, drove gambling out of Little Rock, but unfortunately he died the next year, and the cat came back. The good people of Little Rock had to peg on in their crusade against this vice without newspaper aid, as the successor of Hunt, young Reed from Kentucky, Albert Pike of the Advocate, and DePew of the Gazette, were up to their eyes in political controversy, and the larger questions of "tearing each other down." William E. Woodruff, Sr., was a retired newspaper man for the time, busily working to be treasurer of State. When Featherstonaugh lived in Little Rock in 1838, he found gambling in full swing, apparently the only legitimate business of the place. Woodruff got back to the Gazette after awhile; Pike succeeded in destroying the Times, and these two gentlemen joined in with the citizens and cleaned out the town. Ever since that day, with a few sporadic exceptions of reconstruction days, the vice has been kept under reasonable control.

CHAPTER XV.

Distribution of Settlements in 1820.

In 1820 there were three men of the name of Stuart, or Stewart, in Arkansas, and by a strange coincidence each of these carried the title "colonel," and each had a war record of longer or shorter duration. The name Stuart or Stewart is Scotch, and for centuries has been recognized as the same family name, and there are hundreds of instances where different members of the same family bearing this surname spell it Stuart or Stewart, as the mood affected them. It is a name of high antiquity in Scotland, and adheres to a famous royal family.

Colonel James M. Stewart of Mount Prairie, Hempstead County, has his name spelled in the Gazette of the day in both forms, the spelling Stewart predominating. Two titles were also given him, major and colonel; the former, I apprehend, being won in the war of 1812, and the latter following as an act of courtesy. There are intimations, however, that he was a brevet lieutenant colonel in the same war. He entered Hempstead County in either 1816 or 1817, and was the first clerk of the county in 1818. He came to Arkansas from Tennessee, and died in Hempstead County on February 24, 1825, the most prominent citizen of the county, and frequently mentioned in the columns of the Gazette.

In the same county was another Colonel Stuart, whose Christian name was Abraham. He entered the county in 1818 or 1819. I have not been successful in tracing his military record, but he lived for many years an honored citizen of Hempstead, dying there on August 23, 1836, "at an advanced age and one of the pioneers."

The Gazette noted the marriage on November 24, 1821, of Lounella, daughter of Colonel Stuart of Hempstead County, to William Trimble, United States district attorney. In a previous chapter I indentified Colonel Stuart as Colonel James M. Stuart, which was an error. It was a case of too many colonels on the one hand and too little knowledge of Colonel Abraham Stuart on the other. The Gazette spelling of 1821 of the lady's name was also wrong. Lunetta Stuart married William Trimble, and lived for many years at Columbus, Arkansas, but made her final residence in Texas. William Trimble came to Arkansas from Kentucky in 1819, having been appointed United States district attorney by President Monroe. His first act at Arkansas Post was to draw two indictments for petit larceny, for which he received eight dollars. In the same year he ran for the legislature in Arkansas County, being desirous of sitting in the first legislature of the territory. There were many others with the same desire, but only two, W. B. R. Horner and General W. O. Allen, were successful. The defeated candidates were Bartley Harrington, William Craig, Richmond Peeler, Doctor Robert McKay, Harold Stilwell and William Trimble. Upon his marriage to Miss Stuart he removed to Hempstead County, and in 1823 was appointed judge of the Superior Court, succeeding Judge Selden.

J. L. Stuart of Columbus, Arkansas, is a grandson of Colonel Abraham Stuart, and there are very probably a number of others in that neighborhood carrying the blood, if not the name, of this old soldier and pioneer.

In 1816 Colonel William Stuart located at Davidsonville, Lawrence County. He died on March 3, 1822, leaving a family, whose descendants I have not been able to trace. Besides these three colonels, there was another pioneer of the name of Stuart, who lived in Hempstead for many years. The only reference I have to him, however, is his appointment as commissioner for the sale of lots upon the laying out of the town of Washington. The advertisement bore date October 26, 1824, and the commissioners were Elijah Stuart, John Munn and James Moss. N. E. Stuart was surveyor of Hempstead County from 1836 to 1846, and was doubtless a descendant of either Elijah or Colonel Abraham. James Moss, who was connected with the earliest lot sale at Washington, was county judge of Hempstead County from 1827 to 1832.

THE FIRST TOWN LOT SALE.

So far as the records show, Cadron was the first town to advertise a sale of lots. Nuttal says that a sale was advertised at this place for May, 1818, and thirteen hundred dollars' worth of lots were sold. He called attention to another sale for May, 1819, but does not note the results. On March 27, 1819, he wrote as follows: "Town lot speculations have already been tried at the Cadron, which is yet but a proximate chain of farms, and I greatly doubt whether a town of any consequence on the Arkansas will ever be chosen on this site. There is scarcely a hundred yards together of level ground, and the cove in which Mr. McIlmurry lives is almost impenetrably surrounded by lofty trees." He tells us further that this early town lot bonanza was engineered by four proprietors, not naming them.

In the Missouri Gazette of February 3, 1819, we find the names of these proprietors to have been John McIlmurry, John Chamberlain, James N. Menifee and Thomas H. Tyndall, and that the town they proposed to lay off was on the east side of the Arkansas river at the mouth of the Cadron, "in the center of the best settlement on the Arkansas river." Each of these four men was far above mediocrity, and combined made a quartette of the largest influence in early political affairs. The town of Menifee perpetuates the name of one of them and local traditions and State history immortalize the others.

THE TOWN OF FULTON.

In the Missouri Gazette of October, 1819, and the Arkansas Gazette of December, 1819, a sale of town lots was advertised for Fulton, the proprietors being William O'Hara, a speculator of St. Louis, James Bryan and Robert Fulton. In a succeeding notice of sale Robert Fulton's name was omitted and William Andrews substituted.

The town of Memphis was advertised for lot sale on July 1, 1820, and on July 20 of the same year the town of Currenton was laid off at Hix's Ferry on Current river by Jesse Cheek and Bernard Rogan. The town of Rome was laid off the same year. Beardstown, in Arkansas County, as early as 1819, manufactured leather, William Luckie being proprietor of the tannery.

TOWN OF MOUNT MARIA.

In 1820 William Craig, who kept tavern at Arkansas Post in 1819, and who practiced law for many years thereafter, laid off the town of Mount Maria, on the north side of the Arkansas river, one hundred and fifty miles from its mouth. He reserved four blocks of an acre and a half each for meeting houses, market houses and schools. He offered as a gift twenty lots of three acres each to actual settlers who should at the same time be regular members of the Methodist Episcopal church. At that time there was no Methodist Episcopal church, South, so that this body of the faithful has as much right to claim William Craig as the older one. I can not locate Mount Maria, unless it be the nucleus from which Pine Bluff originates.

The Methodists had a strong church at Henry's chapel on Mount Prairie in 1816, but the Spring River circuit was established in 1815. In 1820 the Methodists had six circuits—Pecan Point, Hot Springs, Mound Prairie, Spring River, White and Arkansas.

All of the preceding towns were laid off before Arkopolis, or, as it is now called Little Rock.

PIONEERS OF LAWRENCE COUNTY.

Lawrence County was established by the Missouri territorial legislature on January 15, 1815, being cut off from Arkansas County, and was then inhabited by several hundred progressive Americans. The earliest settlement dates back to 1804, at the mouth of Poke bayou, a settlement, however, which affected no one save the solitary man who made it. In 1811, and from that on to 1815, when the county of Lawrence was created, a stream of immigrants poured in from Missouri. The earliest settlers were Louis De Mun, William Robinson, William Hix, Sr., Solomon Hewitt, Andrew Criswell, James M. Kuykendall, Isaac Kelley, Charles Kelley and Morris Moore. In 1817 James Campbell was sheriff and Richard Searcy clerk. At

Eleven Points in the same county were William Looney, William Meredith, Massack H. Jones, John Miller and James Hadlock.

At Davidsonville were Polly Taylor, James Taylor, William Cox, Jason Chamberlain, Staples Chamberlain, Stephen Chamberlain, John Lewis, Sr., John Lewis, Jr., Jacob Garrett and Benjamin A. Porter. In March, 1821, Rueben Lewis made an addition to the town of Davidsonville and dedicated five per cent. of the proceeds of the lot sale to the erection of a church, besides giving a lot for the same, and an acre of ground for a cemetery. He who imagines that the art of promoting was born in our day is mistaken. These advertisements also show that schools and churches were looked upon then as the chief additions to a town, and label these backwoods promoters as being, in progressiveness, energy and advanced spirit, every whit as good as any of their followers.

In Spring River township, were Thomas Black, Joseph Hardin, Jacob Hardin and William McAdoe. In Union township John Wells, William Fugett, Henry C. Wells, Jonas Austin and William Jones, a justice of the peace. On Strawberry L. Richie, George Bradley, Mr. Bayliss, James Allen, Napoleon B. Ferguson, James Ferguson, the Revolutionary soldier, Archibald Hodge and John P. Maxwell.

GALAXY OF GRAND OLD MEN.

Old age is honorable. Gray hairs are an honor to any life and a crown of glory to a well-spent life. I have never seen a healthful man that wanted to die, and down deep in every heart is the hope that he may live a long and happy life. The desire to live long is universal and when one finds a number of gray heads in a community the inference is either that they have lived most careful lives or that the locality contains elements conducive to longevity. What shall we say of Lawrence County in early days? In 1830 a census was taken, which showed some remarkable instances of long life. The rules of the United States Census Bureau in 1830, although not so systematic as to-day, required nevertheless that the ages should be classified. Between sixty and seventy years of age at the date of the enumeration were the following Lawrence County pioneers: William Hix, Sr., Henry Murrey, Arthur Murphy, Colonel Stephen

Byrd, Thomas Lewis, John Pierce, Mary Welch, Mrs. Nathaniel McCarroll, Ananias Erwin, William McKnight, Isaac Flaery and James Davis.

Between seventy and eighty years: Nathan Luttrell, Sr., James Boyd, Mrs. Wayland, Peter Taylor, James S. Wortenberry, Daniel Williams, Martin Van Zant and Mrs. Joseph Killett.

Eighty years and upward: John Shaver.

Twenty-one persons were in Lawrence County sixty years of age and upward in 1830. One of the Lewises, thought to be Henry, lived to be one hundred and eight years of age, and John Gould Fletcher, the ancestor of the great Fletcher family of the State, died in 1825 in Lawrence County, an octogenarian. His wife, who was a Lewis, lived also beyond her eightieth year. Nor were large families exceptional. The family of W. B. R. Horner consisted of thirteen white persons and seven slaves. Joseph Martin of Crawford County died March 24, 1841, at the age of sixty-nine having served in two wars, leaving his wife, seventeen children and no slaves, to mourn his irreparable loss. He was born in Albemarle County, Virginia, and lived a strenuous life. In December, 1828, a woman in Clark County gave birth to five living children, three of whom, with the mother, survived the catastrophe and lived to tell the story. James M. Kuykendall died in Lawrence County February 15, 1836, at the age of fifty-four years, twenty-one years of which were passed on Arkansas soil. He came from Kentucky along with the Hardins and served in the Fourth territorial legislature. He was a man of large stature and afraid of no living being. In 1825 he was elected sheriff, succeeding Joe Hardin, and was elected for six successive terms thereafter, dying in office. No other man in Lawrence County has ever held office as long as Colonel James M. Kuykendall.

BATESVILLE ONCE STATE'S BEST TOWN.

In the southern part of the county, cut off in 1820 and called Independence County, were John Read, Perry G. Magness, James Miller, Peyton Tucker, Robert Bean, Stephen Jones and Matthew Adams. When Batesville was laid off, March 10, 1821, Richard Searcy, James Searcy, Charles Kelley and

Joseph Hardin, James Trimble and Samuel S. Hall became residents, and to them the town owes its early progressiveness. For more than twenty years Batesville was the leading town in Arkansas, excelling every other in population, wealth; cultivation, schools and regard for law. Each and every one of its first settlers had been in the territory since 1815, and each and all centered their endeavors on the development of a great and thriving town. Thomas Curran, an erstwhile partner of Terence Farrelly at Arkansas Post, moved to Batesville in 1822, after his marriage to Jane Dodge of Davidsonville. Townsend Dickinson, a lawyer from Yonkers, New York, and one of the first supreme judges of the State of Arkansas, moved to Batesville in 1821. He married there, February 27, 1825, Maria, daughter of Colonel Moore. This wife died at Batesville on February 2, 1836.

In Christian township, Lawrence County, the first settlers were John Shannon, Abraham and George Ruddell. Binks and Henderson Lafferty were prominent young men, the former marrying Sally, daughter of James Miller, and the latter on the same day (August 17, 1821), Nancy Craig.

POPULATION OF THE OLDEST SETTLEMENTS.

The old settlements of Arkansas are best shown by the census of 1820. Lawrence County at that time had nine townships, with the following number of inhabitants: Christian township, one thousand two hundred and twenty-two, the largest and most populous township in the territory; Spring River, seven hundred and fifty-two; Davidson, four hundred and sixty-one; Current River, four hundred and twenty-two; Columbia, five hundred and twenty; Strawberry, six hundred and twenty-one; Lebanon, three hundred and nine; Union, four hundred and seventy-five, and White River, eight hundred and twenty. Two of these, Davidson and Christian, were named after old settlers. Some of these townships are in other counties today.

Phillips County had but four townships, none of them very densely populated: Cache had one hundred and seventy-eight; St. Francis, which included Utica, four hundred and eighty; Mississippi, forty-five and Hopefield four hundred and ninety-eight. Cache, Mississippi and Hopefield townships are in other counties today. Arkansas County, the oldest county in the territory, had three townships: Point Chicot, now in Desha and Chicot counties, four hundred and fifty-two; Mississippi, now in Desha County, eighty-two, and Arkansas township, including Arkansas Post, seven hundred and twenty-six.

Pulaski had six townships: Cadron, seven hundred and seventeen; Crawford, now four or five counties, five hundred and forty-seven; Big Rock, three hundred and thirty-eight; Vaugine, one hundred and twenty-two; Red River, one hundred and sixteen, and Saline, eighty-three.

Clark County had four townships: Caddo, six hundred and seventeen; Warm Spring, one hundred and fifty-three; Antoine, eighty-eight, and Missouri, one hundred and eighty-two. The settlement on the Caddo began with the Barkmans in 1809 and the Hemphills in 1810.

Hempstead also had four townships: Missouri, three hundred and fifty-eight; Ozan, five hundred and sixty-three; Saline, seven hundred and sixty-three, and Monroe, five hundred and sixty-four.

Miller County was not enumerated by townships, but had nine hundred and ninety-nine souls.

These townships are the best and surest guides to the oldest settlements in each of these counties and of the many counties formed therefrom. They are a gauge also to the location of the richest and best lands of the territory as it existed then, excluding the Indian reserves.

Of these enumerated people there were sixteen hundred and seventeen slaves, or about one-ninth of the entire population. The slaves were for the most part in eastern and southern Arkansas, where they gave little trouble to agitators or humanitarians. They became the center of interest, however, in eighteen hundred and thirty-five, when in the constitutional convention, David Walker of Hempstead, by securing representation based on white population and three-fifths of the slaves, also secured a greater representation for Hempstead County with fewer white people than for Lawrence, with a greater number of white people. Had the question of white representation been submitted to the people separate from all other questions it would have carried by a large majority. As it was the people either had to give up statehood or take the mixed representation. The effect was to give a smaller number of white people in south Arkansas a larger influence in State government than a much larger number elsewhere. The question created much contention throughout the State, but was soon forgotten in the march of events.

There were fifty-nine free negroes in 1820 and thirty-nine non-naturalized foreigners.

Such was the distribution of settlements in December, 1820, and in January and February, 1821, when the enumeration was taken by the government, and out of these nuclei of settlements rather than the nuclei of 1810, must come the studies which account for the growth of the State.

1. The pre-United States settlements ended in 1803.
2. The first Anglo-American settlements began in 1806, and subsided in 1811, W. B. R. Horner of Helena being about the last of this wave.
3. The second Anglo-American settlements, beginning in 1814 and running to 1818.
4. The public land wave beginning in 1819, and exhausting its force in 1840.

In the third and fourth waves, the farmers came first, as the great backbone of the settlements; then came the blacksmiths and other artisans; lastly the professional men. In the second wave adventurous merchants were side by side with adventurous hunters and trappers.

CHAPTER XVI.

BENJAMIN FOOY AND FOOY'S POINT—W. B. R. HORNER—ST. FRANCIS AND HELENA.

The Mississippi river region from 1800 to 1819 was a land of adventure, daring and rough living. Calhoun called the river an inland sea and along its banks isolated cabin settlements were made, some prior to 1800, but a much larger number from 1800 to 1812. The river itself was a terror to the early immigrants. Squatting as they did in the almost impenetrable forest jungle along its banks, they were repeatedly driven to higher ground by the recurring overflows, at that time uncontrolled by levees or other hindering obstacles. The river rolled on in majesty and when it pleased spread itself over an area of from fifty to one hundred miles in width, driving deer, bear and other wild animals of the forest to the higher elevations—the wooded islands, as it were, of the ocean of waters.

Fooy's Point, opposite Memphis, afterward called by the Spaniards Camp Esperanza and by the Anglo-Americans, Hopefield, was on high ground, and prior to 1800 was the place of a considerable settlement. Benjamin Fooy was the original settler, followed by the location of a Spanish deputy governor, and then by adventurous Americans. Benjamin Fooy's name will forever stand as the first of the mighty army of settlers on the Mississippi—the first in the van of law and order—the connecting link between the vanishing barbarism of the wild woods and the rising civilization of modern times. His house was ever open to the friendless on the Mississippi, and to it were attracted the wiser and stronger characters of the time. It was in his house, at a period when the whole region was as yet lawless and uncontrolled, that the great Volney wrote his great "Ruin," and the table upon which this volume was written was one of Benjamin Fooy's priceless mementoes. After his death his sons prized it more highly than did their father, refusing an almost princely offer from Judge Overton of Memphis. When the State of Arkansas shall enter systematically upon the preservation and housing of the really great landmarks of her march to power, it will be well for her to hunt up Volney's old writing desk, or rather Benjamin Fooy's old writing table, immortalized by Volney's use in the production of a masterpiece. He who for·decades has had nothing but sneers for the men who came first in the hard life of settlement, will find himself worsted in a combat with Fooy. A character that could attract Volney and hold him in his cabin life for several months is no ordinary man. A house that can boast of being the place where such a book was written is a greater house than the "Big House" of Robert Crittenden.

OTHER CRITTENDEN COUNTY SETTLERS.

Between 1800 and 1812 the region round Wappenocke had gained many additions, none of them, however, equaling in dignity and worth the old pioneer, Benjamin Fooy. Isaac and Samuel Fooy were men of parts and were well known to all river men. Mentford Perryman was another rugged character, dating back almost to the beginning of things, a hunter and trapper known far and wide. Another old resident of the place, John Grace, dated back to 1802. Proceeding down the river the settlements became fewer in number until the present site of Helena was reached, where the settlement of Phillips, Patterson and Mooney presented another air space for civilization. At the Sixty-ninth island of the navigator, Nuttal found in 1819 a tavern kept by a man named McLain. The presence of a tavern indicated a settlement in the neighborhood, for a tavern would not be necessitated by the river traffic of the time. Nuttal says that between this island and the mouth of the St. Francis there was a considerable settlement on the White. He does not name this settlement, but in the first issue of the Gazette of 1819 reference is made to the town of Utica, a town at that time of nearly one hundred people. In the election for delegate in 1819 there were one hundred and two votes cast at Arkansas Post, eighty-two at St. Francis, the township containing the present Phillips County, and the ancient town of Utica; thirty-eight votes were cast in Point Chicot township, the present Chicot County; twenty-six at Hopefield, the present Crittenden County; twenty at Cache township, the present Monroe County, and thirteen in Mississippi township, the present Desha County. This large settlement in St. Francis township extended from the mouth of the St. Francis to where Helena stands, and, in my opinion, the old town of Utica was at the mouth of the St. Francis. It was a town of some possibilities in 1819, but gave place in a very short time to the greater glory of Helena.

TOWNS THAT DWINDLED AWAY.

I have tried to locate Utica exactly, as many marriages were celebrated at this point, and many Arkansas families date their origin from this early Arkansas village. There was a later town, Shirley, in the same neighborhood, but this, like Utica, has faded away. Between the mouth of the St. Francis and a point twenty miles below lived at dates from 1802 to 1812 a fine line of old river men. There were Ebenezer Fulsome, Moses Perry, William Bailey, J. McLean, Jesse Stephens, the last two living near the mouth of Eel river, at its junction with the St. Francis. Sylvanus Phillips lived exactly at the mouth of the St. Francis in 1797, but died near Helena. The Pattersons and Dunns also lived at the mouth of the St. Francis, but the Pattersons soon became identified with Helena. In the same neighborhood lived Wm. Gregory, Patrick Cassidy, Henry Cassidy and Mary Edwards. Three miles below the mouth of the St. Francis lived Edward Proctor in 1803, and ten miles below the mouth lived John LeFevre. On the waters of the St. Francis lived Moses Burnett, Joseph Sevier, Enon Chartreuse and John Taylor. These were of the second wave of settlers, coming between 1800 and 1811, and had increased to eighty-two voters in November, 1819, or about four hundred population for the St. Francis township settlements.

W. B. R. HORNER.

One of the leaders of this settlement was W. B. R. Horner. Sylvanus Phillips and Daniel Mooney came earlier, being there prior to 1800. In the death notice of Horner it is stated that Horner came in 1811 and that he was among the last of the earlier wave of settlement. But while Mooney and Phillips were earlier, they were no more prominent.

W. B. R. Horner was born at Falmouth, Virginia, in 1785, of an old and respectable colonial family. He was twenty-six years of age when he landed at the St. Francis settlements in 1811, and was fifty-eight years of age at his death in Helena on May 11, 1838. He settled in this region before Phillips County was born and was the principal figure in its creation. He was before Helena was, and to him more than any other of the earlier men is Helena indebted for the vigor of her early existence. Horner was a resident of the settlement when it was a part of Louisiana territory and saw that territory die; he lived in the settlement all through its life as a part of the territory of Missouri and all through the life of the territory of Arkansas.

He died just as Arkansas threw off the territorial yoke, and took place among the sisterhood of States. That Horner was one of the quickening forces in all these changes can not be denied. He came to Arkansas a well-educated man, bringing with him all the courtesy and dignity of old Virginia life. He came as a lawyer, thoroughly equipped for a professional career, but without fortune or the blandishments of fame. Whatever of legal business the St. Francis settlement had went to W. B. R. Horner, and in every thriving community there will always be enough real estate, probate and criminal business to insure a young practitioner an honest competency. This was true of Horner at least. He had the confidence of the St. Francis settlement, the Cache settlement, the Mississippi settlement and of the people at Arkansas Post.

THE FIRST ELECTION IN 1819.

When representatives were to be chosen for the first legislature in 1819 there was no lack for candidates. Eight men wanted the place and made strong efforts to get it. Two of these, Bartley Harrington and Harold Stilwell, had been in the territory longer than Horner; in fact, they were almost natives, having lived in the territory from boyhood. Doctor McKay and Richmond Peeler could boast of as long a residence as Horner, and William Craig a year longer. William Craig believed in the old-timers having control and was always outspoken about the upstarts, Crittenden, Scott and Norvelle sent in from the outside to rule them. He demanded that Arkansas offices be filled by Arkansas men, and gave Bates considerable trouble in his first race. General William O. Allen had been in the territory but a short time, while William Trimble was a most recent importation from Kentucky. It was a lively race in the swamps and undergrowth, but brains and character combined won the race. W. B. R. Horner and General W. O. Allen were elected, and two better men could not have been sent to the legislature. The lower house was composed of W. B. R. Horner and W. O. Allen, from Arkansas County; Thomas Fish, from Clark County; J. English and W. Stevenson, from Hempstead; Joseph Hardin, Sr., a revolutionary soldier, and Joab Hardin, from Lawrence; Radford Ellis and T. H. Tyndall, from Pulaski.

Nine choicer spirits never sat around any legislative board. They came from the best families of the United States, from the army of the United States, from backwood's homes. They united blood, brains and adventure in each of their lives and made a better showing than nine-tenths of the succeeding legislatures have been able to make. Allen was killed before his time was out, and the old settler Stilwell, sent in his place. Prior to Stilwell's coming Horner had the distinguished honor of being the oldest resident of the State in the legislative body, but when Stilwell came, all the rest were mere new-comers. Stilwell went back into the dark ages of 1798 and could and did many marvelous tales unfold. William Stevenson seems to have had more legislative experience than the others, and was elected speaker. He did what no other speaker has ever done since, served one day and resigned. His reason was that he had rather shoot than be shot at, and that he had been made a target for one day, which was enough. The question then arose, "Who should be shot at?" Joseph Hardin, Sr. said: "Boys, I was shot at by the British in 1778, and I'm not afraid of your small arms." They elected him, and he gave proof of the qualities which afterward made the Hardin family in Kentucky famous. Allen was the principal thinker and speaker; Horner, the man of the best judgment; English, the man of ideas, while Joab Hardin, Radford Ellis and T. H. Tyndall furnished the local coloring. The upper house, called the Council, was composed of five grand old-timers, Sylvanus Phillips, Jacob Barkman, David Clark, Edward McDonald and John McIlmurry. Richard Searcy of Davidsonville was clerk to the council and a fine young lawyer; J. Chamberlain was clerk to the house, and Sam C. Roane, engrossing and enrolling clerk.

These seventeen men were far more in the public eye than the governor, Miller or the secretary, Crittenden. These fourteen men had been selected by the ballots of freemen to make laws, and they were the only representatives of the elective principle then in being. Wm. Craig said: "The president sent us a governor from New Hampshire and a secretary from Kentucky. That's all right, but as Americans, we like to choose our own cooks."

Largely through the influence of Horner Arkansas County

was divided, and on May 1, 1820, Phillips County was created and named after its patriarch, Sylvanus Phillips, of the council.

W. B. R. Horner was the first representative from Phillips County in the second legislature, and held the place through the life of the third session of that body. He served six years as a territorial legislator, when he was selected as prosecuting attorney for the First circuit, which position he held for five years, when he resigned. He served as clerk of Phillips County from 1820 to 1821. When the office of Common Pleas judge was created in 1821, Phillips County was given three judges, and Daniel Mooney, Benjamin Fooy and W. B. R. Horner were selected for these places, which they held until the positions were abolished. At this time Horner lived at Utica, where he solemnized many of the early marriages. In 1828 he was made the alderman of Helena, which position he held for five or six years. This position corresponds to our office of mayor. He was a lot holder of the old town of Rome, and the owner of much valuable property throughout the State.

OLD-TIME FOURTH OF JULY BARBECUES.

Phillips County held its first Fourth of July celebration in 1821. Several beeves were roasted whole and served in barbecue style. A man who has never attended an old-time barbecue is not a thoroughly educated man. His head may have had proper attention, but his stomach has been neglected. To my mind fully half the sickness of the present age is due to starvation. The idea of economy in living has made wholesome living dangerous. There are too many physiologists telling us what to eat, and what not to eat. Thus through stinginess and fear the stomach is starved. The idea that high thinking and low living are synonymous is one of the modern absurdities. High thinking and the power to do any kind of work well comes from good living, and barbecued meat of the olden days is one of its best types. This Phillips County barbecue was held near a spring in the neighborhood, where a fine quality of Kentucky mint had taken hold, though why the mint patch should be immortalized I can not say. There must have been some beverages of very strong parts, though of this the record is silent. A Kentucky barbecue with the mint left out would be like Hamlet with Hamlet omitted. At this first barbecue in Phillips good order prevailed all day long and everybody was delighted. Toasts were drunk and at the conclusion of each a salute of from three to nine guns were fired. W. B. R. Horner presided at this celebration and made the address of the day. He was assisted by Doctor Smith, Doctor Swanson, N. Rightor, Colonel Spencer and Colonel Mooney. These patriotic meetings were continued in Phillips County for more than fifteen years, and W. B. R. Horner was regularly chosen as the presiding officer.

On the same day down at Arkansas Post another barbecue was held, and Robert Johnson, one of the patriarchs of Chicot, was selected for the following toast:

"Ourselves—Recently collected together from various quarters, may we harmonize in feeling, and with united efforts steadfastly pursue our own and our country's best interests."

Some are ready to criticise the gentleman for emphasizing his private interests. A man that can not steadfastly pursue his own best interests will be lacking in power to pursue his country's interests, and the man who is always subordinating himself to his country's good needs watching, lest the country suffer. Bob Johnson's toast reminds me of another:

"Ourselves—God may have made others prettier and fairer, but I'm sure you'll all agree, he never made a bunch, healthier or squarer."

ST. FRANCIS AND HELENA.

General W. O. Allen was the most active man, and Colonel William B. R. Horner was next in all that transpired in the first real legislature—the one elected by the people. Three-fourths of the motions of this earliest legislative body were made by Colonel Horner. He it was that introduced the bill cutting Arkansas County into two parts, one to hold the old name and the other to be called Phillips County. This act passed in February, 1820, but in all the reports of the secretary of State issued since the days of Jacob Frohlick, the formative day is placed on May 1, 1820.

The county site was originally called St. Francis. Just when the name Helena supplanted it I can not say, but the first reference to Helena in the Arkansas Gazette was on June 23,

1821. Prior to this date the Gazette agent, Colonel Daniel Mooney, was given a residence at St. Francis; on that day and ever afterward, at Helena, Colonel Horner before this was referred to as of St. Francis and after this as of Helena. Now it is more probable that the town changed its name about this time than that these two gentlemen should have moved at the same time from St. Francis to Helena. More than that, the Gazette after June 23, 1821, made no further reference to St. Francis, and before this had never mentioned Helena. St. Francis died, but the town known by that name remained under the new name, Helena.

Thus in 1836 a county site was laid out for Monroe County on Maddux's bay, a lake about four miles from White river and about one hundred miles from its mouth. This county site was called Lawrenceville, and the commissioners advertised a sale of lots on December 11, 1836. Whether Lawrenceville died out or became Clarendon I can not tell, but most probably the present Clarendon is the old Lawrenceville. The commissioners for Lawrenceville were Andrew D. Nance, John R. Dye and Martin Guest. Helena, born in 1821, simply carried on the life of the old village of St. Francis, which lived sleepily and sluggishly through a long line of years back to 1802. Wm. B. R. Horner had lived there from 1811 and continued to live there through the rest of his life. Phillips County ran north to the Missouri line, west to the St. Francis river and south to the mouth of the White. Horner from 1821 to 1826 was an attorney and land agent, advertised in the Gazette nearly the whole time, and had much to do with the settlement of the early land titles. He was postmaster at Helena from 1823 to 1825. Helena continued to be a lazy, sluggish town until 1835, when it began to show a faster development.

THE ADVENT OF NEWSPAPERS.

In 1833 John W. Steele started the Political Intelligencer at Helena, but was induced to transfer it during that year to Little Rock, where it lasted through one bitter political struggle. Steele sold out to Jefferson Smith and Andrew Jackson Hunt, who changed the name of the paper to the Little Rock Times. The people did not like the long name, "Political Intelligencer," and Smith & Hunt did not want an elephant on their hands. Hunt died within a year and Smith took James H. Reed as partner and editor. Hunt started in with one and fifty subscribers, but at his death had a roll of three hundred and twenty-five; in ten months after his death Reed claimed a circulation of seven hundred. This paper was making inroads on the Advocate, owned by Albert Pike, and Pike conceived the idea of adding the seven hundred subscribers of the Times to his own list. He bought out Jefferson Smith at a good round figure, and then proposed to Reed to consolidate the Times with the Advocate under the name Advocate and Times, with Pike and Reed as editors and owners. Reed agreed and between them they got out the best paper in Arkansas from 1835 to 1840.

HOW HELENA WAS BOOMED.

The people of Helena having tasted of newspaper sweets were eager that some one else should enlighten the town. In 1836 William T. Yeomans gratified their desires and for two years got out the Constitutional Journal. Why it was called by so grandiloquent a title will never be known, and there is nothing in any of its issues bearing on constitutional questions. The one thing it did was to "boom Helena." It did this well. It told the world a lot of things that Helena undoubtedly had and a lot of things that Helena did not have. It told of the sleepy age through which the village had passed and then noted the great changes beginning in 1836. It told of new houses, new wharves, new migration and ever so many other new things. Yeomans looked around him at the rising town and then looked into the future. What he saw in this realm induced him to wax eloquent. He declared Helena was to be "the London and Paris" of the Western continent: It was to be "London in size" and "Paris in beauty." Great was the foresight of Yeomans, but too far ahead of Helena to be appreciated at that time. He found himself languishing for patronage. At times he threatened to sell out and at others refused to admit that he ever wanted to sell. He was like the boy with a counterfeit two-dollar bill. Some days he thought it was good and on other days bad. On one of the days he thought it good, it went. So with Yeomans. On one of his blue days Martin made him a good round offer and the paper went to Martin, who suspended it in less than a year.

THE OLD AND NEW HELENA.

Yeomans saw everything old through a minimizing lens and everything new through double magnifiers. Grant that the old Helena was slow, and sleepy, and the new Helena more up to date, the old Helena had many compensations. It was like the old-time clock which sat in the old farmhouse for a hundred years ticking off the minutes to the grand sound: "Peace, Rest; Peace, Rest; Peace, Rest." What a compensation is peace and rest. The grandfather and grandmother sat under its sound at peace with all the world and in most beatific rest. The children grew into refined men and women under the guiding oscillations of an atmosphere measured by the sweet ticking, "Peace, Rest." Every grandchild loved the old clock and imbibed the sweetness of its spirit. The old cat and the faithful dog slept peacefully side by side undisturbed by the ticking of the old clock. But a new age came—an age of bustle, of hurry and of excitement. A little round clock now supplants the old timepiece. The new clock costs seventy-five cents with an alarm thrown in to wake up the household after a dissipation lasting half the night. The new clock is on the mantel and ticks off the minutes in a most up-to-date style, saying "Get-there, get-there, get-there," a variation of the old time "Pot-rack, pot-rack," of the guinea fowl. The Horners, the Biscoes, the Phillipses, the Ferebees, the Mooneys, the Pattersons, the Deshas and other old-timers of Helena had peace and rest, which their descendants have never had under the "get-there" drive of modern law.

THE VIGILANCE COMMITTEE OF 1836.

The Latimers were an old and highly respectable family of St. Francis and Helena. Whether Griswold Latimer entered Arkansas County before Colonel Horner is a question I have not as yet decided, but I am of the opinion that he did. He was of an old Alabama family and well known to all river men. He lived at Utica and reared sons and daughters, who intermarried with the best people of the time. His descendants are in many parts of the State.

In 1836 one of his sons—William Latimer—a most respectable citizen of Helena, was foully murdered by an unknown hand. Even as the gambling element had moved the citizens to most decisive action in earlier days, so this murder moved them to rapid decision. About a dozen men gathered that night at the home of Darby Pentecost, one of the quaintest men of the day. Colonel Wm. B. R. Horner was there and was called to the chair, with William R. Sebastian as secretary.

Horner made a rapid-fire talk explaining the situation and demanding not only that quick action be taken to uncover the murderer, but also that decisive action be had to cleanse the town of all undesirable characters. Honorable Thomas J. Lacy then moved that a committee be named and sent out to bring in all the better class of citizens. That committee consisted of Silas Drury, W. W. Palmer, Robert Maloney and Wm. P. Craig. A recess was taken for the committee to act. The committee scoured the town rapidly, as the sergeant-at-arms scours Washington for absentees from Congress. Every citizen notified dropped everything and went to Pentecost's.

George W. Ferebee, a man who had lived there twenty-five years, moved that three committees be named: (1) A Vigilance Committee to hunt down the murderer; (2) a Finance Committee to raise a reward of one thousand dollars: (3) a Secret Committee for advice.

MEMBERS OF VIGILANCE COMMITTEE.

Colonel Wm. Horner appointed as the Vigilance Committee George W. Ferebee, Miller Irvin, N. Rightor, Thomas B. Handy, Davis Thompson, Thomas J. Lacy, James H. McKenzie, Wm. R. Sebastian, Wm. M. McPherson, S. C. Mooney and S. R. Sumpter. On motion Colonel Wm. B. R. Horner and Silas Drury were added. This was the strongest vigilance committee ever authorized to act by any body of citizens in Arkansas. Every man on the committee was a law-abiding citizen, and every one of them was a terror to evil-doers. This vigilance committee was not to hang nor burn the culprit. It was to discover him, arrest him and put him in jail for trial. A reward of one thousand dollars was also raised and offered for the apprehension of the murderer.

This committee made a raid on the dark corners of Helena and of St. Francis township. All suspicious characters were arrested and put through a merciless examination, but all to no purpose. The murderer was not found. The effect, however, was magical. The bad and suspicious characters left the place and for twenty-five years Helena had no such diabolical outrage to contend against. The pioneers deserve our grateful remembrance for removing from our pathway many of the ruder dangers of an earlier civilization. The descendants of this vigilance committee are numerous and should take an added pride from the fact that their ancestors, when courage was needed, did not shirk from the task.

INCORPORATION OF HELENA.

The old town of Helena had been getting along swimmingly for many years, but in 1836 it woke up to find that it had been "whangdoodled," as Mr. Oliver said of his canal matters. At Little Rock there was a legislature in session and William Russell of St. Louis had a bill introduced to incorporate the town of Helena. The Helena members, thinking of no evil designs, made little investigation and no opposition. When the bill passed and was scrutinized by Colonel Wm. B. R. Horner, the alderman, or, as he was called, "the lord high mayor," of Helena, it was discovered that Russell had incorporated into Helena a lot of his wild land, and was log rolling to have the county buildings moved from their old location to his holdings. Another wave of excitement swept over Helena. The people said they would not be taxed to give an unearned increment of value to a non-resident speculator. But what were they to do? Colonel Horner found a way.

ALL HELENA OFFICIALS ABDICATED.

He advised the town assessor, the town constable, the overseer of the streets and the clerk of the corporation to resign, which they did. He then advised the common council, consisting of George W. Ferebee, James H. McKenzie, Benjamin T. Odle and William Dodson, to do likewise, which they did. Following all this, Colonel William Horner likewise resigned and there was no Helena and no way to create new officials except under the old law, which the citizens resolutely refused to put into operation. A compromise was effected during the year by which the bad features of the new law were abandoned and a new set of officers created. Colonel Wm. B. R. Horner refused to re-enter public life and died shortly afterward.

One of the last acts of Colonel Horner was in the educational field. The school authorities of the town on August 10, 1836, appointed him, with James H. McKenzie and Fleetwood Hanks, commissioners to erect a school house on lot number four hundred and eighty-one of the town of Helena. I do not know whether this building is still in existence, but the citizens of Helena may easily trace the structure.

OTHER MEMBERS OF HORNER FAMILY.

One J. S. Horner began teaching at Helena on April 28, 1836, having been a teacher five years preceding. The ordinary primary branches were taught for six dollars; the grammar branches for eight dollars, and the high school branches for ten dollars a quarter. J. S. Horner gave up the school room in 1837 and became deputy clerk under J. R. Sanford. From 1844 to 1846 he was county judge of Phillips County, and from 1838 to 1842 its county clerk.

Ferdinand S. Horner, William F. Moore and John Swan were appointed by the legislature in 1836 as appraisers of land for the Real Estate bank.

Horner & Tolleson opened a store on July 28, 1836, in a new house belonging to Tolleson, and W. D. Horner was treasurer of the county from 1856 to 1858. In 1835 Amelia Harriet Horner was married at the residence of Colonel Wm. B. R. Horner to J. A. Wherry of St. Louis, the ceremony being performed by Judge Lacy. In 1830 the census noted W. B. R. Horner as the head of a family of thirteen white persons and seven slaves but I have not traced their careers.

I am unable to state the genealogical ties uniting these Helena people of the surname Horner to the pioneer, but if they are not all direct descendants they are of very close kin. The name of Colonel Wm. B. R. Horner can not be disassociated from Phillips County and will forever remain as one of its heroic names. He lived in a rude age, far in advance of his environment. He lived for law, for progression and for righteousness. His descendants are also a vital part of Phillips County.

In the constitutional convention of 1874, the convention that revivified Arkansas and started her on a new career of glory, Phillips County was represented by J. J. Horner, a man whose life and career are household words in eastern Arkansas today. This family first appeared in Arkansas in 1811 and in four more years will have passed the century mark. One hundred years from Wm. B. R. Horner of St. Francis to J. J. Horner of Helena. A century of pulsing life and vigor for all men, but far more important to the Horners of today. The pioneer set a vigorous step—a step which others of the name and blood have sought to maintain with honor and credit. In 1911 the Horners of Helena should hold a reunion and set a step for the century to come. All honor to the heroic pioneer, Colonel Wm. B. R. Horner.

CHAPTER XVII.

Great Cherokee Indian Agents—Matthew Lyon—Edward W. DuVal, and David Brearly.

In 1819 outside of Arkansas Post the most considerable settlement in the State was at Cadron, where about sixty families had gathered. Further up came Pecannerie, the town or settlement where pecans grew abundantly. Here lived the old General William Lewis, who died there January 17, 1825. Originally a Virginian, he was made a captain in the Virginia levies in 1791; a captain in the United States Infantry, March 16, 1792, a member of the Third United States sublegion on September 4, 1792, and was honorably discharged in 1796. A lieutenant colonel of Kentucky Volunteers in 1812 and 1813; brigadier general 1814; resigned 1815. Was among the foremost of the brave Kentuckians in many Canadian battles. Lived for several years in Jessamine County, Kentucky, removed to Arkansas territory settling at Pecannerie in 1819. Dr. Nimrod Menifee, the great dueling surgeon of early days, married his daughter, Harriet, on December 28, 1824.

At Point Remove lived Mr. Ellis and fourteen other families. On Petit Jean were Messrs. Tucker and Major Welborn. At the Galley was a Cherokee village at which Jolly, the chief, had a residence. Between this and the Dardanelle hills lived many half-breeds, with Mr. Raphael, the storekeeper, and at Spadra Bluff lived Mr. Rollin, the United States Indian agent. In the neighborhood lived Mr. Webber, a half-breed, and John Rogers, a respectable and civilized Cherokee.

All this country on the north side of the Arkansas river from Point Remove to the mouth of Frog bayou belonged to the Cherokees, and the government maintained an Indian agency at various places along the river from Old Norristown to Spadra Bluff. All on the south side of the river was open to settlement until in 1820 the government made a treaty with the Choctaw Indians by which all the region west of a line from a point on Red river three miles below the mouth of Little river northwardly to Point Remove was given to the Choctaw tribe and all white settlers ordered to remove. This raised a stir and the people at once wanted to know what their delegate to Congress, James Woodson Bates, had been doing that he permitted the tyrant, John C. Calhoun, the secretary of war, to thus deprive them of vested rights. . As a matter of fact none of them had an original right to locate where they were, but they were located, and being located had rights which they would spill oceans of blood to maintain. General Jackson ordered them removed, however, and they went without spilling a drop. They kept up a great agitation, however, and the politicians saw a great chance for themselves, which they worked religiously, until Congress, without their help at all, moved the Choctaws further west.

The United States in its very earliest history assumed the relation of guardian for its Indian wards, and through more than a century has maintained that relation with more or less of credit. This relation was the result of treaties negotiated with the savages from the very beginning of the republic, which treaties are to a large extent still in force.

The whites, as individuals, wanted the Indian lands, and the government by diplomacy obtained through treaties just what the whites wanted, without making the equities blush too severely. It was a grab game garnished by a show of morality in which the Indians always lost and the whites always gained. To do this, however, the government had to promise to do certain things, and then whether it really intended to do the things or not, to make a show which would have that appearance. There is no proof in all these Indian relations to show that the government really intended to do the vital things it promised, that is, to protect by force the Indians in their new possessions. As a compensation for this double dealing it promised to make certain money payments annually, and to do certain other things which, in the eyes of the multitude, seemed to be the real thing. In order to carry out these money payments and to perform the minor parts of the treaties men were needed on the ground to see that all the government had promised should be done and that no advantage should be taken by contiguous whites of the Indians in their new homes. At first these men thus called to represent the government were called Indian factors, but in time they came to be called by the equivalent name, Indian agents, and by that name they are known today.

These factors or agents were scattered over all the country, wherever the Indians were in actual habitat, and made a most respectable body of United States officers. The older Indian agents were as a rule men of parts, but since the advent of the Civil Service regime they are, almost without exception, men of less than mediocre ability. Arkansas had but one tribe of Indians—the Cherokees—actually within its borders, but these Cherokees were bound to the government by many treaties. The agents connected with this tribe in Arkansas during its occupancy of the soil were Mr. Rollin, Matthew Lyon, David Brearly, Edward W. DuVal and Wharton Rector. Of Mr. Rollin little is known and the services of Mr. Rector will be treated in the chapter devoted to the Rector family.

MATTHEW LYON.

The second of these, Matthew Lyon was in many respects the greatest of them all. Appointed by Monroe as Indian Factor, he came to Arkansas in 1820 and located himself at Spadra Bluff. He performed his duties most satisfactorily, but as the system was young there was little to do; being a man who could not quietly settle down to do nothing he looked about for a new opportunity to distinguish himself. He had to do something or die. His chance came with the agitation which followed the removal of the Choctaws during the first term of Bates in Congress, and just at the beginning of his canvass for re-election.

POLITICS IN THE OLDEN DAYS.

In November, 1820, James Woodson Bates, as the high and mighty delegate to Congress, deliberately sat down in the sanctity of his room in Washington and wrote an ultimatum to John C. Calhoun. One great card of the politicians of the entire West is and has been the writing of ultimatums. When Bates wrote that letter to John C. Calhoun, his admiring constituents gave him the sonorous title, "Junius of the West," a title fitting him as little as any could well have done. He could write, but not like "Junius."

Bates told the South Carolina secretary of war that all that vast region so given over to the Indians had been settled by whites in 1811, and that it had a county government in 1814. This was a mighty stretch of the county government theory, but what was a congressional delegate for but to stretch the Arkansas district of New Madrid County, Missouri, over as vast an area as possible? Accuracy of statement is not political genius, and Bates found it easier to assert than prove.

Bates wound up this paper with these words: "These people (less than two hundred settlers removed) have known government only by its perversions and abuses. I protest against the meditated act, that prostrates their rights, outrages their feelings and treats them as subjects and vassals." Bates fired this straight at Calhoun, who never answered it. He made the treaty; the president signed it and the Senate ratified it. A cool business talk with Calhoun, or the president, or a few quiet words with senators would have changed the whole affair. Bombast failed, but it had a successful run where it was intended to circulate. The letter was not intended for Calhoun, but for the voters in Arkansas in the election of 1821. It was one of the "Home Consumption Articles," which politicians know how to write. They have done nothing, but the people must be led to see how much they had tried to do something.

This Choctaw treaty, however, went into Arkansas politics. Bates had served one term and wanted another. Two hundred voters were a bonanza in an election that totaled less than 2,000. Robert Crittenden had been for Bates in the first election, and was still for him in the second. In the third election Crittenden and Bates no longer played in the same back yard, and Henry W. Conway fell heir to the Choctaw agitation prize, although Bates in the meantime had secured the abrogation of the old treaty and on general principles ought to have been the "Peoples' Pride." He ought to have been beaten in 1821 and ought not to have been beaten in 1823. He had nothing to show in 1821 but the buncombe letter to Calhoun, while in 1823 he had his arms full of accomplished things. Possibly he was beaten in 1821, and the trend of the after-election movements seem to indicate that Bates met his Waterloo in that election, but was saved from its effects by the election officers, who made the people vote the way they "ought to," rather than as they were recorded. It was close, and throwing out ballot boxes was not unknown in 1821, however righteously and rigidly the State may have abstained from the practice ever since.

THE AJAX WHO OPPOSED BATES.

In 1819 several candidates opposed Bates. In 1821 he had but one, and that one, one of the most remarkable men of the United States. James Woodson Bates was pitted against Colonel Matthew Lyon, and was really beaten by him, but Bates and Crittenden had the machinery and knew how to run the machine. Lyon was a good "machinist" himself, but unfortunately he could not enter the power house, where the secret manipulations went on.

On March 21, 1821, the people of Arkansas territory, who read the Arkansas Gazette, were treated to a five-column article on the Choctaw treaty. This document was not a hifaluting ultimatum like that issued by James Woodson Bates. It was a cold-blooded, straight-from-the-shoulder argument, taking issue with President Monroe for signing the treaty, and with Calhoun for drawing it. The article was signed by Matthew Lyon, and all Arkansas wanted to know who he was. To begin with, he was the livelong friend of Monroe and of Calhoun, and his letter had more to do with the after repeal of the treaty than all that Bates or Conway did or tried to do.

Arkansas recognized the fact that whoever Matthew Lyon might be, he was a great and masterly man of affairs. He ignored buncombe and appealed to reason. He had Monroe and Calhoun on the hip, and Gazette readers in the East were quick to see that Arkansas territory had one man at least who could enter the lists of logic, and, without buncombe, convict great men like Monroe and Calhoun of error. The people of Arkansas demanded to know more of Matthew Lyon, and they were informed that he was an appointee of President Monroe, a United States factor or agent for the Cherokee Nation, residing at Spadra Bluff, and who entered Arkansas on February 10, 1821.

MATTHEW LYON AS A CANDIDATE.

The people at once demanded that Matthew Lyon run for Congress, which he did. He made the race and ran well. The official returns showed him a loser by about sixty votes. On October 22, 1821, Lyon proclaimed himself elected, and gave notice to the powers in control that they might expect a contest. He went before the territorial legislature, but that body, largely dominated by Crittenden and Bates interests, took refuge behind the sanctity of the returns. Lyon said the returns were rotten and asked the privilege of making proof. He was denied, although the general impression was that the old man was right. He went to Congress and that body without waiting for Lyon to present proofs, and without giving a hearing, made a report unfavorable to Lyon. The report was based on the fact that Lyon had submitted no proof. Lyon had no notice of a hearing and therefore had not submitted his proofs. Lyon had been in Congress before, not as a delegate, but as a congressman from Vermont, and again as a Congressman from Kentucky. Lyon was genuinely hated by all that part of New England and of the whole country, which afterward made up the Whig party.

Lyon was one of the original Democrats of the United States and was with Jefferson in every fight he had ever made. He was born in Ireland in 1746, and was one of the first settlers of the Green Mountain State, where in time he married a daughter of one of its governors. He took an active part in the Revolutionary war, and was a fighting hero. When Vermont decided to become a State Lyon was a member of its constitutional convention. He was repeatedly sent to the legislature on the anti-Federalist ticket. In 1796 he was sent to Congress from Vermont. The John Adams party soon came into power and Lyon attacked its principles bitterly. One New England member attacked him with a cane on the floor of the house. Lyon wrenched the cane from the assailant and beat him unmercifully. He was attacked the second time and again he beat his assailant with his own weapon. The Federalist party had him before the bar of the house and tried to expel him. Jefferson and his friends balked this movement. They then took him into the courts and mulcted him with a fine, which broke him up financially, but did not quell his energy. New England became too hot for him and he moved to Eddyville, Kentucky, where he was sent again to Congress. In 1819 he moved to St. Genevieve, Missouri and was a candidate against Scott for Delegate to Congress, but was defeated. The Federalists hated him like the devil hates holy water. He was an Irish humanitarian, opposed to aristocracy in every form. He had mental gifts and a superb courage. He was now seventy-five years of age and no longer able to fight the battles of his younger days. In his seventy-fourth year Monroe made him agent for the Cherokees, and in that year he ran against Bates. He died claiming that he was elected, and at this remote period, it may be as well to say, that his claim was supported by the proof. On February 14, 1822, in his seventy-fifth year, he left his home at Spadra Bluff, in a flatboat, made by himself, loaded with furs of the last year's collection, bound for New Orleans, where he arrived safely. He sold his cargo for good prices and bought machinery for a cotton gin, which he was then erecting at Spadra Bluff. The machinery weighed fourteen hundred pounds.

He ascended the Mississippi on his flatboat to the mouth of the White, where he stored his freight, and proceeded on his flatboat to Kentucky to visit his children. Returned on the same boat, and in three months after leaving Spadra Bluff was back at home. He had made a journey of more than three thousand miles in three months, and still there are those who tell us that everything was too slow in the days agone. Matthew Lyon gives the lie to all this and proves that a man is never too old to do great things, until he, himself, comes to see his shadow. What seventy-five-year-old man in Arkansas would undertake that trip today?

Billy Woodruff saw him on his return up the river and said that he could not see that the trip had affected his health. In going down stream his boat frequently ran aground and Lyon was the first man to jump into the river to shove the boat into the stream. On ascending the river he did his full share of the rowing, steering and cordeling.

On May 3, 1822, from Spadra Bluff he wrote a long letter to Josiah Meigs, commissioner of the General Land Office at Washington, an old friend, protesting against the suits brought against steam-boat men for cutting wood on wild lands along the Mississippi river for use in navigating the river. It was a five-column article and very strong in character.

He died at Spadra Bluff on August 1, 1822, in his seventy-sixth year, and is represented in Congress today by a grandson, that stalwart Republican of Iowa, William P. Hepburn. A great grandson of Lyon and a son of Congressman Hepburn was killed in a quarrel on the Frisco Railway in northwest Arkansas and his assailant sent to the penitentiary, to be pardoned afterward by the chief executive of Arkansas.

Such was the life of a man distinguished in three States, and a Congressman elected from each of them, without serving in the last. Among all the grand men of early days, Matthew Lyon stood like a giant. He was an honor to the territory and some mark of honor should be placed over his grave.

COLONEL DAVID BREARLY.

The second Indian agent differed from the first as day differs from night. David Brearly was living in Arkansas as a merchant during the last year of Lyon's life. President Monroe selected him for two reasons: First, for his military career, and, second, for his great business capacity. Colonel Brearly was born in New Jersey in 1786, the son of David Brearly, a Revolutionary colonel. Educated in New Jersey in the best schools, he entered the army of the United States in 1808, being made at once captain in the crack regiment, the Light Dragoons. He served with this regiment three years, when he resigned. He remained at home in New Jersey until the beginning of the second war with Great Britain, when he again offered his services to the United States, and was made lieutenant colonel of the Fifteenth infantry on March 12, 1812; he was promoted on March 12, 1813, to the colonelcy, and was honorably discharged on the 15th of June, 1815. His regiment saw service in all the battles of the war. He re-enlisted January 1, 1816 and was made lieutenant colonel of the crack regiment, the Seventh infantry, with the brevet of colonel from March 12, 1813; on April 10, 1817, he was transferred to the Third infantry, and on April 30, 1817, was made a full colonel of the Seventh infantry. He held this place until March 16, 1820, when he resigned, in order to begin a civil career in Arkansas. Twelve years of active military service had improved his manhood, nurtured his courtesy and developed his executive ability. He knew all the leading military men of the age and was the social equal of any man of the day. For five years prior to 1820 his life had been to a greater or less extent connected with the territory of Arkansas, either at the Post of Arkansas or at Fort Smith.

While colonel he had made many investments in Arkansas lands, and in 1820 cast his fortunes unreservedly with the new territory.

For a year his mercantile enterprise at Arkansas Post prospered beyond precedent and upon the death of Lyon, President Monroe offered him the Indian Agency to the Cherokees. On the condition that he might continue his mercantile business he accepted and in 1822 he removed to Dardanelle, where the new Indian agency had been located. Here he made money and at the same time performed his duties as Indian agent to the entire satisfaction of the government. The Indians had the highest regard for Colonel Brearly, which paved the way for his future greatness in a wider field. He held this place until the 1st of January, 1824, when Monroe, seeking a man to deal with the Creeks and Choctaws of the South, then in readiness for removal to the West, turned his eyes to Arkansas for a man for this new and greater field. Colonel Brearly was most admirably fitted for his new relation. His military training gave him a thorough command of himself and his courtesy and kindness made him a favorite of not only the Indians, but of all with whom he came in contact. He was scholarly, courteous and kind; firm as a rock when principle was concerned, yet yielding and flexible at all other times. He traveled all over the South in his new field of work and was everywhere at home, whether with the great and learned or the poor and unlearned. No man was too great not to be proud of Brearly's friendship and no man was too poor or low to be outside of the pale of his regard. He died in Arkansas in 1837, having spent a greater part of twenty-two years within its borders.

MAJOR EDWARD W. DUVAL.

In January, 1824, Monroe appointed Edward W. DuVal of Virginia and Washington City to succeed Colonel Brearly as Indian agent in Arkansas. Major DuVal brought his family with him and on January 15, 1824, landed at Arkansas Post. After a week's rest there he took a boat for Little Rock, where he remained for another week, when he took passage for Dardanelle. The remainder of his life was spent in Arkansas. Major DuVal was descended from the French Huguenots of Manakin Town, Virginia, and had all the energy, courtesy and force of that ancient people. He was a young man when he entered Arkansas, although the head of a family, and this must be his excuse for many of the weaknesses he showed during the first three years of his incumbency. He lacked the political reputation of Lyon and the military and business parts of Brearly, and to make up for these he at once began to magnify his office, which in turn he thought, would magnify him. Governor Izard was not only the chief executive of the territory, but also superintendent of Indian affairs. DuVal magnified himself by ignoring Izard as superintendent. Whether this was the result of DuVal's initiative, or whether it was the beginning of the government's policy of ignoring State officers, can not be asserted with confidence at this time. Certain it is, however, that DuVal ignored Izard. Now, Izard was not a man to be ignored. He had been a major general of the United States army and was the chief organizing mind in the military propaganda of 1812, the great body of which organization maintains to this day. DuVal failed to report to Izard, as the regulations required, although he reported regularly to Washington. In less than a year, however, DuVal learned his lesson, and for the remainder of his term paid due regard and respect to Governor Izard. DuVal also attempted to control Colonel Arbuckle, but after one effort gave up the attempt in disgust. Colonel Arbuckle let him know that he was the mogul at Fort Smith and that under no circumstances would he take orders from an Indian agent. He would be proud to confer with him, and would be glad to have his advice, but the ultimate decision must rest entirely with him. DuVal was an aggressive man, but at the same time a most sensible man. In less than three years he had worn off all his aggressive bumps so that nothing appeared but the grandly common sense which belonged to the man. From that time on he grew in favor, not only with the Indians, but with all the whites with whom he came in contact.

Colonel Arbuckle loved to drop down to Dardanelle and spend a day with the major, as did the other officers of the fort. On May 22, 1826, Reverend Cephus Washburn was called over from Dwight to perform the marriage ceremony between Captain Pierce M. Butler of the United States army and Miranda Julia DuVal of Washington City. This day was a gala day for Dardanelle, and the Indians were as much filled with wonderment over the great marriage feast prepared by Major DuVal as were the whites.

Major DuVal never neglected his duties as Indian agent. He was absolutely incorruptible, and when his mind was set, absolutely unchangeable. He took a warm interest in the Indian welfare and gave freely of his means and advice for their ultimate development. The Indians came to honor him and love him. He headed many expeditions of Indians from the Cherokee country in Arkansas to Washington City, to enable the Indians to present their claims more fairly to the authorities. Colonel Arbuckle jestingly said, "DuVal had rather take a party of Indians to Washington than to command an army," but at the same time every one knew that each trip that DuVal took to Washington rendered white supremacy that much more secure. He died at his post in 1828 or 1829 and was succeeded by Major Wharton Rector. The descendants of Major DuVal have lived continuously in Arkansas from that day to this, adding honor, dignity and great worth to the State. The names of Lyon, Brearly and DuVal will forever remain an honor to Arkansas and a tribute to the integrity and justice of early Indian affairs.

NEIGHBORHOOD SETTLEMENTS.

The Dardanelle Settlement was mentioned by Nuttal in 1819, and dated back, possibly, to 1817. Its most ancient settler is unknown. On the other side of the river a little lower down was the Cherokee village, the Galley. Old Dwight Mission was established in 1821 on the Illinois Bayou, where it remained until the Cherokees were removed to the West. On November 2, 1829, Pope County was carved out of this old Indian region, the oldest county made from Cherokee soil. Its first officers were—Judge Andrew Scott, County Judge; he had the distinguished honor to have been the first judge of the superior court of Arkansas to arrive on her soil, and with the exception of Judge Benjamin Johnson, to have served longer in that capacity than any other man. He was also first county judge of Pope County and is buried in the cemetery at Russellville, his grave being marked by one of the finest monuments that the State knows.

The other officers first selected to manage the affairs of this new born county were Twitty Pace, clerk; H. Stinnett, sheriff; W. Garrett, coroner, and W. Mitchell, surveyor. These officials held office during the years 1829 and 1830.

Isaac Hughes was the first State senator from Pope County and Judge Andrew Scott the first representative. With the beginning of county government and the removal of the Cherokees settlements went on rapidly. Norristown was founded in 1829, by Samuel Norris of New Jersey, and for a time was a pretty lively town. In 1837 B. H. Martin, John Macbeth, John Wilson, J. H. Newman and Judge Andrew Scott advertised a sale of lots at the town of St. Martin on the north side of the river, seven miles above the mouth of Illinois Bayou and just below the mouth of Big Piney. These gentlemen stated in their prospectus that the site they had chosen was the only one on the river for a great town, and they confidently expected St. Martin to be the London of Arkansas. Norristown, however, was in its way; Scotia sprang into existence; and Dover was born. All these, coupled with the running of the roads relegated St. Martin to the rear.

Just why these incorporators chose the name St. Martin, may never be known. In England there was a great church parish, "St. Martin in the Fields," but there is little evidence that these gentlemen were acquainted with that fact. Possibly the settlement, St. Martin, antedated 1837 by a great many years and received its name from some Catholic father in his ministrations to the Indians. True, B. H. Martin was one of the subscribers to the town lot advertisement, but it is hardly to be supposed that his name furnished the basis for the cognomen St. Martin. Norristown forged ahead and with a most remarkable energy tried to make herself the capital of the State. It is said that she nearly succeeded; that a change of two votes would have dwarfed Little Rock and enlarged Norristown. The coming of the Little Rock & Fort Smith Railway, however, changed the whole state of affairs and brought Atkins and Russellville prominently to the fore. In 1834 Norristown was the county site, which position it held until 1842, when the county of Yell was in part formed from old Pope and the county site removed to Dover.

Dover in 1853 was the most prominent town between Little Rock and Fort Smith, and in that little town was held in that year the first railroad meeting ever held in the State bearing on the Little Rock & Fort Smith Railroad. Men from all parts of the State attended that meeting, and out of it came the Little Rock & Fort Smith Railway. The first church in this county was in the vicinity of the Boiling Spring camp ground, near Illinois Bayou and was established by the Methodists in 1832. The second church was organized at the house of Sanford King on Point Remove in September 1833, and was known as the Baptist Church of Christ. The Cumberland Presbyterians built a church at Shiloh in 1837 near the old Williams camp ground. Among the pioneers of this old county are Andrew Scott and his son, John R. Homer Scott, John Bolinger, Samuel Norris, Robert Davidson, Doctor J. H. Brearly, Thomas Murry, J. M. Crutchfield, John Williamson, Kirkbridge Potts, S. K. Blythe,

Daniel Gilmore, Ben Langford, J. S. Price, Thomas Gardner, R. S. Bewley, John Ridge, Owen Williams, George Roland, Willis Hodges, John Bruton, Mahlon Bewley, Absalom Sims, Merideth Webb, John McCarley, Henry Andrews, Doctor Wear and George Wallace. D. Porter West came with his father in 1839, and in 1903 issued a little book entitled "D. Porter West's Early History of Pope County," which contains much of interest and value to the old citizens of that county. Doctor John Wilson, one of the founders of St. Martin, was the father of R. J. Wilson the merchant of Russellville. Mr. Jacob Shinn, whose name will forever be associated with the development of Russellville and Pope County, did not come in until 1837, when as a child he entered Arkansas with his father, Benjamin D. R. Shinn and others of that name, with Reeds, Harkeys, McNultys, Fowlers, Linkens, Shandys and Brooks, all from North Carolina.

CHAPTER XVIII.

First Authentic Maps of the Territory Showing Roads, Towns, County Lines and Streams—French and German Maps.

A little man comes before the world and blows a trumpet, and then steps aside that another may present himself and be canonized by the public. This is one of the unfortunate conditions that cluster around the making of real history. The men who make real history have not the time to write it, are rarely canonized, never blow a trumpet and are rarely given place in the tomes of historians. One objection to written history has been that its pages have dealt too little with the real workers, or as Junius Jordan says, "those who remain with the pots and pans of every-day life." This trouble roots back into the disposition of the public to enshrine in their temporary affections those who blow trumpets and act comedies or tragedies, more generally farces, upon the stage of public affairs. The real instructors and helpers of the common people are not the trumpeters so much as the obscure workers, and yet the man with a trumpet will get four hundred pages of historic mention to the worker's one. The men who make the dirt roads of a country are its real financiers, its wealth builders and wealth creators; the men who open farms and plant fields; the men who start towns and stay with them through their various stages of development; the men with blacksmith and wagon shops at the cross roads; the men behind the hoe, in short, are the makers of history, and what do we know of them? Only last year the cotton and corn producers added two billions of dollars to our wealth. This was new money—a great, grand, glorious find. Bankers and financiers add nothing to our wealth —they only manipulate it—and generally to our disadvantage. The great orators and great lawyers make no additions to our wealth—they only consume, conserve and distribute.

In the following article I shall go back into the government archives and try to show by authentic maps, surveyors' sketches and other cartographical matter exactly what the pioneers of Arkansas were doing from 1818 to 1830, the roads they were building and the towns they were forming. This will emphasize the magnitude of their labors, unfold the extent of their difficulties and call attention to the debt we owe them for their unrecorded struggles. It will also correct much that has been written and add to our vocabulary of early place names.

MAPS REFERRING TO ARKANSAS.

The first map showing Arkansas as a geographical division was the Lewis map. It had one town named Delaware which was located on the White River. I have never been able to identify it. The Melish map came out in 1816 showing no towns in Arkansas at all. The Varle map came out in 1817 showing two towns, Arkansas Post and Lawrence, as Davidsonville was first called.

FIRST ORIGINAL MAP OF ARKANSAS.

The first sketch map of Arkansas was Watson's map of the military and general land survey, dated Washington, D. C., December 6, 1820. It was made up from matter taken from the surveyor general's office and is absolutely authentic. On this map Helena was called St. Helena, and was not located where it is today. Batesville is recorded under the names Batesville and Napoleon, both names being expressed with the conjunction between them. In 1818, when Schoolcraft was in this place, it was called Poke Bayou, and had a population of fifteen or twenty people. Thus within three years this ancient town of Independence County had three names, Poke Bayou, Napoleon and Batesville. Their high regard for their fellow-citizen, James Woodson Bates, led them to discard Poke Bayou and Napoleon and cling to the word which now identifies the town. Three mills seats in operation were noted on the Watson sketch, located on the north fork of Cadron, and one on Big Creek in section thirty, township two, south, range four east. This shows the original seating place of the great lumber industry which has added so much to the wealth of the State.

Cadron village was noted as a seat of justice of Pulaski County; Davidsonville of Lawrence; Batesville or Napoleon of Independence; St. Helena of Phillips; Little Rock as the seat of government of the territory and Arkansas Village as a former military post and the seat of justice for Arkansas County. St. Helena was in a bend of the Mississippi, about ten miles south of the present location of Helena in territory covered by the surveys and located in township four south, range five east. As this map was made by United States surveyors, it imports absolute verity.

In the extreme southeast corner of the map covering more than the present Chicot County and lying east of the Quapaw line is noted Don Carlos de Villemont's claim, settled at that time by fifty families. None of the southwestern, western or northwestern part of the State is shown, as the object of the map was to enable soldiers holding warrants to locate their bounty lands. The only regions surveyed south of the base line was between Arkansas Village and St. Helena. Bayou Metou has one branch carrying two names, Creus or Little Deep river. No surveys were made north of the St. Francis along the Mississippi. Eel river is noted as a branch of the St. Francis and the lands on both sides of it were surveyed clear to its headwaters. The entire region from the Cherokee boundary line east to the White river and north to Batesville or Napoleon was surveyed, as was all the region on Spring river, Eleven Points and Thomas Fork, tributaries of the Black, and fifteen townships on Strawberry. This map was prepared for office use in 1820 and published in Watson's collection in 1825. It is the oldest map made from record evidence, and is therefore immensely valuable.

THE ORIGINAL SURVEYS.

The surveys were begun in 1819, Nicholas Rightor having eight townships between the White and Mississippi rivers; Charles McPherson had eight more immediately north of those given to Rightor. Stephen Rector, David Nolan, David Deshler, Elias Rector and Wharton Rector had contracts between the Cherokee line and the White reaching up to Missouri. In 1822 and 1823 Henry W. Conway and James S. Conway made surveys along Red river. These contracting surveyors employed a large number of assistants, who in the course of time became citizens of the territory.

BROWN AND BARCROFT'S MAP.

In 1825, E. Brown and E. Barcroft published a map of Missouri, Illinois and the territory of Arkansas from surveys in the surveyor general's office. This map shows Crittenden, Lawrence, Independence, Phillips, Arkansas, Pulaski, Izard, Crawford, Miller, Hempstead, Conway, Clark and Chicot counties. Crawford County began in the southeast corner of township three, south, range seventeen west, and ran due west to a line north and south six miles west of Cantonment Towson, thence north to the Missouri line, thence east to the White river, where the western Cherokee boundary line strikes that river; thence southwest along the western Cherokee line to a point six miles west of Fort Smith on the Arkansas river; thence down the Arkansas to the eastern Cherokee line; thence due south to the beginning. It covered fully one-fourth of the territory and a strip forty miles wide in Oklahoma as we know it. Izard County ran from Independence to the Missouri line and touched Crawford County on the northwest corner, where the White river enters Arkansas. Conway County ran from the Little Red river to the headwaters of the Saline on the south side of the Arkansas. Pulaski County ran east to Vaugine's settlement on the Arkansas, thence around Arkansas County to the White and Red rivers.

TOWNS OF EARLY DAYS.

The present Helena on this map is called St. Helena, and is located where we know it. The only other towns on the map are Villemont, Washington, Crittenden, Biscoeville, Little Rock, Cadron, Post of Arkansas, Harrington Settlement, Vaugine Settlement, Fort Smith, Batesville and Davidsonville. Biscoeville was on the west side of Femchea Caddo in Hempstead County, and Crittenden, twelve miles southwest of Biscoeville on Fommier Creek, also in Hempstead. Henriad's Springs was on a branch of the Little Missouri, about twelve miles northeast of Washington. Eighteen miles west of Washington were the salt works and the Saline landing was about fifteen miles southwest of Washington. No salt works are shown elsewhere, unless the letters S. W., after Wachita in Clark County, mean salt works, and this may have a bearing upon the study of De Soto's travel. It may place the land of the Cayas in the region of Saline Creek, between Big Cofsclose Creek and Washington. Delaware Village and Indian Town are about twenty-eight miles due south of Washington on Red River. Bodcaw is spelled Bodcou. Ten miles southeast of Biscoeville on the eastern side of Femchea Caddo, in Clark County, was the only town in the county, and then called Wachita, S. W., for salt works probably. This town was on the Safreit, and ten miles higher up on the Safreit was a stone quarry. Hot Springs was then in Crawford County. The Tulip was spelled Julip, which shows how tastes have changed. The Ouachita was spelled Wachita. The eastern line of Clark was but thirty miles from the Post of Arkansas, and this explains how Jacob Barkman maintained a home five miles west of the Post, while clearing a final home in Clark. Jacob, John and Asa Barkman, in the census of 1810, were living in Ouachita parish, Louisiana, each having a small family. Jacob in 1814 moved to a farm five miles from Arkansas Post and began hunting and trapping in Clark. He had a second home in Clark in 1818, where he passed the rest of his life. From Ouachita parish, Louisiana, tradition says that he frequently ascended the Wachita to Hot Springs long before he moved to Arkansas Post. Bayou Des Arc was Bayou Des Arques. Fourche du Mas was Fourches a DuMas, which Schoolcraft in 1818 termed a corruption of the legitimate name Fourche a Thomas. On the map the old town St. Francis is identified. It was about four miles above the mouth of the St. Francis and about five miles west of Ship Island.

FRENCH AND GERMAN MAPS.

In the atlas "Deux Ameriques," by J. A. Buchon, 1805, printed in French, Batesville is called "Napoleon," and nothing else. Davidsonville is noted, as is Arkansas Post. The river is spelled Arkansa, as is the teritory. Little Rock is put down as Arkopolis. C. F. Weiland's German Atlas of America, 1824, spells Missouri "Missuri," and Arkansas with a final "s." It makes Crawford County take in all of the Cherokee Reservation. The county site of Miller is put down as Pecan Point and Clark County has no county site. In all other respects it agrees with Finley's map.

In Finley's map of 1826 printed at Philadelphia, Little Rock was on the north side of the river and Arkopolis on the south side. Batesville was called Napoleon. A road from Reynoldsville, Tennessee, ran through Memphis and Little Rock to Hot Springs. Dardanelle was called Dandenai, proving a contention I have always made that the place was named after the Dardennes. Piats Town is put down above Little Rock and the Mount Prairie Settlement is identified as being on the Saline in what is now Benton County. William Rector, however, the surveyor general, in a letter to the land department placed the Mount Prairie Settlement in Hempstead County. In this map the boundaries of Clark County have been changed so as to take in Biscoeville and Crittenden. Batesville has not lost the name of Napoleon and Hot Springs is in Pulaski County. Beardstown is between "Pine Bluffs" and Arkansas Post. Belle

Point, opposite Fort Smith, makes its first bow to a civilized world.

BURR'S COLLECTION.

In Burr's collection for 1839, there is a map of Arkansas made up from surveyors' notes gathered between 1830 and 1839. On his map going up the Arkansas the first town above Little Rock is Cadron, and the next Lewisburg. Then comes Norrisville, Dwight, Spadra Bluff, Johnson, Logan, Ozark, and Van Buren on the north side; Dardanelle, Morrison's Bluff, Crawford and Short Mountain on the south side. No other towns are noted in that region. A road ran from Dardanelle to Petit Jean, thence to Booneville, thence to Zebulon in what is now Pike, thence through Washington to Fulton. Another ran from Logan and intersected this road at Petit Jean. From Little Rock a road ran through Collegeville, Benton, Rockport, Raymond, Clark, Bayou de Rocho, Wolf Creek and Washington to Fulton. From this road at Collegeville a branch ran out through Caldwell Town to Hot Springs. Another road ran from Little Rock through Saline Crossing to Rockport. Another Caldwell Town, about six miles north of the first had a road through Magnet Cove to Hot Springs. From Ultima Thule a road ran east through Paraclifta, Pine Woods, Washington, Ecore Fabre, Cabeans, Bartholomew to Columbia in Chicot County. Five miles north of Columbia on the Mississippi was another Fulton, and ten miles south was Lakeport; twelve miles further south Grand Lake. From Little Rock a road ran on the south side of the Arkansas through Pine Bluff and on to New Gascony, where it crossed the Arkansas and ran down to Arkansas Post to the mouth of the White. Another road left the Post, crossed the river and ran down to the mouth of the Arkansas, thence south crossing into Mississippi, through Bolivar, thence back into Arkansas and on to Columbia. A road ran from Pine Bluff to Hudgens, twelve miles south, where it forked, one branch going to Cabeans, thence into Louisiana, and the other through Bartholomew to Columbia. From Columbia a road ran southwest intersecting the Pine Bluff road to Louisiana, about eighteen miles south of the State line.

From Ecore Fabre a road ran southeast to Union on the Ouachita. A road from Fulton, Hempstead County, ran east to Spring Hill where it intersected the road from Washington south to Lafayette Court House, thence through Conway to Allen's Settlement in Louisiana. Lost Prairie was the only town with no road.

The streams on the map bear the names they now hold except that Tulip creek maintains its old form of Julip creek, a much more savory name. From Little Rock north a road ran through Bayou Meteo, Des Arc, Little Red River, to Batesville, thence to the town of Strawberry River on Strawberry to Jackson, between Spring River and Eleven Points, thence to Fourche DuMas, a town about seven miles from Hix's Ferry and thence into Missouri. From Jackson a road ran east to Pocahontas thence southeast to Crowleys, thence south through Greenfield, County Line, Walnut Camp, St. Francis, St. Francisville, L'Anguille, Martins to Helena. Old St. Francis on the Mississippi disappears and the new St. Francis near where the present Forest City stands takes its place. At L'Anguille the road forked and a branch went southwest to Clarendon. From Dwight a road ran northeast to Clinton where it forked, one branch going to Batesville and the other to Pine Bayou farther up the White. From Clinton a road ran south to Lewisburg. On the Little Rock road at Des Arc a road ran northeast twelve miles to Frankfort, where it stopped. The Congress road, as the military road was called, ran from Little Rock through St. Francis to Memphis, missing Clarendon and Marion. A road from the mouth of the Cache ran east of Clarendon, south to Jacob's Staff, six miles east to Monroe, which had no road, thence east to Helena. Helena on this map is in township two, south, range five east, while on the other maps St. Helena was in township four, south, range five east in the great bend. Oldtown is in township four, south, range four east, outside the great bend. From both St. Francis and St. Francisville roads ran to Marion, one going to Memphis and the other to Greenock, in Mississippi County. No road reached Cornwall still further north and none entered Canadian still higher up. From Batesville a road ran to Sulphur Rock, thence to Pleasant Island and Litchfield, thence southeast to St. Francis, where it tapped the Helena and Memphis road. Another road ran direct from Jackson to Crowleys. From Batesville a road ran northwest through Tecumseh to Pine Bayou then to Izzard, then to Johnson, Yellville, Crooked Creek, Sevierville and Richland to Fayetteville, thence through Cane Hill and Vineyard it reached Van Buren. Cane Hill then was in township fifteen north, range thirty-two west. Another road ran from Johnson through Carrollton and War Eagle to Fayetteville.

From Fayetteville a road ran north through Hubbard and Osage to Sugar Creek, Missouri. Another road swept south from Fayetteville to Mountain, thence west to Cane Hill. A road ran from Little Rock on the north side through Cadron, Lewisburg, Point Remove, Dwight, Scotia, Spadra Bluff, Johnson, Ozark, Pleasant Hill and Cotocton to Van Buren. From Morrison's Bluff on the south side a road ran west through Mountain to Crawford, thence on to Fort Smith. A road also extended from Van Buren to Fort Smith, while another ran from Vineyard out to Lee's Creek. This is a large map and the foregoing contains every town and road as laid down at that time. The only error that I note, and this may not be error, is the location of Oldtown. I take Oldtown of this map to be St. Helena of Watson's collection. The locations on the Watson map were made by government surveyors and St. Helena is there placed in the bend of the Mississippi river, with that river on both sides of it and a part of Mississippi, Coahoma County, between it and Arkansas.

ST. GENEVIEVE-BATESVILLE ROAD.

Above New Madrid was the older French town, St. Genevieve, which likewise attracted to itself rich and educated Virginians, Marylanders and Pennsylvanians, and from which many men afterwards migrated to the newer territory of Arkansas. St. Genevieve is also bound to Arkansas by a closer tie; near it was one of the principal ferries over the Mississippi, by the aid of which the vast throng of emigration found its way from the older States into Louisiana. To accommodate this tide of travel a road had been cut from St. Louis to St. Genevieve, and from St. Genevieve to Hix's Ferry on the line between Missouri and Arkansas. These roads formed one continuous line, started about 1765 and finished about 1800. Soon after 1800 the road began its prolongation southward and ever southward, to make way for the ever increasing flood of dissatisfied men and women, seeking a land of promise and of rest in southern Missouri and Arkansas. On each side of this road in Missouri, towns sprang up far into the interior on branch roads which the wanderers established, the direct fruitage of the old St. Genevieve and Little Rock road, or as it was called then the National road.

Just when Hix established a ferry is not known, but it was certainly prior to 1808. This ferry was necessitated by the extension of the National road and brought the first English settlers of northern Arkansas into that region. It was a noted place of crossing in the olden times and the beginning point of that other great road on the south side of the river on to where the immigrants built Davidsonville, then on to where they built Batesville, and on to Little Rock, then on to Fulton. It was a grand thoroughfare, the builder and maker of north, central and south central Arkansas. I have traveled it from Hix's Ferry to Little Rock, and it is the best long road in Arkansas today, but not what it ought to be made. That road, could it speak, would tell of long caravans of covered wagons bringing men and women, who became the ancestors of the wisest and best of Arkansas' present population. When it was a new road, a mere thread zigzagging over the face of the earth, old Colonel Walker road over it on horseback to attend the legislature at St. Louis.

Down that road in 1819 came James Woodson Bates on a blooded horse—a young lawyer, poor, as a lean turkey—but brimful of brains and purpose, riding to his destiny. Down that road on another splendid Kentucky charger rode Robert Crittenden, another youngster of power and purpose, the then secretary of the backwoods commonwealth and its acting governor. Down that road rode Andrew Scott with his head filled with Blackstone, ready made by the midnight lamp of study to oil the wheels of justice and start the courts of Arkansas. That old road carried civilization to a large degree into Arkansas. Ashley, Miller and

Letcher got to Arkansas Post by water, but Bates, Crittenden and Scott came by way of the so-called National road.

CARAVANS OF PIONEERS.

Over that road from 1808 to 1830 went caravan after caravan of covered wagons filled with men, women and children, and accompanied by slaves, horses, cattle, sheep and troops of dogs to found for themselves a new empire—a new government of larger, freer and ampler scope and power. In all the wide world there is no fairer region than that between the Strawberry and Current rivers. To the west and northwest rise in granduer the mighty Ozarks, whose tops lose themselves in the distant skies, while to the south and east stretch out into glorious perspective the undulations which lose themselves in the Arkansas and Mississippi. Where in all the world can a body of rivers be found as limpid, clear and beautiful as the White, the Black, the Strawberry, the Eleven Points and the Current? The attractiveness of the region brought French pioneers there as early as 1750. Who will ever tell the story of the Janis family on the Black or of the other old Frenchmen who lived and died in this romantic region? It is no wonder that Alice French, or as she is better known, "Octave Thanet," loves that locality, and clings to it with the fervor of a Mohammedan clinging to his shrine. The land is full of poetry, romance and history and the old National road is the key to its treasures. When Arkansas shall put aside politics and rise to the majesty of a great State creating highways of indomitable purpose and power, this oldest of Arkansas highways will be made one hundred feet wide of the best macadam clear across the State from the monumental landmark, Hix's Ferry, to that other monumental landmark the town of Fulton.

In what a most romantic field was Hix's Ferry placed! In the land of the Osages then, and afterwards in the land of the Cherokees. Bands of savages from either nation traveling on errands of peace or war converged from all directions to the ford where Hix's ferry came to be. Here these barbarous and half-civilized tribes camped, and here they danced their harvest, their peace or their war dances. Here tradition still points out the spot where these savages clashed with themselves, or with the whites who first crossed the lines. All through the region are mounds holding their heads aloft in dignified attestation of the earlier Indian habitat. All around Cherokee bay are Indian relics of profound historic character, which in the future will furnish the world, and I trust at the hands of Arkansas genius, romances and historic theses of marvelous interest and worth.

SCHOOLCRAFT ON NATIONAL.

Schoolcraft and Drummond struck the National road in the winter of 1818-19 at Poke bayou, afterwards Napoleon, and the present Batesville. They put up with Robert Bean, the earliest merchant of the town, and a man whose name is associated with pioneer life in many States. The first white child born in East Tennessee bore the name, Bean, but whether its parents were of kin to Robert Bean I can not say. Certain it is that either Robert Bean or a son organized a body of Rangers in Independence and Izard Counties in 1832 or 1833 who attached themselves to the expedition of Captain Bonneville, which made fame for itself in what is now Oklahoma. It was on this expedition that Washington Irving gathered materials for two of his excellent books, and in this way through either Robert or Mark Bean, North Arkansas connected itself with a glorious enterprise. Schoolcraft and Drummond were two of the earliest "tramps," known to Arkansas history. They tramped from Batesville to St. Genevieve about the time that Congress was creating the territory of Arkansas. Schoolcraft's boots hurt his feet and he could not make time, and as Drummond had to be in the East at a certain time, by mutual consent, they separated, Drummond walking to make time, and Schoolcraft taking it more leisurely to save his feet. At Strawberry, Schoolcraft found a village of fifteen buildings scattered along the banks of the stream, including a grist mill turned by water, a whisky distillery, a blacksmith shop and a tavern. I am of opinion that this was not the first distillery in Arkansas, although it may have been. Down on Oil Trough Bottom, or as Gerstacker called it, "Oil Trove Bottom," Magnus had a distillery, which I think was the first in the State. I have tried to find a reason for the name Oil Trough, but have not found a satisfactory one, and I am inclined to believe that the real name was the one handed down by Gerstacker and not the one which marks that splendid bottom today. Ten miles beyond this village, Davidsonville, Schoolcraft stopped at Dog Wood Spring on the divide between Strawberry and Spring river, where he was entertained by that old pioneer, Major Haynes, who represented Lawrence County in the fourth territorial legislature, when Robert Bean was speaker and David Barber, clerk. Schoolcraft was amazed at the improved farms and houses which skirted the road on either side. Ten miles from Spring river he entered a region where he found wheat, rye, oats, cotton and tobacco, all flourishing in the same field. He crossed the Spring river in a canoe, and at eleven o'clock the next day reached the Eleven Points, which he also crossed in a canoe. He spoke of the Fourche at Thomas, and remarked that even at that early date the American emigrants had corrupted it into its present form, Foosh-e-da-Maw. Those who would connect this little stream with the great French name, Dumas will be hit hard by this explanation. He did not speak of Fourche de Mun, a stream immortalizing the name of old Robert de Mun, the early French settler of Davidsonville. The testimonial of Schoolcraft to the hospitality of early Arkansas has already been noted, and this trip over the old National road is of additional interest. At that time L. Ritchie was magistrate at Davidsonville, and one of his earliest official acts was the marriage of Napoleon B. Ferguson to Elizabeth Allen. As early as 1820 another old pioneer preacher was on the Strawberry, Reverend James Larrimore, a Baptist preacher from Virginia and Kentucky. On February 1, 1820, he married George Bradley to Eleanor Bayliss, at the home of the bride near Davidsonville. In 1788, General Morgan of Virginia, began a settlement on the Mississippi, which received the name New Madrid and grew rapidly. Morgan had received an extensive grant from Spain, rich in special privileges and abounding in promise. The prominence of Morgan in the revolutionary war, together with his social position in the lower Shenandoah Valley, made it easy for him to induce settlers to leave the old Virginia heaven for a new home on the banks of the mighty Father of Waters. The men who settled that town and neighborhood were the creme de la creme of Virginia, and one can but wonder why they made the change. Men of wealth abandoned the aristocratic counties of Frederick, Page and Berkely, taking with them their families and all their property for the Wild West. With them went rich Marylanders and Pennsylvanians, thus importing into New Madrid, a ready made colony of intelligence, wealth and power. The peregrinations of the Bowie family from Maryland to Louisiana, must be unravelled, if the gnarl is ever straightened, by a study of the New Madrid rolls. Rezin and David Bowie were at New Madrid before 1800, and both proved settlement between that place and St. Genevieve between 1800 and 1808. Stephen and Amos Byrd, whose descendants in after times were found in Arkansas, had a home on Randall's Creek on the road leading from St. Genevieve to Little Rock, and on Byrd's Creek as early as 1800. Randall was a rich man from the Shenandoah Valley whose children migrated to Arkansas. The earthquake of 1811 which destroyed New Madrid left hundreds of people without homes, and the government to provide for these, issued New Madrid certificates, which authorized their holders to locate on unoccupied lands in Missouri and Arkansas. Many of those were located in northern Arkansas and in the neighborhood of Little Rock. Thus the building and destruction of New Madrid were intimately associated with the development of Arkansas.

CHAPTER XIX.

LONGEVITY OF THE PIONEERS—SOME OLD MARRIAGES AND MARRIAGE CUSTOMS.

There is a sentiment running through American history which seems to sustain the dictum that the West was peopled by young men and that the gray-heads stayed at home. Out of this has come the distinctions of the "Wild and Woolly West," and the "Cultivated East." I have lived in the East seven years and have traveled a great deal throughout the world and have corrected some of my own impressions, and am now writing to change a general impression.

LITTLE ROCK AND WASHINGTON.

Washington has more people, Little Rock more refinement; Washington has more wealth, Little Rock more independent good livers. Washington has more negroes than Little Rock has white people and negroes combined, and the negro question will eventually be settled by their moving to Washington and the whites moving to the States. There are ninety thousand negroes here and "more a-comin." Washington has more official, and Little Rock more real society. There is no better system of education in Washington than in Little Rock, and there are a far greater number of gawks, cranks and half-educated people here than in Little Rock or any other first class city of the country. Civil service finds a roosting place for thousands who can just pull through, but when they are through have a life job without corresponding mental improvement. They do one thing forever, which dwarfs without making them specialists. The president of Princeton University has pointed out that the tobacco chewers of the West are the greatest thinkers of the country, and that there is a close inter-relation between the sawdust spit-boxes of the cross roads and a high order of thought. Government clerks never think; it would be suicidal so to do. They do as they are told and in exactly the manner they are told, and have a dozen high mucky-mucks standing over them to see that they do it. They can't think and hold their jobs. Other people in the West are too busy reading the papers and making money to have time for rumination and chewing the cud. When young men were told to go West and grow up with the country it was not generally known that the old men of the country had been acting on that advice for fifty years. In fact, the West was peopled by men over forty-five years of age to a far greater extent than by people between twenty-six and forty-five.

OLD MEN NOT AFRAID TO MOVE.

It is generally believed that old men become more and more cautious as they advance in years and less and less adventurous. I understand how difficult it is to properly generalize the class of old men, but those over forty-five will come much more nearly forming a single class of old men than those under forty-five will the single class of young men. If there are to be but two classes, the forty-fifth year is a distinct line of cleavage. More men and women over forty-five years of age entered Arkansas prior to 1830 than did the men, women and children under forty-five. Men begin to live the really strenuous life at about forty-five, and do more really good work for the next twenty years than they did from twenty-five to forty-five. It is too great a task to enumerate all the men and women between forty-five and seventy years in Arkansas in 1830, but their aggregate 'was much larger than those between twenty and forty-five.

WORK OF THE HALF-CENTURY EMIGRANTS.

Men and women of forty-five years or older piloted the long caravans of covered wagons that entered the State in territorial days; they entered the lands; they cleared the lands and built the cabins. In those days people younger than these were to be seen, not heard. There were exceptions of course, but the rule was as I have stated. Young lawyers and politicians came in droves of one and two, while the old people came in caravans.

I have in a previous chapter picked out the men over sixty years of age in Lawrence County, but found the task too great for the entire territory. I have changed the age to seventy or more and present the following list, as official and authentic, for the entire territory in 1830. It proves that old men in that day were not afraid to make long journeys, not afraid to make a new home in the wilderness. These old men and women are the ancestors of thousands of our best citizens and are entitled to the special mention I give them.

Lafayette County had three men between seventy and eighty —George Hubbard, Morgan Cryer and John Berry.

Izard County had nine—John Deerman, John Hargrove, Abraham Wood, Sr., Mrs. Abraham Wood, Samuel Davis, John W. Stewart, Mrs. Winnifred Chisolm, Webb E. Hayden and Joshua Martin. Towering above all these was old Jacob Wolf, between eighty and ninety.

Phillips County had four from seventy to ninety—John Royall, Mrs. John Royall, John Ward and Mrs. John W. Hunt.

Hempstead County took the premium for grand old men and women. There were three from seventy to eighty—Mrs. John Wilson, William Bailey and John Chairs. There were two between eighty and ninety—Mrs. Ambrose Hudgins and Mrs. Benjamin McDowell—while four men and women answered to their names with ages between ninety and one hundred. This grand old quartette of nonogenarians was John Haleman (possibly Holman), Mrs. John Haleman, Mrs. William Reed and Mrs. Abraham Stuart.

Conway County had two from seventy to eighty—Henry Siscoe and Mrs. Margaret Kuykendall—while John Aplin registered between eighty and ninety.

Hot Spring County had two old people between seventy and eighty—L. Belding and Mrs. Jonathan Irons.

Sevier County had a quartette of septuagenarians—John Dollarhide, Mrs. John Dollarhide, Mrs. David Fareen and Benjamin Clark. She also had two octogenarians—David Fareen and Mrs. Benjamin Clark.

Pope County, my own native heath, had two between seventy and eighty—Mrs. Jessie Burton and Elijah Baker.

Away up in Washington County, where the boast has been that the men live forever and the women never die, there were eight between seventy and eighty, but none older—James Fisher, Mrs. Alexander Williams, Jacob Pyeatt, Mrs. John Casey, John Estes, Henry Click, Samuel Vaughan and Mrs. Samuel Vaughan.

In Clark County they were limited to septuagenarians, but they beat Washington County in number. The roll contains ten names—Mrs. George Overban, Mary Dickson, Benjamin Crow, John Little, Jonathan West, Charles Cox, Mrs. Charles Cox, John Elkins, Nancy Biddix and Mrs. Joseph Galbreath.

Jefferson County was exceedingly short on longevity and had but one person seventy years of age—Mrs. Samuel Waters.

Miller County had one from seventy to eighty—John Roberts —and one from eighty to ninety—George C. Wetmore. Major Wetmore was reported to have been killed by the Indians in 1822, but this proves that to have been false.

Independence County had four persons from seventy to eighty, Col. William Johnson, David Vance, John Minyard and Morgan Magness. Samuel Caruthers was between eighty and ninety.

In Pulaski County none but septuagenarians, were enrolled. These were: Samson Gray, Thomas Massengill, Asher Bagley, Patrick Flanakin, John Bailey, Valentine Miller, William Duncan and Margry Harris. Six of these old men of Arkansas were Revolutionary soldiers, Benjamin Clark, Morgan Cryer, John Holman, David Vance, Asher Bagley and Charles Pelham.

FOURTH OF JULY, 1822, AT BATESVILLE.

On this ocasion the whole county turned out and a grand jubilee was held. They read the Declaration of Independence, and Townsend Dickinson, a young lawyer from Yonkers, New York, afterward supreme judge of the State, made a speech which "set the boys wild." Among the men who responded to toasts were men that afterward added fame and honor to Arkansas. There was Richard Bean, one of the men from Tennessee whom Schoolcraft has named. Colonel Richard Peel was there and kicked harder than his descendant, Sam W. Peel, ever did against taxation without representation. John Colley, with his coon skin cap, tickled the State officers with compliments. James Trimble drank to the health of the territory and wished that it might soon become a State. There was no height of impudence to which these jovial sons of the forest would not go. James Trimble came from Kentucky in 1815. His wife, a Culpepper, Virginia, woman died in 1836. Major Joseph Taylor, fresh from Cynthiana, Kentucky, paid a glowing tribute to the pioneers. He unfortunately died the next year and was buried with Masonic honors, before there was a lodge in the State. Richard Holaby toasted Governor Miller, and Colonel James Boswell pushed up Statehood. Townsend Dickinson looked askant at the daughter of Major William Moore (whom he afterwards married), and made the speech of the day. William Ramsey pitched into the Choctaw removal and Charles H. Pelham paid a tribute to young Robert Crittenden. Charles Kelley and Major William Moore boomed Batesville, while Aaron Gillet toasted John C. Calhoun and nominated him for president. The red-hot speech, however, was made by Major David Magness. His toast was: "May the hand wither and rot that plucks one feather from the tail of the Bird of Freedom to adorn the crown of royalty." A man that couldn't make a speech on that question at that time was not much of a speaker. Major Magness filled the bill and roused Independence County to the heights of patriotism.

After the speaking was over the fiddles were brought out and the dance began. It was a grand gathering of fair women and brave men and all went merry as a marriage bell. The whole affair was impromptu and enthusiastic. Independence County couldn't give that celebration today. There are too many critics in these modern times to do things grandly large in a truly off-hand way. There must be committees and a bevy of grand marshals, and a regiment of good lookers to grace the platform—a phalanx of fuss with little feathers.

WEDDING FEASTS OF LONG AGO.

While camp meetings, barbecues and Fourth of July celebrations gave vent to the social proclivities of early Arkansas, illustrating their good nature, good humor and camaraderie, nothing so well illustrated these points of vantage as the weddings and infares of the early days. These were the great events of the neighborhood and were celebrated with all the pomp and ceremony of backwoods civilization, a civilization in some respects, in the matter of wedding festivities particularly, far in advance of the civilization of today. The wedding supper then, given at the house of the bride, meant something to eat; something substantial, wonderfully tasteful and altogether abounding. In the center of a long table, running diagonally across the large old-fashioned generous room, cake stands were placed one above the other to the height of three feet, containing cakes of the most toothsome kind, made at home by cake makers and not bought at a bakery, each tier of cake flanked by rows of small glasses, each filled with a different colored jelly, all topped with a bouquet of hundred-leafed roses, sweet pinks and lilacs. At one end of the table was a young pig cooked whole lying in a dish as you have seen live pigs in a trough, flanked by dressing made savory with sage, thyme and parsley, with a small nubbin of roasting ear held between its feet and nose, and its tail curled saucily over its naked back; this pig being a thoroughbred of early Arkansas days before modern degeneracy had developed the razorback and straighttailed variety. At the other end a turkey hen sat in state upon a gorgeous platter surrounded by stuffing with hard-boiled peeled eggs protruding, as though the fowl were preparing to hatch a glorious brood. This was not the modern "nature study" of imitation eggs and learned palaver, but the real turkey on a nest of real stuffing and eggs equally as real and altogether true to nature. Then there was the great platter of cold ham, and that other of sliced lamb, and numerous dishes of chicken salads—all of which made a first course better than any three courses of the modern menu, whose essence is physiological culture and parsimonious economy.

Time fails to enumerate the pyramids of cream potatoes, the bountiful dishes of butter beans and cucumbers, and the huge tureens of gigantic roasting ears. All down the aisles of these substantials were tumblers of stick candy of all colors and sizes, very much like the barber poles that grace the avenues of our cities. The only new things advertised for the occasion were egg puffs, known today as sugar kisses. These were an innovation lately brought up from New Orleans, and were carried home as souvenirs to furnish social diversion for the following month.

"FLOAT" WAS THE DESSERT.

For dessert another huge tureen, holding about ten gallons, contained that savory production called in those days "float," which modern learning classifies as "egg-nog," without contributing a particle to the excellency of the old-fashioned float. This was before ice cream could be bought done up in tin squares ready to be served with a wafer or nabisco, and the float fully made up for this possible lack. There was enough on these tables, taken separately, to serve five or six hundred guests, as guests are served today at swell receptions at our capital, where one teaspoonful of chicken salad upon one small lettuce leaf, one cheese straw, two salted almonds and a stuffed olive is considered a superfluity of most gorgeous abundance. We have today physiology and starvation coupled with choice intellectual pabulum, socalled, making a somewhat dubious feast of reason coupled with a flow of soul. Our Arkansas ancestors had plenty to eat, cooked in generosity and served with fervor. They got their physiological service from the force which came from good food well cooked, and the pleasure which came from the knowledge that no one need fear that a second helping would exhaust the supply.

THE SECOND DAY FEAST.

An exact copy of the wedding feast came the next day at the infare, which was held at the home of the groom. Thither went the friends and neighbors for twenty miles around in the old-fashioned lumbering coaches, in heavy buggies and wagons, and on horseback. They all ate like they loved to eat and no one was the worse for it. Nervous prostration was a thing unknown in Arkansas in the days of groaning tables and bountiful living. Emaciation had not come and health was so distressingly prevalent as to make the practice of medicine unprofitable. Old Doctor McKay at Arkansas Post in the year 1819 earned less than ten dollars and changed his business for another which carried a percentage. Nerve prostration came in with physiology and regulated eating and has kept splendid pace with their ruinous teachings. A man's stomach in the good old time worked full time, giving beauty and strength to the body and far more intellectual impetus to the mind than modern eaters display who starve the body to enrich the mind. The old Latins had an idea that soundness of mind was in some way connected with sound bodies, and the soundest bodies are those that not only digest good food well, but glory in doing it. A little weasley, shrunken, half-starved body was never designed to carry anything but a weasly, shrunken and half-starved mind. Poor living may suit those who want to save money, but it was never designed to develop an immortal mind.

NOTABLE EARLY MARRIAGES.

Such weddings and infares were common in early days throughout Arkansas, Missouri, Tennessee and Kentucky. Marriage to a young man meant a most momentous occasion in life and was celebrated with all the dignity of a feast. Following are some of the marriages of 1822 and 1823:

On December 20, 1822, George W. Scott, afterward United States marshal at Little Rock, was married to Ann Dodge, daughter of General Henry Dodge, at St. Genevieve, Missouri.

In the same year the following marriages were celebrated at Arkansas Post: Robert Brooks to Clemence Polet, in June; Achille Godin to Manette Felicity Valliere in July; both these marriages were celebrated by Judge Scott. In April of that year at the same place John Taylor was married to Eliza Webb. On June 19, 1821, Squire Petty in Mississippi township united Isaac Copeland to Nancy Bridgman in holy wedlock; on July 4, 1821, Joseph Bonné was married to Miss Billeate in Pulaski County by John Dodge; on May 28, 1821,Joseph Bennett was married to Margaret Montgomery in Mississippi township at the mouth of White river by 'Squire Petty; in June, 1821, William Kepler was married to Mary Folson, both of Clark County; on February 11, 1820, Charles Ewel was married to Borradell Latimer at St. Francis by Judge W. B. R. Horner. On December 25, 1822, William Franklin was married to Elinor Lockert, daughter of James Lockert, in Pulaski County; on February 19, 1823, John Taylor to Judic Imbeau, daughter of Monsieur Joseph Imbeau at Arkansas Post; in February, 1823, Zechariah Lorance to Betsy Harold, daughter of Abner Harold at Little Rock; on February 28, 1223, Andrew Hemphill to Margaret Welch, daughter of Robert Welch in Clark County. On October 22, 1821, in Vaugine township, Pulaski County, Creed Taylor was married to Utalie Vaugine, daughter of Major Francis Vaugine; on March 21, 1822, at Jackson, Missouri, Henry Sanford clerk of the Lawrence County Court, to Maria

Daugherty; on June 24, 1822, Andrew Fentor to Sidney Dean in Clark County; on the same day James Scarborough was announced as having been married to Betsy Fentor, but the next week's paper said that this wedding did not come off. On July 17, 1822, in Pyeatt township, Pulaski County, Smith Kellum was married to Jane Pyeatt, daughter of Jacob Pyeatt; on January 8, 1833, at Long Prairie, Joshua Morrison was married to Margaret Bradley, stepdaughter of William Woodward; on March 25, 1823, Reverend Isaac Brookfield was married to Nancy Campbell in Lawrence County.

These were all noted weddings of the day and time, adding much to the pleasure and well-being of the neighborhoods at the time and to the glory and growth of the State since that time.

CHAPTER XX.

Early Election Practices.

The Gazette began its existence in 1819 at Arkansas Post in a small house owned by Richmond Peeler. In less than a year it moved out to the main street opposite the store of David Brearly, a Revolutionary soldier from New Jersey and a prominent soldier, at that. There the Gazette stayed until its removal to Little Rock. Its first resting place in the capital of the territory is not clearly disclosed, but on January 7, 1824, the paper's habitat was more clearly defined. On that day the management let the people know that the day of log and frame houses was over for the Gazette, and that thereafter the headquarters of the great newspaper emporium would be in the new brick house—the new two-story brick house—a few rods west of the tannery, or tanyard. Much speculation has been indulged in as to the oldest brick house in Little Rock, and writers seem to have fixed the brick house era as beginning in 1825 or later. Henry W. Conway had a brick kitchen and outhouse in 1823, and the Gazette occupied a two-story brick house in 1824. The issue of the paper making the announcement does not state that the Gazette would occupy the first brick house built, or the only brick house then standing in Little Rock, which seems to authorize the inference that "there were others." Doubtless there were, and the date of the notice of January 7, 1824, would certainly place their construction in 1823, if not earlier. This brick building of the Gazette was on the northeast corner of Markham and Scott.

THE BRICK TAVERN.

Isaac Watkins kept the earliest tavern, possibly, in the village of Little Rock, which, after his demise, was not again used for a tavern for several years. Matthew Cunningham moved to Little Rock in 1821, having come from Missouri to Arkansas Post in a wagon, which he advertised for sale at that place. How he transferred himself to Little Rock is not known, but he got there, all the same. On January 7, 1822, he advertised for private boarders, and kept a fashionable private boarding house for several years. On October 10, 1825, Nick Peay, from Shelbyville, Kentucky, opened a house of entertainment in the Isaac Watkins tavern stand on the river front, which was a noted place under his management for many years. These, however, were all frame houses, as were several other minor taverns and boarding houses that existed for a longer or shorter period between 1819 and 1825.

The habit of locating physicians in hotels is an ancient one, and on December 21, 1821, Doctor C. Baker advertised his place of business at "Watkins' hotel." Alan Mars & Company advertised themselves on February 28, 1822, as ready for brick and stone masonry contracts. In 1823 a two-story brick building was put up on Main Street about half way between Markham and Second streets, which was at once occupied as a hotel, and continued as such for more than fifteen years. This was the first brick hotel in Little Rock, but it is not standing today. Just opposite was another two-story brick house, also put up in 1823, which was used as a store. All of these brick structures were in existence when the Gazette took the new brick two-story building on January 7, 1824. How many brick residences there may have been I have not been able to determine, but in all probability there were several.

Some time in 1821 Christian Brumbach and Benjamin Clements formed a partnership as bricklayers and plasterers, which partnership lasted until October 31, 1822. This firm advertised frequently for bricklayers, and there is little reason to doubt but that in 1822 and 1823 they put up many brick houses, which are still standing or have given place to other structures under the rapid march of improvements. It is certain that the era of brick houses in Little Rock began long before 1825.

FIRST JUDICIAL HANGING.

Judge Pope in his Early Days places the first judicial hanging as of date May 21, 1828. This was the execution of William Strickland at Little Rock for murder. The judge was mistaken upon the point of priority in the honor of hangings, as there are several recorded instances of judicial hanging prior to 1828, and a great number of others that by all the rules of the game ought to have transpired, but by vicious practices were kept from the realm of fact. In the year 1820 Thomas Dickinson, a farmer owning three hundred acres of land on Old river, made an unprovoked assault upon a neighbor and killed him. He was arrested, tried, convicted and hanged at Arkansas Post in the year 1820. This is the first duly authenticated "necktie party" of the territory of Arkansas, and a terrible warning to evil doers.

EARLY ELECTION SCHEMES.

From the very first day that the territory boasted an existence there was an all-prevalent desire on the part of early arrivals and on the part of the "old residenters" to do their country service by holding one or more of its offices. In the first days of the territory one office was not enough, and really ambitious citizens not only wanted, but were permitted to have, two or more good, fat jobs. Robert Crittenden could act as a governor, run the secretary's office, practice law and conduct a real estate office. This led some one, who signed his name "Farmer," to publish a two-column article in the Gazette on November 17, 1821, protesting against it. This writer said: "There is no people more degraded and unfortunate than those having a practicing lawyer for governor." He also objected to Sam C. Roane acting at the same time as United States district attorney and as president of one of the legislative bodies, and to Brigadier General Hogan, a commissioned officer of the United States, holding a seat in the legislature. His objections had a great influence on all after elections, and effected a reform, except that Crittenden never relinquished his power until he was forced out by General Jackson in 1829. In 1819 William Craig, an old resident at the Post, began to size up the new coming officeholding class, and in July, 1820, flagellated them severely in the Gazette. He did not object particularly to their holding office, and that without the consent of the people, but he did object to their dabbling in other business. He said they gave one hour to the public business and nine hours to their own pockets. That they were "claim sharks," of the meanest order, and that the people of Arkansas territory were entitled to a cleaner deal. The newcomers looked upon the older citizens as a sort of uncivilized barbarians upon whom they might prey with impunity, and their greatest field of operation was in the buying of claims.

ELECTIONEERING DEVICES.

When the first legislative election came there were many candidates. They harangued the voters, as they do today and used many practices which have since been legally declared to be corrupt. Whisky was a powerful stimulant upon the minds of the electorate. The man who set up the most free whisky was the man of the greater intellectual caliber, and the quality of the whisky cut no figure, except that all grades of decent, first-class whisky were barred out. Only whisky that would befuddle quickly and accurately was up to the standard, and in close races there were always a sufficient number of sots to turn the scales in favor of the intellectual giant, who knew where to locate his jugs and how to manipulate them successfully. The whisky scheme was detected first and the clean voters blacklisted the man who used it. Then came the cheap cigar age of electioneering expedients. Here, also, none but the worst grades were in use. The office-wanting class seemed to think the electorate a lot of unthinking blocks, not only ready to be bought, but to be bought by cigars that cost fifty cents a hundred. They lacked not only the decency of clean practices, but the generosity of a real grafter.

In the old three days' elections all the sots of the neighborhood were secreted by the office-seeker, who was not ashamed to work that way, kept full of mean whisky for two days and hauled to the polls on the third to plump in their unpurchasable votes for their friend. Others had their pockets stuffed with cheap cigars and at the right moment voted a free vote for the cigar candidate.

MORE CRITICISM FROM CRAIG.

In the very first election old William Craig denounced these practices, and like Ossian prophesied the downfall of the class using such schemes. On July 1, 1821, he said: "The new-fangled mushroom politicians will be left to their own shame, and to smoke their own segars." He seemed to think smoking an abomination, but the smoking of candidates' "segars" a mental, moral and physical poison. The giving of cigars and drinks to the voters has survived through all the years since 1820 and is proof positive that Darwin was wrong in his doctrine of the survival of the fittest. The question of drinking and smoking is not involved in the discussion, as every man has the moral and legal right to determine that for himself, without subjecting himself to criticism. The bald question is "Can a clean candidate, one who has never before been found extending the courtesies of smoking and drinking to anybody, when he announces himself for office, all at once begin treating the electorate promiscuously?" The mind and conscience of the people have answered this with a strong negative, and the corrupt practices' acts of many States have made the promiscuous treating of voters illegal. Candidates still treat their constituents, but so guardedly as to avoid the operation of law.

CHARGES IN ODEN-CONWAY RACE.

In the race between Robert Oden and Henry W. Conway it was charged by the Odenites that Conway used whisky and cigars, while the Conwayites retorted that Oden did far worse. It was charged that Oden kissed all the babies he came in contact with in that race except the "pickaninnies." Conway's detectives found out that every time Oden left Little Rock on his canvass he carried out a carpetbag full of trinkets of little or no value, but which he distributed judiciously among the children, the wives, daughters and mothers of the voting population. It was charged that he cleaned up all the unsalable gewgaws of Little Rock and scattered them throughout the rural regions. He was overwhelmingly defeated, which would seem to argue that the voters thought more of their whisky and cigars than they did of the pleasure that might be given their feminine adjuncts. Or it might be said that they were getting the graft of both sides—the men got whisky and cigars from one candidate and the women of their families got the gewgaws. In all such expedients only the "floaters" are involved and to the honor of Arkansas be it said that this class, although dominant in localities, has never had a very great influence on a general election. In the legislature of 1825 a certain question was carried by the judicious distribution of a boatload of sugar-cured hams among the legislators. The recipients of the hams were spotted and in the next election the question of "Ham or no Ham" played a most important part.

The Gazette published several cards from pork-packing establishments, wanting to know how many boatloads of hams would be required for the legislation of the territory during the next session of the legislature. One cargo laid up at the mouth of the White on its way to New Orleans, dickering with Little Rock persons as to whether to bring the cargo up to the capital or take it on down the river. It went to New Orleans and the question soon died away.

No age has ever been exempt from corrupt practices, nor has any country. They had a wide latitude in early days, but were as emphatically denounced then as now. Fewer legislatures have been bought in Arkansas than in Massachusetts and New York, and the debauching of the electorate has never been so general in Arkansas as in Massachusetts or New York. The campaign funds of party politics are the bases of corrupt practices and until they are absolutely abolished and the elections left entirely to the will and determination of the electors these practices will go on. The management of campaigns by and through committees having a treasury is the essence and core of corruption and should be abolished by law.

CHAPTER XXI.

GOVERNOR GEORGE IZARD.

In the fall of 1825 Governor James Miller went back to New Hampshire and was elected to Congress from that State and was appointed collector at the port of Salem. He was loaded down with offices and honors. He took the collector's place and resigned his governorship of Arkansas and his right to a seat in Congress.

He and Robert Crittenden, the acting governor, are credited with setting up the territorial government, oiling it at periodical moments and seeing that it did not jump a cog now and then.

When Miller went out there were those who thought Crittenden should go in, and Crittenden might have been of that opinion, though there is little to show for it. One thing is certain, however, he did want to be secretary for the territory. He was called Cardinal Wolsey, and he tried to follow in the footsteps of that illustrious character, without copying him in any particular save in his fall. There were those in the territory who opposed him for secretary, prominent among them being Judge James Woodson Bates. These two used to play in the same back yard, but now they refused to walk on the same side of the street. Bates had more sense, but less political sagacity. He had the better education, legal and otherwise, but had far less prudence. Crittenden used the gloved hand while Bates used the mailed fist; besides, Bates loved a toddy. Crittenden as acting governor appointed several justices of the peace and many militia officers. In other words, Crittenden had a machine, while Bates had nothing but his own intellectual and moral parts. He gave Crittenden considerable trouble and kept him awake all night frequently dodging twenty-four pounders, but he couldn't keep him from being appointed secretary of the territory.

IZARD APPOINTED GOVERNOR.

The president, James Monroe, who had the appointing power, selected Major General George Izard of South Carolina to fill the place of governor, and he made a most admirable selection. His greatest difficulty was in securing his acceptance. Monroe desired some one who had character and strength sufficient to bring order out of the chaos. Things in Arkansas were not lovely by any maner of means and an iron hand was needed. Izard needed no office, being a man of independent means; his associates were the leaders of the country and his sentiments were decidedly adverse to going to Arkansas. Monroe prevailed, however, and Izard accepted.

George Izard really organized the territory of Arkansas. His predecessors, the governor and the acting governor, simply set the machine up and put it into bungling operation. They touched the high places, as it were, and substituted words for things. They had a militia so-called which consisted of a brigadier general, who lived at Fort Towson, and an adjutant general, who was sheriff of Arkansas County. They had colonels galore, and that was the sum and substance of the "milish," except the neighborhod organizations. They had no men, no guns, no ammunition, no arsenal, no rules and really no militia.

IZARD THE GREAT ORGANIZER.

In point of education, George Izard was unquestionably the superior of any man that ever sat in the governor's chair at Little Rock in either form of government, State or territorial. Born in Richmond, England, he graduated at the University of Pennsylvania, an honor man in 1792. He then attended the military schools at Kensington, England; the University of Edinburgh, and the French military schools, at Marbury and Metz. More than that, he was a man of sense. He had the caliber that took on education with out becoming a fool. He had a sound organizing mind to begin with, and he enriched this with all that the best schools of organization could offer. The results of the war of 1812 are traceable to George Izard's masterful power of organization, more than the work of any other man, or that of any other twenty men combined. It was he that supplied the military organization act of 1812, which was taken by the supreme authorities and put into practice. Under this act Captain George Izard was made Colonel of the Second Artillery, with Lieutenant Winfield Scott as lieutenant colonel and William Lindsay as major.

IZARD HAD NO SUPERIOR.

Concerning Colonel Izard, Birkhimer in his history of the Artillery of the United States says:

"There was not in the United States his superior in military knowledge. Educated in the military schools of France, he had, by several years' experience in the army, supplemented by study and reflection, methodically digested in his mind the whole subject of organization and supply. This fact made his counsel particularly valuable at the beginning of the war, upon which, with little preparation, the government had now embarked. Both the colonel and the lieutenant colonel of this regiment rose to the grade of general officer."

Colonel Izard was in a short time promoted to the rank of brigadier general and Scott succeeded him as colonel of the Second Artillery. George Izard was the son of the patriot and statesman, Ralph Izard, of South Carolina. Ralph Izard was a grandson of one of the founders of the Palmetto State and the name has always been an honored one. It was given also to Ralph Izard to have a splendid education. He was a graduate of Cambridge, England, and lived for many years in England and France. While at Paris he took sides with Arthur Lee against Silas Deane and Benjamin Franklin in their famous controversy. Returning to America, he secured for General Greene the command of the Southern Continental Army, and then pledged his entire estate to enable the Continental Congress to purchase the ships of war in Europe. He was a delegate to Congress from South Carolina in 1782 and 1783, and a senator from the same State from 1789 to 1795, when he was paralyzed. Few grander men have ever lived than Ralph Izard, and in the same category stands the name of his illustrious son, George. His father married a De Lancey of New York, which gave George two currents of blood, each representing the best of two widely differing sections.

In 1814 Major General George Izard was in command on Lake Champlain and on the Niagara frontier, where in September at Sackett's Harbor he received an urgent call from General Jacob Brown to come to his relief at Fort Erie. Izard moved up to Black Rock and crossed the Niagara, camping within two miles of Fort Erie. Ranking General Brown, he took supreme command and prepared to march against General Drummond, who had retreated to Queenstown. At Chippewa, Izard vainly tried to draw Drummond out, but that astute general retreated further inland. Izard then blew up Fort Erie and recrossed the Niagara. For this he was severely criticized by the New England stay-at-homes, but supported by the War Department. When the war was over, he, in 1816, issued a volume entitled "Official Correspondence With the War Department," which added a great deal to his stature as a military and scholarly man.

When this man of affairs reached Little Rock he found everything in confusion. The governor was in New Hampshire and the acting governor in Washington. Izard asked how they managed in this way and was told that everybody did pretty much as he pleased anyway and that they got along fully as well without governors as with them.

IZARD DRAWS THE REINS.

Izard soon ascertained that things were running pretty loose. Money to pay the Indians was in the shape of a draft locked up in Crittenden's desk awaiting his return; other moneys were at the mouth of the Arkansas in Crittenden's name awaiting his signature. Vacancies in various offices were hanging fire and the people doing without officers awaiting Crittenden's return. Indian agents were withholding their reports and a spirit of unrest was abroad in the land. The Quapaws had not been paid and the Indian agents were arrogating unlawful and arrogant powers. Izard as an organizer soon had everything in good working order. Indian agents fell back to their lawful places and soon made quarterly returns, accounting for every dollar. The Quapaw chief, Heckaton, said that Izard was a white man of the right kind and worthy of everybody's confidence. The Choctaws were moved to the West without a particle of friction, and south Arkansas was entirely clear of Indians. Izard then took up the Cherokee question and during four years laid down plans which eventually removed every Indian from the State.

Izard was a clean man and a well-dressed man. He knew the world and was equally at home in a king's palace or an Indian hut. His speech was clean and his heart spotless. The only present he would ever allow a man to make him was a razor. When he left Europe he had more than twenty of these tools, and when he moved to Arkansas he selected seven and had them marked with his name and the day of the week. He never entered his office in the morning without a clean shaved face and his example had a wonderful influence on the birds' nests which many men of the time sported on their faces.

LITTLE ROCK COULDN'T MAKE CHANGE.

The United States treasurer sent Izard drafts for $10,000 to pay Indian and other claims. These he took to the business men of Little Rock, there being no banks, who told him that all the money in town put together wouldn't total $10,000. Izard had to send a messenger to New Orleans to have these drafts cashed, a most expensive as well as dangerous proceeding.

THE CRITTENDEN-CONWAY DUEL.

The old-time honesty could not be impugned, but it wouldn't pass muster today. If a messenger entrusted with money in those days ran short he appropriated from the trust funds, and sometimes made it up promptly, but sometimes did not. Izard had to sue one messenger for using the trust funds and wait nearly a year for the money. The duel between Conway and Crittenden grew out of this habit. The treasurer at Washington handed Conway in 1824 about $7,000 to hand to the governor of Arkansas to pay the Quapaws. Conway ran out of money before reaching Little Rock and used some of the money. He called on Crittenden, the acting governor, and asked him how much he would need. Crittenden said about $6,000. Conway said that he was glad of that, as he had used a part of the money given him at Washington, but had $6,000, which he paid, and Crittenden gave a receipt. The other $1,000 was strictly accounted for several months later. When Conway ran for Congress in 1824, his second term, nothing was said about this matter, but when Robert Oden ran against him in 1826 he made this his bill of particulars. Conway answered him and admitted all that Oden charged. He said that the treasurer of the United States was the man to object if any wrong had been done, and not Oden. In his explanation, however, he said that Crittenden had consented for him to keep the $1,000 for a short time. Crittenden denied this and said that he had no right to consent or to object. That the money was not his and that the treasurer had not authorized him to demand anything of Conway. That he simply took the $6,000 and receipted for it without expressing an opinion one way or the other. Conway still claimed that Crittenden consented and the people soon forgot Oden's charge and began to discuss whether Crittenden consented or not, a question not connected with the race. Conway won the election and followed it by a bitter card denouncing Crittenden, which brought a challenge and Conway's death.

This affair coupled with Izard's fixed rules requiring prompt reports and settlements, broke up the habit of using public funds for private purposes, even though the use was apparently righteous and necessary. To keep from sending $10,000 drafts to New Orleans Izard succeeded in having the drafts sent in $500 denominations, which were easily handled by the merchants of Little Rock.

IZARD ORGANIZES MILITIA.

Izard began a real organization of the militia. He got guns and then men. He laid the foundation for the arsenal. He furnished the rules and regulations, having done this before for the entire United States. Drilling went on regularly and many men who became famous in the Mexican war received their earliest tutelage in Izard's militia companies.

Civil officers were held to a strict accountability and his administration was in every sense a great and wise one. During his administration of affairs in Arkansas his family remained in Philadelphia, where, in 1827, his wife died. After Izard's return to Little Rock he gradually succumbed to a disease that had followed him through life. He died November 22, 1828, and was buried on the lot where the Peabody school now stands. His death was a blow to Arkansas. He had elevated the territorial government to the highest rank and had made troops of friends. Could he have lived for a few years longer (he was but fifty-one at his death), he would in all probability have represented the State in the highest councils of the nation. As it was, Arkansas stood well with all other people and was looked upon as a great and growing commonwealth. The good work begun by Izard was most fortunately continued by John Pope, which made the organization absolutely complete.

Thus sleeps on Arkansas soil one of the greatest constructive minds of the United States. His work still lives in the organization of the United States army and his influence is still felt in the State where he died. There are few brighter spots in Arkansas history than the short four years George Izard was its governor. May his memory ever be revered and his example emulated.

CHAPTER XXII.

ROBERT CRITTENDEN.

Robert Crittenden was a Kentuckian and was immensely proud of the fact. Virginians first made "State pride" a sine qua non, and the changes have been most vigorously rung on the F. F. V.'s of the Mother of Commonwealths. Kentucky was the eldest daughter of Virginia and some of her children, when they could make no other boast, fell back upon the claim that they were born in Virginia. To be a Mayflower descendant was a great thing in New England, but it never meant half so much as being born in Virginia meant in Kentucky. That fact alone covered a multitude of sins and was thought to be sufficient to unlock all gates, even the golden gates of heaven.

Kentucky was settled by people from all the Eastern States, with Virginians preponderating. The Crittenden family may be said to be a Kentucky family, with Virginia antecedents, all the glory of the family having been made in Kentucky, however, and very little in Virginia.

The family lived in Woodford County prior to 1800 and were its pioneers, increasing in wealth as the hemp of Woodford projected itself into the markets of the world. My grandfather preferred the uplands of the adjoining county, Anderson, to the levels of Woodford, and therein he committed a crime against his descendants, although Anderson County got even on distilleries.

Robert Crittenden was born in Woodford County, Kentucky, in 1797. John J. Crittenden, the one to whom the family owes its greater fame, was also born in Woodford County in 1787, ten years prior to the birth of Robert. Both studied law and both were eminent in their profession. Robert became an ensign in the Second United States Rifles in 1814 and was honorably discharged in June, 1815. He served about thirteen months with credit to himself and honor to his country. Henry Crittenden of the same county enlisted in 1812 and served three years, rising to the rank of captain in the Seventeenth infantry. These were all of the Crittendens who held official position in the War of 1812, but quite a number of the name became prominent in military affairs during the next century. George Bibb Crittenden graduated at the military academy in 1833 and rose to the rank of major in the United States army, being cashiered in 1848. He joined the Southern army in 1861 and rose to the rank of major general. Thomas Leonidas Crittenden never went to the academy, but as a private joined the regular army in 1836, from which he rose to the position of major general in the United States army. It will thus be seen that the family has been well represented in all the wars of the United States since 1812 and that it is a family of high martial instincts.

ROBERT CRITTENDEN IN ARKANSAS.

In his twenty-first year, a young, ambitious and briefless lawyer, Robert Crittenden was appointed by President Monroe, secretary of Arkansas territory at a salary of $1,000 a year and the privilege of doing all and every other sort of business, not conflicting with his secretarial duties. The duties of the office were not onerous, even though he had to act as governor, as there were but five counties, and these with a regular quota of officers. Crittenden accepted the place as the best possible opening for a young lawyer, and to his credit it may be said that he made a good secretary, and when called on made a good acting governor. No fault can ever be found with Crittenden's performance of duty. He was a good officer, one of the very best. His sins were of another nature and had nothing whatever to do with the words misfeasance or malfeasance in office. He arrived at Arkansas Post in 1819 and on July 4 Governor Miller not having arrived, organized the territorial government of Arkansas, as acting governor, in conjunction with Charles Jouett, Charles Letcher and Andrew Scott, judges of the Superior Court. The whole work was finished in less than three weeks and Jouett and Letcher vamosed, never to return, and a doubt exists as to Jouett's presence.

Crittenden at once formed a partnership with James Woodson Bates in the practice of law and the dealing in real estate. Bates was soon put on the bench, and this partnership was dissolved. Bates left the bench and ran for Congress, being elected by a close shave. The partnership was re-formed and continued for three years most profitably to each. Bates wanted a third term, but did not say so. He was in Washington most of the time and did not keep his weather eye open on the Arkansas clouds. Crittenden resolved to beat Bates and found three candidates ready to make the race; in fact, already announced and working for the place. Crittenden believed that if Trimble, Eskridge and Conway all ran, Bates would have clear sailing and set about to get two of them out of the way.

THE GREAT INTRIGUE OF 1823.

Crittenden asked Trimble, Eskridge and Conway to meet him in Judge Roane's office, and requested Judge Roane to be present. Crittenden made quite a talk and after arguing with Trimble and Eskridge for quite a while induced them to withdraw, which they did, agreeing to support Conway. Crittenden afterward alleged that Conway promised to have but one term and not to run again. This Conway denied and Roane, when called on to prove Crittenden's assertion, made a good Conway witness. One need not study far to ascertain Conway's change of front. He outwitted Crittenden, Eskridge and Trimble. After the cabinet council referred to above Conway went up into Missouri and met Bates. He asked him: "Are you going to run for the third term?" Bates said: "No, Conway; you are the man for the place." Conway said: "No, I'll not run; you are the man." Thus Arkansas without knowing it furnished the originals for the two great characters, "Gaston and Alphonse," and unconsciously verified the adage that there is no new thing under the sun. Bates and Conway parted, so Bates said, with the understanding that neither was to run until a further consultation, and that if Bates decided to run Conway was not to run. Conway said that Bates gave him a clear field over his (Conway's) protest and that he proceeded to make good. He went to Batesville and saw Colonel Hardin, who told him that Independence County was for Bates, but that if Bates was not going to run, as Conway said, the county would support Conway. Conway having the whole field to himself repudiated his one-term stand and ran the second and third times, winning in every case.

BETTER LAWYER THAN POLITICIAN.

Crittenden stuck far more closely to the law than to politics, and succeeded most admirably at the bar, while failing most egregiously in politics. He made money and spent that money in beautifying Little Rock. He built a fine house and with a most generous hand dispensed the most lavish hospitality. He was clean of speech, clean of dress, open handed and open hearted. He was the best loved of all men among his votaries, and the most hated man in Arkansas among his adversaries. What was his trouble?

He had all the arts of the politician without the wisdom of the statesman. His ambition extended to a mere parceling of minor appointments rather than a leadership based on reason or the exercise of superior talent. He preferred to marshal men through personal obligation rather than lead them by an appeal to conviction. He did not lack eloquence—a great and commanding eloquence—an eloquence, however, more fanciful than logical—more imaginative than practical. He lacked an orderly control of his mind and this to a large degree destroyed his influence upon political subjects. His greatest defect was that he mingled too little with the masses of men, and was therefore without knowledge of the great mainsprings to human action. He was an inborn aristocrat and a whig to the core. To the multitude he was therefore an iceberg, and to him, the multitude was an unthinkable quantity. He was above them and this feeling of eminence barred his entry into the great domain of human nature.

Evidence is not lacking of his desire to dominate the governors of the territory, and of a bitter resentment on his part for the governors who resented his dictation.

DID NOT HOLD FRIENDSHIPS LONG.

Judge Bates is authority for the saying that Crittenden dubbed James Miller "The Old Fool," and gave as a reason the tendency of Miller to think for himself. That the relations between Izard and Crittenden were strained is well known, but the reasons for their polite estrangement have not been enumerated with exactness. That Crittenden expected the appointment of governor in 1825 and did not get it seems to have been accepted as a sufficient reason for the lack of camaraderie between these men. If so, both men were of a smaller caliber than history has accorded them and unworthy of a lasting public esteem.

The real reason must be sought in the abnormal propensity of Crittenden to control, and the abnormal propensity of Izard to think for himself and follow his own bent.

Evidence is not lacking also to show that Crittenden was without constructive ability in his management of those relations which lead up to permanent and powerful friendships. He was check by jowl with Elijah Morton in 1819, but sundered from him as far as the poles in 1820. It was to his influence in 1819 that Bates owed his small majority. So intimate were these men then as to be partners in law and in real estate.

HIS DUEL WITH CONWAY.

In 1823 Crittenden paved the way for Conway to beat Bates. Conway and Crittenden were close friends in 1823. Conway secured Crittenden the commissionership to negotiate the Quapaw treaty, and suggested his name to the president as governor in 1825. In 1827 Crittenden was for Oden, against Conway, and took the stump for Oden, not on the high plane of civil service, but on the supreme issue of personal altercation. When Oden was defeated Crittenden pursued the personal phase of the controversy on the field of honor, with fatal results to Conway.

Had there been but one estrangement between Crittenden and his close friends no general conclusion would have followed.

But the estrangement of Morton, of Bates, of Conway, and, in a lesser sense, of Miller and of Izard—all seem to point to a mental objectiveness on Crittenden's part to subordinate himself officially. Nor were his lesser friends permitted to shine by their own light—they were to be mere pawns in his hands—nothing more.

THE CONWAY-SEVIER DYNASTY.

There was no real reason for the rise of the Conway-Sevier dynasty. Crittenden was on the ground before the Conways—before the Seviers. He had the advantages of place and a wider acquaintance. He was more eloquent than either, yea, than all of them, and with a rational program ought to have succeeded. The Conway-Sevier dynasty could never have had an initial place had Crittenden adhered to Bates in 1823. His act then drove the Bates faction to Conway in 1827. Ambrose H. Sevier would not have been a debatable quantity in 1827 and 1833 had Crittenden's policy from 1819 to 1825 been one of higher political thought. The Conway family, from 1820 to 1827, had no abnormal influence in Arkansas affairs. Ambrose H. Sevier was not a gigantic power until 1836. He held his position up to that time, not through family influence and ramifications, but solely and alone through his better knowledge of human nature. Henry W. Conway, in 1823, first sprang the idea of rotation in office, and quietly rang the changes on being a poor boy making his own way. The people elected him. Sevier ran in 1827 as a Whig, and is recorded in Washington as a Whig until 1836. He told the people about coming to the territory in 1820 as a mere boy—an orphan, friendless and alone. He told them that he had grown up among them and was not afraid to submit his claims to their judgment. All the speeches of Henry W. Conway from 1823 to 1827 were exactly the kind of speeches Henry Clay was making at that time. All the measures Conway got through were public improvement measures, for which Clay spoke and voted. The men who were afterward called "rock-ribbed Democrats" all voted and spoke against Conway's measures. The same was true of Sevier up to 1836.

FELL AS DID WOLSEY.

Crittenden solidified the Conway-Sevier influence by a supreme lack of high organizing sense, and laid the foundation for the great family influence which sprang up after 1836, and which it took the State twenty years to destroy.

Not only did he lay the foundation for this family control of political affairs, but he also undermined the foundations of the Whig party in Arkansas. James Woodson Bates was driven to be a mugwump. Henry W. Conway died before he had to make a choice, but up to the day of his death was as good a Whig as Crittenden. Sevier was originally a Whig, but Crittenden made him a straightout Democrat. Dictation was Crittenden's greatest weakness and led to the nickname "Cardinal Wolsey." Even as the great cardinal went down carrying his friends with him, so Crittenden went down, burying the Whig party under the ruins of the temple.

In every relation of life save politics Robert Crittenden was a great and illustrious man, and in that field would have shone as a bright and particular star but for his abnormal self-esteem. As a lawyer, he attained particular eminence and died after a triumphant nine hours' exposition of a great and notable case.

He married on October 1, 1822, Miss Ann Morris of Frankfort, Kentucky, a woman of most excellent understanding and the highest social position. For his wife, Crittenden always had the highest affection and in his family relations was sans peur et sans reproche.

His death occurred at Vicksburg, Mississippi, on December 18, 1834, in his thirty-seventh year. That death cast a gloom over the entire State, and both friends and enemies united in testimonials to his personal and professional worth. He had in him the elements of greatness and worked out for himself a position second only to that achieved by John J. Crittenden, the greatest of that name.

CHAPTER XXIII.

CHESTER ASHLEY—THOMAS WILLOUGHBY NEWTON.

On October 11, 1620, the Mayflower from England landed at what is now called "Plymouth Rock," with a passenger list that has become the foundation for membership in one of the most exclusive societies in the United States. The basis of this society is blood descent from some one of the passengers of this ship, and as a matter of historical interest this list as printed in the New England Historical and Genealogical Register of fifty years ago is reproduced here. It is the oldest passenger list for New England and registers the entrance date, not of Puritanism, but of Pilgrim Puritanism into New England. Pure English Puritanism came later and the difference was more of degree than of kind. The Pilgrims had lived in Holland awhile and had worn off the keen edge of controversy; the English Puritans came direct from England fresh from the arena of controversy and battle, and were pious, plucky and pugnacious. The essence of Puritanism in every age has been, not so much the purity of the inner individual life as the formal regulation of the outer social life. The Catholic and Episcopal churches presented dogma standardized by councils and a hierarchy. The Puritans presented dogma standardized by local communes. The standards differed materially, and each destroyed to a degree the right of private judgment. No pope and council ever ruled with a more rigid iron hand than did the Puritan elders, ministers and councils of New England. God Almighty gave ten short commandments from Sinai; the Puritans enunciated ten thousand or more and enforced them with remorseless rigidity. They regulated everything from the dress of the body to the food for the soul, and pronounced upon the desirability of their citizens with the same ease and glib facility that the president of the United States now discourses upon the same theme.

Everything had to be regulated and the regulators were the chosen high priests of a political and religious hierarchy, which ruthlessly trampled upon all opinions and judgments not in accord with their narrow judgments. Puritanism died a slow death under the hammer of enlightenment, but the spirit of regulation it brought to life has survived its demise.

Senator Spooner in a short verse lampooned the present Massachusetts, and most vividly recalled the older days of severity and repression. He said in the Senate hall:

> "Hail Massachusetts!
> The land of the herring and cod,
> Who swaps her Adams for Douglas
> And worships her Lodge as God."

THE ORIGINAL PILGRIMS.

The Pilgrims of the Mayflower were:

John Carver, Mary Carver, his wife, and Jasper Carver.

William Bradford and Dorothy, his wife.

Edward Winslow, wife Elizabeth, son Edward, grandson John and George Soule.

William Brewster, wife, two children, a daughter-in-law and a grandson.

Isaac Allerton, wife and four children.

Miles Standish and wife.

John Alden.

Samuel Fuller and William Butten, his servant.

Christopher Martin, wife and son.

William Mullins, wife and three children.

William White, wife and two sons, Resolved and William.

Edward Thompson and Richard Warren.

Stephen Hopkins, wife and four children.

Edward Doty and Edward Leister.

Edward Tilley, wife and two children.

John Tilley, wife and child.

Francis Cooke and John, his son.

Thomas Rogers and John, his son.

Thomas Tinker, wife and family.

John Rigdale and wife.

Edward Fuller, wife and son.

John Turner and family.

Francis Eaton, wife and son.

James Chilton, wife and daughter.
John Crackston and son.
John Billingston, wife and two sons.
Moses Fletcher, John Goodman, Degory Priest, Thomas Williams, Gilbert Winslow, Edward Margeson, Peter Brown, Richard Britterige, Richard Clarke, Richard Gardiner, and two seamen, John Allerton and Thomas English.

THE ASHLEY FAMILY.

The Ashley family of England had representatives in both the major and minor gentry of England and among the yeomen. According to Hinman, the only one of the name to locate in New England, prior to 1800, was Robert Ashley, a Puritan from England, but not of the ultra type. He settled at Springfield, Massachusetts, and was the lineal ancestor of Honorable Chester Ashley, possibly the greatest of the name in America, and one of the greatest senators Arkansas or any other State has ever produced. The name of Robert Ashley's wife was Mary, but her family name is lost in oblivion. Robert had five children, David, Mary, Jonathan, Sarah and Joseph. David married Hannah Glover and had eleven children, of whom one, Samuel Ashley, became the father of Reverend Joseph Ashley, graduate of Yale and minister at Sunderland. The son of Reverend Joseph Ashley, Stephen, had a son, William, born at Leverett, who became the father of Chester Ashley, who was born at Amherst, Massachusetts, in the latter part of the eighteenth century. In about 1805 William Ashley removed to Hudson, New York, from whence, in 1809, Chester was sent to Williams' College, from whence he graduated in 1813. At Litchfield, Connecticut, under the guiding hand of the famous judges, Reeve and Gould, he prepared himself for the profession of law.

SETTLES IN ARKANSAS.

Recognizing the great advantages offered by the West, he in June, 1819, opened a law office at Edwardsville, Illinois, and advertised for practice in that district and in Missouri. The overtowering importance of the new territory of Arkansas was soon brought to his attention and determined him to make that region his permanent home. In the latter part of 1819 or early in 1820 he was at Arkansas Post, and in 1820 had a merchant's license for the village of Little Rock, and had also swung his shingle to the breeze as an attorney at law. Robert Oden was at that time the greatest lawyer in Little Rock, being the only one there, and without much business or hopes for business. With the coming of Ashley, two great lawyers had the entire community to themselves. The town was noted for its suburbs; in fact, had more suburbs than anything else. But Ashley and Oden, not being overburdened by the demands of high social life, managed to keep their heads above water, and their hopes burning for an overwhelming future. Other people were coming—at least other speculators were coming. Two great bodies of speculators, and a caravan of smaller fry, covered the location of Little Rock with overlapping and conflicting claims, and spread the same over the nonpartisan ground which afterward became famous under the name of Argenta. Ashley and Oden in their rude log law offices smacked their lips with delight as these conflicting claims, backed by pugnacious promoters, began to claim the attention of the courts.

RIVAL TOWNSITERS.

Each of the great speculating companies had its cohort of surveyors and each laid off a town, one town being laid off on top of the other. One town was called Little Rock and the town on top of it was called Arkopolis. Everybody was busy. The Little Rock crowd swore they would fight it out on that line if it took all summer. The Arkopolis crowd said, "Me, too." The word "crowd" must not be taken in its modern sense. All the people put together would not have numbered one hundred souls. Ashley and Oden told the speculators to keep cool and not bite off their noses to spite their faces, that the whole matter would have to be thrashed out in the courts, but that in the meantime they had better get together and agree upon one name for the town and some method of neutrality, the observance of which would tend to invite prospective purchasers to make the place a permanent home.

WHEN LITTLE ROCK WAS NAMED.

They patched up a truce, agreed upon the name, Little Rock, and parcelled out the territory accordingly. All was fair on the surface now and Little Rock began to fill up. During the year 1820 another lawyer, William Quarles, located at Little Rock; up at Batesville James Woodson Bates and Richard Searcy were practicing; while down at Arkansas Post Robert Crittenden, Colonel Walker, Kelly & Maddox, Sam C. Roane and William Craig were trying to practice. From 1820 to 1825 the bar at Little Rock increased very rapidly with Chester Ashley at its head. Speculation went on, yielding large profits to those who were shrewd enough to be on the right side. The settlements of the conflicts growing out of the wave of this speculation gave all good lawyers an abundance of fees. Chester Ashley had that sort of judgment, and that character of investigation, which always kept him on the safe side of his speculations; he also had that character of education, legal and otherwise, which made his judgment most valuable to the courts and his clients. With these he brought the courtesy of the Ashleys of the major gentry and in a comparatively short period of time became not only a wealthy man, but a man of affairs and honors. On July 2, 1821, he went up to Potosi, Missouri, where he was joined in holy wedlock to Mary W. Elliot, one of the loveliest characters of early Arkansas history.

WON FAME AS A LAWYER.

His fame as a lawyer soon covered Arkansas, not without the usual stabs of envy and the strokes of calumny and enmity. No successful man can escape these and no great man can avoid them. They are the tribute which men of lesser power always pay to greater genius. He kept out of politics and attended strictly to his own affairs. From 1820 to 1848 his name was written in the largest character of letters upon everything connected with the betterment of Little Rock, and with much that made for the development of the State. Kind and thoughtful, he made and kept friends; profound and learned, he baffled and destroyed his enemies. Having made his estate secure he at last listened to the importunities of his friends and was sent to the Senate of the United States. His rank there is known to all men and needs not my puny pen to enrich it. Here he died and at Washington was given a most dignified state funeral.

Whatever may have been the antecedent greatness of the name Ashley, certain it is that he was the greatest of its great. Born of a Puritan family, he practiced its principles without advocating its regulatory rigidity. He had profound convictions, and at proper times never hesitated to express them, but he scorned that system of regulation which would regulate all the affairs of men by the puny arm of a single narrow creed or a single narrow party. He was a Democrat by conviction, and as a Democrat lived a pronounced life among his fellows. He recognized, however, the value of Whiggery, and had many pronounced friends among the most thoughtful of that great party. He was a great man in every sense of the word and an honor to the State of his choice, if not of his birth.

THOMAS WILLOUGHBY NEWTON.

Thomas Willoughby Newton, Sr., lived a strenuous life in Arkansas, beginning in 1820. He came from Alexandria, Virginia, being about seventeen years of age at the time. When a youngster of seventeen leaves an old town like Alexandria for a new life in the woods it is but fair to say that he had strenuous blood in his veins. Some Newtons lived at Norfolk, Virginia, among whom was Thomas Newton, born in 1769, who, being liberally educated, represented Norfolk in Congress from 1801 till 1830, and then served one term afterward. He died at Norfolk in 1847.

There was also a Willoughby Newton of Westmoreland County, Virginia, who, with a limited education, represented his district as a Whig in the Twenty-eighth Congress.

The relation of these two men to Thomas Willoughby Newton of Alexandria cannot be told by me, but the identity of names suggests something of kin.

Neither of these two eminent Virginia Newtons lived as eventful a life as our Arkansas Newton. He was born at Alexandria in 1803, and had but a limited education. He had the "three R's" well and was a good penman. He entered Arkansas in 1820 and began his career riding the one-horse mail from Arkansas Post on the north side of the river to Cadron. He did not deign to stop at Little Rock, that being too small a place. He not only carried the mail on this star route, but he used his wits for better things. He made an impression on Crittenden, on Bates, on Samson Gray and on all the prominent men of that time.

Politics cut no ice in 1820 and all men lived together in the love of the Lord and goodfellowship. Newton attended to his business and was soon sought by McKinney as deputy superior court clerk, which position he held for years. He was also postmaster for awhile in 1824, and from 1825 to 1829 was clerk of Pulaski County. During this time he had studied law with Crittenden and had become a full-fledged lawyer. He had a most amiable and sunny disposition, which brought him friends. Even in his worst Whiggery he had troops of Democrat friends. He counted Colonel Walker out as the law directed, which led Walker to dub him a "stripling from Virginia;" Newton answered that stripling as he was, he was the equal of any cashiered officer. He was fearless, brilliant and most energetic.

NEWTON AS A LETTER WRITER.

In the period of 1824-30 a mania existed in Arkansas for card writing in the Gazette over assumed names. Even Bates used this plan, as did all the earlier prominent men of the State except Tom Newton. He signed his own name and seemed to be proud of it. He never wrote cards about himself, nor very frequently in defense of himself. He loved Bob Crittenden, however, as a brother; lived at his house for a long time and was his constant associate. Whenever an anonymous writer attacked Crittenden, as they did every week of the world, sometimes deservedly, but more frequently the opposite, Newton defended Crittenden—and to his credit, be it said, he did it well. His pen was not polished, but it was strong. His English was good and he knew human nature as expressed by the heart feelings of the age. He knew the people also and could worst far better thinkers and writers than himself. His tilt with Bates was strong, but Bates got the laugh on him. Newton said in the beginning of his card that, unlike his opponent, he was not college bred—that he lacked the graces of a finished education. He claimed for himself a more humble origin and said that he walked fearlessly on every part of his native heath, defying all oppressors and backbiters. Bates retorted that he used the wrong words; that he should have said: "Like his predecessor of old he walked the Hounslow Heath, seeking whom he might devour." Newton was dubbed the Knight of Hounslow Heath ever after that, and frequently complimented Bates on his skill at turning trumps. On the field of honor his troubles were never his own, but a part of the heritage growing out of his close relationship to Crittenden. He was adjutant to Crittenden at the treaty with the Quapaws, and aide-de-camp to General Bradford in 1826.

In 1829 he went to Shelbyville, Kentucky, and married Mary K. Allen, daughter of Colonel John Allen of that place, and a hero of the war of 1812. He rose to the rank of general and no man stood higher in the estimation of Kentucky people than General Allen. Newton followed the fortunes of his wife and remained at Shelbyville practicing law. In 1837, however, after the admission of Arkansas to the Union, Newton brought his wife back to Arkansas, making it his home. He became cashier of the State and Real Estate bank and lived through the fortunes and misfortunes of that institution.

GIVEN MANY POLITICAL HONORS.

He always had a strong penchant for political affairs and was frequently honored by the political parties. He was clerk of the council in the Third territorial legislature in 1823 and also in 1825, 1827 and 1828. He was elected as a Whig to the fifth State legislature and served in the Senate from November 4, 1844, to November 4, 1848. When Archibald Yell resigned his seat in Congress to become colonel of the Arkansas volunteer regiment in the Mexican war, Thomas W. Newton was elected to fill the unexpired term and served as a Whig in the Twenty-ninth Congress. He died in New York City in 1853.

Thus we have a most strenuous life, beginning as mail boy in the backwoods in 1820 at seventeen and ending in the halls of Congress. Thomas W. Newton, Sr., was an honest man and a most cheerful one. He loved his fellows and was an optimist of the highest rank. Everybody loved him. His sons were Robert Crittenden Newton and Thomas Willoughby Newton, Jr., the former being dead and the latter a citizen of Little Rock, whose name is known to all sons of Arkansas.

THE NEWTON GENEALOGY.

Thomas W. Newton, Sr., of Arkansas, was the seventh in lineal descent from Thomas Newton of Kingston-upon-Hull, England. Thomas Newton of Kingston-upon-Hull, had a son, John Newton of the same place, master and mariner, who settled in Westmoreland County, Virginia, about 1660, where he died leaving a will dated August 19, 1695, and recorded July 28, 1697. He appears to have been married twice, the name of the first wife being unknown to me, while that of the second was Rose Gerrard of Virginia. Three sons were the fruits of the first marriage, all born in England, from the eldest of whom the Arkansas Newtons, so far as they descend from Thomas Willoughby Newton, claim descent, while the Willoughby Newton line of Virginia, including the late Bishop Newton descend from the last marriage.

The eldest son of John Newton of Kingston-upon-Hull was John Newton of Westmoreland County, Virginia, who was brought by his father to that region about 1660, passing the rest of his life in that county. He married a woman whose surname is lost but whose Christian name was Elizabeth and died leaving a will dated March 1, 1721, and recorded May 30, 1722.

The second son of John Newton of Westmoreland County was William Newton of Stafford County who married Margaret Monroe of Virginia of the same family as that of President James Monroe. His will was dated June 16, 1784, and recorded sometime in 1789. William Newton left a son, John Newton of Stafford County, who married Mary Thomas and died after the year 1798. John Newton left two sons, William Newton being the eldest and John Newton the second. William Newton married Jane B. Stewart of Maryland and left a large family among whom were Commodore John Newton, Commander of the

Hornet, whose second wife was a Miss Izard of South Carolina, Thomas Willoughby Newton, the subject of our sketch and Fenwick Newton.

From John Newton, the second son of John and Mary (Thomas) Newton, who married Sarah Pollard of Virginia, there descended a daughter Jane P. Newton who married John H. Crease and moved to Arkansas. John H. Crease was State treasurer of Arkansas from January 10, 1849, to January 26, 1855, and from February 2, 1857, to February 2, 1859, and reared a family in Arkansas. His third daughter, Mary A. Crease, married George Claiborne Watkins, Chief Justice of the Supreme Court of Arkansas.

OTHER NEWTONS OF ARKANSAS.

The first cadet credited to Arkansas at the Military Academy at West Point was James Hamilton, son of a merchant at Arkansas Post and Little Rock. He withdrew the same year, and G. W. Hardin of Batesville, was appointed in his stead, but failed to report. In 1827, James Scull, son of the pioneer at Arkansas Post, was appointed, but he found the military life too strenuous and withdrew in 1828. In 1828 Fenwick Newton of Pulaski was appointed, but there is no record of his further progress. Arkansas from 1820 to 1830 held a very low rank at West Point, although all the boys who reported stood their entrance examinations upon arriving.

Before Thomas W. Newton, Sr., was registered in Arkansas there was a man named John Newton living in Pulaski County on the north side of the river. He was a man of family, and seems to have had an estate. When Crawford County was laid out in 1820 the first court was held in a storehouse belonging to Basil and Larkin Newton. I suppose these were brothers, and were possibly sons of John Newton of Pulaski. The latter died in December, 1822, at his house in Pulaski County, and on November 11 of the same year Jane, wife of John Newton, died in the same county. In July, 1825, Basil Newton of Crawford County took administration upon the estates of John and Mary Newton. In September, 1829, Larkin Newton drifted into Hempstead County and on that day married Mary Ann, daughter of John Wilson of that place. He was at that time serving as clerk of the court, piecing out the unexpired term of Colonel J. M. Stewart. The after-history of Fenwick, Basil and Larkin Newton is unknown to me, but they doubtless have many descendants in various parts of the State.

Jesse Newton of Drew County was an honored citizen of that bailiwick, but came into the State at a much later period. James Newton of Calhoun County in 1850 may have been a descendant of Larkin Newton, but this is merely assumed.

CHAPTER XXIV.

The Superior Court of Arkansas—Andrew Scott—Benjamin Johnson.

When the territory of Arkansas was created provision was made for a court to be styled "The Superior Court of the Territory of Arkansas." This court was to consist of three judges, and on March 3, 1819, President Monroe appointed as these judges Andrew Scott of Missouri, Charles Jouett of Michigan and Robert Letcher of Kentucky. The records of the office of the secretary of State at Little Rock show that in July, 1819, under the act of Congress creating the territory, this court met at Arkansas Post and in conjunction with Robert Crittenden, the acting governor of the territory, proceeded to put the new government into operation. There was little to do and, so far as the records show, these men did that little in a very short time and adjourned. The book containing the legislation passed by that so-called "first legislature" could be written by a good typewriter in three hours. Records which can not be denied show that Charles Jouett was elected president of the body, and yet there are equally undeniable records proving that Charles Jouett never set foot on the soil of the territory of Arkansas. Hempstead in his history of the State says that after the adjournment of this body two of the judges, Jouett and Letcher, left the State, never to return. This may be the actual state of affairs, but from what follows it will be made clear that either Jouett never entered the State at all or that the Grand Jury which indicted him was absolutely ignorant of the English language.

INDICTMENT BY THE ARKANSAS POST GRAND JURY.

The Grand Jury of the Superior Court of Arkansas at its June term at Arkansas Post in 1820, Judge Andrew Scott being the only judge present, after bringing in an indictment against Robert Oden for fighting a duel with General Allen, and another against the seconds of that duel, brought in a third indictment against Charles Jouett, one of the judges of the Superior Court of the territory. The latter indictment was more in the nature of a complaint and was designed to represent certain facts in the strongest light possible, rather than to bring him to the bar of justice for any crime. This Grand Jury represented to the court that Charles Jouett, who for more than twelve months had held the appointment as judge of the Superior Court, without having taken his seat on the bench, was thereby obstructing the course of justice and should be reprimanded or removed.

It is true that Judge Jouett could have sat in the first legislature as its president without taking his seat as judge of the Superior Court. This is hardly probable, however, as he was appointed judge of the Superior Court, and as judge became ex-officio a member of the legislative body. In the nature of things he had to take his seat as a member of the court first, and this indictment negatives that. But this is not all. William E. Woodruff in the columns of the Gazette, a month or two later, set out that Judge Letcher had gotten sick of the Arkansas country and retraced his steps to Kentucky without setting his foot in the territory. This is very strong language and but for the emphatic record of the acts of the first legislative body, which contains his signature, together with that of Judge Jouett, would be taken in any court of law as proof positive that neither of these judges ever set foot on Arkansas soil. In the same article Mr. Woodruff has this to say of Judge Jouett: "It is still remembered here that last spring (1819) Judge Jouett was driven from the territory by a swarm of mosquitoes, at the mouth of the White river, while on his way to this place, and within eighteen miles of his destination." Language can hardly be made stronger than this, and would seem to prove that Charles Jouett, despite his signature to the acts of the first legislative body, never qualified as judge of the Superior Court, and was never inside the territory of Arkansas, except his landing at the mouth of White river and his judicial combat with "gallinippers" of that region, in which the insects got the advantage.

The first Superior Court of Arkansas, from July, 1819, to January, 1821, was constituted and made up solely and alone of that man who never flinched from duty, Judge Andrew Scott. As long as the court remained at Arkansas Post, Judge Scott performed all the duties of this court, and remained one of its honored members after the removal of this court to Little Rock. Benjamin Johnson of Kentucky was appointed judge of this court in the place of Jouett in December, 1820, and arrived at the Post shortly afterward. Joseph Selden was appointed in the place of Letcher in October, 1820, proceeded to the University of Virginia in the same month, where he was married to Miss Harriet Gray of Albemarle County, Virginia, and with her set out for his new post in the territory. He arrived there on December 24, 1820. Judge Johnson arrived shortly after this and in early 1821 the first full court sat at Arkansas Post.

The most comprehensive definition of a court is that it is a tribunal for the settlement of disputes. It is an institution set up by wise government to furnish a remedy for the grievances of orderly life. This is its older and most comprehensive function. Without sacrificing this under modern refinements it has come to be a tribunal for the settlement of disputes between rival authorities. The Superior Court of the Territory of Arkansas from 1819 to 1836 had little to do with questions other than the settlement of disputes, and from the nature of the population of the territory, its sparsity and its poverty, it never gained a position of eminence. There was little to do, and that little had nothing whatever to do with those questions which give greatness to a tribunal.

There was an apparent exception to this in the settlement of the Spanish land grant claims, but as will be seen hereafter, the court failed to take the right side of the question, failed to measure up to any standard which would have attracted to it the title "great," and therefore the entire body for the entire period must be classed with those necessary institutions which fall under and never pass beyond the claims of the word mediocrity.

In the constitution of this court in 1819 three judges, Scott, Letcher and Jouett, were appointed to administer the United States law in the territory, and to act as an appellate court from the judgments of such inferior judges as should be created by the territorial legislature. The original defects of this Superior Court was its numbers. One man would have done far better than three, and for the first year one man really did all the work. Jouett and Letcher showed up at the organization of the territory, and then quit, leaving Andrew Scott as the sole judge for the remainder of the year, 1819. Scott's identify with the territory of Arkansas began in June, 1819, and terminated only with his death.

As a citizen no one in the territory or State has ever entitled himself to higher rank or merit, cleanliness and public enterprise. Descended from a Virginia and Missouri family, he brought into Arkansas an escutcheon entirely clean.

JUDGES WERE ALL TOO YOUNG.

Another objection to the Superior Court of Arkansas was the fact that all of its members were young men. Scott had just passed his majority, and when reappointments were made to fill the places of Jouett and Letcher, two young men, Robert Selden and Benjamin Johnson, were selected. No matter what the antecedent training of these men may have been, and no matter what their family connections were, they were entirely too young for the responsible position of judges of a superior court, unless that court was of the most secondary importance. Robert Selden was a Virginian, a descendant of a Revolutionary colonel, possessed of all the elements of a great and good man. Benjamin Johnson represented the same characteristics, but descended from an illustrious family in Kentucky. Selden brought to Arkansas the old Virginia idea of social superiority, which as a young man he had not the prudence to conceal. The same remark to a lesser degree applies to Andrew Scott. Both were fond of social eminence, both prided themselves on their gentlemanly instincts and both possessed tempers which their youth forbade them to control. Johnson, while the equal in birth and social standing of either of his associates, cared less for the honor attached to ancestry, and still less for the honors society usually confers. Johnson owned a fine plantation several miles from Little Rock, where, surrounded by his slaves, his friends and his family he created a society of his own, and kept aloof from the entangling jealousies of Little Rock life. Selden and Scott lived in town and were thrown for their lighter amusements upon the facilities which the society of the town at that time afforded. Bridge whist was not then in vogue, but card playing was as popular then as now, and both Selden and Scott prided themselves upon their skill in a social game, the social games of society, and not those of the gambling hells.

JUDGES QUARREL AT CARD TABLE.

Judge Pope, upon the authority of John R. Homer Scott, the illustrious son of Andrew Scott, has given us as a reason for the unfortunate animosity which sprang up between Judges Selden and Scott, the statement that in a game of cards Selden used what at the most can only be called rude language to the partner of Judge Scott. Scott and his partner seemed to have been winning, and Scott's partner, an unnamed lady of Little Rock, triumphantly claimed superiority in words addressed to Judge Selden. It is said that Judge Selden replied, "That is not so." or "That is not true," or words to that effect. The lady took offense and showed it by a resort to tears. This appealed to her partner, Judge Scott, who at once demanded of Judge Selden that he apologize to the lady he had offended. Judge Selden was rude, and, as a Virginia gentleman, should have apologized at once without the request of Judge Scott, and should have done it gracefully and freely.

But this little act of rudeness was no excuse for what followed. Judges Selden and Scott were representatives of the highest court in the land, and were expected to set the highest example of good citizenship. The laws forbade dueling and this little incident was no excuse for two eminent judges to so far forget themselves as to resort to a duel to settle an insignificant dispute. The Little Rock Gazette of that time seems to indicate that there were other causes than the one already narrated, but does not state them. Selden did not apologize, and Scott did not challenge him at once. A stiffness grew up between them, and for many months they sat upon the bench together, side by side with Judge Johnson, without speaking to each other. It was thought that the men were antagonistic in temper and that they would never agree, and although a duel was hinted at in the earlier stages of the coolness, no such calamity was expected later on, as time had removed both men so far from the incident.

JUDGE KILLS ASSOCIATE IN DUEL.

Early in the year 1824 Judge Scott challenged Judge Selden to fight a duel, the meeting place being opposite the mouth of White river in Mississippi. Dr. Nimrod Menifee was the second of Judge Scott and surgeon for both parties, and James Woodson Bates, second for Judge Selden. Pistols were used and the distance was ten steps. Judge Selden fell at the first fire, and Scott escaped uninjured. No one regretted the affair more than Judge Scott, a man whose life both before and after was in every respect above all reproach. The act is chargeable first to the youth of the parties and the prevailing sentiment at that time that the duel was the only honorable way for gentlemen to settle their disputes.

DUEL PREVENTED SCOTT'S CONFIRMATION.

Scott's second term expired in 1827, and he was nominated by the president of the United States for a third term. The friends of Judge Selden, however, succeeded in the Senate of the United States in having his appointment not confirmed. The bar of Little Rock, at a public meeting shortly after this act of the Senate, passed a series of resolutions condemning the Senate of the United States for its action and commending Judge Andrew Scott for his ability, cleanness and character. He was designated as the leading judge of the Superior Court of Arkansas. This terminated his connection with the Superior Court bench, but he was at once appointed by Governor Izard as judge of the First Circuit Court of the territory. He held this position until 1831, when he retired to his plantation at Scotia, in Pope County. He represented Johnson and Pope counties in the Constitutional Convention of 1836, and was a member of the Territorial House of Representatives from Pope County in 1831. He acquired a fortune in private life and was at all times the most distinguished citizen of Pope County. His monument in the cemetery at Russellville is one of the finest creations of art, an honor to him and to his distinguished son, John R. Homer Scott, who erected it. The greatest judge on the superior court bench from 1819 to 1827 was Judge Andrew Scott.

SUCCESSION OF SCOTT AND SELDEN.

To succeed Judge Seldon, the president appointed William Trimble of Kentucky, who remained on the bench for several years. We have the authority of Robert Crittenden for saying that no man upon the Superior Court bench made as much money as did Trimble. He was a fine business man, in fact a better business man than a judge, and all his ventures in business were successful. Crittenden said that he left the State in 1832 with about $20,000 in gold. His character was above all reproach, although his legal acumen was not equal to that of either Scott or Johnson. He was succeeded on the bench by Edward Cross. In 1827 S. P. Eskridge was appointed to succeed Judge Scott and remained upon the bench for many years. He was a Presbyterian of the strictest type and also a most successful business man. He had lived in the territory since 1821, in which year, as a commissioner, he ran the famous Choctaw line. He was the first judge appointed by Governor Miller in the First circuit in 1823, which position he held until 1827, when he was advanced to the superior court bench. He was prominently identified with almost every interest of eastern and northeastern Arkansas. He lived in Crittenden County and died at his residence on December 1, 1835. He was a native of Virginia and one of the staunchest of Arkansas' early citizens. In 1828 the superior bench was enlarged to four, and James Woodson Bates appointed to the place. Upon his removal in 1831 the bench resumed its old numbers with Johnson, Cross and Eskridge as its members.

JUDGE JOHNSON'S ONE MISTAKE.

Judge Benjamin Johnson held the position of territorial judge from December, 1819, until 1836, when the State was admitted into the Union, a longer period than that of any other man. Each year of his life he added to an originally good judgment and increased his hold upon the law. His only break was in 1827, in the decision of the Spanish Land Grant cases, which was cured by a graceful overruling of his own decision a few years later and a greater caution throughout the rest of his long life in the investigation and application of precedents and legal authorities. When the State was admitted into the Union it become entitled to a United States Supreme Court judge, and in all the United States no man could be found fitter for the place than Judge Benjamin Johnson. He had had sixteen years' experience upon the Superior Court bench of the territory of Arkansas; he was connected by birth with the ablest families of Kentucky and of the nation, and had the natural qualifications of attention and study so essential to the progressive career of a great judge. He served as United States Supreme Court judge in the State of Arkansas for thirteen years after the creation of the State, and died rich in this world's goods, rich in honor, and rich in the esteem of the entire people of the State. His son, Robert W. Johnson, served the State with honor in the Senate of the United States, and his son-in-law, Ambrose Hundley Sevier, held the same position. Such was the old Superior Court of the territory of Arkansas, and such were the men it brought into Arkansas.

GENEALOGY OF BENJAMIN JOHNSON.

Judge Benjamin Johnson was descended from an old Virginia family. His father, Robert Johnson, was born in Orange County, Virginia, on July 17, 1745; in the same county in 1770 he was married to Jemina Suggett; he afterwards moved to Kentucky, dying at Warsaw in Gallatin County on October 15, 1815. Eleven children were the fruits of this marriage: Betsy, James, William, Sally, Richard M., Benjamin, Robert, John T., Joel, George W., and Henry, two girls and nine boys. Betsy married

General John Payne in Orange County, Virginia, on June 28, 1787, and died in November, 1845, leaving thirteen children.

Sally married General William Ward at Great Crossings, Kentucky, on December 28, 1795, and died August 25, 1846, leaving eight children.

Of his elder brother, Richard Mentor Johnson, little need be said. In 1812 he was made Colonel of the Kentucky Mounted Volunteers and gained distinguished honor in Upper Canada. Congress by an act of April 4, 1818, resolved: "That the President of the United States be requested to present to Colonel Richard M. Johnson a sword as a testimony of the high sense entertained by Congress of the daring and distinguished valor displayed by himself and the regiment of volunteers under his command in charging and essentially contributing to vanquish the combined British and Indian forces under Major General Proctor, on the Thames, in Upper Canada, on the 5th day of October, 1813." He was a representative in Congress and a Jackson Democrat in the Tenth, Eleventh, Twelfth, Thirteenth, Fourteenth and Fifteenth Congresses; a United States Senator from Kentucky succeeding John J. Crittenden; he served as Senator from March 3, 1819, to March 3, 1829; served again in the Twenty-first, Twenty-second, Twenty-third and Twenty-fourth Congresses; was Vice President of the United States from 1837 to 1841, being chosen by the Senate; he was defeated for the same office on the Democratic ticket in 1840; he died at Frankfort, Kentucky, on November 19, 1850.

Another older brother, James, served with distinction in the war of 1812; was a large contractor for supplying troops on the Mississippi and Missouri Rivers in 1819, 1820; represented a Kentucky district in the Nineteenth Congress and died at Great Crossings, Kentucky, August 14, 1826.

John T. Johnson, a younger brother was born in Scott County, Kentucky, where he was admitted to the bar; represented that district in the Seventeenth and Eighteenth Congresses; was Judge of the new Court of Appeals of Kentucky for many years; joined the Christian Church and became one of its most noted preachers, preaching throughout the Mississippi Valley, in Arkansas and at Little Rock. He died at Lexington, Missouri, December 18, 1857.

Of the further career of his elder brother, William, and his other younger brothers, Robert, Joel, George W. and Henry, I am not advised.

We have been told by Arkansas historians that Benjamin Johnson was the youngest member of a family of distinguished men. The above genealogy proves this to be untrue. We have also been told that Richard Mentor Johnson served fifteen years in the lower house of Congress, while the records show a service of twenty years. The order of a man's birth and the number of years he may serve in a given position may not be important; but where they are stated as historic truths they should at least be accurate. Another narrative makes a brother of Judge Benjamin Johnson kill the great Indian Chief, Tecumseh, and another brother serve as Vice President of the United States, when the truth is that these brothers were identical.

Judge Benjamin Johnson was born in Scott County, Kentucky, on the 22d day of July, 1784, and was married to Matilda Williams in the same county on September 8, 1811. The Judge died at Lexington, Kentucky, on October 2, 1849, and was buried in Mt. Holly Cemetery at Little Rock. Eight children were born to Judge Johnson and his good wife, Matilda. They were as follows:

1. Juliette E. Johnson, born October 12, 1812, married to Ambrose Hundley Sevier at Little Rock on September 26, 1827, and died on March 16, 1845, being buried at Little Rock. Four children were the fruits of this marriage, Annie M. Sevier, Mattie J. Sevier, Elizabeth Sevier and Ambrose H. Sevier. Of these, Annie M. Sevier married General and Governor Thomas J. Churchill on July 31, 1849, and became the mother of six children: Abbie, Samuel J., Ambrose S., Juliet J., Emily and Matilda.

2. Robert Ward Johnson was born July 22, 1814, married Sarah S. Smith, daughter of Doctor George W. and Sabina Dubb Smith of Louisville, Kentucky, March 10, 1836, died July 26, 1879, and was buried in Little Rock. Robert W. Johnson was born in Kentucky, attended the common schools and the college at Bardstown, Kentucky; graduated in law at Yale College; admitted to the bar and began practice at Little Rock; was elected to the Thirtieth, Thirty-first and Thirty-second Congresses as a

Democrat; elected United States Senator to succeed Solon Borland, serving from December 5, 1853, until he withdrew from the Senate to align himself with the Confederate States in 1861; Confederate States Senator from Arkansas from 1861 to 1865; after the war removed to Washington, D. C., where he engaged in the practice of law until his death. His children were: Charles who died in infancy; Benjamin S., born October 29, 1841, married December 19, 1878, to Lina Vandegrift of Delaware, and became the father of Adeline C., who died in infancy, and James V. Johnson, who with his father, Benjamin S. Johnson, are prominent practitioners in the department of law at Little Rock; George J., who died in infancy; Robert W. Jr., who died at eighteen years of age; Francis born September 5, 1847, married to May F. Curran, October 14, 1873, and died September 22, 1902, leaving children, Alice, Sophia, Elsie, Ada May and Robert W.; Sally F., born February 12, 1849, married Joseph Cabell Breckinridge of Kentucky, December 1, 1869. Her children were—John C., Laura, Robert W. J., and Benjamin J.

3. George Junius Johnson died early in life unmarried.

4. Benjamin S. Johnson married Amelia Smith and died April 20, 1857, leaving no children.

5. Richard H. Johnson was born February 22, 1826, married Annie Newton, daughter of Thomas W. Newton, Sr., on February 22, 1855, and died in 1891. His children were Matilda, Sevier, Allen N., Mary, Junius J., Sidney, John A., and Anna. All of these children are dead, except John A. Johnson who lives in Little Rock.

6. James B. Johnson, born February 16, 1828, married Mary W. Cocke, niece of Governor John Pope, and was killed in the Confederate Army in 1862. His children were: Matilda, James Watt, and Irene, all of whom are dead.

7. Charles E. Johnson, died o. s. p.

8. Irene M. Johnson was born April 27, 1835, married Doctor John A. Jordan and died in August, 1878. Her children were: Matilda, Robert W., Mary, Irene and Maude J.

It will thus be seen that Judge Benjamin Johnson while tied to a distinguished family in Kentucky was also the head of a distinguished line of descendants whose names are connected with every line of development in Arkansas.

CHAPTER XXV.

AMBROSE H. SEVIER—WILLIAM S. FULTON—PRE-EMPTION.

Ambrose Hundley Sevier owed much to heredity. His family on the paternal side had for more than a thousand years occupied places of honor and trust in both church and State in the great kingdom of France. His great uncle, John Sevier, had carved for himself an immortal name in the creation of the State of Franklin and the making of the great commonwealth of Tennessee. The father of John Sevier, who spelled his name Xavier, its French form, was born in France, but on account of religious differences emigrated to Rockingham County, Virginia, where in 1745 John Sevier was born. In this same rugged county of Virginia, the bee hive of restless and ambitious spirits, was born Valentine Sevier, another immortal Tennessee name, and also several other brothers' among whom was the grandfather of A. H. Sevier.

John Sevier's fame rests upon the confidence of his friends and neighbors, engendered by his unselfish and patriotic devotion to duty. Wherever John Sevier went there went all his neighbors and friends, and out of his pocket, which was never reimbursed, went the money which these friends and neighbors needed in the execution of their enterprises. John Sevier was the idol of his neighbors and friends and knew men as few other men of his age knew them. Valentine Sevier sacrificed boy after boy in the East Tennessee conflicts with the Indians; with but two left, he sent these into the Cumberland district to help his friends there, where they were both butchered by the savages. In the agony of his heart the old man wrote back to a brother in Rockingham County: "Send me one or two of your boys. My boys are all gone, except some little ones they left, and the old man is so lonely." The wail of Ossian is no whit grander than this wail of old Valentine Sevier in the mountains of East Tennessee. In answer to this request, one nephew, with his wife, moved to Greene County, Tennessee, to comfort the declining years of this majestic old uncle, who was, with the exception of his brother, John, the proudest figure of that day.

CLASSICAL EDUCATION IN THE MOUNTAINS.

This boy, the father of Ambrose Hundley Sevier, married in Greene County, Susan Conway, whose nephews afterwards, became famous in Arkansas. In Greene County, in the year 1801, at the very time when his great uncle, John, was governor of the commonwealth, A. H. Sevier was born. For nineteen years he lived in Greene County and was there educated. He was classically educated in the mountains of East Tennessee. And he who conceives that a classical education may only be had inside great collegiate walls needs to undeceive himself. He who believes, like Alfred Bushnel Hart, professor of history in Harvard College, that the puritans of New England furnished the leaven which leavened the whole lump of American civilization, needs to undeceive himself. The civilization of the great West and South owes less to puritanism, to New England, than to any other cause. In fact, the very purest puritanism existed in other colonies, and while the narrow puritanism of New England made more noise, the broader puritanism of the other colonies produced a greater effect.

When Doak, the great Presbyterian puritan of North Carolina, established a college in East Tennessee before 1800, he was planting the leaven which should contribute most to Tennessee civilization. This college had the same Virgil, the same Caesar, the same Xenophon, the same Cicero, the same Legendre and the same Bible that any college in the world had, and its teachers were masters of the books, a thing that may not be said of all the professors who hold place in the greater institutions of today. A. H. Sevier in East Tennessee received a classical education, and upon the death of his father and mother received a very small estate. Not satisfied to live surrounded by an aristocratic kin, unable to move in the same circle with them, and looked upon by them as poor relations, Ambrose H. Sevier, in his nineteenth year, moved to Little Rock, Arkansas. We are not left to conjecture as to his condition upon arriving there. On April 25, 1825, in a speech to his friends in Little Rock, he used these words: "In my orphanage and boyhood I emigrated to this country, where I had neither friends or fortune or family connections." He was not making a speech for political buncombe, for the election was over and he had won. It was a speech characteristic of old John Sevier and of young Ambrose Sevier, or, as he was called in Little Rock, "Don Ambrosia." It was a speech to the people in which he rehearsed his life for five years in their midst, and in which he acknowledged his obligations to them for taking him into their confidence and honoring him with their support. It was not the speech of a demagogue, tickling the people for future gain, but a speech from the heart, a Sevier speech of the type of old John, in which truth and honesty predominated. There are those who think that Sevier's rapid promotion was due to his gifted father-in-law, Benjamin Johnson, and to his great kin, the Conways and Rectors. As a matter of fact, instead of these making Sevier, he, in all truth, may be said to have made them. It was Representative Sevier who saved Benjamin Johnson in the Congress of the United States, and it was the same Sevier who had a name and power before the Conway-Johnson family became the political rulers of the State.

SEVIER'S RAPID RISE.

He studied law in Little Rock, which is not to his discredit. He had the same Blackstone, the same Chitty, the same Stephens, that he would have had in a great law school, and as good teachers as any law school of that day afforded. He was a student and that explains the whole question. While others were enjoying themselves Sevier was studying his tasks, or visiting among the common people, whose heartthrobs found an answering echo in his own. He was a full-fledged lawyer in 1823 and had for his first case the defense of Russell in the great slander suit of Hogan v. Russell. He lost, but made for himself a character and a name. His friends were Chester Ashley and Robert Crittenden. He was clerk of the House of Representatives in the second legislature in October, 1821, and earned in that way the means necessary for his support. His manly common sense won for him the esteem of the people and in 1823 he was sent to the House of Representatives from Pulaski County, and returned again in 1825 and in 1827, in which session he was speaker of the house. Such a career for a poor orphan boy is absolutely remarkable, and bespeaks for him talents and virtues of the very highest order. During this time he held partnerships with Crittenden, with Ashley and with Trimble.

Political issues were of little moment, but in all the essentials of a party he was a Whig, as were the great body of the aristocratic slave holders of that period.

In fact, he is credited as being a Whig in his first term as delegate to Congress by the registers of that body. The enmity between him and Crittenden was not yet born, for in 1824 Crittenden, as acting governor, appointed him as prosecuting attorney for the Second Judicial District, and in the same year aide-de-camp to the governor, with the rank of lieutenant colonel, from which he obtained the title Colonel Sevier. In the race between Conway and Crittenden Sevier supported Conway, and upon his lamentable death entered the field as a candidate to fill the vacancy. In this race Crittenden supported him, but from that time on Crittenden's way diverged from that of Sevier. Sevier became a Democrat and Crittenden a pronounced Whig. It was not likely otherwise than that Sevier should become a Democrat. His whole life had been spent with the people. He knew their trials, their sentiments, and was one with them in their hopes. For years he had been an intimate associate of Sampson Gray and in his company had mingled with the common people everywhere.

He had the aristocratic tendencies of his Whig friends and relatives, but had the sense to know that these tendencies were antagonistic to a republican form of government.

SEVIER'S DEFEAT OF CRITTENDEN.

His greatest race for office was against Crittenden. Crittenden was more eloquent Sevier the more forceful; Crittenden made preparation for literary effect; Sevier for a natural effect; Crittenden sacrificed matter for a period; Sevier sacrificed his periods for his matter. Both were learned men, both honest, and both good looking. Sevier's knowledge of men gave him the advantage and he won by an overwhelming majority. From 1827 to 1836 he was constantly in Congress as a delegate from the territory, and while there made friends in both parties. In fact no man had a greater influence than did he. In 1836 he was sent to the Senate of the United States and remained there for twelve years. In the Senate he took the very highest rank, and maintained it. As chairman of the Committee on Foreign Relations he was recognized as a power with few equals. His speeches in Congress are models. When the pre-emption law was before the Senate of the United States in 1841 he made a speech, which should be in all the school readers of the State. In that he described the common people as he knew them and to their credit. He argued for the emancipation of men from the grade of operatives to that of managers. He argued for a freer life upon the farm. He argued for Arkansas and for the great influx of population which this bill would surely bring. He described as no other man on the floor did, or could, the kind of people that were going West in covered wagons. He drew a parallel between the covered wagons of the Yankees seeking a new home and that of the North Carolinians on the same quest. It was humorous and far more creditable to the Yankee than to the North Carolinian.

His apostrophe, however, to the North Carolinians was eloquent to the extreme. He pictured his early boyhood home, where for nineteen years he could look from his door over Buncombe County, North Carolina, and told his North Carolina friends who opposed the bill that while they might be ashamed of their own sons and daughters, that he was not. He said they were a good sort of people and that he wanted more of them, both Yankees and North Carolinians, in Arkansas. He then told of his association with North Carolinians as a man, from Wilmington to the mountains, and while honoring them and loving them, he assured the senator from North Carolina that he would not blush, nor dread to make a comparison of his constitutents upon the public lands with the best his State afforded, gauged by any standard of virtue, intelligence or worth, which he or others might choose to suggest. His speech upon the civil service had exactly the right ring and was head and shoulders above the twaddle which modern civil service reform has given the world. He believed in the spoils system, the very system that obtains, despite all civil service law. He said: "But as for Democrats, they expect to be turned out from one end of the country to the other. And for one, I should disown them as party associates if they whimpered over their removal." He was answering Henry Clay, and that great man, after the answer, hurried to his side to express his congratulations. There was a manliness about Sevier which no one could doubt. He was a man of the people without being a buffoon or a demagogue, and in the matter of the division of the offices, conscientiously believed that the party in power should have their exclusive control. In 1848 he was sent as minister to Mexico, and in the same year died at his plantation in Arkansas. On September 27, 1827, he married Juliette Johnson, daughter of Honorable Ben Johnson of the superior court, and his children may be found in the chapter on Judge Benjamin Johnson.

In whatever capacity Sevier was placed to serve he rounded it out with dignity and honor. His private life was above reproach and in all the attributes of greatness was sound to the core. He inherited much and in a new environment hammered himself up to the fullest stature of a great man.

PRE-EMPTION SPEECH.

Senator A. H. Sevier in his great speech on pre-emption in 1841 before the Senate of the United States said:

"Public sentiment in the new States demands a change in the disposition of the public lands, and, sooner or later, public sentiment will control. On this subject there is a collected moral force, which can not and will not be resisted. And is it not our duty to respect this public opinion? Is it not our duty to promote the peace and happiness of every member of our Union? And in accomplishing so high and so noble a purpose, does it become us to stand out upon mere trifles? What are a few dollars, more or less, to the national treasury, in comparison with such absorbing questions?

"And, lastly, is it not our duty, as far as in us lies, to make every citizen in every State a freeholder—an independent and happy man? What spectacle is there so pleasing to a virtuous and feeling heart?"

This was a great speech of a great man on a great question, and is of lasting importance to one who tries to grade the intelligence of Arkansas in early times. The extract is but a part of the speech, but it is enough to lead us to intelligent conclusions as to the speaker, and through him, as to the men behind him, and who stood for him. Webster may have had a quality of eloquence more refined and more exhaustive, but no whit greater than that of Sevier in cogent and forceful utterance, in comprehensive knowledge of the finer play of human nature, in an understanding of the loftiest soul forces and the power of human spirituality. He was on the borders of a great, and hitherto, untried problem—the disposition of the lands of a continent. Is it not proof of his disinterestedness that he stood out boldly and fearlessly for the individuals—the men in homespun—the pioneers? Today he might be criticised as a Socialist, but in that good day such a classification was unknown. What loftier utterance has ever been made by any statesman than Sevier's words, "Is it not our duty, so far as in us lies, to make every citizen in every State a freeholder, an independent and happy man?" And with this grand old pioneer may we not all say, "What spectacle is there so pleasing to a virtuous and feeling heart?"

Grand old Sevier! Yea, verily, Grand old Arkansas! He was not a diamond dropped in a sea of dirt, nor was he alone, among his fellows in the territory, a master of correct thought and rightful action. The pioneers of Arkansas were all diamonds in the rough, great hearts and souls living in the woods. There were gamblers and thieves among them, as a matter of course, for wherever mankind has rested there these degenerates have been found. Gamblers and thieves, however, never chose a Sevier for their leader, for he was not of their kind. The great population of the territory and State was honest, and Sevier represented that element, and in his day a man from Arkansas was in any part of the world the peer of any man from any section of the Union.

The question he discussed so ably was a most comprehensive one, and the happiness, thrift and wealth of the United States have come more from the way in which America handled this question than from any other single source, except that of American freedom.

PRE-EMPTION LAWS.

Between 1801 and 1841—a period of forty years—sixteen separate pre-emption laws of greater or lesser comprehensiveness were passed by Congress. In 1838 the selfish effort was made to confine the benefits of pre-emption to citizens of the United States, but it failed. In 1843 the right was extended to all citizens, but limited to land which had been surveyed. The acts of 1853 and 1854 permitted the pre-emption to extend to unsurveyed lands in California, Oregon, Minnesota, Kansas, Nebraska and New Mexico. All the lands of Arkansas had been surveyed prior to the passage of these laws. The necessity of protecting settlers on the public domain and of giving preference right to persons desiring to make homes thereon became strongly apparent in the period 1830-40. During that decade the population of Arkansas increased more than two hundred and twenty per cent.

The receipts of the government from cash land sales during that period were eighty-one million, nine hundred thirteen thousand and seventeen dollars; and in the year 1836, the record year of our whole history, twenty-five millions, one hundred and sixty-seven thousand eight hundred thirty-three dollars, and represented a sale of thirty-two million eight hundred thousand acres of land, an area greater than the State of Ohio.

FREE SOIL

After 1850 we hear less of pre-emption and more of free soil, but we must never forget that Sevier in Arkansas is entitled to a meed of praise for cheap lands equal to that which Missouri ascribes to Benton for free lands. When my history of the United States was up for adoption for State use in Missouri the Adopting Board made three ultimata, viz: a full page picture of Lincoln, another of Grant and still another of Thomas H. Benton. The three pictures went into the book and during ten years more than one hundred thousand copies of the book were sold. In my native State, the State whose honor I have upheld on two continents, no more than thirty counties ever adopted the book, proving two things, (1) that a prophet is never without honor save at home, and (2) that Arkansans are not as proud of Sevier as Missourians are of Benton.

The Free Soil Democrats in 1852 at Pittsburg put into their platform a plank demanding the granting of the public lands in limited quantities free of cost to landless settlers. From this on to 1862 the question became national and a part of the platforms of all parties. In 1860 Andrew Johnson of Tennessee introduced a homestead bill into the Senate of the United States, by which all actual settlers, being heads of families, should have the right to a patent for one hundred and sixty acres of land by settling upon it and remaining upon it for a period of five years. The house had already passed another bill, but upon conference the Senate bill was accepted, and passed both houses.

HOMESTEAD LAW OF 1862.

James Buchanan, an Eastern Democrat, vetoed the bill to his everlasting dishonor and discredit. The present law was passed in 1862, and Abraham Lincoln, a man who, like Sevier, knew the settlers on the public lands, made haste to sign it. The entries under this law from 1862 to 1880 numbered four hundred sixty-nine thousand, seven hundred eighty-two, and the area settled amounted to fifty-five millions six hundred sixty-seven thousand and forty-four acres. Nearly five hundred thousand heads of families were thus made freeholders and given the peaceful and happy condition so aptly outlined by Mr. Sevier. Today the president, the secretary of the interior and the commissioner of public lands, under the cry of "fraud" and the further cry of "hold the lands for actual settlers," have promulgated rules and regulations which virtually destroy the law of 1862. Reform may go too far, and it does go too far, when it makes it harder for an honest man to obtain the benefits of the law than it ever did for a dishonest man to bring it into contempt. There are cases today in Arkansas of cash entries made under the timber and stone act as far back as June and October, 1906, which have been held up by the department during all these months, with not even an inspector ordered to this good hour to make an investigation, and I can give names and letters from the commissioner as late as January 25, 1908. The land system of the United States has had the ability and experience of Hamilton, Jefferson, Madison and Gallatin, and is the best known to the world.

SENATOR WILLIAM S. FULTON.

Senator Fulton, a colleague of Sevier, was a Marylander, who had lived in Tennessee and Alabama before his appointment to the gubernatorial chair of the territory of Arkansas, being the last to hold that position. He was born in Cecil County, Maryland, June 2, 1795; graduated from Baltimore College in 1813; started the study of law under Williams Pinckney, but gave it up to serve in a company of volunteers at Fort McHenry; after the war moved with his father's family to Tennessee and finished his law study with Felix Grundy, military secretary to General Jackson in his Florida campaign in 1818; moved to Alabama; appointed by Jackson, Secretary of the Territory of Arkansas in 1829, succeeding Robert Crritenden, and Governor in 1835-6. He was elected to the United States Senate in 1836, and died August 15, 1844, during his second term. He, like Sevier, took quite an interest in the public land laws, and when Tom Benton's great pre-emption bill was before the Senate, made a speech of considerable importance, and which contains a fair view of how the public lands were manipulated under the old law. He said:

"Mr. President—Under the present system all lands subject to sale are put up at auction. And what is the result? The moment the proclamation issues, speculators put their agents to work. They obtain the numbers of every valuable tract to be sold. They meet together at the sale. They form a company and agree to bid off all the good land offered. They accordingly purchase it at a fraction over the minimum price, as they have no competitors. Immediately after the public sale they have an auction among themselves, and each one purchases the tract he wishes to buy and pays for it in proportion to its value, or as there may be bidders who come into competition. The proceeds of the sale are divided amongst the company and the speculators realize all the profits of your auction system."

This was the much-lauded system which Eastern men clung to with an almost fanatic regard, opposing all pre-emption laws for its maintenance, and with equal force opposing the homestead law. The speeches of these Eastern men were selfish to the extreme and placed the treasury of the United States, which was not really benefited by the old law, as Fulton has shown, above the future advantages which a liberal pre-emption law or a free soil law would bring the entire country. These same Eastern men denounced the settlers on public lands as criminals, although Sevier, Benton and Fulton lifted their voices in vain to tell them that these public land settlers were equal in point of worth, integrity and enterprise to any of those who took pleasure in denouncing them. Senator Fulton said:

CHARACTER OF THE OLD PIONEERS.

"They are not known to senators or they would not thus be maligned. Arkansas was organized as a territory when nearly all her citizens were settlers on the public lands. Go to your land offices and you will find that men who have been members of Congress, and have filled the highest stations in the old States, have settled upon the public lands and have obtained titles to their lands as pre-emptioners. For generosity, capacity to endure hardship and noble daring no people are equal to the pre-emptioners of the South and West. They go there with their wives and children poor and penniless, and in a year are found in a snug cabin surrounded by a cultivated field, with an abundance of everything necessary to support life. From this humble beginning by the exercise of industry and perseverance, they soon become independent, and in time become the best and worthiest of the inhabitants. To secure homes for men like these is the end of my political ambition, and as an act of justice, I ask the Senate to protect the settler, the maker and builder of commonwealths, from the greed and rapacity of the most selfish of men, the speculator in public lands."

Thus from the mouths of both Senator Sevier and Senator Fulton is the character of the old pioneer blazoned to the world. It is a character which brings no blush of shame, and although made without a coat of arms, forms the basis for the most illustrious quarterings which heraldry can give.

CHAPTER XXVI.

JOAB HARDIN—THE BENTLEYS—MAJOR WELBORN—ABNER HAROLD—COLONEL THOMAS MATHERS—THE ARKANSAS TRAVELER.

Joab Hardin was a fair representative of an old family in Kentucky, that was pioneer in the commonwealths of Pennsylvania, Kentucky, Illinois and Arkansas. The expedition of George Rogers Clarke took many Kentuckians into Illinois, who afterward made that State their permanent place of residence. When General William Rector surveyed Illinois under the land laws, soldiers from all parts of the Union, especially from North Carolina, Virginia and Kentucky, entered Illinois, and located their claims. This made Illinois Democratic during all the earlier years of its history, especially the southern part, which on this account was called by the abolitionists who flocked to the northern part, Egypt. Some of the most thrilling history of the United States from 1820 to 1860 was fought out in southern Illinois by these Southern emigrants, who carried with them into their new homes their peculiar ideas as to slavery and other things. Along with these went soldiers from the Northern States, equally as pugnacious as their Southern friends, who created contests most bitter and lasting. Some of the greatest names of modern Republican history spring from men and women of southern Illinois, who up to the beginning of the war were Democratic in political faith. Generals Grant and Logan were Democrats until the exigencies of the war made them Republican.

THE PROLIFIC HARDIN FAMILY.

The name Hardin is a contraction of the older name, Harding, and both forms root back into colonial Pennsylvania, Virginia and Maryland. Some of the members of families using both forms of spelling are to be found in all the Southern States. Joab Hardin was born in Virginia, moved to Kentucky and then to Arkansas. He served in the War of 1812, but was more of a politician than a soldier. Like his kinsman, Old Ben Hardin, of Kentucky fame, he believed it less sinful to fight with his tongue than with guns. He settled in Lawrence County, Arkansas, in 1818, and at the first election in the territory began to run for office, a trait characteristic of the Hardin family, if not of the human family. He not only ran, but was elected, and served in the first and second Territorial legislatures.

He had not the Hardin gift of eloquence, but was a speaker very hard to down. He could talk well on his feet without notes, being master of human nature and well acquainted with the foibles of mankind. He fell in with the Cadronites in their effort to make Cadron the capital of the State, and it was to his influence that the measure finally carried. He owned lands not only in Lawrence County, but also in Pulaski County in the neighborhood of Cadron. In 1823 he moved from his Lawrence County home down into Pulaski County, into what is now Conway County, and without any effort whatever became the most influential man in that part of the county. On account of this influence they called his settlement "The Hardin Settlement of Pulaski County," and when townships were named the one containing this settlement took old Joab's surname, which name it holds to this good day. When Conway County was formed Hardin township fell into that county, and in 1873 was set off into Faulkner County. The town of Conway forms the center of the old Cadron settlement, while the Cadron mills were located in another settlement, now called Matthews township. In October, 1824, Joab Hardin died in Hardin township, Pulaski County, and John Lindsey Lafferty, then living in Pulaski County and in the same township, administered upon his estate. John Hardin represented Hardin township from Conway County in 1844. In this way the Hardins go back to the beginning of things.

THE BENTLEY FAMILY.

George Bentley came to Arkansas territory in 1819, and settled on the Arkansas river in the Pecannerie settlement. A fine grade of pecans then grew in that neighborhood, from which the name was derived. The father of George Bentley was a member of the Fifth Virginia Continental Line and rose to the grade of captain. He served from 1776 to 1779 and was also a lieutenant colonel in the Indian war of 1799. He was mustered out in 1800 and died shortly afterward. His son, George, was a sturdy pioneer in Arkansas history, but kept out of politics. He made money in the early history of the State, and was considered one of the best of the old citizens of Conway County. A township carries his name. He had a daughter, Nancy, who was quite an accomplished woman, who died at Pecannerie in 1821. He also had a son, Joseph, who died at the same place February 14, 1825. The mails at that time went from Davidsonville through Batesville to Cadron, and thence down to Arkansas Post, once every two weeks. In March, 1821, through the efforts of George Bentley, a new route was established, beginning at Cadron, running through Arkopolis, thence south to the Ouachita. Colonel Bentley had another daughter, a most promising woman, who was married on September 23, 1823, by Reverend Mr. Arnett, to Colonel Thomas Mathers of Pulaski, now Conway, County. There must have been other sons who married, as both the name and the blood still exist in Conway County, where for nearly ninety years it has contributed to the development of that region.

MAJOR WELBORN AND OTHER PIONEERS.

This old soldier came from Virginia to the Arkansas region in 1817, and was well located on the Arkansas river when Nuttal passed up in 1819. He acquired his title as major in the War of 1812, and was one of the most vigorous citizens of the old Pecannerie region. In a trip to the southwestern part of the State lassoing wild horses in 1822 he was killed by the Indians. This is one report; in another report it was noted that he escaped, and in still another that he was killed and scalped by the Indians. I am not able to say which report is correct, but his prominence was sufficient to give his name to a township in the county, the thriving town of Morrilton, I believe, being its center. Major Welborn and General Lewis were firm friends and contributed much to the respectability and power of this old settlement. It was then a part of Pulaski County, and the most prominent citizens of the settlement, in 1822, other than Welborn and Lewis, were Thomas White, John Hibbin, Timothy

Harris, William Frazier, William Lackey, Jacob Slinkard, James Titsworth, Thomas Hibbin, George Bentley, Adustin Rogers, George Carden, John Belcher, Larkin Womack and Samuel McCall.

ABNER HAROLD.

Another old pioneer in that part of Pulaski which is now Faulkner was Abner Harold. He appears to have been Kentucky born and to have entered the territory in 1820, locating in the neighborhood in which he lived and died. He was a man of most forceful convictions, of splendid influence among his neighbors and friends, but without political aspirations. Modest, unassuming, honest and industrious, Abner Harold made a fine impression on the neighborhood in which he lived and was in every respect one of the most respectable citizens of Pulaski County. In February, 1823, a daughter, Betsy, was married to Zechariah Lorance, very probably Lawrence. Going out the Arch street turnpike toward Cockmon's sawmill, a citizen of today will pass a little creek called Lorance creek. This would seem to indicate that the name, Lorance, whether originally Lawrence or not, still clings to Arkansas as a place name, and would indicate that the surname Lorance was a part of the earlier territorial history. Very probably the pioneer Zechariah Lorance lived upon this creek, or, if not, some of his descendants. Abner Harold must have had sons and grandsons to perpetuate his name, since in more modern times one of the most distinguished lawyers of the State carries that name and roots back as to his forbears into this old Faulkner-Pulaski County settlement. The vigor of the grandfather or great grandfather, if these be the exact relations, is most aptly shown in the strong native parts of this illustrious descendant.

COLONEL THOMAS MATHERS.

This old soldier was born in Cumberland County, Pennsylvania, that thriving county of which Carlisle is now the county seat. He won a colonel's commission in the War of 1812, and located his land warrant in Pulaski County in 1820, where he built a mill which was known far and wide as Cadron mill. He at once became one of the leaders of the settlement, and was considered a good catch, by all the respectable girls of the neighborhood.

In 1823 he was married at Pecannerie to Mary, daughter of George Bentley. Colonel Mathers served in the third territorial legislature from 1823 to 1825, and was clerk of Conway County from 1832 to 1836. He died at his home at Cadron Mills in 1839. Other old settlers of Pulaski County in the Conway County region were Judge W. G. Saffold, David Barber, James Ward, Judge B. B. Ball, J. I. Simmons, James Kellam, James Barber, Reuben Blunt, John Houston, William Ellis and E. W. Owen.

"THE ARKANSAW TRAVELER."

Conway County was named after Henry W. Conway, the second delegate to Congress from Arkansas territory, and was formed out of Pulaski in October, 1825. It was originally much larger than its present boundaries indicate. A large part of the Cherokee Indian purchase was added in 1828, while large subtractions were made and given to Pope and White in 1853. Besides the ones named, Gregory township, Griffin, Higgin, Howard, McLaren and Nichols carry the names of other old settlers of that region. Faulkner County was not created until 1873, and was named for Colonel Sandford C. Faulkner, a wealthy planter of Chicot County, the author of the famous colloquy and piece of music entitled "The Arkansaw Traveler." Edward P. Washburn of Pope County has painted in oil this famous scene as told him by Colonel Faulkner. The painting was said to be a fine piece of art, and found place for many years in the parlor of Colonel Faulkner at Little Rock. I do not know where this historic painting is lodged at present, but in deference to Colonel Faulkner, and as an honor to Arkansas' earliest artist it should find place in the archives of the State.

NO INJURY TO STATE

It has been said that this literary production of Colonel Faulkner has been an injury to the State. This is a very shortsighted view of the question. In my opinion no community can ever be permanently or temporarily injured by any mere work of humor, and as a piece of humor, broad, it is true, "The Arkansaw Traveler" has never been excelled. Instead of injuring Arkansas it has carried that name to the remotest parts of the earth, and has exploited a type of easy-going citizens common to all localites the world over. The type needed excoriation, which Colonel Faulkner gave with a gloved but not a mailed hand. No living man in any part of the world has extended the range of the type to include all the citizens of the State, and the idea that it does so' has originated in the mind of those who claim it has injured the State, and not elsewhere. Colonel Faulkner deserves honor for the fidelity with which he has delineated the type, and Mr. Washburn an equal honor for perpetuating it in oil. "The Arkansaw Traveler" has a niche in the temple of fame from which it can never be dislodged, and is in no sense a reflection upon the energy and masterly parts of the great mass of the population which has contributed to its growth and power.

CHAPTER XXVII.

Reverend Cephas Washburn.

In 1819 Nuttal found settlements on both sides of the Arkansas river in the neighborhood of what is now Dardanelle. The whites lived on the south side of the river and the Indians on the north. There was quite a large village located on the north side made up of Indians exclusively which was called The Galley. The chief of the Cherokees was named Jolly, a half breed of respectable talents, who had made quite a reputation in Tennessee and Mississippi. The Indian agent at that time was Mr. Rollin, who lived at times at The Galley, and at other times at Dardanelle and at other points on the river. In 1820 he was succeeded by Matthew Lyon, who made his home at Spadra Bluff. During his administration the government built an Indian house at Dardanelle and upon the death of Lyon, Edward Duval, who succeeded him, moved into this agency house where he remained for many years, combining the duties of Indian agent with those of postmaster.

Quite a friction was engendered between Duval and Governor Izard as to the management of Indian affairs, the rendering of accounts and other minor items, but the friendship of these gentlemen was never impaired. There was a half breed Indian storekeeper at The Galley in 1819, and another half breed, Walter Weber, lived at the foot of the Dardanelle Hills. At The Galley lived John Rogers, one of the most respectable of the civilized Cherokees, and one to whom that nation is much indebted for its development and growth. Colonel David Brearly, a Revolutionary soldier and also a soldier of the regular army, moved in 1821 to Arkansas Post, where he opened quite a large store. Four years later he opened a store at Dardanelle and still later at Norristown, a vigorous town on the north side, which made a hard fight in later years for the position of capital city of Arkansas.

THE FOUNDING OF DWIGHT.

Reverend Cephas Washburn, a Congregational minister of New England, was sent by the Board of Missions of the United States to Arkansas in 1821 to open a mission school among the Cherokee Indians. A place for the mission was selected at a point on the Illinois bayou, which, in honor of Timothy Dwight, president of Yale College, was named Dwight, and is now known to all the people of the State as Old Dwight, and is in the present Pope County. The erection of buildings was begun in 1821, and continued for several years. Doctor Washburn brought with him six teachers, all from New England, and began a work at Dwight, whose influence is still apparent among the Cherokees in Oklahoma. On his road to his mission he stopped at the village, Little Rock, and preached a sermon. His description of the capital at that time is so well known as to demand no repetition here. He went on up the river and opened a school which was of distinct advantage to the Cherokees, who were already the most advanced Indian nation of the country. That school was continued at Dwight until after the removal of the Cherokees to the Indian Territory. Under the same management it was continued for several years afterwards for the white people, and many of the most distinguished men of the Arkansas valley in early days were educated at that place.

Reverend Cephas Washburn, president of the mission and school, descended from a New England family whose history goes back to the very earliest colonial days. The Washburn family was not only an old one on American soil, but one noted for its distinguished sons and daughters, whose names and histories have added luster to American art, politics, religion and law. The spelling of the name varies from Washbourn through Washburne down to its modern and settled form, Washburn.

Reverend Cephas Washburn was an alumnus of Yale College, and in naming his Indian mission honored its illustrious president, the chief executive of the institution while he was a student. The transition from the New England climate to that of Arkansas was noted by many climatic diseases, the one which gave the most trouble being the ague. The assistants at Dwight from 1821 to 1826 were Alfred Finney, Mr. Orr, Jacob Hitchcock, Asa Hitchcock, Ella Stetson and Nancy Brown. Cephas Washburn's name in the Cherokee language was "Ookuquahtuh," but none but the Cherokees ever used it.

Reverend Cephas Washburn was an Indian Educator in Arkansas and the Indian Territory from 1821 to 1847. Coupled with this he preached the gospel, but did not assume a regular charge until late in life, when his age precluded further active educational endeavor.

THE FAR WEST ACADEMY.

In 1844 he was the chief spirit in the organization of the Far West Academy in Washington County and president of its first Board of Trustees. These trustees came from all parts of the State and were as follows: Hugh A. Anderson, Robert A. Mecklin, Joseph M. Hoge, James Boone, William D. Cunningham, David Walker, John Harrel, Edward Freyschag, Samuel Newton, Benjamin Pearson, Alfred W. Arrington, Joseph P. Moore, Thomas J. Pollard, William T. Larrimore, Isaac Murphy, Andrew Buchanan, Matthew Leeper, James Orr, Muloin A. Lynde, George W. Paschal, Edward Cunningham, David McManers, James Lockridge, Aaron W. Lyon, John McMillan, James M. Moore, William W. Stevenson, Benjamin F. Thompson, A. R. Banks and J. S. Phelps, the latter being from Springfield, Missouri. One of these was afterward a member of the United States Senate from Arkansas, and another one of its best governors. Aaron W. Lyon was the president of Batesville Academy and a most prominent educator in early times. The whole list is a distinct roll of honor and shows the remarkable influence of Cephas Washburn among the really strong men of the day. The land for this academy was in Prairie township, Washington County, and was donated by Solomon Tuttle, J. M. Tuttle, W. D. Cunningham, John Pollard, J. P. Moore and Allen Moore. The fundamental rule of the school was that the Bible should be the standard of morals and religion.

WASHBURN'S WORK STILL LIVES.

Any conservative estimate of the character and life work of Cephas Washburn will fall short of accuracy. He was a man of purpose, distinct religious purpose, animated by the loftiest desire to aid the Indians. He was educated to the highest and best degree and thus enabled to realize his purpose. He was undoubtedly disinterested and his long and distinguished career in Arkansas left him a poor man, a fact somewhat discreditable to the State he helped. However, this was as he would have had it to be, as under no circumstances would he put his own interests above those of the public. He strengthened the Cherokee character as no other man did and gave direction to Arkansas character as few others did. His work remains in the civilization of Arkansas and Oklahoma, although his name to most Arkansans is completely unknown. He was one of the State's best characters and deserves a niche in its Valhalla when it comes. He died at Little Rock on March 7, 1860, having spent thirty-nine years in Arkansas.

EDWARD P. WASHBURN, ARTIST.

He was one of the earliest pastors of the Presbyterian church at Fort Smith, and while stationed there, his son, Edward P. Washburn, began to exhibit that mentality which stamped him as an artist in embryo. In a previous chapter I have referred to the talent of this young man, but unfortunately called him Charles P. Washburn. Having forgotten his name, I referred to Judge Pope's Early Days and adopted his error. The salary of Cephas Washburn at Fort Smith was not sufficient to justify him in sending Edward to the studio of some eminent artist in Europe, and the boy was left to develop his own talents under his own intuitions. The father of J. F. Weaver of Fort Smith was at that time a merchant at that place and a great admirer of young Washburn. Being in Philadelphia, replenishing his mercantile stock, he bought an artist's outfit of painting material, which upon his return he presented to the young man. This was as great a delight to young Washburn as the consent of Benjamin West's Quaker parents was to Benjamin, when they agreed that he might have time and place to develop his God-given gift. As a return for the kindness, young Washburn presented Mr. Weaver with a picture he had executed, representing the Bay of Naples. This picture was prized by Mr. Weaver, but in a removal in 1871 it was unfortunately misplaced and lost. Washburn gave Mr. Weaver another picture, which is now at the house of J. F. Weaver of Fort Smith, the editor of the Fort Smith Elevator. This picture represented Fort Smith in the early fifties and was the joint production of young Washburn and William Quisenbury, an old-time Arkansas editor and artist, whose pseudonym was "Bill Cush." It is said that Quisenbury made the drawing while Washburn added the color.

THE ARKANSAW TRAVELER.

About this time Col. Sandy Faulkner's inimitable story, "The Arkansaw Traveler," made its appearance and was as popular in a day as "After the Ball" or "Annie Rooney" ever dared to be. Edward Payson Washburn listened to the story of Sandy Faulkner and decided to sketch it. The house or cabin in the picture which he made originally stood on the bank of Illinois bayou near Dwight, but not a trace of it exists today. I was born in a log cabin on Illinois bayou in 1849, and have heard the story repeated from my earliest recollection. In my flights of oratory and rhetoric my mother took pleasure in bringing me down to earth by pointing to the old cabin of Washburn's picture, saying, "My son, don't fly too high. There was where you were born." She meant, of course, that I was born in a house exactly like the one which Washburn painted into his picture, and any house on Illinois bayou at that day would have met the conditions. I have never claimed that I was born in the identical house painted by Edward Washburn, but I was born in a log house very like it and very close to it. Neither am I ashamed of the old log cabin in which I was born, but on the contrary I have reason to be proud of it. From papers on its walls I learned to read, and when I was six years of age I presented myself at the doors of the Louisville, Kentucky, graded schools, then in charge of that accomplished educator from New England, Doctor George Chase, the founder of the graded school system in the West, and I was put in the fourth grade. As a six-year-old boy I started in the Louisville graded schools in the fourth reader, and am indebted to that old Arkansas log cabin for the fact that I never saw the first, second or third reader in my school life.

So much for the early Arkansas cabins, the cabins made famous by the painting of Edward P. Washburn. The boy on the hopper in the picture is said by the family to be Joe Brearly, son of David Brearly of Norristown. Others say that the boy was George F. Dodge, but the version of the family is more likely the correct one. The man on the horse was said to be Colonel Faulkner himself. In this way with real models which he carried in his mind, young Washburn worked Faulkner's fiddle story into the picture as we know it. At least this is the traditional account as told by the Washburn family today. The boy on the hopper was not demanded by Faulkner's philosophy, and was Washburn's conception pure and simple, a decided addition to the picture.

BOTH WASHBURNS BURIED IN MT. HOLLY.

Edward Payson Washburn was born at Dwight Mission in the Cherokee nation, November 17, 1831, and died at Little Rock March 26, 1860. He and his father both died at the house of Doctor R. L. Dodge, in the same year, and both are buried in Mt. Holly cemetery. The grand-daughters of Reverend Cephas Washburn are now living at Russellville, Arkansas, viz.: Mrs. George Black and Mrs. Dodd, wife of C. W. Dodd, editor of the Pope County Record. The original sketch of the Arkansas Traveler is held by Mrs. Black. It has been laid away for years and is now somewhat defaced. It was exhibited at Eureka

Springs last summer at the annual meeting of the Arkansaw Travelers' Association. Mrs. Black is also the owner of an oil portrait of Edward Washburn, and also of his father, Cephas Washburn, both life size. She has also a scrap book containing many newspaper references to both father and son at their death.

It is said that Rev. Cephas Washburn was called upon one night while located at Old Dwight to visit the bedside of a dying Indian. After prayer and other religious ceremonies, the dying man revealed his identity and claimed to be none other than the famous renegade, Simon Girty. I doubt the validity of the claim, but if it shall turn out to be a truthful one, Arkansas contains the grave of one of the most notorious white renegades known in Indian history.

CHAPTER XXVIII.

Major Isaac Watkins.

Buckle was a firm believer in the doctrine of a great natural law so dominating all special laws, that given all the special laws acting on a man's environment it became possible to foretell each man's action at every period of his life. This theory was needlessly attacked by many divines, as in general terms its truth is unassailable. Its uselessness as a doctrine, however, lies in the fact that only Omniscience can see the multiplicity of natural special laws acting on a man's personality and that therefore only Omniscience can foretell. Buckle simply said, "If you will make me Omniscient, I will tell you how you will act in every conceivable situation."

It is a general law that a certain number of men will become bondsmen for other men. Special laws determine who these men are to be. It is a general law that a definite number of these bonded men will fail to perform their bond as stipulated and that the bondsmen will suffer. Special laws determine the failures, and only Omniscience can foresee them. It is a general law that the sufferers under the mortification of loss will migrate to other localities, wherein their pride shall not suffer and recuperation go on under changed and more peaceful conditions. Thus the movements of population are influenced by the bankruptcies of the world and by the added loads bondsmen are forced to carry.

It was this that gave Arkansas the citizen, Major Isaac Watkins, father of Chief Justice George C. Watkins, and his most interesting family, wherein Arkansas was a distinct gainer and Kentucky the loser. The Watkins family was an ancient family of England belonging to both the major and minor gentry, and the old fashioned box shaped tomb of Major Isaac Watkins in Mt. Holly Cemetery, Little Rock, blazon the words:

"Haud Immemor.

"Isaac Watkins, Gent.

"Born in Virginia, April 10, 1777.

"Died in Arkansas, Dec. 13, 1827."

The migration of the earliest propositus to Virginia was in the latter part of the seventeenth century, and the habitat, Cumberland County, afterwards Powhatan. Thomas Watkins settled on Swift Creek and his will was probated in June, 1760. His eldest son, Thomas of Chickahominy, Virginia, married a sister of Claiborne Anderson, who was also a descendant of William Claiborne, the first Secretary of the Colony.

Thomas of Chickahominy had a brother, Benjamin, who represented Chesterfield County in colonial assemblies, and was a member of the convention of 1776. He was a friend and correspondent of Samuel Adams and John Hancock, and the grandfather of the famous Benjamin Watkins Leigh.

The youngest son of Thomas Watkins of Chickahominy was also named Thomas. He married in 1763, Sallie Walton, sister of George Walton, signer of the Declaration of Independence and Governor of Georgia. A descendant of George Walton became Governor of Florida and father of Madame Octavia Walton Le Vert of Mobile, Alabama.

FOUGHT IN WAR OF 1812.

Major Isaac Watkins, the subject of this sketch, was the youngest son of Thomas and Sallie Walton Watkins and the first of the family to migrate to Kentucky. His father died while he was quite young leaving but a small estate and a large family. His mother remarried and moved to the neighborhood of Shelbyville, Kentucky, taking her younger children with her. Here Isaac Watkins grew to manhood and became a man of influence and wealth. In 1812 he served as a soldier and rose to the rank of Major. No man had a fairer reputation in Shelbyville than he did. He had been assisted to a most accomplished education by his uncle, Francis Watkins of Virginia, who married the heiress Agnes Woodson, daughter of Baron Woodson, a great landholder of that region. With a sound education and all the polish of an old time Southern gentleman he could not refuse to aid his friends and in a weak moment in 1820 signed a bond for a large amount for a friend, which bond he had to pay.

CAME TO LITTLE ROCK IN 1820.

This stripped him of the larger part of his fortune and he with a remnant thereof in 1820 came to Little Rock to recuperate. In December, 1820, he lived in a log house while putting up the first frame residence in the town. This residence was finished early in the summer of 1821, and was used by Major Watkins as a hotel for several years, and was said by W. E. Woodruff, Sr., to be the only eligible location for a public house in the town. It was called The Little Rock Tavern, and may be identified from the fact that in 1825 it passed into the hands of Mr. Nick Peay, who continued it as a public house for many years. On June 20, 1822, Major Watkins announced to the people in the columns of The Gazette the completion of a horse mill at Little Rock, being the first structure of the kind in the town. It would grind six bushels an hour by a little pushing of the horses, and fifty bushels of good meal a day. The mill was constructed by Joseph Thornhill, an intelligent carpenter of the town, but who had never built a mill. Under the direction of Major Watkins, Thornhill is said to have built one of the best mills of those times. Thornhill amassed wealth and died in 1826, appointing Bernard Smith, Major Watkins and William E. Woodruff, Sr., as his executors.

HEIRLOOM FURNITURE STILL IN EXISTENCE.

The furniture for the most part which Major Watkins used in his log cabin as well as in his larger frame mansion was brought from Kentucky, and was of the most elegant kind, a sad reminder of his more prosperous days. It is worthy of note to say that an old Chippendale clock, some sofas, tables, miniatures and portraits, brought by Major Watkins from Kentucky to Arkansas, are still in the possession of his descendants at Little Rock. In addition to his town property, he bought a large tract of land on the north side of the river, about three miles below the town, which he cleared and put in a high state of cultivation. It is also worthy of note to say that the north side of the river in the very earliest days had more attractions for emigrants than the south side. United States Marshal George W. Scott bought a plantation on this side of the river about a mile above town, and built a brick house on it which was finished in October, 1824. This was certainly the first brick house on the north side, and in all probability the first brick house in Pulaski County, outside of Little Rock. Some local antiquarian may be able to point out its present location. It was built by Christian Brumback.

Major Watkins in 1821, 1823 and 1825, set banquets for the men who celebrated the birthday of our independence during these years. One of these banquets was set in the gallery of the old court house, and accommodated one hundred persons, being presided over by Governor Izard. At the celebration of 1823 Watkins was the presiding officer, and at each of these celebrations he responded to a toast. On the fourth Saturday in July, 1824, the first Baptist church of Little Rock was organized at his house, Reverend Silas T. Toncray, presiding, with Major Watkins, clerk.

FIRST BAPTIST ASSOCIATION.

In November, 1824, the first Baptist Association of Arkansas was formed at the State house, the same officers presiding. The churches present were Little Rock, Salem, Clark County and Pecannerie. This association was called the Little Rock Association of Regular Baptists. Major Watkins remained clerk of the church and of the association for many years. In 1825 he made his only race for the legislature, being a candidate for the council, against General Edmund Hogan and Colonel A. S. Walker. He was too good a Baptist to be a good politician and lost out. In those days it was not much of a recommendation for a politician to be a church member, and the Baptist church did not look with favor upon its members running for office. The same may be said of the other churches. The change between that time and today is no better marked in any particular than in this. In 1827, Governor Adair of Kentucky, visited the Hot Springs and was entertained by Major Watkins at his residence in Little Rock most sumptuously. Governor Adair commanded the regiment in which Major Watkins held a commission.

MAJOR WATKINS WAS ASSASSINATED IN M'LANE'S STORE.

In December, 1827, while Major Watkins was seated in McLane's general store in Little Rock, a man named John Smith, with a rifle on his shoulder, walked in and began talking with the proprietor. Having thus engaged his attention, Smith deliberately turned, brought his rifle to a charge, and fired its contents into the body of Major Watkins, who sat not ten feet away. Major Watkins died within an hour. In the excitement following the shooting, Smith passed out the front door, leaped on his horse and rode toward Crystal Hill. He passed the night with General Hogan, who knew nothing of the shooting, and in the morning rode to the south. The posse following Smith did not discover until morning that he had ridden toward Crystal Hill, and when it reached there Smith was well out of the way. A reward of five hundred seventy-five dollars was offered for the apprehension of Smith, but he was never arrested. W. E. Woodruff of the Gazette, after stating that Watkins was one of the first permanent settlers of Little Rock, went on to say that beyond all question he had done as much for the improvement of Little Rock as any other man. It appeared that on the preceding day Watkins had been to his plantation and had found that some of his stock was missing. He traced it to the cabin of John Smith, found the dead carcass of one of his hogs, and immediately charged Smith with the theft. Smith did not resent it then, but took his revenge as we have stated.

HIS DESCENDANTS PROMINENT.

Major Watkins was married twice, both times in the State of Kentucky, His first wife was Paulina Thurston, who died shortly after giving birth to a son, who afterwards became Doctor Robert Anderson Watkins of Little Rock, and who on June 28, 1827, married Mary W. Nash, daughter of Doctor John T. Nash of Florissant, Missouri. Robert A. Watkins, was the first secretary of State under the new constitution, serving from September 16, 1836, to November 12, 1840.

Major Watkins took for his second wife Marie Toncre of Kentucky, a lady of Huguenot extraction, and who came with him to Arkansas. The children of this marriage were: Honorable George Claiborne Watkins, who became chief justice of the supreme court of Arkansas, and Mary Eliza Watkins. George Claiborne Watkins married Mary A. Crease, the third daughter of John H. Crease, State treasurer of Arkansas, and Jane P. Newton, his wife. Mary Eliza Watkins married John J. Clendennin, afterward one of the supreme judges of the State of Arkansas.

When Major Watkins moved to Arkansas he brought with him Miss Mills, a neice of his wife, who on November 14, 1827, became the wife of William E. Woodruff, Sr., the editor and founder of the Arkansas Gazette.

After the death of Major Watkins, his wife remarried, her husband being Reverend W. W. Stevenson, a pioneer Methodist preacher at Little Rock, but who afterwards joined the Christian church, becoming a noted minister therein. Mrs. Stevenson died at the residence of her son-in-law, Judge Clendennin, on the 21st of March, 1874, in the eighty-first year of her age, having lived in Little Rock continuously for fifty-four years, a longer continuous residence than any other citizen before her time, and, in all probability, since her time. Her husband died in California in his eighty-ninth year. Mrs. Stevenson was one of the best women who ever lived in Little Rock. She was first last and all the time a Christian, and her home was at all times a home of missions and for all the ministers of all denominations. When the Scientist, Featherstonaugh, was in Little Rock in 1838, he found no place of public lodgment at all suitable for a gentleman. Mrs. Stevenson, hearing of his dilemma, threw open her house to him, where for several months he prosecuted his studies, leaving a high testimonial to the admirable good character and magnificent womanhood of Mrs. Stevenson. Such is a brief record of the antecedents of Chief Justice George Watkins, possibly the ablest man that Arkansas has produced.

The following is taken from the files of an old newspaper:

"Died. In this city on the morning of the 21st of March, 1874, at the residence of her son-in-law, Judge Clendennin, Mrs. Maria Stevenson in the eighty-first year of her age.

"This brief notice records the death of the oldest female resident of our city. For fifty-four years she has been a continuous resident of Little Rock, and during all that long period she graced the community by her hospitalities, blessed the poor with her charities, and the stricken in sorrow and affliction with her love and advice. Enjoying through most of her long life uninterrupted health and favored with more than an ordinary intellect, she met the troubles and trials of her early frontier life with firmness and fortitude and was able to assist, counsel and advise those who sought her in their troubles; always a Christian, her house was the home of the mission and the ministers of all denominations. She lived to see her children and children's children grow up around her, anxious to minister to her wants, and surrounded by them she calmly passed away to the rest prepared for those who here have so well done the Master's will.

"Mrs. Stevenson was born in Williamsport, Maryland, in 1793, and when quite young moved with her parents to Kentucky where she married Major Isaac Watkins, of Shelby County, with whom she and her infant son, the late Judge George C. Watkins, and her niece, Mrs. Woodruff, the wife of the venerable William E. Woodruff, resided. In 1820, she removed to Little Rock where she had always since lived."

CHAPTER XXIX.

Slave Holders of 1830.

It is a most interesting study to connote the rise of the slave interest in the United States. From a few squalid slaves planted on the shores of New England in the earliest days of the colonies, the institution spread Southward, hunting a more congenial clime, until, after a century, its habitat was found in the Southern States, and its quasi enemies in the original New England States. The inhospitable climate of New England did not favor slave labor, nor did its more inhospitable shores. The more generous climate of the South, coupled with its lands of superabundant fertility, made that region a heaven for not only slave owners, but for the slaves.

It is a waste of time at this day to discuss or even seem to discuss the advantage of slavery to such negroes as were caught up in Africa and subjected to its malign influences in the American colonies. The negro of America today is the product of slave institutions, and by as much as he surpasses any set of negroes in his original African home, by that much is he indebted to American slavery. I have met negroes in all parts of the world, negroes who had slave antecedents and negroes who had not; the American negro of slave antecedents is immeasurably superior to all these and infinitely superior to his brethren that he left in Africa two hundred years ago.

Slavery may be illogical; it may be inhumanitarian; it may be against all conscience, propositions I do not care to discuss, but, it certainly prepared the American negroes for higher estates than have been held by the negroes of any other country, taking the negro of a country as a whole. They have improved in language; they have improved in dress; they have improved in manner of living, although there is yet a tremendous room for improvement; they have improved in mentality; they have improved in business relations, and high and above all other things, they have improved morally and spiritually. Give the devil his dues. Let slavery be crowned king of African development, so far as the same gives evidence in American affairs, and let the old slave-driver, the schoolmaster of African civilization, hard-hearted though he may have been, be given a crown of laurels for the absolute success of his work.

No set of schoolmasters that the world has known has done as much for a race as the African slave-drivers of the South did for the African race. The African was made in every respect more decent, more respectable, more lovable, more able to do a man's work in the race of life, although the Republican party emancipated him a trifle too soon, a few minutes before the hatching bird would have pipped the shell for itself, and emerged a thoroughly self-respecting bird. As it is, the African is puzzled to know whether he owes most to his old owner or to the Republican party. The Republican party freed him, the slave owners of America gave him whatever parts he possessed which entitled him to freedom. The mere ipse dixit of a party cannot confer manhood; the antecedent elements of manhood, wherever they may be found in the American African race, must be sought for in the Anglo-Saxon homes of the South, among its educated men and its eminently lovable women.

NORTHERN OVERSEERS HARD TASKMASTERS.

It is a well-known fact that the hardest slave-drivers were the overseers and that the kindliest friends the slaves had were the masters and mistresses. As a rule the overseers were either Northern men or men of Northern antecedents. They are and always have been the best bosses of human labor, getting more out of it on harsher terms than any bosses of the world, and they are now bossing the white labor of America with the same inexorable fatality that they bossed the slave labor in the good old days before the war. They were conscienceless. They made the negroes work, and the best paying plantations were those in the hands of Northern overseers. All such plantations were detested by the Southern slaves. They hated to be bought by a Southern slave owner who maintained a Northern overseer. They traveled from master to master when their own masters were in bankruptcy asking them to buy them and promising the most faithful service. The reason for their importunity was that if they were not so bought that other slave owners with a Northern overseer would certainly get them, and these poor darkies hesitated to fall into his hands.

But the great majority of the Southern slave-owners were either their own overseers, or had Southern overseers, or had even negro overseers. That old pioneer, Titsworth, of Logan County, Arkansas, owned between one hundred and two hundred negroes, and was a very prince of good fellows. His own negroes loved him, and all the negroes of the surrounding plantations when they had to be sold, surreptitiously sought out Titsworth and begged him to save them from the fiendish hands of the Northern overseers. To the credit of Titsworth be it said, that he always gave the negroes a squarer deal than Roosevelt or any other Republican has ever given them since. Titsworth's plantation was a very Eden for the negroes, and the slaves he owned had much more nearer a heaven on earth than any other negroes have had at any other time or place before or since. When you are hunting for old-time men who have done something for humanity in the largest and best sense write down Titsworth's name of Logan County. He was a man among men, the equal of any other man, whether his name was Roosevelt, Taft or Bryan.

The whole South was full of Southern great hearts like Titsworth, who put to blush John Temple Graves, the great orator of Georgia, who reasons with his tongue and not with his brain, and who seems to think that Roosevelt is in love with the South, when, in fact, Roosevelt knows no god but himself. Roosevelt hates the old slave-holders and holds himself immensely their superior. As a matter of fact, as men ran then, the old slave-holders of the South had no superiors. They were honest; they were truthful; they were full of the milk of human kindness; they gave every man a square deal in reality and not ostensibly as a mere party pretext; they were clean; they led a clean government and gave the world its finest examples of integrity, leadership and honor. All hail the old-time Southern slave owner, not only for what he was himself, and for what he made his family, and for what he made the old South, but for what he made of the negro himself. When the honors are divided by a just judge the old Southern slave-holder will get so much that the frazzle that is left will not hurt the other fellows.

SLAVES OF PULASKI COUNTY.

The Fletcher family, consisting of Richard M., Henry L., Frederick and John, in 1830 owned thirty-three slaves, a greater number than that owned by any other family in the county. Do family traits inhere? Is it worth while to study family history? Is there any reason why a family should be great in one age and weak in another? There are reasons and they can only be ascertained by a comprehensive system of family history. Why should the Fletchers be great in 1800? Why should they be the most solid people of the country in 1830? Why should they hold their own in 1870 and give Arkansas two as solid men as it has today? Why are the Fletchers still solid today? Only a most comprehensive study of sociology and family history can in any sense answer these questions.

The greatest individual slave holder of Pulaski County in 1830 was Benjamin Trotter, who held twenty-three slaves in his own right, and was everywhere known as the most humane slave owner. If any of Trotters negroes are alive today they are entitled to be heard, and if all the good things that happened on Trotter's estate had been told with reference to the negroes alone several books as large as the Bible would have been required. Old Ben Trotter was one of the makers of Pulaski County, a tremendous factor in the development of Arkansas.

The next greatest slave-holder of Arkansas territory was Judge Benjamin Johnson, who owned twenty-one slaves, one-half of them being under fifteen years of age. A negro from one to fifteen years of age was worth all the way from one hundred dollars to one thousand dollars, while a negro from fifteen to forty was worth from one thousand dollars to three thousand dollars. Is it any wonder that the negroes themselves who brought three thousand dollars on the block should hold themselves superior to the poor white trash who could not earn fifty cents a day?

The next greatest slave owner in Pulaski County was Lawyer John H. Cocke, who owned fourteen, and Samuel Taylor who owned the same number.

The Lindsey family came next, having thirteen negroes, and these Lindseys, sons of old Caleb Lindsey, of Virginia, spelled their name in the good old-fashioned way, with an "e" and not an "a." More great Lindseys in England today spell their name this way than the other, but this is all a matter of taste. The Lindsey negroes, however, were a matter of dollars and cents.

AMBROSE SEVIER'S RAPID RISE.

Standing next below the Lindseys stood old Archibald McHenry and James Walker, with twelve negroes each, and mighty fine negroes they were. All near the two thousand dollar mark. Then came the Honorable Ambrose H. Sevier, with eleven slaves in 1830. In 1820 he came to Arkansas a poor, friendless orphan boy; in 1830 he was a good lawyer, a delegate to Congress, the son-in-law of Ben Johnson, and the owner of eleven slaves. A pretty good march for a poor boy in ten years. True, his slaves were for the most part under fifteen years of age, being household maids for the most part, and it may be true that old Ben Johnson gave him the most of these, but they were Sevier's negroes all the same, and he took all the glory and honor for them. Ben Johnson's negroes were Kentucky negroes, and were in a sense F. F. V's., but none of the Arkansas negroes ever yielded precedence to them. It was said that one of McHenry's negroes could whip any five of Johnson's negroes, but that they were afraid to do it lest the judge should get the law on them.

The following persons in Pulaski County in 1830 each had nine negroes: Elinor Lockhart, Wharton Rector and John Pope. The following had eight: Robert Crittenden, James Lemon, George W. Scott and John Evans. The following had seven: Nicholas Peay, Allen Martin, John D. Mosby and David Rorer. The historian who made Judge David Rorer an example of the happy-go-lucky kind seems to have reckoned without his host. In this way a large lot of veritable history, so-called, is made.

Old David Rorer ranked with the elite in 1830, and would rank there yet were he alive to row his own boat. I have skipped another old Pulaski County slave-holder, Samson Gray, the son of a Revolutionary soldier and who had eleven negroes. Quite a number of Pulaski County citizens owned five negroes or less. Chester Ashley owned three under fifteen years of age, and had one free negro in his family, thirty-five years of age. Billy Woodruff, Sr., owned three, all under fifteen years of age, which shows that Arkansas citizens from Long Island and Massachusetts were not ashamed of the peculiar Southern institution, and owned slaves and treated them equally as humanely as the manufacturers of Long Island and Massachusetts treat their employes in factories and manufacturing establishments. If any of the old negroes belonging to any of these old men of Pulaski County are alive I should be pleased to hear from them, in order to gather from their lips a few more ideas of the grandly good old times in Arkansas from 1830 to 1890.

CHAPTER XXX.

THE FLETCHERS.

In the Review of Reviews for November, 1907, is a picture of Horace Fletcher, in turn whaler, explorer, miner, sharpshooter, gymnast, merchant, traveler, philosopher, philanthropist, author and originator of "Fletcherism," or how to eat so as to live royally, which book every dyspeptic should read, and which picture every one interested in the inhering likenesses descending to members of the same family even after all trace of the relationship is lost, should see. My object in adverting to this picture is primarily to call attention to the heredity of family likeness, although the common ancestor may have lived three hundred years ago, and his descendants, widely scattered, may be unable to trace any tie of kin or bond of family union; and, secondarily, to animadvert upon the superior claims of common sense over legislative control, or pure food laws, in securing and maintaining a proper degree of health.

When I opened the Review of Reviews last November and let my eye fall upon the picture of Horace Fletcher, my mind at once recalled "Uncle Tom Fletcher" of Little Rock. The likeness was not only faithful, but singularly striking. My mind soon corrected this impression by a glance of the eye at the signature beneath the picture, and from a reading of the accompanying matter. Had there been nothing but the picture, however, I am of opinion that I should have called it the picture of Thomas Fletcher, despite the plug hat on the table and one or two other minor details.

PIONEERS AND MAKERS OF ARKANSAS.

To show how strong this likeness really was, I covered up the signature and submitted the picture to my wife, who at once said: "What a fine picture of Uncle Tom Fletcher!" Stranger than this, it so happened, that John Fletcher, the distinguished son of Thomas Fletcher, dropped into my office in Washington, and I made the same test upon him. Now John Fletcher is one of the most modest men in the world, more is the pity, and he hesitated; that hesitancy proved to me that he, too, was just ready to say: "How did the picture of my father get into this book?" His controlling modesty produced by the fear of being vain, led him to say: "The face is familiar to me," and I said, "Oh pshaw!" John laughed. He then pointed out to me minute points of pose, facial resemblance and other particulars common to his father and to the picture, which led me to see that he saw the striking resemblance of the picture to his father, but like a good lawyer, would not commit himself.

STRIKING FAMILY LIKENESS.

I have also been informed that Honorable Thomas Fletcher of Pine Bluff, erstwhile acting governor of Arkansas, bore a most marked resemblance to Uncle Tom Fletcher of Little Rock. Here are two strong sets of facts of family likenesses, or inhering resemblances in families of the same name, yet claiming no kin, and these facts prove a kinship of nearer or remoter degree. In the matter of Thomas Fletcher of Pine Bluff there is an explanation, based on a much nearer kinship to Thomas of Little Rock than any that can be suggested as to Horace Fletcher. Thomas Fletcher of Pine Bluff, erstwhile acting governor, descended from the Fletchers of middle Tennessee, remotely connected to all branches of the various Arkansas Fletcher lines. Joshua and Peter Fletcher, brothers, entered Arkansas in 1811, and settled on the Mississippi river, in what is now Mississippi County. Peter Fletcher remained where he settled and became the head of a prominent family in that county, one of whom became prominent in the legislative history of the State. Joshua Fletcher for some cause left Arkansas and moved across the river in 1819 into what is now Shelby County, and held many positions of county honor in his new home. He was a member of the first Grand Jury that ever convened in that county, and was a respectable citizen in every particular. The land archives of the government show that Joshua Fletcher actually made his settlement in Mississippi County, Arkansas, in 1802; that he abandoned it in 1806, and returned to it in 1811, leaving it finally for Tennessee in 1819.

In 1815 John Gould Fletcher settled on Fourche de Thomas, Lawrence County, now Randolph, and died there in 1825. These old people doubtless knew their relationship to each other, but the younger descendants of the present day have lost the trace. The resemblance of Thomas Fletcher, grandson of John Gould Fletcher, to Thomas Fletcher, acting governor, and who hailed from middle Tennessee, proves a consanguineal relationship, and back in antiquity somewhere the ancestors of Horace Fletcher and of the Arkansas and Tennessee Fletchers unite to form one line. I have not traced Horace Fletcher's lineage sufficiently to even name an approximate time for this union. The Fletcher physiognomy, however, is so marked as to prove a family tie.

FLETCHERS DATE BACK TO 1620.

I am certain that no Lindseys were in Virginia on February 16, 1623, the date of the first census ever taken in America. It is interesting to note that this most venerable roll shows John and Richard Fletcher as among the living at that date, and what is more valuable as separating the Baldwins in Connecticut from those of Virginia, is the fact that Thomas Baldwin was then living at Jordan's Point, Hugh Baldwin on the Main, John Baldwin at Jamestown.

Thomas and two William Baldwins at Elizabeth City. On the roll of Virginia adventurers made up in London in 1620 stands the name of John Fletcher, contributing fifty pounds sterling and John Fletcher & Company, seventy-five pounds sterling. Thus the Fletchers and Baldwins connect themselves with the oldest American colony and the first settlement of America. Old Isaac Baldwin of Pulaski County, 1820, is very probably a descendant of these Jamestown Baldwins.

Lawrence County presented many attractions to settlers seeking new homes in the early part of the last century. That two days work in the Arkansas district would contribute as much to the support of a family as a week would do in the North and East was prevalently believed at that time, and had much to do with the migration of the period. Another element which had a large effect on the Tennessee migration was the excitement in that State over the removal of the Cherokees to the West. Indian agents told great stories of the St. Francis, the Black and the White river regions to the Indians in Tennessee and North Carolina, and young Tennesseeans hearing these stories took dogs and guns and started on exploring expeditions. Returning, they had still larger stories to tell which resulted in whole families pulling up stakes and starting for Arkansas. They were either Indian fighters or sons of Indian fighters and were inured to the hardships of hunting, trapping and fighting. For twenty years Middle and East Tennessee had gone through the horrors of Indian butcheries, and the cessation of hostilities brought such a stagnation as to cause many of the more hardy ones to want to move. In other cases, the emigrant wanted to find a region where there were not so many people, where they could have more elbow room.

HENRY LEWIS FLETCHER.

This man, born on the Watauga in 1788, entered Arkansas before 1815 and settled on Bayou De Mun in Lawrence County. Along with him came his father, John Gould Fletcher, who died in what is now Randolph County in 1825 or 1826, in his sixty-sixth year. The father of John Gould Fletcher was Richard Fletcher, of the Washington district on Watauga, who was a pioneer in that region. The pioneers of Arkansas never underwent the privations and horrors that the pioneers of East Tennessee had to undergo. In 1779 men from Virginia, Maryland, Pennsylvania and North Carolina began to settle on Watauga, where for thirty years they had to fight for their lives. They were cut off from the protection of the colonial governments and in self-defense formed governments of their own. In 1775 the Washington District of Tennessee had all the forms of an independent government and addressed a petition to the Assembly of North Carolina reciting that they had organized a government; that they had sent troops eastward to help the colonies' in their affairs and had directed other troops to quell the Indians. The petition respectfully asked to be made a part of North Carolina, and to be given a chance to aid that colony repel British aggressions. This petition is marked "Filed July 20, 1776," and it must have been prepared early in that year. About one hundred names are affixed to it, among them being those of John Sevier, Valentine Sevier, and the ancestor of our Arkansas family, Richard Fletcher.

In the next session of the North Carolina Assembly, later in 1776, Washington District was represented by delegates, so that this petition had its effect. This government must not be confounded with the State of Franklin, formed on the same grounds by the same men later on. It was a government, however, which stood for American Independence, and the action of these signers contributed to the success of the American arms.

The Watauga settlement is the only settlement in the United States where a Tory was not permitted to live. Richard Fletcher was one of the original patentees to lands on the Watauga in 1775. It is said that every able-bodied man on Watauga rode with Sevier to King's Mountain, but I have not been able to find the muster roll of the heroes.

In all probability Richard Fletcher was one of them, and it is certain that Surgeon David Gould, father of Richard Fletcher's wife, was a member of the Virginia Continental Line. Others of the name from the mountain regions of North Carolina who participated in that war were Thomas Fletcher, John Fletcher, Reuben Fletcher, Nathan Fletcher, William Fletcher and Abner Fletcher. What relationships these bore to Richard Fletcher,

I can not say, but in all probability the relationship was close, as they all hailed from the same region. Richard Fletcher died and was buried on the Watauga; John Gould Fletcher, probably the revolutionary soldier named above, died in Arkansas and was buried on the De Mun; Henry Lewis Fletcher, born 1788, died in Arkansas, and was buried on the Saline in 1840, leaving children, Thomas, Henry L., John G., Jeff L., Richard, and several others most prominently identified for fifty years with every interest of the State. Henry Lewis Fletcher, Sr. married in 1815, Mary, daughter of Caleb Lindsey, a Kentucky pioneer, on De Mun, and very probably the first old field school teacher of the State, as his brother, Eli, was the first local preacher of the Methodist church in Arkansas, beginning on Strawberry in October, 1815.

FLETCHERS IN PULASKI BEFORE 1830.

The census of 1830 shows Henry Lewis Fletcher a resident of Pulaski County, with one person in the family from forty to fifty years of age, one from thirty to forty, six children and eight slaves. This put upon his shoulders the responsibility for the support of a family of sixteen persons. Men of Arkansas for the last fifty years have mingled with the sons of this old pioneer and are in condition to estimate his mental and physical vigor. Figs do not grow on thorns, nor do such men as the later Fletchers come from insignificant ancestors. The vigor of the old Watauga struggles was perpetuated in the lives of the grandsons and great-grandsons. Strong men do not come from castles alone. The cabins of the West have been splendid hives for thousands of our best moral, mental and physical leaders.

In the same census there was Thomas M. Fletcher, born between 1800 and 1810, with a family of three children, all living in Pulaski County. Eli Fletcher, born in the same period, with a wife and one child, lived in the same township. Richard Fletcher, born between 1790 and 1800, with a wife and six children, lived near. I suppose these were all brothers of old Lewis H. Fletcher and sons of John Gould Fletcher, the pioneer in the cabin on the De Mun.

Away up in Randolph County at the same time lived John Fletcher, born between 1780 and 1790, with a wife and seven children. This John was either the eldest of old John Gould Fletcher's children or the second child. Near him lived Levi Fletcher, born between 1800 and 1810, with a wife, no children and two slaves. Thus of all the progeny of John Gould Fletcher, a great and mighty race, there were but two who owned slaves in 1830, Henry L. Fletcher of Pulaski County and Levi Fletcher of Randolph County.

Just who Captain Fred Fletcher of Old Crawford County was, I cannot say, but he was surely a descendant of John Gould Fletcher. He lived around Cadron and organized a company of cavalry in the spring of 1824 for Indian activity.

When John Gould Fletcher left the Watauga Settlement he went to Stewart County, Tennessee. There his son John married a Skinner, a daughter of the proprietor of a very extensive iron works which flourished there in that day. In that neighborhood the Fletchers and Lindseys began to intermarry, and in the after migration to Christian County, Kentucky, and to Randolph County, Arkansas, went together. Caleb Lindsey, the father of Mary Lindsey, who married Henry L. Fletcher, had in addition to Mary, six other children; Betsy, who married Martin Fletcher, a brother of Henry L. Fletcher, and who died in Pulaski County in December, 1826, Abijah Davis and Richard Fletcher administering upon his estate; John Young Lindsey, who married Jennie Davis; Agnes Lindsey, who married Richard Fletcher, another brother of Henry L. Fletcher; Sally Lindsey, who married Will Williams; Caleb Lindsey, who married Rebecca Brilhardt, and another daughter who married Doctor Hoover at Davidsonville, in 1824. Henry Lewis Fletcher died in Saline County in 1855. Caleb Lindsey, Sr., died in Pulaski County in November, 1826, Sarah Lindsey and John Y. Lindsey administering.

The sons of Henry Lewis Fletcher were Thomas, John Gould, Henry Lewis, Richard, Jefferson L. and Martin Franklin.

Martin Franklin Fletcher died several years ago in Camden leaving a son, Wiley Lewis Fletcher who married Pauline O'Connell, and had one daughter, Olivia Fletcher, who is now the wife of C. W. Cherry of Little Rock. Upon the death of

Wiley Lewis Fletcher, his widow, Mrs. Pauline Fletcher, became the wife of Dr. Lindsey of Little Rock.

THE LATE THOMAS FLETCHER.

Of the sons of old Henry Lewis Fletcher, Thomas was next to the eldest, having been born in Arkansas on the De Mun, April 8, 1817, dying in Little Rock in February, 1900, being eighty-three years of age, all of which were spent on Arkansas soil. Who will write the biography of Uncle Tom Fletcher? There is no one better fitted for the task than his gifted son, John, the attorney in Little Rock. To write that history will be to write almost all the history of Arkansas, but there has been no character on Arkansas soil more worthy of an extended biography. Born in Randolph County in 1817, he came with his parents into Pulaski County in 1825. The old homestead was cut off by the legislature into Saline County in 1835, but in 1844, after his marriage to Lucinda Beaver of Henderson County, Kentucky, Uncle Tom moved into Pulaski County, where he remained until his death. He served as sheriff of Pulaski County from 1858 to 1862, and in 1862 was sent to the State legislature; was a member of the Confederate legislature in 1864, and in 1866 was re-elected sheriff of Pulaski County; licensed to practice law in 1868, and candidate for the Democratic nomination for governor in 1878. It was in this race that Uncle Tom disposed of one of his opponents by a fatherly shake of the head and the words: "As to my friend, Smithee, he's young; he can afford to wait." To which Smithee innocently retorted: "True, I can afford it, but that is not the question. Can Arkansas afford it?" As an appointee of President Cleveland, he served as United States marshal for the Eastern District of Arkansas with credit to himself and to the administration. No more vigorous man ever lived in the State, and he will forever remain a fine type of the old regime of honest, earnest, able men.

Lucinda Beaver, wife of Thomas Fletcher, was a daughter of Stephen Beaver, born February 10, 1823, in Lincoln County, Tennessee. Stephen Beaver entered Tennessee in the first decade of the nineteenth century from Beaver County, Pennsylvania. Two other daughters of this old couple married Arkansas gentlemen, Sarah and Nancy; Sally marrying John Moose, becoming the head of the noted family at Morrillton, and Nancy who married John Milner and became the head of a family in South Arkansas. The wife of Stephen Beaver was Nancy White, whose father, as well as Stephen Beaver, are said to have been soldiers in the Revolutionary War. The children of Thomas Fletcher and Lucinda Beaver who lived to rear families were five in number:

1. Henry Lewis Fletcher, who married Cumi Smith, and had two children, Thomas Milton Fletcher, a physician at Paris, Arkansas, and Mary C. (Fletcher) Daniel, who lives at Palarm, Arkansas.

2. Richard Fletcher, deceased, who married Lillie Dea Butler, and had three children; Elizabeth married Allen Johnson, who died leaving a daughter, Elizabeth; James Richard Fletcher, who married Mary Collins in October, 1907, and Lillie Dea Fletcher, who married Mr. W. C. Cherry of Nashville, Tennessee, in June, 1907.

3. John Fletcher, attorney at Little Rock, who married Mary Emily Moose, a granddaughter of John and Sally (Beaver) Moose, and had one son, Thomas. They reared another boy, Ellis Ford.

4. Nancy A. Fletcher, who married J. B. Miles, and died leaving a daughter, Nancy, who married W. M. Tatum, and became the mother of several children.

5. Caleb Lindsey Fletcher married Elizabeth Medlock, and died leaving one daughter, Alma Elizabeth Fletcher, who is still unmarried, and living in the old homestead at Ninth and Cumberland, in Little Rock.

Richard Fletcher served in the Sixth legislature from Pulaski County, with Charles P. Bertrand and Peter L. Crutchfield as associates. He was then sent to the Senate and served through the Eighth and Ninth legislatures. Jefferson and Henry never sought office, but were fine types of manly citizens. Henry Lewis, Jr., born in 1833, married Susan Bricelin in Pulaski County and died in 1896, his wife being still alive. Her father was Milo Bricelin and her mother, Pamelia Baldwin, a daughter of Isaac Baldwin of Pulaski County. I was well acquainted with Henry L. Fletcher, Jr., and have known no man for whom

I had a higher regard. His daughter, Mary Pamelia Fletcher, is one of the best women of Little Rock.

John G. Fletcher was possibly the most prominent banker the State has ever had, and was most prominently connected with every great enterprise that had for its object the permanent uplift of the State. This is a short resume of the Fletcher family from 1770 to the present time. It is a clean, refreshing record of the Wataugan principle, "Independent thinking coupled with a clean life, leads to competence here and happiness hereafter."

THE LEWIS FAMILY OF LAWRENCE COUNTY.

The career of John Gould Fletcher, who died in Randolph County in 1825 or 1826, is not fully developed. Its greater part was spent in the mountain fastnesses of western North Carolina, southwestern Virginia and east Tennessee. He was probably in the Revolutionary war and was certainly connected with all the Indian struggles on Watauga. He saw his brother, Thomas, scalped by Indian savages, together with his nephew, Thomas, and had ground into him the principles of an actual struggle for existence which developed all the latent powers of manhood. He married a Lewis, one of the family that for heroism and privation stands unequaled in historic fact. When the sentimental and fictitious strenuosity of Theodore Roosevelt shall have been forgotten the strenuous lives of the Lewises will remain. Five statues of the Lewis men adorn the Washington monument in Richmond, Virginia, and all Virginia, Kentucky, North Carolina and Tennessee history abounds with their names. The battle of Point Pleasant, in Virginia, is a monument to the courage and leadership of five Lewis boys.

John Gould Fletcher married into this family on the Watauga, and in that neighborhood spent the greater part of his married life. In that neighborhood in 1772 the family of William Lewis, consisting of himself, his wife and five children, were brutally murdered by the Indians. Two small children, a boy and a girl, were carried into captivity and afterwards ransomed by the pioneers of the Watauga. Thirteen of the Lewis family were in the Revolutionary war from North Carolina and more than twice that number from Virginia. The old town of Davidsonville in Lawrence County was laid off by the descendants of the Tennessee Lewis family, and the blood of the family is carried by more than a thousand of Arkansas' sons and daughters.

CHAPTER XXXI.

Edmund Hogan.

The Hogan family dates back in Georgia history to the ante-revolutionary days, and the father of Edmund Hogan, the subject of our sketch, was a wealthy and prominent Georgian during the Revolution and the days that followed. Both he and his son were members of the Georgia legislature, and Edmund was a brave soldier in the war of 1812. In 1817, before the creation of Pulaski County, Edmund Hogan removed from Georgia to the Territory of Missouri, and settled in what is now Pulaski County, at Crystal Hill. He brought with him several slaves and a large amount of money. In fact he was reputed in the earlier days of the county to be one of its richest men, but owing to his generous disposition and the numerous land suits engaged in by him he had lost at the time of his death a large amount of his wealth. He bought the pre-emption claims of Thomas Pharr, near the lands located by John Carnahan, and erected thereon a fine residence and numerous other buildings. It was the handsome residence of Edmund Hogan, as well as the fine elevation of Crystal Hill that led Governor Miller to make his residence at that place, and to urge it as the most suitable location for the capital of the State.

Edmund Hogan was the first justice of the peace appointed by the authorities of the Territory of Missouri in Pulaski County upon the formation of that county in 1818, which position he held for many years thereafter under the laws of the Territory of Arkansas. In this capacity he celebrated many of the early marriages of the territory, the most prominent of which was that of Henry P. Pyatt, son of the pioneer, to Miss Carnahan, daughter of Rev. John Carnahan, the first Presbyterian preacher of the territory, on February 10, 1820. Crystal Hill was then the center of fashion and intelligence of Pulaski County, and also the center of the religious influences which even at that early date were beginning to permeate the territory.

BRIGADIER GENERAL OF ARKANSAS MILITIA.

Edmund Hogan in the war of 1812 made a good sollier, and when his record was presented to President Monroe, upon the death of Brigadier General Allen, he was appointed on March 24, 1821, as brigadier general of the Arkansas militia, which position he held until 1825, when he was succeeded by an appointee of President Adams, namely Brigadier General Bradford of the regular army, then stationed at Fort Smith.

General Hogan took great interest in his military position, and in conjunction with Governor Miller tried to bring the militia of the State to a high degree of perfection. He was not successful, however, save in towns like Arkansas Post and Little Rock. He made a fine appearance in his regimentals, as did the subordinate officers. At that time there were quite a number of soldiers who had served in the war of 1812 in the territory, and it may be said with a large degree of truth that the militia of the Territory of Arkansas from 1821 to 1825 was largely made up of this soldiery. The territory contained several men who had risen to the rank of colonel in that war, and hundreds who had been majors, captains or lieutenants. They were all of the Western type, free and easy in their manners, very outspoken in their conversation and therefore very hard to control. They were not bad men, but men of independence of character and very tenacious of their opinions. General Taylor of the regular army, or as he was familiarly called, "Old Rough and Ready" was of this type of men. When General Scott issued his tactics in 1835, or thereabouts, a copy was sent to all the inferior officers of the army, among whom was General Taylor. Taylor looked at it, turned over all its leaves and then remarked: "This is another of Scott's novels." He then pitched it into his trunk and commanded his army according to his own rules of warfare upon tactics which suited him and the soldiers of the West.

Hogan had considerable force of character, and being a superior soldier managed to control the combustible elements of which the militia was formed at that time, and to make of them most serviceable soldiers. They were never called into action, but had there been occasion, Hogan's soldiers would have made a record. Hogan also had to contend with numerous land claimants, whose attorney was Colonel A. S. Walker, a foe not unworthy the general's steel. Both men were given to bluffing to a large extent, but both were brave and true as steel. Hogan spent a large part of his money to defend his holdings and a still greater sum to maintain his position in the community according to his ideas of the demand of a gentleman and general. He entertained lavishly, and was one of the most popular men of early Arkansas history.

BITTER POLITICAL CAMPAIGN.

One of the most bitter contests known to Arkansas history occurred in 1825, when Colonel A. S. Walker was pitted against General Edmund Hogan for a seat in the council of the Fourth Territorial Legislature. Invective was largely indulged in and feelings aroused, which were not quieted by time. By throwing out one township Hogan was declared elected by the narrow majority of thirteen; Walker would not stand for this and a new election was ordered in which Walker was elected. Many prominent citizens of the county were drawn into the controversy on one side or the other, and out of it grew the lamentable circumstances which led to the general's death. In the canvass for the legislature of 1827, three candidates were before the people, Colonel Walker, General Hogan and Judge Scott. Pretty much the same canvass was made this year as had been made two years before, except that the invective was greater and the atmosphere considerably hotter. Hogan was elected and everybody settled down to quiet life not thinking that a great tragedy was on the eve of enactment. So far as Walker was concerned he appears to have dropped out of the limelight, and Judge Scott to have taken his place. After the election was over the people resumed the usual tenor of their ways, and on the surface everything appeared quiet.

In 1828, on May 31st, a great public hanging occurred in Little Rock, at which men gathered from far and near. When the hanging was over the crowd dispersed, those living at a distance taking their horses and riding away. Judge Scott after witnessing the execution wended his way to the store of McLane & Badgett on the west side of Main street. Here surrounded by a number of Little Rock citizens he was discussing the circumstances of the hanging, when General Hogan entered the store.

The general was a man weighing nearly three hundred pounds, tall and straight as an arrow, and with a physique as powerful as that of a lion. He always made a fine appearance either on foot or on horseback, and was a man of almost superhuman strength. Judge Scott was a small man, not weighing more than one hundred and thirty pounds, and as weak as General Hogan was strong. Scott was a giant in mental furniture, but a weakling in the matter of physique. Nobody expected the difficulty, not even Hogan or Scott. The conversation went on, both Scott and Hogan taking part in it, at times, and neither showing any animosity one to the other. As conversations ordinarily do, this one soon diverged from the hanging to politics, and before the men knew it they were discussing the old Walker and Hogan race. This seemed to revive in the mind of General Hogan something that occurred in the triangular race between himself, Walker and Scott. He turned to Scott and accused him of writing a letter into one township derogatory to the character of Hogan. Scott at once informed the general that he had been misinformed. Hogan reiterated the statement and said that he believed that it was true. Scott denied it again, and remarked that if he made it as a statement of his own that it was false.

HOW HOGAN MET HIS DEATH.

Both men were standing up. No sooner had Scott made the last remark than Hogan, with a powerful sweep of his arm, felled Scott to the floor, where for an instant he remained in an apparently senseless condition. As he revived he struggled to his feet, and Hogan squared himself for another blow. As Scott arose he very dextrously unsheathed a dirk from a sword cane which he carried, and before Hogan could strike the second blow, had plunged the dirk several times into the body of General Hogan. Hogan fell and expired within an hour. Everybody was amazed and likewise horrified. Judge Scott was arrested by his brother, United States Marshal George Scott, and taken before an officer for trial. The facts as stated above were there proven, and the court held Hogan to have been the aggressor and released Judge Scott. It was everywhere remarked that the blow of Hogan would have killed an ordinary man. Thus perished one of the oldest and best citizens of Pulaski County. Judge Scott, while regretting the circumstance, always held that he could not have done otherwise than he did. Both men were thoughtful, humane and most progressive citizens, and the entire community was shadowed with gloom over the lamentable affair. The residence of Hogan at Crystal Hill was noted by Nuttal in 1819, and from that time on until the date of his death was one of the best known residences in the county. William Hogan was married in Pulaski County on March 25, 1825, to Mary Rankin, but whether he was a son of General Hogan or not I am not informed.

General Bradford held the position of brigadier-general from 1825 until the date of his death in 1826, when he was succeeded by Colonel John Nicks of Crawford County. General Nicks was one of the strong characters of early Arkansas history. He represented Crawford County in the House of Representatives in the Third and Fourth legislatures, and was noted for his strong common sense and sterling courage.

CATERED TO ALL TASTES.

The first county seat of St. Francis County was called Franklin, and was located at a point which before that had been known as the "old Cherokee village." It was near the United States road from Memphis to Little Rock, and two miles from the St. Francis river. Its first public buildings were begun in 1832. The inducements offered by the people for settlers were two:

First—A respectable Bible Society for the improvement of those who felt desirous of promoting the cause of religion.

Second—A race course for the recreation of those who devote a portion of their time to the scenes of high life in connection with the respectable jockey club.

CHAPTER XXXII.

THE "TWO P" ARCHITECTURE—THE MARTINS.

One of the quaintest conceits of family history is the famous "Three Brothers Theory." One came over and settled in New England; another in Virginia, and the third further south. The conclusion drawn is that all of the name descend from these brothers. This is unmitigated bosh. Another is the Northern and Southern "branch" theories. This is greater bosh than the other. Every man of the name came over at any time formed the prepositus of the branch, and the branches do not descend from any one man in the North and another man in the South. I read a short time ago that all the Williams in the United States descended from some old emigrant up in Massachusetts. What humbug! There were at least five Williams in Virginia before the Mayflower ever came to the rock where—

> The Puritans landed and fell on their knees
> And then—on the Aborigines.

All of these Williams had families, and there is no proof that the original immigrants were related. So it is evident that there are several thousand Williams in the United States not descended from the New England stock, who can claim an older residence in America. I have spent eleven years on the Williams pedigree in order to gratify a certain fair lady who was born a Williams, but who in deference to me, changed her name to Shinn. After all sorts of investigation, running through years, I landed her line in unbroken continuity in an old log cabin of David Williams, Jamestown, Virginia, of 1609. There were other Williams' there then, viz.: Thomas of Jordan's Point Henry of the same place, Robert of the plantation above and

Rowland of Brick Row, and for one hundred years afterwards hardly a ship landed without one of the name, each becoming the prepositus of a line. Then after other years I ascertained that the David Williams of Jamestown, Virginia, was not the ancestor of my wife, but that another David of the eastern shore of Maryland of 1660 was the ancestor, which brought in another distinct line of ancient Williams. So of coats of arms. These are property and descend to the issue of the original grantees or creators. The collateral kin have no title whatever. If a coat of arms is two thousand years old, there is a greater possibility that all of the name may claim it, but it is not sure. One must prove his lineal descent from an armored ancestor before he can claim the arms. Then the coat of arms of a father may be changed by the son, and again by the grandson. All descendants of the father may claim his armorial bearings, but they may not claim those of the son or grandson.

ARKANSAS ARCHITECTURE.

Every age has produced an architecture, which in a sense characterizes the age and comes to the dignity of an order. The seven orders of ancient architecture have been made the theme of many articles and are well known, as is the Colonial style of early America. Not so well known, however, to the literary world, is the architectural order established by early Arkansas pioneers. It is hardly true that this order was the evolution of pure Arkansas thought since it found place everywhere in the Mississippi Valley. It has never been named, and for continuity of thinking I propose to label it the "Two P" order of architecture, the latest, if not the most prevalent style of house building. It derived its name from the significant fact that it consisted of two pens and a passage. Logs round or squared were notched and laid on each other until a pen of the required size was laid about eight feet high; then another pen was made about twelve feet from the first and built to the same heighth. Then longer logs were laid over both pens so as to make a passage between the pens. Then the whole edifice was covered with clapboards and the structure was complete. These houses were immensely popular and covered Arkansas in 1830. In one pen cooking and eating went on, and the other contained the piano and harpischord. The sitting room where melons were cut and horses swapped, was in the passage. The sleeping apartments were in the loft, reached by a cleat ladder on the sides of the pen. More great men and women of early times were reared in these double log pens with a passage than in castles or marble fronts. In fact a boy or a girl coming from these last establishments was looked upon as a doubtful quantity.

Then the furnishing of the pen and the passage was a triumph in every particular. Modern writers lampoon it for incongruity, but what of that? Are there no incongruities today? What relation does a Louis XIV set of exquisite chairs in a modern parlor bear to an antique oak dining room set? Or how connect a Brussels carpet with cheap plush parlor sets? What relation has a silver sugar bowl to a fifty cent set of plates? True there was incongruitiy in the old time houses, but let not the guilty descendants of their owners throw the first stones.

MUSIC OF THE THREE P'S.

In old times as you sat in the passage you heard the music of pigs, poultry and the piano. Horrid, you say! Well, I don't know. Many old pigs made better music than scores of modern pianos. Any old time piano player in the log cabins had the art of playing instead of thumping, and pigs and poultry ceased grunting and cackling to listen to the grander music. Our ancestors had cornmeal products side by side with custards. Our filet mignon de Meyerbeer combines the tenderloin with toad stools and chicken gizzards. In the old houses you could see sand, sawdust and silver, tubs, teapots and tapestry, metals, mosquitos and mahogany, gourds, gimlets and geraniums. Happy combinations! Wonderful ideas! In our modern style we combine saloons, saliva and sacristans; pewter, pomatum and priceless prints; feather beds and finger bowls; bats, balls and Bibles, and so on to the end.

OLD TIME MOTHER WIT.

In Conway County there happened to be a neighborhood of old timers who came in 1819; near by was another band of immigrants from Illinois who came in 1830. The first set having lived on the soil eleven years were natives and held their heads high above the other set. They had to worship God in the same house, but they sat on different sides. Sometimes the women met but they did not mix. They always clashed. One day an old maid from the Illinois set got out of humor and said: "You sisters on that side of the house are the most cantankerous people I ever saw. I have seen sassy people, but of all sassy people in the world Arkansassy people are the worst." Amidst loud applause from her side she sat down. Then another old maid from the other side got up and said: "I hate noisy people, and of all the noisy people in the world the Illinoisy ones are the worst." Great was the applause on the other side. Here we have the genesis of the modern womans' clubs of the State and their motive. The idea is always to do the other fellow before he does you, and if he does get his oar in first, come back with remark called for brevity, "The Retort Courteous."

The humor of the old Conway Club was that the young people of these two factions had to intermarry, and the children were not only "sassy" but "noisy," which accounts for a great deal of our modern history.

But mother wit was not confined to the female portion of the communities. Some of the boys had all of it, and their mothers very little. There was William R. Miller of Miller's Creek. He was born on the soil and was a holy terror as a boy. Some wise heads said "That he would come to no good end," while others said, "Pshaw, Bill Miller will be governor; mark my words." Now putting aside the reflection that the two remarks coincide, let us look for the future governor's style. In 1836 the Van Buren campaign was on and Bill Miller, a sixteen-year-old boy, seeing young Fent Noland, an ardent young Whig, approaching him on the boulevard of Batesville, yelled out:

"Hurrah for Van Buren."

Fent Noland immediately replied:

"Hurrah for a jackass."

To which the future governor roared:

"That's right Fent, you holler for your candidate, and I'll holler for mine."

This made Bill Miller the hero of the Democrats, and Fent Noland his life-long friend. Miller had to wait a long time for his reward as governor, but he finally made his mark.

OLD TIME CRITICAL ACUMEN.

In a newspaper of New York City, bearing date, 1822, I found an article which said that the editor of the Little Rock Gazette, William E. Woodruff, had criticized Noah Webster for putting the word "lengthy" in the dictionary. "What are we coming to?" asked Woodruff. "If the word is permitted to stand, the next edition will authorize the word 'strengthy.'" The New York journalist said that "Our contemporary in the Great West is right about the matter, but old Noah will have his way." One does not read far in Billy Woodruff's thesaurus of Arkansas happenings before he concludes that the editor was a most thoughtful man, and that his range of subjects were very great and his method of treatment original and profound. He educated a lot of Arkansas printers, who under the laws of nature came to have papers of their own and then turned upon the old man to rend him. He was as brave as Julius Cæsar, and was never the first to cry, enough.

OLD GAZETTE MARRIAGE POETRY.

The Gazette of May 29, 1839, contained the following:

"On May 28, 1839, Allen Martin of Pulaski County was married to Mahala Rowland, daughter of Thomas Rowland of Saline County, by Rev. J. W. Moore."

Then the Gazette followed with this gem of poetry, which the Martins may put in their scrap books, if they choose, and other benedicts may follow suit.

> Huzza for the married men true,
> Huzza for the men who have wives.
> It's better to stick to your dearie like glue
> Than single to live the days of your lives.
> So down with the bachelors, gloomy and sad,
> Up with the married men, merry and glad.

OLD PULASKI PIONEERS.

The Martins date back to 1817, coming in with that grand old guard "Rector's Surveyors." The family on Little Rock soil is older than Little Rock, and is a strong and reputable family today. It has been largely a family of surveyors and their work has established lines and monuments which in their totality make the security of Arkansas. A Martin married a Daniels, daughter of Wright Daniels, September 16, 1820, at Little Rock. Who this was I do not know. Certain it is that one Allen Martin was on the north side of Arkansas river in 1819, but whether he was the lucky man to marry this fair woman, I cannot say. Wright Daniels was one of the oldest settlers of Pulaski, a most industrious man, the owner of a grist mill, and the father of beautiful daughters. Jared C. Martin on January 25, 1827, married Mary, daughter of John Douglas. Here are two old Martin marriages, brothers, which form stems for two great families, James Martin died in 1826, and Martha Martin, his widow, and Allen Martin were appointed executors. This James may have been a brother of Allen and Jared C. Martin.

Ezekiel Douglas and his son, John, settled in Pyatt township, in 1819, but John Douglass in 1820 entered land five miles below Little Rock, at a time when only one log house stood where Little Rock now stands. At the same time, three Martins, known to be brothers, were in the neighborhood, Hutcheson, Allen and Jared C. Hutcheson ran a ferry boat and was probably the one that married a Daniels. This was James Hutcheson Martin, who in addition to running a ferry kept an inn on the north side of the river. He died in February, 1826, at the house of Reuben J. Blount, and his widow married Judge David Rorer in March, 1827. Allen and Jared C. erected a tombstone to Hutcheson in 1857. Allen Martin was county surveyor of Pulaski County from 1825 to 1830, and Jared C. Martin county treasurer from 1840 to 1842. Allen Martin was sheriff from 1836 to 1838, and member of Arkansas Legislative Council, 1831-33, while Jared C. Martin was member of the Arkansas legislature from 1842 to 1844. On September 13, 1829, a double funeral was preached at the house of David Rorer by Rev. S. T. Toncray, commemorative of the death of Wright Daniel and James Hutcheson Martin. There was a known fourth brother of Hutcheson, Allen and Jared C., named Andrew, who was judge at Jackson, Missouri, and who died there September 6, 1834, aged forty-two years. These old pioneers, Martin, Daniel and Douglas, have left a most honorable line of descendants, who still do honor to the State.

ALLEN MARTIN.

Since writing the above, I have received from Miss Mahala Isabella Martin of Midland, Texas, and a daughter of old Allen Martin, the following matter which I publish entire:

"Our father, Allen Martin, son of John Martin and Elizabeth (Allen) Martin, both from near Belfast, Ireland, was born in Washington County, Georgia, November 10, 1801.

"His father moved with the family to Louisiana territory and settled near Jackson, Cape Girardeau County, Missouri. In this new home Allen's father died in July, 1808, leaving him to work and study under the care of his mother until he was seventeen years old. That year, 1818, he, with his own chain, compass, etc., helped survey the route from Memphis, Tennessee, to Fulton, Arkansas, said route known as the military road. He then returned to his mother's home full of desire to come to Arkansas territory. About 1821, he and his brother, Jared Carswell Martin, came to Little Rock country, at that time only one little log cabin on the site of the now beautiful city of Little Rock, secured land round about what is now known as Mabelvale, made some improvements and returned to Missouri.

"Their mother moved with them to their new home one and one-half miles apart, and died in Allen's home in 1840 on the 28th of June—seventy five years old. Allen's first marriage was to Mahala Collins Rowland in 1839, May 28th. On July 17th, 1840, she died, leaving a son nine days old. He married (the second time) Maria Shackleford Rowland, who had cared for the little boy, John Rowland Martin, since her sister's death, this marriage occurring on May 24th, 1842.

"Allen Martin was a very accurate and successful civil engineer and sectionized a large part of the State of Arkansas, and was a trusted reference for facts and conditions all over the State of Arkansas as long as he lived. His memory was remarkably faithful, so much so that he could even recall different things he was doing the day his first wife was born.

"He and his brother, Jared, with whipsaws, sawed the necessary planks for flooring, doors, etc., needed in the construction of their log homes. They burned brick and built chimneys, some of which are still standing. In 1857, Allen with his family left the home of thirty-six happy years to move to Red River County, Texas, where he settled ten miles east of Clarksville.

"Allen was always full of public enterprise, ever doing something to help his neighbors and further the welfare of his community. He loved the Methodist church of which he was a faithful member from 1842 till his death in 1872."

This is a splendid letter and will be prized by not only the descendants of Allen Martin, but by all the descendants of old John and Elizabeth Allen Martin. It is incorrect in minor particulars. The military road was not established until 1824, and the road indicated by Miss Martin was the continuation of what was then called the military road from St. Genevieve, Missouri, to Little Rock, Arkansas, upon which work from Little Rock to Fulton, Allen Martin was engaged in 1818. He was afterwards employed in surveying Conway's military road, 1824-5, from Memphis to Little Rock.

There was another brother, John Martin, who entered Arkansas at a very early date and settled on Poke Bayou, fifteen miles from Batesville, where he lived until driven from home by the events of the Civil War, to the home of his daughter, Elizabeth Mahala Watkins, wife of Dr. Owen Watkins of La Crosse, Izard County, Arkansas. He died there in September, 1864, almost seventy-six years of age. When John Martin, the ancestor of this family left Georgia, the governor of that commonwealth in a testimonial under the State seal certified to the fair name of John Martin and stated that he was a faithful soldier in the war for American Independence. His sons, John Martin and James Hutcheson Martin, were volunteers in the war of 1812 and did honorable service for their country.

Jared Carswell Allen stuck to Pulaski County and left the following well-known descendants:

1. James Allen Martin, who married Huldah T. Toncray, daughter of Silas T. Toncray, the pioneer Baptist preacher. James Allen Martin was a material addition to the State's progress, and no history of value will ever omit his name. He was honest, just and courageous, and all religions were bettered by his existence. He belonged to the Christian Church, however, and that body of people throughout the State owe much to his consistency and general good character. He left three children to honor his name.

2. William Andrew Martin, who married Sue R. Hamlet and left three children.

3 Mollie Douglas Martin, who married James Jared Martin, her cousin, son of John Martin of Poke Bayou. I know no better law than the one that the husband is a full half of his wife, and following that law and speaking for my wife, I note Mollie D. Martin as one of the best of Little Rock's splendid women. There were five children of this marriage.

4. Jared Carswell Martin, who married Fanny Foy, daughter of William Foy. He has now three living children, one of which, Blanche, is a graduate of Vassar.

5. Henry Gibson Martin, who married Clara Davis, and though without children, are a couple standing among the very best of the citizenship of Little Rock.

I knew the descendants of Jared Carswell Martin, and without disparaging the merits of descendants of John and Allen, desire to say that, in my opinion, no better people ever lived.

Thomas Rowland was one of the pioneers, as was R. N. Rowland. The latter was county surveyor of Pulaski County from 1830 to 1832, and from 1836 to 1838. Thomas Rowland was a public spirited man and one of the incorporators of Benton Academy, Saline County. G. Douglass was county surveyor from 1838 to 1840, but of his relationship to Ezekiel Douglas, I am not advised.

CHAPTER XXXIII.

Henry L. Biscoe.

Are we wiser today than the pioneers? It is no answer to this to say that everybody finds it natural and easy to deplore and to denounce the errors and crimes of past times. But are we at the same time finding it easy and natural to abandon the prejudices and predispositions of today? What we do is right, because we are at the helm, but when we shall have passed away will not our very righteousness be condemned by those who follow us? In other words, have our heads grown larger or smaller during the century of our existence as a State?

Professor Carl Pearson and Dr. Bernard Hollander, together with various hat manufacturing establishments, say that our heads are larger today than they were one hundred years ago. This may be good news, and it may be bad news. There have been large heads in Arkansas which were admittedly good heads, a good example being that of Senator Garland. On the other hand, there have been large heads that were disappointing to say the least. It must be admitted that there have been a great number of small heads in Arkansas, who have really done wonders. It would be so manifestly unjust to particularize that we let it go at that. Roughly speaking, alertness of intellect belongs to the small head; profundity to the large head.

Admitting that exceptions abound, we would suggest that large heads are slow and sure, but there is no proof that we today have a greater number of these in proportion than had the pioneers. If the deliberations of large heads usually result in conclusions that are sound morally as well as logically, then large heads are just what Arkansas wants. No doubt the heads of a considerable section are today as they were in the past, far too small, as the historical expression "cymlin head," bandied in legislative halls and the newspapers, fairly proves. It is this section that has probably yielded measurements to the learned doctors and professors, to say nothing of the hatters, and if this is true the finding that heads are growing larger is absolutely good news, providing always that the skulls are not growing thicker.

AN OLD ARKANSAS PIONEER AT HELENA.

One of the earliest large heads to come to Arkansas was that carried on the shoulders of a young man from Richmond, Virginia, whose name was Henry L. Biscoe. He came early in 1819, before Governor Miller had reached the territory, and took residence at Arkansas Post, where he announced it as his intention to stay. He had no office under the government, nor did he seem to want one, although his life was checkered with office-holding years. His people, back in Virginia, were of the most respectable kind and his education had therefore been the most liberal. His career, however, had to be made, and Richmond at that time was crowded with well-educated, ambitious young men, who might and would win, but who would have to wait a very long time for their laurels. Elbow room is a great thing, and it is a sign of a great mind for a young man to decide that his home field is too crowded for his rapid development, and who casts aside his easier and more settled life for the greater and harder ordeals of a life in the woods.

Such a man was Henry L. Biscoe, who left Richmond soon after Congress had created the Territory of Arkansas for a home at Arkansas Post. He lived at Arkansas Post during the greater part of 1819, and in 1820 he divided his home between the Post and Clark County. There was some close connection between Clark County and Arkansas Post, not fully disclosed by the records. Why Jacob Barkman should maintain a home five miles from the Post, and another in Clark County is not now known, but the fact remains that he did. Colonel Walker was an Arkansas Post man as to residence, and at the same time sheriff of Hempstead County. S. M. Rutherford was a clerk for years at the Post, and maintained a home there even after opening an office in Clark. Sam C. Roane had a home at the Post, another in Clark, and still another in Pulaski. Henry L. Biscoe was appointed clerk of the Circuit Court of Clark County in 1820, which position he held until 1823 when he was appointed assistant United States Marshal. The town of Biscoeville was named for him in 1821.

HIS CAREER AS MARSHAL.

Mr. Biscoe was a man of indomitable courage and inured to every variety of hardships. One of the most picturesque and dangerous expeditions ever undertaken by an Arkansas official was one cast upon him while assistant marshal and which involved the arrest of a half-breed Indian, Tom Graves, who had violated the national law in Clark County and fled to the Indian reservation in the West. Believing that the Cherokees had grown contemptuous of the white courage, and that, if the law of the whites was to be vindicated, and the rule of the whites perpetuated, Biscoe held that a supreme example was necessary to impress the natives and prevent the recurrence of similar crimes, and that this half-breed should be brought back to Clark County and made to suffer the consequences of his acts. Biscoe prevailed and the old rule of "good riddance" as applied to a refugee was set aside and pursuit ordered. There were no Bertillon measurements then, no rogues' gallery of pictures, no telegraph lines, and no railway trains, and Biscoe had to seek his man as a dog hunts a rabbit. Biscoe set out for the West on a fine horse, being well armed. At Fort Smith he heard that his man was over in the Cherokee country to the east, as the Cherokees then inhabited nearly all of north Arkansas. He turned his steps toward the Cherokee country, where he arrived in good time to locate his man. He found him somewhat protected by the favor of the Cherokee chiefs and braves, and was told that it was dangerous to attempt an open arrest, as the unthinking Indians would certainly espouse the half-breed's cause. Biscoe sat down among the Cherokees to win their favor by a course which soon ingratiated him into the esteem of all the savages. Dressed in the moccasins and accoutrements of a trapper, Biscoe made a fine appearance, and his ready use of the rifle made the Cherokee braves his warm friends. Gaunt and thin of figure he would have arrested attention anywhere by the impressions he conveyed of endurance, skill and independence. He kept his eye on his man all the time, but did not disclose his mission. Warily he waited and at a favorable moment, when he was separated from his comrades by a distance they could not easily overcome he arrested him and hurried him, despite his bullying protestations to the Arkansas river, where he quickly crossed, and directed his movements toward Little Rock.

The Cherokees missed Biscoe and one of their men went to Fort Smith, where, learning the truth, they threatened war against the whites, but were appeased by good council. When the Indians calmly investigated what their compatriot had done they agreed that he ought to be punished, and that he had no right to flee into their reservation to avoid his just deserts. They also applauded Biscoe for outwitting them, although had he disclosed his intentions openly they undoubtedly would have opposed him. Biscoe lodged his man in jail in Little Rock and then took him down to Clark County, where he was tried and convicted. Terror was king throughout that long ride, but its effects were only visible on the face of the half-breed—to Biscoe it was simply an excursion in the woods.

While Biscoe was assistant United States marshal his old friend, S. M. Rutherford, was sheriff of Clark County and then sheriff of Pulaski County.

BISCOE AT HELENA.

In 1825, Henry L. Biscoe flung aside the official restraint of the assistant marshal's place and moved to Helena, where his old friends, Horner and Rutherford, had preceded him. The lives and fortunes of these three men were most strangely intermingled. He had scarcely got a foothold at Helena, when he was elected to the House of Representatives of the Fourth Territorial legislature for the years 1825-27. During the same years he held the office of county clerk for Phillips County, and from 1827 to 1831 was sheriff of the county, to which office he was re-elected in 1832 and held it until 1836. When the territory became a State in 1836, he was elected by Phillips County, along with his old friend, George W. Ferebe, to represent that county in the convention which formed the first constitution for the State. His education and talents, coupled with his observations and experiences in the backwoods of the West, gave him power and influence among his fellows, a power and influence which he used for their betterment and the permanent development of the State. He had gathered to himself considerable money and his influence extended throughout the State. He had been made colonel of one of the militia regiments in the 20's, and in 1834 purchased a new printing outfit and started a paper, the Helena Democrat, with William T. Yeomans as its manager and editor. Biscoe was opposed to Governor Pope and the columns of his paper did valiant service in creating popular opinion against the governor. Biscoe wanted to be governor and had he succeeded in demolishing Pope would, in all probability, have attained his end. Congress, however, stood by Pope, and Biscoe then turned his attention to the question of Statehood. No paper in the State did better service for the advancement of the Statehood sentiment than did the Helena Democrat, and as a reward Phillips County sent him to Little Rock to join in the making of the first constitution for the State.

THE BISCOE FAMILY.

Colonel Biscoe was a married man and left quite an interesting family. His wife, Phebe, died at Helena November

30, 1828. One of his sons, Captain Cameron N. Biscoe, is still living at Helena, the father of several children residing at the same place. A daughter of Colonel Biscoe married Major General T. C. Hindman of Helena, a distinguished Confederate soldier and a distinguished congressman of the United States. General Hindman was assassinated in Phillips County shortly after the war, leaving a family of children, Miss Blanche Hindman of Suwanee, Tennessee; T. C. Hindman of Nashville, Tennessee, and Colonel Biscoe Hindman of Louisville, Kentucky. What relation Henry L. Biscoe of Little Rock, of the firm of Biscoe, King & Company, was to Colonel Biscoe, I am not advised, but from the similarity of names I would take him to be either a son or a grandson. This, in brief, is the record of one of the most prominent of the early pioneers. He lived a clean life and died with an honored name, which his descendants have kept unsmirched to this good hour.

CHAPTER XXXIV.

CALEB LINDSEY—OTHER LINDSEY FAMILIES.

The Lindseys in America are a widely distributed people, but are of pure Scotch descent, although many of them found a resting place in Ireland before coming to America. The old earldom of the Lindseys became extinct in the fifteenth century, but the clan shows no sign of present extinction. An American has written a history of the Lindseys in America, confining herself in the main, however, to proving that David Lindsey of Northumberland County, Virginia, represented the oldest migration to America and that her line descended from that David. Neither proposition has been established absolutely, since David's will shows but one child and that a daughter.

She has made one interesting point, however, and that is a tabulation of ninety-nine different ways of spelling the word,

It may be that David Lindsey of Northumberland was the first immigrant to America, but the fact is not yet proved. There is a grant of land to David Lindsey of Northampton County, Virginia, in 1657. There is no proof, however, that the David of Northumberland and the David of Northampton are identical. The whole Chesapeake Bay divides these counties.

There is an undisputed grant, however, in Gloucester County, Virginia, to James Lindsey in 1674, and another in the same year in Middlesex County to John Lindsey. I have not investigated the relationship of this John and James, but have investigated the descendants of James of Gloucester in order to help the great army or Arkansas Lindseys to a glimpse of their blood. The life of James Lindsey of Gloucester, like all other lives, rests on tradition and fact. The tradition is that James Lindsey entered the James river with the second or third fleet that came to America, and the tradition is probably true. That the fact is that in 1674 he owned three hundred and ninety acres of land in Gloucester County, while John owned seven hundred acres in Middlesex. The inference is that these men were brothers, but it is not proved. Who James Lindsey married is not known, but he had four male children, Caleb, Joshua, Adam and William.

ANCESTOR OF ARKANSAS FAMILY.

We are not interested in the last three in this article, but they have an army of descendants not noted in the Lindsey book. The eldest son Caleb married in Gloucester County and had two sons born, James and Joshua. Joshua remained on the ancestral estate in Gloucester, while James removed to Caroline County on the Rappahannock. He married either in Albemarle or Caroline County Sarah Daniel, the daughter of William Daniel. He was born in 1700 and died in Caroline County in 1782. The children by Sarah Daniel were Caleb, born 1733; John, James, William, Jacob and Daniel. James married the second time to Miss Ware, and had another son, Reuben Lindsey. Of these eight boys, Caleb removed to Essex and Albemarle, and thence to Rockbridge; John removed to Halifax County, North Carolina, as did Jacob. The others remained in Virginia.

The Port Royal Lindseys of Caroline County, Virginia, are descended from James of Gloucester through his fourth son, William, and have given the world two great military men, Colonel William Lindsey, who rode with Light Horse Harry, and Colonel William Lindsey of the Second United States Artillery. The O'Neals of Arkansas descend from James of Gloucester, through Adam, his third son.

Caleb, born 1733, married in Albemarle County Sarah Carlton, and had Caleb, James, Joshua, Carlton, Archibald and probably Eli. Caleb, born 1767, married in Rockbridge County, Virginia, Sarah, daughter of John Young, and with his brothers, James, Joshua, Carlton, Archibald, Eli, and a large company of others, set out for the West between 1790 and 1800. Their first resting place was in Christian County, Kentucky, where in 1810 the census of the United States locates them with large families of children and slaves. Here Carlton, Archibald and Joshua died. Carlton was the eldest child, born 1760, and left eleven children. In 1814 or 1815, Caleb, James and Eli moved their families to the territory of Missouri, settling on Fourche de Mun in Lawrence County. Caleb afterwards moved into Pulaski County, where he died November 23, 1826. Caleb's widow, Sarah, and his brother, James, were in Pulaski County in the census of 1830, being between sixty and seventy years of age.

CALEB LINDSEY'S CAVE SCHOOL.

Caleb Lindsey, born 1767, married Sarah Young, about 1790; he was commissioned a justice of the peace in Christian County, Kentucky, on March 9, 1812. He was a surveyor, as was his father in Essex County, Virginia, and the records of Christian County show that in 1813 he was authorized to resurvey a tract of land four hundred acres, and in November, 1814, he had his tract recorded. This ends his official record in Kentucky, and the census of 1820 shows no Lindseys in Christian County. He is noted of record in Arkansas Territory in 1819, and the traditions of the family place his entrance into Lawrence County in 1815. He was a man of varied parts and a fine type of the educated pioneer.

In a cave in what is now Randolph County he gathered the children of the neighborhood and taught them the elementary branches. Uncle Tom Fletcher, who was born in Randolph in 1817, always gave Caleb Lindsey the credit for what education he had. When we look at our splendid Architectural triumphs in school buildings and compare them with Caleb Lindsey's cave—God's own handiwork—we are moved to exult over our progress. It is a progress—a great and triumphal progress in architecture, and also in opportunities. Whether education has advanced is another story, as Kipling says. Garfield, in choosing a building, said: "Give me an old three-legged bench in a log house with Mark Hopkins as teacher and I'll get an education." So with the hardy pioneers. Give them a cave and Caleb Lindsey as teacher and they got education enough to grease the wheels of the highest civilization and push the backwoods State into prominence. In noting what a later age has done, it will be well to remember that greater things were done in an earlier age by the graduates of the cave and log house schools. The lives of Jackson and Lincoln show that great men come from educational institutions of very low architectural degree.

Caleb Lindsey had six children, four girls and two boys. One of these boys, John Young Lindsey, was a pioneer Baptist preacher in Randolph, Pulaski and Saline counties. His monument is the men and women he put on the road to righteousness and the godly life he lived himself. Today after services the pewholders invite the preacher home to dinner—that is, they are supposed to do this in some parts of the country. They don't do it in Washington. All the traditions of the country about the best chickens for the preacher fail to materialize in Washington. If the preacher gets chicken there, he buys it out of his salary, and eats it close communion style, with his own family. Not so with old John Young Lindsey. He preached until he was through, an hour, or two hours, or more, and then invited the whole congregation over to his house for a dinner that was worthy of the gods. His congregation never found fault with his long sermons, and he never insulted it by using a manuscript. He had something to say, and knew how to say it, and then talked it over with the brethren over a feast of good things. He was a grand type of the pioneer Baptist preacher, and would have been an honor to Virginia, but in his day Virginia was persecuting all saints who did not happen to be of the Episcopal brand, and his father and people found freedom in the rising empire of the West.

THE DANCE FIRST, THEN THE SERMON.

Eli Lindsey began preaching on Strawberry in 1814 and his circuit ran from Little Red river north to what is now Missouri. He was a Methodist, and had his own methods. Colonel Magness states that the visits of Eli to Oil Trough Bottom were irregular; that he attended all the house raisings, log rollings, quiltings, marriages and frolics. He would encourage the young people to dance and after they were through would preach to them. At the end of the year 1815 he reported ninety-five members in his circuit. In 1816 he visited the spot where Batesville now stands and found a man named Reed in possession of a new house he had just finished for a store. Lindsey asked the privilege to christen it, which was granted. He sent out to Miller's creek, to Lafferty's creek, to Greenbrier, and all around, and notified the folks to come out. They came with their guns, and a fine old crowd it was. Colonel Miller and his boys, Colonel Peel and Sons, the widow Lafferty and sons, Major Robert Magness and his army of boys, the Craigs, Ruddells, Trammels, Beans, Gillets, Holabys, Trimbles and Kelleys were all there with their guns stacked around the walls. Old Eli began his sermon and in a short time the dogs started a bear. Old Eli said: "The service is adjourned in order that the men may kill that bear." They rolled out with alacrity, mounted their horses, pursued Bruin and killed him. They then went back to the new house, where Eli "thanked God for men who knew how to shoot and for women who knew how to pray," and finished his sermon.

Whether Eli and Caleb were brothers I cannot say with confidence. Long after both were dead there was a young Eli Lindsey, about the same age as John Young Lindsey in Saline County.

INTERMARRIED WITH FLETCHERS.

Of Caleb Lindsey's daughters, three married Fletchers; these were Mary, Betsy and Agnes. The fourth daughter, Sarah, married Dr. Huber at Fourche de Thomas in 1825. The eldest daughter, Mary, married Henry Lewis Fletcher in 1815, and left a family of ten children, Honorable Thomas Fletcher of Little Rock being the second child born in 1817. Of old James Lindsey, who came in with old Caleb, I am not so well informed. He was alive in 1830, living in Pulaski County, as was his wife, and both were then nearly seventy years of age. In his neighborhood lived a number of younger Lindseys from thirty to forty years of age. These were Eli, John Young, Carlton, Samuel and Walter, all married and blessed with children. This is a clean, authentic line connecting these Lindseys in unbroken chain to James Lindsey of Gloucester County, Virginia, of 1623-1674, and with the Earl of Lindsey of the fifteenth century.

DESCENDED FROM NOBILITY.

There is quite an army of Lindseys, descending from the Earl of Lindsey now living in Arkansas, who descend in another way. They carry the blood and are of remote kin, but of the clan. These are Colonel Lindsey, the Tripletts, the Embrees, the O'Neals, the Whites and a host of others whose line I will take up at some other time. All these, however, are later additions to the Arkansas trunk, coming in fully thirty years after the advent of the Gloucester-Caroline-Albemarle-Rockbridge line. They trace through the Northumberland-Fairfax line, and the trip of their ancestress, a widow with children, from Fairfax to Jefferson County, is a splendid story of privation and heroism.

Senator Lindsey of Kentucky, the most eminent of the name in the United States, traces through Rockbridge straight to Scotland, going backward, and straight to Frankfort, Kentucky, coming the other way. The old pioneer, Isaac Lindsey of Davidson district, afterward Sumner County, Tennessee, traces through the Halifax (North Carolina) line back to James of Gloucester County. All the Lindseys of Virginia were of gentle blood.

The second family of Lindseys to enter Arkansas was that of Isaac of Hempsteady County, who, in 1823, was declared by the sheriff of the county delinquent for State and county taxes, to the extent of $5. Tax dodging is a very common thing today, but there is little evidence to show that it existed in Arkansas as early as 1823. The long list of delinquents published by the sheriffs and collectors is neither evidence of residence in Arkansas nor of tax dodging. These lists at the best simply show that certain men, residence unknown, had made claims for lands in Arkansas, which claims had been allowed. There is no evidence to show that for the major part these claimants ever made an actual residence in Arkansas, or that they, as foreign land holders, preferred to abandon their lands to paying taxes thereon. This is all there is of record to show that Isaac Lindsey of Hempstead County was ever in that county. He may have been, but the inference is that he was not, and that he preferred to forfeit his land claim to paying a $5 tax claim. I have not been able to find other Lindseys in Hempstead County as early as 1823, nor immediately thereafter, and I am inclined to believe Isaac Lindsey was never a resident of the State. If I am wrong in this, and there are descendants of Isaac Lindsey in south Arkansas who can prove my error, I shall be under many obligations to them, or to anyone else, if they will kindly do so.

The third man of this name actually entered Arkansas, lived in it for eleven years, and died leaving a family whose descendants still honor the State. A young man, Peter Lindsey, left Fairfax County, Virginia, in 1825, and traveled overland to what is now Jefferson County, Arkansas. He spelled his name "Lindsey," although descendants of the same family in Virginia today are sticklers for the spelling, "Lindsay." Why anyone should prefer the suffix "say" to "sey," I am absolutely unable to determine.

The aristocratic Lindseys of England, Canada and America, up to the year 1850, all spelled their names "Lindsey," and the real value of the suffix "sey" is of transcendently greater historic importance than that of "say." In an article of this kind I cannot go into the reasoning which supports it.

Peter Lindsey's journey from Fairfax, Virginia, to Jefferson County, Arkansas Territory, was most romantic, and would make a fine basis for a real historic novel. His life in Arkansas was not eventful, as he died in Jefferson County on February 7, 1839, at the age of thirty-six, leaving a wife and children. He lived long enough to acquire an estate and his children intermarried with the best people of the State. From 1838 to 1840, William H. Lindsey was judge of Jefferson County. He could not have been a son of Peter Lindsey, although he may have been a brother. The O'Neals of Jefferson County, also from Virginia, were also descended from the Fairfax Lindseys, and were most prominent in Jefferson County affairs from 1833 to 1840.

The Virginia Lindsey pedigree is most aptly illuminated in Vols. X, XI, XII and XIII of the Virginia Magazine, and much pertaining to the general line of Lindseys is therein included.

MORE AS TO REV. CEPHAS WASHBURN.

It is so easy to forget. It is so easy to let slip one or more of the essential features of a record. In Cephas Washburn's record there is no reason for naming one set of granddaughters without naming all of them, and Miss Clara B. Eno of Van Buren, very kindly called my attention to the lapse. She informed me that Cephas Washburn has a granddaughter, Mrs. Mary Washburn Henderson, at Prior's Creek, Oklahoma. Biographers and historians are credited with a full cup, and they must walk very carefully or the liquor will run over. I ought to have known possibly, that Mrs. Henderson was alive and a granddaughter of Cephas Washburn, but I am frank to say, I did not. The credit for the perfected line is therefore due Miss Eno, a lady I have known and respected for more than twenty years, and whose intelligence and patriotism is an honor to the State she so vigilantly represents.

ALMOST FORGOTTEN KING'S MOUNTAIN HERO.

On June 28, 1840, in Johnson County, Arkansas, the death of Major Henry Francis was noted, be being then eighty-three years of age, and, what is more to the purpose, the last of the King's Mountain heroes. Major Francis was a citizen of patriotic tendencies and a warm friend of the old pioneers, Samuel Adams, Sr., and John Williamson. What his family connections were I do not know, but he doubtless left a family whose descendants may still be found in Johnson County. The Daughters of the American Revolution would do well to hunt out the grave of this old hero and mark it in some suitable manner. It is a false idea to think that memories are perpetuated solely and alone by marble shafts coming from the hands of great sculptors and costing an immense sum of money. There are memorial shafts over all the world which have been made by loving hands from the rough rock of the neighboring hills, and these memorials are of equal value with the more artistic. The Daughters of the American Revolution at Van Buren cannot find the grave of James Phillips, a revolutionary soldier, and the founder of Phillips Landing, the original name of Van Buren. The cemetery in which Phillips was buried in 1829 is now in all human probability in the very center of the bustling city of Van Buren. It is enough to know, however, that the revolutionary soldier Phillips died there, and was buried there in the very center of his last forceful endeavor, and a monument made of Crawford County stone, of which there is a superabundance, will not only honor the soldier, James Phillips, in the highest degree, but honor the Daughters of the American Revolution at that city and every citizen who shall contribute his part to the erection of a monument at any point within the corporate limits of Van Buren.

JACKSON COUNTY PIONEERS.

William H. Glass first settled on the Mississippi river, five miles below the mouth of the St. Francis river, in the days of the French domination in 1802. He proved his concessionary right before the United States commissioners in 1806-7, but was denied a grant. He persisted and under the ten years' settlement act obtained his land. Where he came from and his after-history is unknown to me. Hiram Glass was an early settler on White river, and may have been his son. Jackson County was formed in 1830 from Independence and Lawrence counties and Hiram Glass lived in the northern part of the new county Jackson near where Swifton now stands. One of the earliest townships of Jackson County was named for him, and he was the first county judge of the county, while from 1832 to 1836 he was its coroner.

One of the most active men of Jackson County from 1823 to 1850 was John Robinson. He came into the State as a surveyor under General William Rector, and did a great amount of contract work throughout the territory, entering land for himself in both Independence and Lawrence counties. He was county surveyor for Jackson County from 1830 to 1834, and its county judge from 1834 to 1836. He was elected by his fellows to represent Jackson County in the convention which formed the first constitution of the State and was generally considered a man of excellent judgment. John Robinson was also county judge of the county from 1844 to 1850, but could not have been the pioneer. James Robinson was also of Jackson County and may have been a brother of John. He was sheriff from 1835 to 1838 and from 1838 to 1842. He also served three times in the legislature of the State. Much of the early history of this region is wrapped up in the lives of these two men, and the early progress of the county was largely due to them. Other prominent pioneers of Jackson County were Judge E. Bartley, J. C. Saylors, who was clerk for eight years; Isaac Gray, sheriff for ten years; M. Copeland and A. M. Carpenter.

John Robinson, the pioneer aforementioned, came to Missouri territory, from whence he finally drifted into Arkansas territory where he died. He was in 1834 placed on the pension rolls of the United States as a survivor of the Pennsylvania militia in the Revolutionary war, and was at that date seventy-seven years of age. When he died I am not advised, but his grave is in all probability near Swifton in Jackson County.

Near him rest in Lawrence County the Revolutionary patriots James Ferguson, eighty-two years of age in 1833, and James Vanzant of the Pennsylvania Continental Line, seventy-eight years of age in the same year. Near him also to the northwest are the graves of five Revolutionary patriots in Independence County: Lawrence Angel, of the North Carolina Continental line, seventy-one years of age in 1833; John Carothers, of the South Carolina militia, eighty-eight years of age in 1834; Benjamin Hardin, of the North Carolina militia, sixty-nine years of age in 1833; David Vance, of the Virginia Continental line, seventy-five years of age in 1834, and John Weldon of the South Carolina Continental line, seventy-five years of age in 1834. Thus eight duly accredited revolutionary soldiers sleep in what was once old Lawrence County, being not only soldiers of the American Revolution, but pioneers of the new territory Arkansas. They are entitled to a double monument at the hands of the people of Independence, Lawrence and Jackson counties, and the Daughters of the American Revolution of these counties or the daughters of the pioneers of these counties should see to it that their graves are fittingly marked.

Besides the grave of James Phillips, in Crawford County, there also rest within its bosom the two brothers, Isaiah Mobley and Clement Mobley, who were on the pension rolls in 1835 from Crawford County, as surviving soldiers of the South Carolina militia in the Revolutionary war. In addition to John and James Robinson, Pioneers of Jackson and old Lawrence, there was a William Robinson in Lawrence County as early as 1815, who was appointed one of the commissioners to select a location for a court house, his associates being the oldest pioneers of the region, Lewis De Mun, William Hix, Sr., owner of Hix's Ferry; Solomon Hewett, Andrew Criswell, who married a daughter of John Lafferty; Isaac Kelley and Morris Moore. The sheriff at that time was James Campbell.

CHAPTER XXXV.

THE BRILHART AND DAVIS FAMILIES—MARRIAGES AND DEATHS.

Brilhart is an old German name ante-dating the campaigns of Cæsar on the north of the Rhine. For twenty centuries or more people of the name lived in the Rhine region, cultivating the graces of King Gambrinus and wearing wooden shoes. In about the year 1720 Jacob Brilhart, with his frau and little kinderlings, migrated from the oppressed German States to the Quaker land of Pennsylvania. They came to be called "Pennsylvania Deutch," and with true German frugality prospered and waxed fat. Jacob, Jr., a son of Jacob, Sr., was attracted to North Carolina in 1760 and settled in Lincoln County. He was blessed with a family of nine children, one of whom, Jacob, had a family of seven in 1790. One of the seven, also named Jacob, a great-grandson of the emigrant, went back to the old Pennsylvania home, and while there enlisted as an American soldier in the war of 1812 and served his time. In 1816 the government gave him a land warrant, and he started west to locate it in the wilderness of Illinois. The influx of land-grabbers was too great for the quiet Jacob Brilhart, and lands in Missouri Territory being more inviting, he crossed the river and drifted southward until he found a place that suited him in what is now Lawrence County. Here he drove down his stakes and made a home.

DAVIS FAMILY IN LAWRENCE COUNTY.

At that time, 1817, there was a man, Benjamin Davis, forty-seven years of age, living at Strawberry. Near him lived Eliphas Davis, about the same age with a family of ten children, and also the widow Elizabeth Davis with a family of eight. Samuel Davis, about fifty-seven years old, also lived in the county, as did Charles and David, each about thirty years old. It will thus be seen that there were quite a number of the Davis family in Lawrence County in 1817, and at this late day it is impossible to untangle the degrees of relationship. Where the Davis family came from I cannot say, but it is reputed to have come from Kentucky to Arkansas, and from North Carolina to Kentucky. It is certain that North Carolina could have furnished two regiments of the name Davis in 1790 without calling on the other States. The first census of North Carolina gives four hundred and four families of the name, with an average of five persons in a family, or two thousand and twenty Davises. Some of these may have formed the Lawrence County settlement.

UNION OF THE BRILHARTS AND DAVISES.

Young Brilhart was smitten with the charms of one of the young Davis girls and married her. The father and mother lived on their little farm near Strawberry, where in 1822 a daughter was born. Jacob Brilhart and wife both sickened and died in 1826, and the infant daughter was taken by her grandmother Davis to her home and reared.

The attractions of Pulaski County on the Saline were at that time beginning to depopulate Lawrence County, and in 1831 Grandmother Davis moved to that neighborhood. Rebecca Brilhart grew to womanhood on the Saline, a gem of the forest and a picture of life. She knew every dale and glen of the neighborhood and made toys out of the soapstones before modern industry gave them a value. Under the guidance of a noble dame Rebecca Brilhart was trained to think, to act and to grow symmetrically.

THE SALINE OCTOGENARIAN.

Eighty years is a noble span for a single life, and she who makes it is one of the immortals. Rebecca Brilhart died in Little Rock in 1903 at the ripe old age of eighty-one. All of that life was spent in Arkansas. In 1838, about seven miles from the quiet town of Benton, Rebecca Brilhart married Caleb Lindsey, a son of Caleb Lindsey of Lawrence County, and a brother of John Young Lindsey of the Saline. It was a great and notable wedding. The Lindsey negroes were sleek and fat, and the Lindsey and Davis homes noted for their hospitality. Marsa Caleb was to bring home the young mistress, Becky, and every negro added something to the festivities. The wedding dinner was superb and the infare an immense affair. Rebecca Brilhart did well, but Caleb Lindsey did better. A noble woman is God's best gift to man, and Caleb Lindsey got a noble woman for a wife.

DOWN IN ASHLEY COUNTY.

How Americans drift from place to place! Ashley County was opening up and Caleb Lindsey, as the youngest child, went where chances for growth were greatest. Here he prospered, but in 1856 sickened and died. The widow Lindsey never wavered. She had seven children born, three of whom lived to be honored citizens of Arkansas. All through the horrors of the Civil war Rebecca Lindsey kept her family intact. In 1866 she doffed her widow's weeds and married Cornelius Carlock, also a man of German extraction, but with an ancestry of more than one hundred and fifty years of American life on North Carolina soil. The Carlocks of Cabarrus County were once the leaders of the county, and the grandmother of the writer was Rebecca Carlock, of Rowan-Mecklenberg-Cabarrus County, a sister of the father of Cornelius Carlock, and my father wore her name, Josiah Carlock Shinn.

Rebecca Brilhart Lindsey Carlock was a fine specimen of the old Arkansas womanhood, and could have given novelists and historians much valuable matter had they deemed it worth while to consult her. She lives in the memory of a troop of loving children and grandchildren, and in the high esteem of hundreds of friends. Her three sons, Harrison B., Rezin W. and Allen H., all married and reared families. Harrison B. Lindsey is living in Ashley County, the honored father of five children. Dr. Rezin W. Lindsey is a familiar figure on the streets of Little Rock today, and is represented in the law by a son, Edwin W. Lindsey. Allen H. Lindsey died at Portland in Ashley County in 1887, leaving a son, Guy A. Lindsey, at the same place.

Thus Rebecca Brilhart and Caleb Lindsey both cover the same habitat. Both lived in Lawrence, Pulaski and Ashley, while the mother lived to a grand old age.

ORIGIN OF THE PROVINCIAL.

Are the fathers greater than the sons? Are the mothers superior to their daughters? In flesh and blood, no; in opportunity, yes. All the fathers and mothers of 1810-1830 had seen something of the world; their children and grandchildren had not. The cosmopolitan sense is far more ennobling than the provincial. The pioneers were cosmopolitan and their immediate descendants provincial. The old people, the pioneers of Arkansas, had seen much more of the world than their children and were to that extent broader and better educated. No education can quite equal that of travel and changed residence, and in this sense the people of Arkansas from 1830 to 1860 suffered. They had great, broad, generous parents who knew the world, but they themselves lived in a province and acquired the idea, in part at least, that the province was the world. They needed only the mellowing influences of contact with other people to make them broad, generous and tolerant, as great in every sense as their fathers, the pioneers.

Jacob Brilhart may have been poor in worldly goods, but he was rich in observations and experiences. He had been in North Carolina, Pennsylvania, Illinois and Arkansas, and had served in the army. He was rich in all the elements of greatness and transmitted these to his daughter, who carried them forward to her children.

HEMPSTEAD COUNTY SETTLERS.

One of the earliest settlers of Hempstead County was Matthew Fountaine of Virginia. He came in 1816 or 1817 and settled on Mount Prairie, west of Washington. This prairie is historic, being the oldest settled part of south Arkansas. The national road was out thereaways in 1819, but the settlement ante-dated the road and a godly settlement it was. The oldest church edifices of the State belong to the Catholics, but the oldest Protestant church house was Henry Chapel on Mount Prairie, built in 1816 or 1817. It was Methodist in belief, but Christian in practice. All bodies of people worshipped freely within its walls. Exclusiveness had not yet set in, and it was generally believed that a Methodist and a Baptist had an equal chance if they behaved themselves.

While Eli Lindsey was the first Methodist preacher in Arkansas, Mr. Henry was the second, and to him is Henry Chapel indebted for its existence. He preached for many years all over south Arkansas and contributed in no small degree to the civilization and moral growth of that region. His wife died in Hempstead County in 1826, and to her influence and excellent character is much of the early Methodist growth attributable. Mr. John Harris was the third Methodist preacher, coming in 1820 with a circuit extending from Little Rock to Missouri.

MARRIAGES AND DEATHS.

The woman of the future is far less interesting than the girl of the present. Thus thought our Arkansas ancestors, and so think we. Lads and lassies have glorified every age of the world, and marriage has everywhere been honorable. There have been three historic forms of marriage: First, marriage by capture. This was a most ancient form, but still prevails in some regions; second, marriage by purchase, a very common form today, but always vehemently denied; third, marriage by espousel, or by fascination or love. This is the holiest form of wedlock, and the form that prevailed most largely in the marriages we enumerate below. Whether each and all of those I collate were celebrated by the espousal and the engagement ring, I cannot say, but in all probability each one of them was. The people of the elder Arkansas day were far more particular about the "Trulofa," or the ring ceremony, "I plight my troth," than we are. In Southwestern Ireland, a marriage today is not considered valid unless solemnized with a ring, and the laborers of Eastern England express their faith in the mystic efficacy of the "Golden Arrabo" in terms almost worshipful. It was said by an old Arkansas pioneer that every matron, no matter how poor, always wore a wedding ring. Hundreds of backwoods mothers were able to repeat and did repeat with pride Herrick's old lines:

"And as this round is nowhere found,
To flaw, or else to sever,
So may our love as endless prove,
As pure as gold forever."

And hundreds of Arkansas fathers today remember the old couplets or posies their mothers used:

"Our contract was heaven's act,
In thee my choice
I do rejoice.
I will be yours
While life endures,
If you deny, then sure I die."

In one old Arkansas paper was this couplet:

"I did commit no act of folly
When I married my sweet Molly."

It is said of Bishop Thomas that he married his fourth wife with a wedding ring that had for its posy the following words:

"If I survive, I'll make them five."

SOME EARLY SUPERSTITIONS.

Very few of the old Arkansas rings carried posies, although their wearers were great hands at quoting them. The plain golden ring was the almost universal form and grew out of the saying of Queen Mary, who, rather than have a wedding ring with jewels on its surface and engravened with a foolish couplet, "chose to be married with a plain hoop of gold like any other maiden." Our grandmothers wore this ring on the third finger of the left hand, because at that time there was believed to be a channel of connection between the ring finger and the heart. Lemnius said "the small artery is stretched from the heart to this finger." Many an old Arkansas mother has aroused her daughter from a swoon by pinching her ring finger and rubbing saffron on her wedding ring. It was the saffron and the pain together that wrought the cure, and not the mystic artery. It was said of an Arkansas physician that he dosed his patients with gin and sulphur, because it made them cheerful, and always attributed the cheerfulness to the sulphur. After marriage suppers in early Arkansas days the younger lassies observed the following superstition: She would sleep on a pillow over a piece of wedding cake cut by the bride from her bridal cake and passed three times through her bridal ring. She was sure to dream of her future husband.

One old Arkansas bachelor got off the following, which was by no means original:

"A spaniel, a woman and a walnut tree,
The more they are beaten the better they be."

Another compositor in Phillips County, desiring to make fun of a certain girl who had possibly jilted him, got off the following non-original, two-century-old couplet:

"Fair and foolish, black and proud,
Long and lazy, little and loud."

ARKANSAS MARRIAGES 1820-30.

The following marriages were celebrated in different parts of the territory prior to 1831: At Arkansas Post, on August 9, 1826, Francis Vaugine, Jr., to Odelle Paulette, the ceremony being performed by Judge Eskridge. In January, 1827, at the same place, Major Francis Vaugine to Madam Mary Deruseaux, widow of Monsieur John B. Deruseaux, an old French pioneer. In Crawford County, on December 12, 1827, Honorable James Woodson Bates to Mrs. Elibabeth W. Palmore, daughter of Ben Moore, Sr. On June 17, 1826, at the residence of Chester Ashley in Little Rock, by Rev. S. T. Toncray, Joseph Henderson, a merchant of Little Rock, to Ann Eliza, daughter of Ben Elliott of Washington County, Missouri. At Long Prairie, Hempstead County, on December 21, 1826, James Sevier Conway to Mary Jane, daughter of John Bradley of Wilson County, Tennessee. At Arkansas Post, January 23, 1824, Ignace Bogy to Desire, daughter of Francis Michel. At Walnut Hills, Moses Starr to Eliza, widow of P. J. Cady, late of New York. At Arkansas Post, on April 28, 1828, Albert

Berdu to Mary Goceaux. In Welborn township, Pulaski County, Adustin Rogers to Mary Cardin, on May 18, 1824. At Little Rock, June 17, 1824, James Gibson to Priscilla Clanton, and on August 15, 1824, Jacob Thorn to Lavina Porterfield. At Arkansas Post, on July 22, 1824, John Whittaker to Mary Greenwait, and on the same day at the same place, Asa H. Kemble to Margaret Scipes. On August 28, at the same place, Pierre Pono to Amelia Brinsbach; on December 5, Eli Evans to Polly, daughter of Thomas Burris; and on January 17, 1825, Francis Limoneaux to Madam Barbe Benette. At Pecannerie, February 14, 1825, William Lackey to Sarah Harris. In January, 1825, Paul Vaugine was married to Jane Wolff by Judge Scott. On August 29, 1829, Archibald Hubbard to Charlotte Fooy, daughter of Judge Fooy of Crittenden County. At Cane Hill, Washington County, March 16, 1831, John Piatt, late of Pulaski, to Miss Eliza, daughter of Widow Buchanan of Lincoln County, Tennessee. On the same day at the same place, by Rev. A. Buchanan, John Stephenson to Nancy, daughter of Samuel Pitman. On August 4, 1831, Edward Cross, judge of the Supreme Court, to Laura Frances, daughter of Ben Eliott of Washington County, Missouri.

The earth holds more dead bodies than it numbers living souls. It is a mighty charnel house—a universal cemetery. The pioneers died and no mark remains to tell where they were buried. In this work we shall number some of the ancient deaths and mark their general resting place. It may comfort some soul, besides aiding others to perfect a record of their family lines. To live in hearts we leave behind is not to die, and my work is to help the dead to that sort of immortality. In the larger realm of thought each departed friend is a magnet attracting us to another world. These friends lie in graves which are the general meeting places for all mankind; places where all distinctions are leveled—vast ante-chambers to immortality.

At Arkansas Post in the Spring of 1820, Solomon B. Judd from Colchester, Connecticut, sickened and died and was there buried. He was a young man prospecting for a home. At the same place on July 21, 1821, Wm. O'Hara, a rich speculator from St. Louis. There also on July 11, 1821, Judge Seldon lost an infant daughter. The judge consoled himself with the remark, "Whom the gods love die young." In September, 1821, Jonathan R. Brown from New York died at Little Rock, and in the same months Mrs. Ann Greenwalt, an old settler, died on her farm five miles from Arkansas Post. In the same month at the residence of Wright Daniels on the Arkansas river, Lewis Rouse passed away. In September, 1819, Moses Graham, sheriff of Pulaski County, died at his residence, having lived in Arkansas about three years. John McLain died in Hempstead County in 1819, and William McDonald administered on his estate. At Davidsonville, Stephen Chamberlain died on August 6, 1821. He was from Vermont and quite a prominent man. In Richland in Arkansas County in 1831, James Currin died at a very advanced age, having been for many years a resident of that section; like a fire he flickered out, but sparkled long after they thought him gone. In 1821, two brothers from Kentucky, Joseph and Andrew Colville, died; the former in Miller and the later in Pulaski County.

In the same year at Arkansas Post Martha D. Long, wife of Zachariah Long, late of Versailles, Kentucky. Michael D. Robinson from Nashville, Tennessee, died in Hempstead County in 1823, and Madam Imbeau, wife of Monsieur Imbeau, died at the Post. In December, 1820, Jacob Jones died at Little Rock, being fifty years of age. On February 8, 1823, Asenath Stuart, daughter of Col. Wm. Stuart, died in Lawrence County. At Pecannerie on May 28, 1824, Eliza, wife of Thomas White, and on September 25, William, son of Colonel William Lewis. In Independence County there were several deaths in 1824: Betsy Millsaps, wife of Reuben, in November; Mrs. Stephenson, wife of William, and Mrs. Dodd, wife of Thomas D., both died in November, as did a Mrs. Griffith. Crystal Hill in January, 1825, Mark Westland, a native of Austria, and Hiram Green, both passed away. Joseph Bentley, son of George, died at Pecannerie in February, 1825, while William Woodward passed away in Hempstead County on November 2, 1824, leaving a wife and children. He migrated from Tennessee to Long Prairie, then in Missouri, in 1816, and filled offices under the general government. He was one of the first common pleas judges of Hempstead County. Samuel Faulkner, late of the steamer Spartan, died in August, 1825, at the house of James H. Martin, aged thirty years. Dr. R. H. Fenner died in Little Rock in February, 1824. At Arkansas Post in her twentieth year, on January 14, 1820, Paulina Colville. The family seems to have been located there several years, and she was doubtless of kin to the brothers mentioned above. In June, 1820, Major Noah Lester, a United States army officer, died at Little Rock. Jairus Berry from Courtland County, New York, with his family, entered Arkansas in 1820, and at the mouth of the Arkansas river his wife was taken sick and died. She was buried at that place. William Wilson arrived at Little Rock in 1820 from Orange County, New York. In October of that year he died, leaving a wife and three children, who remained in Arkansas. In December, 1820, Dr. William Orr from Missouri, a friend and relative of Judge Andrew Scott, died at the Scott residence and was buried in Little Rock. Abraham Beck, formerly of New York, died at Arkansas Post on September 5, 1821. He had just opened a branch of the Western Land Agency. Betsy Barkman, wife of Jacob Barkman, died at the farm five miles from the Post on August 2, 1821. Jacob Barkman seems to have had a home in Arkansas County, while blazing a way for his later and lasting home in Clark County. In Hempstead County in February, 1829, Joseph Paxton from Virginia, being fifty years of age, passed away. Thomas Knox, who moved to Chicot County in 1826, died there in 1829. At Arkansas Post on August 22, 1839, Elizabeth, wife of Wigton King, died in her fifty-eighth year. In Miller County, on November 21, 1829, Claiborne Wright died in his forty-fifth year, leaving a wife and children. Sylvanus Phillips died at Helena October 31, 1830, aged sixty-five. He was one of the oldest Arkansas pioneers, dating far back into the previous century. On July 25, 1831, at Van Buren, James Phillips, a soldier of the Revolution. These all lie very probably in unmarked graves, over which the plow-share of progress has run so deep and often as to make their identity impossible.

CHAPTER XXXVI.

THE LAFFERTY FAMILY.

When you come to consider an Irish pedigree you have your hands full. The Hebrews have their genealogical lore in as fine shape as any other knowledge and the Bible redounds with genealogical lines. The only people that can compare with the Jews in clear-cut accuracy of genealogical acumen is the Irish—the genuine Irish—of the oldest Ireland. They run their family lines in bold assurance straight back to the Garden of Eden, and then defy Huxley to show a better parentage. The monkey theory never bothered an Irishman. He says: "Well, Huxley doubtless sprang from a baboon. He looks like one and acts like one. But as for me, I'm from Killarney, and my people came there straight from the Garden of Eden." It was an Irishman in Arkansas who, after listening to an Englishman boasting of his descent, said: "Well, it may be true that you blarsted Englishmen came over with Noah in the ark, but we, sons of Erin, came over on our own account. Our ancestors ran an independent line which put Noah out of business."

Burke's Peerage is a good old book, but it looks like thirty cents when put side by side with Rooney's Irish Families. The Englishman, like Byron's ocean, stops with the shore, but the Irishman proves his descent from the most hoary antiquity. Take the old pioneer, John Lafferty of Lafferty's creek, in what is now Independence County, but was then the territory of Louisiana. His father was from Donegal, but his ancestors could show an unbroken line from King Milesius of Spain, two thousand years before Christ. The Lafferty family in Ireland were Labbertachs before St. Patrick drove the snakes out of the island. Their coat of arms was an unquartered shield of gold, in whose center was a full-grown tree of everlasting green, the tree of life, in whose boughs was a crown of gold, the emblem of their kingly descent. Descending from King Milesius, through the line of his son, Heremon, a scion was at length found, Brian Labbertach, who was one of the kings of Ireland in A. D. 350. The Irish spelling has gone through many successive changes, from Labbertach, through Lafertach, Lavertach, Laferty, Laverty to Lafferty of modern times. All Laffertys or Lavertys who are not clean Irish are descended from another son of Milesius and trace through Gaul to Britain before Julius Cæsar led his conquering legions to battle. These became the English Lavertys. Those who remained in Gaul became the De la Fertes, who entered England with the conqueror. So all the Laffertys of the world are of one blood, and spring from old Milesius, a direct descendant of Adam and Eve, and one of the earliest pioneers to go west and start a country from which Columbus went still farther west to find America. The John Lafferty of 1810 in Louisiana, now Arkansas, sprang from the Irish line, from King Brian Labbertach, the heroic snake fighter of Ireland before the Saxons had discovered England. My friend Thomas Lafferty, of Little Rock, is of the same family, but he is not descended from old Arkansas John of 1810.

The Lafferty coat of arms is ancient and singularly characteristic. It lays the English peerage in the shade and chuckles and chortles. The Lafferty crest is still more remarkable. It is an arm akimbo holding a fine tempered Toledo blade on whose point fixed through its tail is a venomous snake coiling itself around the blade and killing itself on its sharp double edges in its mad and vain effort to strike the Lafferty hand. Saint Patrick may have driven the snakes out a hundred and fifty years later, but the Laffertys had lots of fun killing them before St. Patrick was born.

IMMIGRATED FROM IRELAND.

John Lafferty of Independence County came over with his father from Ireland a mere boy, at the time of the great exodus to North Carolina from 1740 to 1770, and settled with the Irish clans in western North Carolina, in what was then Rowan County, now Rutherford. In his seventeenth year he joined Captain Smith's company in Colonel Thomas Polk's regiment, the Fourth North Carolina Continental Line, and served three years in the Revolutionary war. He enlisted June 10, 1776, and was mustered out June 15, 1779, in his twentieth year.

History leaves him for a few years at this point, but family traditions link him with the Cherokee troubles of 1785 in western North Carolina, carrying him over into Tennessee. History finds him in Tennessee in the Cumberland district in 1790, when he married an Arkansas pioneer, a Lindsey, of pure Scotch blood. She may have been a daughter of Isaac Lindsey, the first regularly appointed justice of the peace in the Davidson district in 1783, being one of the guard of honor, who were given lands in 1782 without price. There were six hundred and forty of this grand guard, and John Lafferty himself may have been one, but unfortunately the complete roll is not recorded. This Isaac Lindsey was made ranger in 1786 and was a noted pioneer character. Whether John Lafferty married his daughter, or the daughter of Benjamin Lindsey, who was scalped in 1784, may never be known, but it is certain that he married a sister or cousin of Caleb and of old Eli Lindsey, the pioneer Methodist preacher of Arkansas on the Strawberry, the Current, the Black and the White in late 1785.

John Lafferty lived for many years in Tennessee near the Kentucky line and all his children were born there. He was a rover of the grandest type. His hunting and trapping carried him all over Missouri, Louisiana, Arkansas and Kansas. He was on friendly terms with the Cherokees of later days and with them hunted and trapped incessantly. In 1810 he brought his family to what is now called Lafferty's creek, in Independence County, and settled on the barrens in a little log hut, which in after days was one of the most famous of Arkansas. That cabin was then in Louisiana, but it lived on through the days of Missouri territory, Arkansas territory into the life of Arkansas State. Political divisions may change, but the log cabins do not change with them. In 1814 the tocsin of war called John Lafferty back to Tennessee, and with Jackson he marched to New Orleans, where he was wounded, and from the effects of which he died in his cabin home on Lafferty's creek in 1815. A hero of two wars sleeps somewhere in the barrens of Union township, Independence County. This ends the mortal career of the Irishman, John Lafferty, but opens the career of his

Scotch wife, the Widow Lafferty, and the mainstay of Methodism in the Lawrence County of early days.

LEADERS IN ALL GOOD WORKS.

Eli Lindsey preached everywhere in his most original way. Caleb Lindsey, another brother, taught school in a cave up on Fourche de Mun, while the Widow Lafferty, a sister or cousin of these boys, kept open house on Lafferty's creek, encouraging the pioneers to live godly and righteous lives and rearing a family of splendid boys.

In 1808 when the Commissioners were taking proof to settle titles growing out of settlements made prior to 1803, John Lafferty proved a settlement on White river for six hundred and forty acres of land made in 1802. This claim was not allowed because it had not been continuously lived upon for ten years. He also made proof in 1813 for another six hundred and forty acres in the Paoli Fields or White river, proving a continuous settlement from 1807 to date, which was allowed.

A caravan of Laffertys and Criswells left Tennessee in 1807 with teams and wagons for Memphis, Tennessee, at which place they built a boat and went down the river to the mouth of the White; from this point they went up to the Post of Arkansas where they laid in a supply of furniture, salt, flour and everything necessary for a long life in the woods. They then went back to the mouth of the White and made their-way up that stream to the Paoli Fields.

John Lindsey Lafferty and Margaret Lafferty, a son and daughter of John and Sarah Lafferty, were with this party, Elizabeth Lafferty, another daughter, married a man by the name of Kelley in Tennessee and formed another part of the caravan. Elizabeth Kelley died at the mouth of the White river, where she was buried, while the husband kept on up the river with the Laffertys, dying a few years after he reached the destination. The trip from East Tennessee to Independence County, Arkansas, took six months. There was a young man named Criswell with the party who on March 13, 1813, married Margaret Lafferty. He was born in South Carolina in 1791 and died in Izard County, October 31, 1844; his wife, Margaret, died February 23, 1868, and was buried near Philadelphia Church in the same county. They were both members of the Methodist church.

One son of this marriage, Cyrus J. Criswell, is still living far out on Rock Creek in Montana. There he owns five thousand acres of land, sixty head of horses, three hundred and fifty head of cattle and one hundred calves. He is about six feet high, of a light complexion, splendid blue eyes and weighs one hundred and seventy pounds. He remembers his grandmother, the widow Lafferty, as a very small woman, but one of remarkable courage and splendid force of character. Besides these three children of John and Sarah Lafferty, there were four other boys, Henderson, Austin, Binks and Lorenzo Dow Lafferty.

When Schoolcraft and Drummond passed down the White river in 1818, they stopped and stayed all night at the Widow Lafferty's house, which they stated was thirty miles below Williams' and five miles above a Mr. Jones on the same river. Her farm was said to be on the right banks of the river, where she had been living for many years. Schoolcraft found Mrs. Lafferty very much excited, as were all her neighbors on that side of the river. She with others had improved farms, farms upon which they had lived for a long time, but which under the treaty made with the Cherokees they were to be forced to relinquish. Mrs. Lafferty was making arrangements then to move across the river to another farm which belonged to her deceased husband, now in Izard County, and upon which she died in 1832.

Thus the good work of this little woman found place in Schoolcraft's narrative, and her other life work was most splendidly exemplified in the lives of her sons and daughters. Lafferty's creek in that region perpetuates the name of old John Lafferty and his family to this good hour.

The Lafferty boys from 1815 to 1830 were the leaders in all good works. The eldest boy, John Lindsey Lafferty, was a noted pioneer of Van Buren County. He was born February 20, 1794. In 1836 he contested the seat of W. W. Trimble in the constitutional convention and was successful. He was in the legislature of 1838-40, and was the first county judge of Van Buren County.

In 1862, in that most trying legislature when John Harrell was speaker and Alden M. Woodruff clerk, he represented Van Buren again. He then joined Colonel T. D. Merrick's Tenth Arkansas Regiment and marched with General Bragg. He died before the war was ended in his seventy-fifth year, leaving a splendid family of children, whose descendants are among the prominent men and women of the State.

Judge John Lindsey Lafferty was certainly married once and he may have been married three or four times. The evidence points to several marriages. His first wife was Lucinda Bagley, to whom he was married in 1817, who died after giving birth to a son, Vaughn Burr Lafferty, who lived for many years with his grandfather, Asher Bagley, in Saline County. His other sons were Wesley Rufus, George Lorenzo, John Redman, Henderson Green, Austin Dallas and Alfred Wright. John Redman died in California in 1872; the others are all dead, excepting Alfred Wright, now living in Brownsville, Cleburne County, Arkansas. Their mothers' names are unknown to me.

Vaughn Burr Lafferty, married Eritha McCaleb of Hickman County, Tennessee, a granddaughter of that other old pioneer, Joseph Hutcheson, of Saline County, Arkansas. Vaughn Burr Lafferty settled in Dallas County, where for years he was the neighborhood peacemaker and advisor. Born in Arkansas, he lived on its soil eighty years, dying on Christmas Day in 1898. Vaughn Burr Lafferty learned surveying under Henry W. Conway, possessed most excellent judgment, was a good debater and a strong States' rights Democrat. He was prominent with Simon P. Hughes in the early Grange movement. He was born August 16, 1818, in Independence County and was married on April 3, 1842. His wife was the daughter of John McCaleb of Saline County, Arkansas, and was born in Hickman County, Tennessee, January 30, 1819, and died August 18, 1872, being buried at Holly Springs, Arkansas, where a suitable stone marks her last resting place. She was known to be an excellent Christian woman. V. B. Lafferty died December 25, 1898, at Lester, Arkansas, where for fifteen years he had been merchant, postmaster and justice of the peace. He is buried in Greenwood cemetery, Camden, Arkansas, and his grave is marked with an appropriate stone. The sons of V. B. and Eritha Lafferty were:

1. Lafayette Samuel Hempstead Lafferty, born January 29, 1843, and who died at New Madrid, Missouri, February 11, 1862, a member of the 12th Regiment Arkansas Volunteers, C. S. A.

2. John McCaleb Lafferty, born in Dallas County, Arkansas, February 10, 1845. He was a Confederate soldier, a comrade of Ex-senator Jones, a physician for fifteen years at Chidester, Arkansas, and for the last twenty-four years connected with the United States railway mail service. He married January 12, 1871, Nancy Minerva Hairston, who was born at Holly Springs, Arkansas, August 15, 1848, a daughter of James and Mary (Vaughn) Hairston, both natives of Fayetteville, Tennessee. Their children were: (1) Mary Eritha Lenora Lafferty, born October 4, 1875, married December 22, 1903, Dr. Jeter Lafferty Rushing, and had one child, Mary Elizabeth, born October 19, 1906; live at Chidester, Arkansas; (2) John Yandell Lafferty, born October 14, 1879, married Bessie Phillips in March, 1904, and had one child, John Lewell, born January 17, 1905; John Yandell Lafferty holds a responsible position in the baggage and express department of the Iron Mountain Railroad and is located at Little Rock; (3) Vaughn Elbert English Lafferty, born April 23, 1881, A. B. of Hendrix College, physician, now holding responsible position in Charity Hospital at New Orleans, Louisiana.

3. Druzilla Jane Lafferty, born March 9, 1847; married James Rufus Brazeale March 19, 1871, and died September 1, 1900. James Rufus Brazeale, son of Benjamin Franklin Brazeale, was born in Ripley County, Mississippi, April 10, 1838, and died June 3, 1895; Druzilla Jane and her husband were both members of the Methodist Church, South, and are both buried at Sardis Church in Dallas County, Arkansas; he was a farmer and a Mason. Their children were: (1) Isabelle Eritha, born

February 11, 1872; married January 5, 1896, London L. Knight, and have three children, Vaughn Alberta, Eritha Elizabeth and John Felix; live at Fordyce; (2) Mary Eliza Ann, born July 25, 1874; married February 14, 1901, William David Hall, and became the mother of two children, Martha Druzella and Cora Mildred; live at El Dorado.

4. Eritha Elizabeth Lafferty, born March 1, 1849, and died September 19, 1859.

5. Sarah Elender Lafferty, born May 10, 1851; married Alexander Tolbert Nailor in October, 1876, he died in December, 1879, leaving no children; his wife married Maston Decatur Fletcher of Lonoke County, Arkansas, in December, 1881, who died February 5, 1905; she died October 4, 1901; they were members of the Christian Church and are buried at Hamilton postoffice in Lonoke County; the children by the last marriage were: (1) Lloyd Lafferty Fletcher, born May 18, 1883; a farmer married and lives near Stuttgart, Arkansas; (2) Anna Gertrude Fletcher, born June 25, 1884, married November 10, 1901, to Benjamin Franklin Leonard, a farmer of Lonoke County; now living near Hillsboro, Texas, with two children, Lloyd Decatur and Cleo Gertrude; (3) Kathleen Fletcher, born May 9, 1886; married November 21, 1907, to William Orr Whitlock, a farmer near Hillsboro, Texas; (4) Arky Vaughn Fletcher, born in August, 1891, and is still unmarried.

6. Vaughn De Kalb Lafferty born December 31, 1853; physician, zealous Sunday school worker and lecturer; member Masonic fraternity and of the Methodist Church, South; represented Saline County in the Legislature of 1888 and died March 1, 1891. He was buried at Bryant, Arkansas. Unmarried.

7. Mary Mariah Lafferty, born March 29, 1856, and died December 30, 1872.

8. Arky Burr Lafferty, born April 3, 1859; married November 9, 1879, James Oliver Reinhardt, who died in September 1887, without issue; the widow married on October 28, 1890, James Wilkinson Hopper, a locomotive engineer, born in New York City, September 6, 1839, and for many years connected

with the Iron Mountain and Texas Pacific Railways; he died March 12, 1906, and was buried in Greenwood cemetery, Camden, Arkansas.

John Lindsey Lafferty was nearly seventy years of age at the time of his enlistment in the Confederate army—a magnificent age and a magnificent cause combining to round out his eventful life. It is said that at the battle of Shiloh, Judge John Lindsey Lafferty was chosen to carry the flag at the head of the regiment,—and that running some twenty or thirty paces ahead, he would turn about ever and anon to cheer his comrades forward. The Stars and Bars were a glorious incentive but the long flowing white locks of this grand old man made a most picturesque figure and inspired his comrades to the loftiest deeds of daring. His descendants are entitled to look upon their ancestor with the most fulsome pride and Arkansans of all shades of opinion will certainly justify them.

Another son of John Lafferty, the pioneer, was Jacob Binks Lafferty, who in 1825 married a daughter of old Colonel James Miller of Miller's creek, Independence County, and a sister of ex-Governor W. R. Miller. Binks had a daughter who married twice, her last husband being Rev. William Atchley Maples of Carroll County.

Another son, Henderson Lafferty, married in 1825 a daughter of that other pioneer, Colonel Craig of Greenbrier. He was one of the greatest of the early Arkansas Methodist preachers, and possessed many of the characteristics of his uncle, Eli Lindsey.

Another son, Austin F. Lafferty, married in Independence County and reared a family.

The youngest son of the pioneer was Lorenzo Dow Lafferty, commonly called "the Rover." He went to Texas and there published a book entitled "The Life and Adventures of Lorenzo Dow Lafferty," which was published by a New York house, and dealt largely with the romance of early Arkansas life. He married Elvira Chriswell and had children; Martha, Matilda Jane, Sarah, Eliza, Eva, Margaret, Francis, Burwell, Dow and Albert Glenville.

The boys of old John Lafferty were an honor to his name, and stand as monuments to the sturdy virtues of the widow Lafferty. The Berkshire Hills of Massachusetts never turned out a more honorable, a more vigorous, a more patriotic set of boys than came from the old Lafferty cabin on the barrens of Independence County.

When honors are fairly divided John Lafferty of Lafferty's creek, the hero and pioneer, will be entitled to a full share; and the Widow Lafferty, the great Methodist mother of the barrens, will be crowned with laurels.

THE LAFFERTY ANCESTRAL MOTTO.

John Lindsey Lafferty, in marrying Lucinda Bagley, married a daughter of a soldier, then drawing a pension, who had served in the First regiment of the New Jersey Continental Line. The descendants of John Lindsey Lafferty are thus doubly tied to patriotic ancestry. Asher Bagley died in what is now Saline County, and his daughter, Lucinda Lafferty, died in Van Buren County on April 23, 1840, in her thirty-ninth year. John Lindsey Lafferty also served in the Eighth Arkansas legislature in 1851.

For the edification of all the Laffertys of Arkansas, I print their ancient motto in Irish and Latin. If they cannot understand it, that is their misfortune. There is no law against an American or Irish descent studying his ancestral tongue.

The Lafferty motto as engraved on their arms was:

O Dhia Gach an Cabliar—
Nec Timeo nec Sperno—
Min Sicker Reag.

THE HALL FAMILY.

William Hall, Sr., was born in South Carolina, sometime in the year 1769. Of his parents we have no record, save that his father came from Ireland. When quite a young man he went from South Carolina to Georgia and settled a farm near the county site of Forsyth County. In the year 1794 he married Mary Hamilton and became the father of ten children, John,

Alexander, George, Sarah, Samuel, David C., Mary, Jack, James and William, Jr. With his family he entered Arkansas in the spring of 1834, settling in Dallas County, seven miles west of Holly Springs; at a later period he moved up near Tulip, at which place he died on July 20, 1854; his wife died in 1865, and both were buried at Old Tulip. Of this old pioneer family but two are living; Mary and Sarah have their homes near Cedarville, Crawford County, Arkansas. George, Jack and William, Jr., died during the Civil war; Samuel died in 1854, and John and Alexander died sometime in 1890. David Clark Hall was born in Forsyth County, Georgia, August 20, 1822, and came with his father to Arkansas in 1834; he was married on December 26, 1844, to Martha Ann Dickinson, to whom was born nine children; (1) Mary Kate, born June 22, 1846, and died August 9, 1871; (2) James T., born March 8, 1848, died May 25, 1897; (3) Sylvester D., born October 8, 1849, now living in Dallas County, Arkansas; (4) Robert D., born August 14, 1851, now living at Arkadelphia, Arkansas; (5) Martha D., born July 22, 1855, died September 17, 1859; (6) Edward M., born December 12, 1857, now living at Arkadelphia, Arkansas; (7) Charles G., born August 18, 1860, died July 31, 1879; (8) William D., born January 4, 1863, now living at El Dorado, Arkansas; (9) Sally, born January 14, 1867, died June 4, 1867.

David Clark Hall and his wife lived near Tulip, Arkansas, where his wife died on August 29, 1871. On December 21, 1871, he was married the second time to Mrs. Lucy H. Kittrell. Three children were born to this marriage, Ida V., Luta G., and Geneva K. David C. Hall continued his residence in Dallas County until the latter part of 1886, when he moved to Arkadelphia, where he died May 24, 1887. His last wife still lives at that place.

CHAPTER XXXVII.

The Kaufmans, Coffmans and Cuffmans.

All names as they run through the centuries change form, and no name is as difficult to identify through all its ramifications as is the name Kaufman, Coffman or Cuffman. There can be little doubt but that these three forms represent the name of the same old German family, the Kaufmans. In Rupp's Thirty Thousand Germans who landed at Philadelphia during the 18th century the name Kaufman appears many times, but the name Coffman or Cuffman is not to be found. They were Palatines and in the main shipped from Rotterdam to Philadelphia. The first on Rupp's list was Henry Kaufman in 1727; then John Kauffman in 1737; then Hans Jacob Kaufman in 1738, and in the same year John George Kauffman. From this on until 1764 eighteen other males bearing the name, Kauffman or Kaufman, entered Philadelphia, and in 1750 Solomon Caufman is presented. In 1764 Conrad Korfman came over. This is enough to show that the German spelling of the word is either Kauffman or Kaufman.

Now note the transition. I have followed up the immediate after history of many of these emigrants of Rupp and find that when these Germans bought lands, or did other business which brought them into contact with the English Colonial office holders of Pennsylvania, Maryland or Virginia, that the word Kaufman immediately changed to Coffman on the American records. The Germans simply spelled it one way and the English record makers another.

In the history of Lancaster, Pennsylvania, the county to which nearly all of these Kaufmans as enumerated by Rupp made their way, I find that one, Michael Kaufman, migrated from the vicinity of Greensted, Hesse, on the Upper Rhine for America and entered Lancaster County at sometime between the years 1710 and 1719. The history states that Michael died soon after leaving a son, John, and a daughter, Elizabeth, and that their guardian bought of Penn's Commissioners, a large tract of land in the vicinity of Landisonville, upon which John Kaufman settled. All that is known of Elizabeth is that she married Christian Stoneman in 1734. John Kaufman died leaving three sons, Christian, Michael and John.

Old Michael Kaufman did not die soon after, but on the contrary migrated to the Shenandoah Valley, Virginia, in 1727 or 1728. In Wayland's German Element in the Valley it is set out that Michael Kaufman of Lancaster County, Pennsylvania, bought lands of Daniel Stover at Massanutting in the Shenandoah Valley in 1729. It appears that Stover had made false representations to Kaufman in Lancaster County, Pennsylvania, by and through which Kaufman with a part of his family was induced to enter the Shenandoah. At that time no one lived in the valley of the Shenandoah, and Michael Kaufman in making this settlement of Massanutting earned for it the title which history accords it of "The First Permanent White Settlement West of the Blue Ridge." After the settlement was made and the Germans were beginning to make a show it was found that Stover's grant was defective, and the Virginia Colonial Council upon petition of these German settlers quieted their title and gave them lawful latitude to develop and prosper. This is now in Page County. In 1736 a deed is recorded showing that Michael Coffman lived on the south side of the Shenandoah river adjoining Martin Coffman's land at Elk creek. In the same year Michael Coffman bought other lands on the Shenandoah, and in February, 1737, Martin Coffman of Pennsylvania bought six hundred acres of land on the Shenandoah. In the same neighborhood were several Coffmans and in that neighborhood the name has prevailed for more than one hundred years. One of the trustees of Woodstock Academy at its incorporation was Samuel Coofman in 1817. In Hening's Statutes the charges fixed by the legislature of Virginia for a ferry from the land of John Coffman in the county of Shenandoah across the south fork were fixed by law on December 7, 1796.

Martin Coffman died in 1748 leaving a large estate and between that and 1800 many entries of land were made for Coffmans by the name of Martin, David, Augustine, Andrew, Jacob and John. Some of these are spelled Coffman and others Coofman, yet all descending from the old German, Michael Kaufman. It is my opinion that the spelling Cuffman is a corruption of the Coofman, which in turn was a corruption of the spelling Coffman, all being corruptions of the original spelling Kauffman or Kaufman.

In Arkansas Christopher Kaufman, known to have come from the Shenandoah valley inhabited and cultivated six hundred and forty acres on Kaufman's Bayou, Arkansas County, from 1803 to 1806, and from 1809 to 1812 in person, and by tenants from 1806 to 1809 and was granted six hundred and forty acres under the act of Congress of 1814. Under the same act George Kepler proved that he had possessed and cultivated two hundred and forty arpens from 1801 to 1813 on the Lake of the Prairie, bounded above by Coffman and below by Lavergne. From this it is evident that the old spelling in Arkansas County for Christopher was both Kaufman and Coffman. Nuttal adverts to Kaufman's Bayou but nearly all of the later spelling confirms Coffman. Christopher Kaufman died in Arkansas County being one of the earliest pioneers of that region, but as to his family I am not further advised. The name Kaufman and Coffman as place names are landmarks in Arkansas history.

OTHER COFFMANS.

C. T. Coffman, the present county judge of Pulaski County, says that his great grandfather was named Andrew Coffman and that he emigrated from Virginia to Granger County, Tennessee, prior to 1800. That he ended his days in Granger County living to be eighty-four years of age. He had a son, Andrew Coffman, born in Granger County who in 1852 migrated to Hot Springs County, Arkansas, where he died about the year 1884. This Andrew Coffman had a son, Hugh W. Coffman, the father of C. T. Coffman, who was born in Granger County, Tennessee, in 1821, moved to Carroll County, Arkansas, in April, 1854, where he now lives (1907) at the age of eighty-six. Hugh W. Coffman states that his grandfather, Andrew Coffman, was a soldier in the Revolutionary war and that he has often heard him narrate his experiences growing out of that struggle.

All this is right and all wrong. The Nashville, Tenn., Military Grants from North Carolina show that Andrew Coffman was granted on October 22, 1872, 200 acres on Lick creek in Green County and not Granger.

THE CUFFMANS.

The traditions of this family as gleaned from old settlers of Sumner County, Tennessee, are that Pavatt Cuffman was born November 30, 1782, probably in the Shenandoah valley, Virginia. The traditions are that the father of Pavatt Cuffman was named Thomas Cuffman, and that he was born in Virginia, that he either married there or in North Carolina a woman by the name of Pavatt, and that he died either in Virginia or North Carolina. It is certain that he left a wife and two children, Thomas and Pavatt. I have not been able to identify this particular Thomas Cuffman, but I feel assured that he descends from Michael Kaufman of the Shenandoah valley.

Personal investigation since the above was written shows Thomas Cuffman a surveyor of roads in Sumner County, Tennessee, in 1796, and as serving on a petit jury in 1797. This leaves little room for doubt that the father of Pavatt Cuffman was Thomas Cuffman, the traditionary ancestor. The records also show that this Thomas Cuffman was from Shenandoah County, Virginia, which virtually makes him a descendant of Michael Kaufman, the pioneer. He died and was buried in Sumner County, Tennessee.

It is unfortunate that the census rolls of Virginia for 1790 and 1800 are lost, as they would throw much light on the settlement of this region. The census of Virginia for 1810 for Shenandoah County, which at that time included Page and a part of Rockingham, contains the names of twenty-six Coffmans, each of which represented a head of a family. Besides these there were three Pavatts. The court records of Shenandoah County as to the marriage licenses of the dates 1780-1800 are not available, and it is not therefore possible from these sources to determine which of the Coffmans married a Pavatt, or Pavett as it is sometimes spelled. We shall assume therefore that the traditional Thomas who married a Pavatt was the real Thomas and the facts show that he was a grandson of Michael Kaufman, the original settler of 1729 through Martin Kaufman, his son. Thomas Coffman married a Pavatt between 1770 and 1800, dying in the same period. The traditions of the family now remaining in the valley show that as early as 1780 men of the name began to emigrate to the west, but I have not been able to find from those sources the migration of Thomas Coffman and his two sons. In the census of 1820 for Tennessee, the earliest extant, the names of Pavatt and Thomas Cuffman appear as follows:

"Purvat Cuffman, one male six to ten, one sixteen to twenty-six, one twenty-six to forty-five, three females six to ten, and one female twenty-six to forty-five, with four slaves."

Thomas Cuffman also appears immediately after Purvat as a married man but without children or slaves, both man and wife being between twenty-six and forty-five. No other Cuffmans appear in Sumner County and as there was no one enumerated in either the family of Pavatt or Thomas over forty-five, the inference is that the Widow Cuffman was dead at that time.

Of Thomas Cuffman, the younger brother, little further is known. The official war records show that Thomas Cuffman, so spelled in one place, and Thomas Coffman, in another, served in the War of 1812 in Colonel John Coffee's Regiment of Tennessee Mounted Volunteers in Captain John W. Byrn's Company. He left Sumner County shortly after his marriage and the traditions say that he went to Arkansas. Beyond this nothing is known.

Pavatt Cuffman was born November 30, 1782, and migrated with his father and brother to Tennessee between 1790 and 1795. In 1807 he married Jane Kinsall, daughter of Moses Kinsall, who came with his family to Sumner County, Tennessee, in 1796. A sister of Jane Kinsall married Colonel Montgomery of Sumner County, Tennessee, who was from Virginia. Pavatt Cuffman was a physician of the old style and did an extensive practice in Sumner and adjoining counties; he stood high in the community where he lived and had many substantial friends. He was noted for his honesty, fair dealings and for his charity. He was also a farmer, and was counted very well to do for a man of his day and time, owning a considerably quantity of land and a large number of slaves. He died September 14, 1840, and was buried in the family burying ground on the old Cuffman homestead near Hendersonville, Tennessee. He was the father of six children, Iantha, Eliza Ann, Josephus, Julia Jane, Benjamin and Mary Martha.

Josephus Cuffman, the oldest son and third child was born March 19, 1814, in Sumner County, Tennessee; he was reared on a farm and at twenty-two years of age enlisted in Captain William Trusdale's Company, Second Tennessee Mounted Militia, and served as a private in the Florida War of 1836. He was twice married: First, to Mary A. Smith of Sumner County; second, to Mary E. Carroll. Five children were born to the first marriage, Benjamin Franklin, Mary Jane, David Pavatt, Robert M., and Daniel W. The children of the second marriage were Rowena, John H., James M., Joida, Almeda and Almira.

Mary E. Carroll, the second wife was a daughter of Wiley Carroll and Polly Hunnicutt, who was a daughter of Bartlett Hunnicutt and Sally Holt, both North Carolinians. Bartlett Hunnicutt served as a private in the War of 1812, and Gabriel Holt, father of Sally Hunnicutt was reputed to have been a Revolutionary soldier.

The following testimonial of the family physician of Josephus Cuffman is worthy of perpetuation and will be appreciated by his Arkansas descendants: "Josephus Cuffman was born in Sumner County, Tennessee, March 19, 1814. He died October 27, 1869. He was a man remarkable for his love and devotion to his family. He had raised to majority four sons and one daughter, and leaves six little ones, the youngest two being but three weeks old. He was a man of the strictest honesty in all his dealings, and of stern and unbending integrity. As a husband he was one of the kindest and most devoted; as a parent, ever ready to advise, assist and protect his children; as a neighbor, kind and obliging; as a man and friend, true, faithful and ever ready to assist. He has gone to his grave leaving many to mourn his loss, and all may profit by the contemplation of his honesty, and his affection for his wife, children and friends. James Franklin, M. D. October 28, 1869."

John H. Cuffman, son of Josephus Cuffman by the second marriage was born in Sumner County, Tennessee, educated in that county and Hickory Flat Institute, Kentucky; he graduated from the Medical Department of Vanderbilt University in 1889, and removed to Arkansas the same year. He is now located at Gurdon engaged in the general practice of medicine, at the same time being a surgeon for the St. Louis, Iron Mountain & Southern Railroad, and the Gurdon and Ft. Smith Railroad. He married Mary E. Littlejohn of Dallas County, a descendant of one of the pioneers of that region. Her father, Alex W. Littlejohn was the boy companion and life long friend of Ex-Senator James K. Jones.

Another son of Josephus Cuffman, James M. Cuffman, is a resident of Nashville, Tennessee.

CHAPTER XXXVIII.

Augustus Hill Garland.

Augustus Hill Garland was well born and had furnished to his hands many of the elements out of which greatness is evolved, but his success is not to be attributed to these alone, nor to any considerable degree. His father, Rufus King Garland, was a Virginian of Scotch-Irish descent, of a family whose respectability extended through more than a century of Virginia's colonial career, and who in his young life removed to North Carolina, and afterwards to Tennessee.

At that time there was living at Lexington, Henderson County, Tennessee, a young woman named Barbara Hill, who, born April 10, 1811, near Louisburg, Franklin County, North Carolina, was destined to exercise a tremendous influence upon the life and fortunes of Rufus King Garland. She had removed with her parents in her tenth year to Tennessee and had finished her education at the female academy in Lebanon. In 1827 at Lexington, Rufus King Garland married Barbara Hill, and not long after their marriage they removed to Tipton County, Tennessee, near Covington where they resided for a few years. In this place they prospered and here three children were born.

1. Elizabeth John Garland, born December 1, 1828, who married Captain Robert P. Cook, of Virginia antecedents, born Bedford City, Virginia, March 31, 1815, a pioneer of Arkansas who settled near Brownstown, Sevier County in 1836, and who died at Arkadelphia on the 15th day of June, 1880. The mother died at the same place December 31, 1896. The children of this marriage were Robert T. Cook, now a prominent citizen of Hot Springs; Garland Cook of the St. Louis, Iron Mountain and Southern Railroad, now living in Little Rock; Fanny Cook who married Dr. Ware, a presiding elder of the Methodist Church, South; Laura Cook, who married Eli McDaniel of Arkadelphia, and Barbara Cook who never married.

2. Rufus King Garland, Jr., was born May 22, 1830, and in his after life, became a prominent character in Arkansas a noted lawyer and a great politician, and who married Isabelle Walker, the accomplished daughter of David Walker, the wealthiest man in his day in Hempstead County; he owned a thousand acres of good land, was a first class lawyer, a planter and a recognized preacher of the Methodist Church. Rufus King Garland, Jr., lived a long life in Arkansas, but died without descendants. He died at Prescott, December 12, 1886.

3. Augustus Hill Garland, the youngest child, born June 11, 1832, whose further life is the object of this sketch.

He inherited from his father and mother a strong mind and a strong will. The conservation of that will marked him for a life of greatness, and the exercise of that will brought the realization. Before he was a year old his parents moved to Arkansas and settled upon a farm near the present town of Garland, in Miller County, then in Lafayette County. Upon this farm his father died within a very short time, and upon that farm, overlooking the Red river, was buried. Thus it happened that young Garland never knew much of his father, but notwithstanding this always held his memory in the very highest esteem. So strong was this sentiment that he was frequently charged with ancestry worship, a charge that he never took the pains to deny. It is true that he never visited near Garland, in any part of his after eventful life, even after his mother had remarried and become the head of a great house in Hempstead County, without going to the grave of his father, and with uncovered head standing before his last resting place. On one occasion he put up at the Russell residence on the opposite side of the river for the night, announcing to his host that he desired to be called early in order that he might cross the river and pay his accustomed visit to his father's grave. His host told him that such an arrangement would be useless, for at the last rise of the Red river the banks upholding the cemetery had been undermined and all the graves washed away. This affected Mr. Garland very much, and kept him from retiring until long after midnight. He walked backwards and forwards over the veranda of the old house and was frequently overheard to say, "Would to God I knew where to find his bones."

What I propose to do first is merely to consider a little of Garland's life prior to the events which gave him a prominent State character, the sure forerunner of his national character, and then to refer to any other facts and circumstances which may help us to account for his greatness as a man and as a statesman. I do not wish to be impudent, nor shall I be servile, believing, however, with Lord Beaconsfield that it is better to transgress through impudence than servility.

The first great fact to remember is that Augustus H. Garland was in every essential a monument to Southern character and therefore a true representative of all that is good in American worth. He was an American to the core, and this Americanism found root in that other circumstance that he was born in the South.

He was born in Tennessee—a fact that may and may not be of importance. It is also a fact that before he was out of his swaddling clothes he was taken by his parents to Arkansas—a fact of greater importance possibly than his birth date and place. What he would have been under a life tutelage in Tennessee, no one can say—no one can guess. He might have worked out a greater stature and then again he might not. His greatness came to him by and through his Arkansas mantle and not through the clothing of his Tennessee birth. He was proud of his Tennessee lineage, but prouder of his Arkansas home. The one was accidental, while the other was to the greatest extent the result of his own volition. Whenever you are in your next fit of depression about Arkansas and most piously wish yourself a denizen of a greater State, it may be well to do a little stock-taking and calculate your profits as well as your losses. Garland, as an Arkansan, lifted the State to a higher pedestal of honor and power, and this is all to your good. You can, if you choose, do likewise.

GARLAND A TYPICAL ARKANSAN.

Garland was not only an Arkansan, but a typical one; one of the very kind that many Northern men make a point of disliking. He lived in Arkansas while it was a territory and knew the pioneers and was thoroughly well acquainted with pioneer life. He lived in Arkansas under every one of its constitutions and was therefore a good constitutional Arkansan. He was a "before the war" Arkansan, a "through the war" Arkansan, and a first-class "after the war" Arkansan. He lived in South Arkansas and was educated there in good old pioneer schools. His mother was Arkansan to the core and his father was buried on Arkansas soil. His mother remarried one of the old type of Arkansas gentlemen, Judge Thomas Hubbard, a prominent attorney of Hempstead County, prosecuting attorney from 1828 to 1832, and judge of the Sixth Circuit from 1854 to 1856, and it is no discredit to the stepfather to say that he loved and honored the stepson to as great a degree as a father could honor a son.

Shortly after the death of his father, his mother, Mrs. Barbara Hill Garland, rented out the Red River farm, and with her children and servants, settled a new home in the hills, some thirty miles from the farm, which she called "Spring Hill," at which place in 1837 she was remarried to Judge Hubbard. The residence at Spring Hill was maintained until 1844 when it was transferred to Washington, Arkansas, where it was continued until the death of Judge Hubbard in 1865.

Augustus H. Garland received his early education from his mother and step-father, two characters most admirably adapted to this end. He also attended schools at Spring Hill and Washington, and was afterwards sent to Bardstown College, at Bardstown, Kentucky, where he spent six years. His intellectual habit of mind exhibited itself early, and formed the basis for that strong tie which always existed between his step-father, Judge Hubbard, and himself. He was an omnivorous reader and went to college with a larger miscellaneous stock of reading than was usual for one in those parts, and in this sense he was like Edmund Burke. I can not say that he read no novels, for that would be a charge against his emotions; nor that he eschewed poetry, which would be to attack his intelligence; I suppose he was like all other sturdy boys, an omnivorous reader of novels and poetry, in which sense he is again comparable with Edmund Burke. Certain it is that he read much history, which at that time meant Rollin, Plutarch, Irving, Burke and Macauley—a far better course than most young men take today. A master of Plutarch is already a master of historic thought. He also read Blackstone—long before he had taken the notion to read law. His scholarly stepfather was doubtless the cause of this excursion into the greatest law book that has ever been penned. A master of Blackstone is fixed in the saddle of the science of law and no pernicious bucking of the steed can unhorse him. Among the students at Bardstown he stood high. Father Hill of St. Louis, who was a teacher at that institution, in his after life, said of General Garland: "That Gus Garland had one of the greatest minds of any student that ever appeared at Bardstown."

After graduating he returned to the residence of his stepfather in Hempstead County, learned as to the schools, but undetermined as to a vocation in life. His mother had her way and he was given freedom to choose for himself. Judge Hubbard, however, bided his time and in time had his way. For a year Garland taught school in Sevier County, but being possessed of a strong penchant for clerical work, returned to Hempstead County and took a place in the office of the county clerk. Specimens of his work are not handed down to us, but traditions are full of glow as to their worth. He was not fixed in his political principles, but his leaning was to the Whigs. When one looks at the record of Whiggery in Hempstead County, from 1835 to 1855, he has no dificulty in explaining this leaning. That county was for years about evenly divided between the Democrats and Whigs—one party succeeding at one election, and the other at the next, the only exception being in favor of S. T. Sanders, the county clerk, who held office from 1838 to 1868, through the vicissitudes of all parties and the favorite of all men. About this time, the date of Garland's entrance upon a career, the Democrats had been in power for two years and the Whigs felt that it was their turn next. He was a favorite of Judge Hubbard and also of Mr. Sanders, and the Whigs thought that with their help they could make Garland the treasurer of the county, a thing which appealed to his young mind and won his consent. This, however, brought the iron hand of the stepfather down and carried the mother with it. Judge Hubbard forbade Gus Garland to run for county treasurer, and the mother united her prayers to her husband's remonstrance. Gus backed down, entered Judge Hubbard's office and began the serious study of law. In after years Garland asked his stepfather why he had so vigorously opposed his taking a county office. The judge answered: "For this reason. You had a legal mind and you owed it to yourself and the people to develop it. Had you been elected treasurer, you would have remained treasurer all your life, and the triumphant leadings of your mind would have been stifled."

HIS MARRIAGE.

The society of old Washington was possibly the most cultivated of the State, and in this young Garland spent his young boyhood and manhood. He had for his friends the ablest and best Whigs and Democrats of that day and was surrounded by as high a class of womanhood as the world has produced. Captain Simon T. Sanders, a North Carolinian by birth, and the most popular man in Hempstead County at that time, had a most accomplished daughter, Sarah Virginia Sanders, whose love was won by A. H. Garland, and who became his wife. The union was blessed with eight children, four of whom died in infancy, while four reached maturity. Sarah Virginia Garland died at Little Rock in her Scott street residence in 1879 and was buried in Mount Holly cemetery.

Garland was an American also in his love for debate and was most fond of this class of educational societies. He was unquestionably the possessor of great powers of illustration, explanation and expatiation. He was not great in the reservoirs of critical learning, but was in every sense a virile, vigorous thinker. Being admitted to the bar under the advice of his stepfather he removed to Little Rock, where he formed a partnership with Ebenezer Cummins, under the firm name of Cummins & Garland. Judge Cummins at that time was the leading lawyer of Little Rock and the fortunate master of a large and lucrative practice. Within a year Garland had acquainted himself with the demands of this practice, and, at Cummins' death, shortly afterward, succeeded to this practice in its entirety. Thus before he was twenty-eight years of age he was in possession of one of the most lucrative law practices in the State of Arkansas, and but for the breaking out of the war in 1860 would possibly have become the richest practitioner of the State.

HIS FIRST VISIT TO WASHINGTON, D. C.

In his little book, "Experience in the United States Supreme Court," Garland has himself told of this first visit to the capital of the country. He says: "In December, 1860, when I was half way between twenty-eight and twenty-nine years of age, I left Little Rock, Arkansas, to come to the Supreme Court for the purpose of attending to the case of McGee v. Mathis, and several others. At that time it required nearly an entire week to make the trip from Little Rock to Washington." At Washington he put up at the Kirkwood house, which afterward came to be known as the Palais Royal, and is now refitted and known as The Raleigh. Accompanied by Reverdy Johnson on the 26th of December, 1860, he was enrolled as an attorney at law, solicitor in chancery, and proctor in admiralty. He did not visit Washington again for five years, his next appearance being in the Test Oath cases, wherein he blazoned his right to stand as a national character and laid the foundations strong and secure for his after greatness. But between his first and second trips to Washington much of historic moment intervenes, which we shall now turn aside to examine. The four cases filed by Garland at this time involved the impairing of the obligations of contracts by State law, and the Circuit and Supreme Courts of Arkansas had decided adversely to Garland. These cases slumbered at Washington for six years, but through Garland's untiring efforts were finally decided in his favor. The amount involved financially was large to the extreme, and, if no war had come, the decisions in his favor, according to Garland's own statement, would have enabled him to retire from practice, but owing to the war they profited him nothing.

GARLAND IN THE CIVIL WAR.

He left Washington on January 15, 1861, and arrived at Little Rock a week later. Here all was turmoil and excitement. Men were preparing for war, and Garland was borne with the people into its seething center. A constitutional convention was called and he was elected a member thereof from Pulaski County. This convention held sessions from March 4 to March 21, 1861, and from May 6 to June 3 of the same year. In the meantime the Southern Confederacy was formed and on May 10, 1861, the Arkansas convention sent R. W. Johnson, A. H. Garland, H. F. Thomasson, Albert Rust and W. W. Watkins as delegates to the Provisional Confederate Congress at Montgomery, Alabama, Garland receiving the highest vote. Here, Garland lived in the same house with Alexander H. Stephens and formed a friendship which was only terminated by the death of the distinguished vice president. At the general election in 1862 Garland was elected to the lower house of the Confederate Congress from the Third district of Arkansas, and at the general election in 1864 was reelected from the same district. The delegates to the lower house from Arkansas, who sat with Garland, were Thomas B. Hanley, G. D. Royston, F. I. Batson and

R. K. Garland, his brother. During his second term in the lower house the Confederate legislature of Arkansas, after a spirited contest between him and Albert Pike, elected him to the Confederate Senate, which caused him to resign his place in the lower house, where he was succeeded by D. W. Carroll. Thus, A. H. Garland served in the Provisional Congress of the Confederacy at Montgomery, Alabama, and also in both the upper and lower houses of the Confederate Congress at Richmond, Virginia, during the entire life of the Confederacy. The history of this most remarkable body has not as yet been written, but when the future historian shall outline its work in its entirety it will challenge the admiration of the world. To legislate for an armed struggle of the magnitude of the Civil war in a territory surrounded and blockaded by the enemy at every point and to carry that struggle successfully through a period of four years will not only merit but command impartial attention. With the downfall of the Confederacy, Garland went back to Little Rock to find himself absolutely impoverished. His negroes were gone; his property worthless, and his splendid practice absolutely destroyed, while military law dominated the entire land. He had to live, and in July, 1865, made a trip to Washington, called upon President Johnson and with much amiability besought him to grant a pardon, wiping out all of Garland's sins of omission and commission growing out of the Civil war. Reverdy Johnson, the man who had introduced him to the Supreme Court five years before, seconded the efforts of Garland, and Johnson issued the pardon. It was a huge document, of which Garland was proud, as in his language it virtually made him a new man. Going over to the Supreme Court, he dug up the papers he had filed there years before and resolved to prosecute them to the end.

THE TEST OATH IMPEDIMENTA.

One thing, however, stood in his way as it stood in the way of all lawyers of the South. On January 24, 1865, Congress had passed an act disbarring every attorney from practice before the Supreme Court of the United States or any Circuit or District Court of the United States unless said attorney should take the iron-clad oath of July 2, 1862, which recited that he had never borne arms against the United States, nor voluntarily given counsel, aid or encouragement to persons in armed hostility to the government. This act of Congress was made a rule of court in March, 1865, and Garland found himself although able and willing to practice, without the right to enter a single district, circuit or the United States Supreme Court. He said to Reverdy Johnson, "I am going to fight the constitutionality of that law, and I desire your counsel and help." Johnson, with his usual generosity, replied, "I will help you gladly, but will take no fee." Garland was afterward advised to secure the help of Matt Carpenter, who answered in almost the same words that Johnson had used.

Garland went home, prepared his petition to the Supreme Court attacking the constitutionality of the law and filed a brief, which formed the basis of the after arguments made by Garland, Reverdy Johnson and Carpenter. No greater State paper has ever been filed in the Supreme Court than Garland's brief. He argued that exclusion from the practice of law or from any other vocation in life for past conduct was a punishment for said conduct; that a bill of this character was of the nature of a bill of pains and penalties and therefore within the constitutional inhibition against the passage of bills of attainder and therefore unconstitutional. He also set up many other points which made the law unconstitutional on the ex post facto side. He argued strongly also that attorneys were not officers of the United States, but officers of the particular courts which enrolled them and were responsible solely to them, and could only be deprived of their special office by the judgment of those courts, after opportunity to be heard had been afforded. That their admission and exclusion to and from the practice of law were judicial powers, absolutely outside the range of congressional action. He further argued fully and forcibly the nature, extent and effect of executive pardons and in every item carried the court with him.

On the evidential side he showed his admission in an Arkansas court and his continuance on the Arkansas roll of attorneys; he showed the intervention of the Civil war, secession and his alliance with the Southern cause; his membership of the lower house of the Confederate Congress and afterward his membership of the Confederate Senate. It was impossible therefore for him to take the oath of July 2, 1862, or to obey the rule of the court of March, 1865; he filed the pardon granted by the president in July, 1865, which gave him a clearance against all offenses against the United States and their effects. He showed that he had taken the oath required by the pardon and annexed to it, and argued that all other oaths were unconstitutional.

When he got ready to go on to Washington to argue the case he found himself without money. He dropped in to the office of S. H. Tucker, the moneyed man of the town, and told him that he wanted $100, for which he could give no security except his note. Tucker looked at him a minute and said, "Gus, what would you do in Washington with $100? You would look shabby." Then turning to his clerk, he said, "Give Garland $500 and take his note for it. There is no security, but I believe the money will be repaid." The money was repaid.

The case was known as "Ex parte Garland," and was argued for Garland by Garland himself, by Reverdy Johnson, Matt Carpenter and Mr. Marr, an attorney from Louisiana. For the government it was argued by Attorney General Sneed and by Henry Stansberry, special counsel. The case attracted wide attention, as it involved the return of the old Southern lawyers to practice before the Supreme Court. Johnson and Carpenter were giants, but Garland proved his right that day to stand side by side with these men. Matt Carpenter said: "Garland, you have this day, stepped from a provincial to a national field."

The Supreme Court was constituted then as follows: Chief Justice S. P. Chase, Justices James M. Wayne, R. C. Grier, Noah H. Swayne, David Davis, Samuel Nelson, Nathan Clifford, Samuel F. Miller and Stephen J. Field. Justice Field delivered the opinion of the court, from which Justices Swayne and Davis dissented. The case will be found in Fourth Wallace, a book abounding with questions of great constitutional moment. From this it will appear that seven justices decided with Garland, maintaining every contention that he made, while two dissented. For some reason Garland in his little book, "Experience in the Supreme Court," printed in 1898, held that but five judges were on his side and four against him.

James G. Blaine, in his "Twenty Years in Congress," stated that there was a strong disposition on the part of Southern Democrats in the convention which nominated Mr. Seymour to nominate Judge Chase, as he had favored the application in ex parte Garland to admit their lawyers to practice in United States courts. Garland said that Blaine was mistaken, that Judge Chase, the chief justice, was a dissenter. The records, however, show that only Swayne and Davis dissented and that Blaine was therefore right.

Garland was now not only a pardoned man, but admitted to the right to practice law in all the United States courts, and the right which he gained for himself inured to every lawyer of the South who had been disbarred. This brought Garland prominently before not only the Southern bar, but the entire bar of the United States. This episode was in all probability the greatest act of his life, and if he had done nothing more, would entitle him to rank among the very greatest men of the United States. Credit should also be given to those grand men, Reverdy Johnson and Matt Carpenter, and Arkansas has special reason to forever remember their names.

THE RECONSTRUCTION PERIOD IN ARKANSAS.

Returning to Little Rock, he set about to resume the practice of law and to this end formed a partnership with James White and L. C. Nash under the firm name of Garland, White & Nash. A few months later, Mr. White died, and the firm became Garland & Nash. Some years later the firm was dissolved, Nash going West, and a new partnership was formed with Sterling R. Cockrill, under the firm name of Garland & Cockrill. When what was called the Rebel legislature met in 1866, John T. Jones and Andrew Hunter were elected senators of the United States. Hunter resigned in a short time and Garland was selected in his place. While Garland had been fortunate in conquering his way into the Supreme Court he was not able to overcome the political antagonism of the United

States Senate. Both he and Jones were denied admission to that honorable body at that time. From 1866 to 1874, Garland's life was devoted to his law practice. In 1868 he was sent by the Democracy of Arkansas at the head of its delegation to the Democratic convention at New York city, the convention which nominated Horatio Seymour. While there he had a picture taken, which in after years was used by a Tennessee artist, Miss Crawley, for painting the portrait which now hangs in the State house at Little Rock. Garland always liked this picture and used it in his little book, "Experience in the Supreme Court." There is another picture of Garland which adorns the walls of the Department of Justice at Washington, but which his friends say is not a true portrait.

HIS GREAT LETTER TO VICE PRESIDENT STEPHENS.

In the same year, after the election was over, Senator Garland wrote a letter to Vice President Alexander H. Stephens, a copy of which he kept and which is now in the possession of Mr. R. T. Cook of Hot Springs, Arkansas. On account of its importance it is reproduced entire:

A. H. Garland.
L. B. Nash.

GARLAND & NASH.
Attorneys at Law.

LITTLE ROCK, ARK., Nov. 9, 1868.

My Dear Mr. Stephens:

The election on last Tuesday, the 3d inst., has resulted in the choosing of General Grant to the presidency of the United States. which I have been expecting for the past two months, and I do not, for one moment, suppose that you are astonished in the least, at this result. Grant will go into office with influence and weight of character sufficient to destroy the liberties of the country as well as the country itself in a very short time; and so too, he will have it in his power, if disposed, to arrest the tide that is now upon us, and to restore the country to peace and order, which in a few years would bring us prosperity again as a nation. It is with him, in my calm and deliberate judgment, to accomplish one of these alternatives. If he follows the programme and the wishes of the party whose candidate he was, ruin, red ruin, will be the consequence, and that at no distant day; if on the other hand, he follows his own judgment and tries to administer the government according to the constitution, and in justice to all, he will rescue us from destruction, and lay broad, deep and permanent the foundation for our future well being.

Which will he do? I know so little of General Grant as a public man, I am utterly unable to form a satisfactory opinion to myself as to this. I know him personally, but not well, and he says nothing on public matters; but I have always heard he was a man of sense, and particularly a man of his own will and judgment. From his acts towards our soldiers and others in trouble after the surrender, I can not think him a bad man at all, but rather a fair minded man. Of course much has been said of and about him, during the late political contest, by his opponents, that they themselves in their cool moments do not believe—the results of, I suppose, what is called *political license*. Now then, whatever tinge or coloring may have been given to his feelings in passing through the recent ordeal of an election, which under the most favorable auspices is always trying, he must, now that the storm of battle has cleared away, reflect calmly upon what lies before him. Certainly he is not a fool, and certainly he would like to live in history as the savior of his country rather than its destroyer. We all believe him as ambitious as Cassius, and he might aspire to that praise Cicero claimed he would be entitled to in saving Rome from Cataline's machinations—that is, saving Rome would give him more honor than the founder of Rome had. If his ambition is at all purified and well directed, the idea of saving the institutions of his country and living hereafter by the side of Washington, might well move him in a direction altogether different from that desired or expected by his *party* friends. We must bear in mind, that we now had it that Grant was a republican or a radical until he and the President, summer before last, got at outs, and it was by no means certain until then, that he would be with the republicans, but on the contrary, some of our friends were fondly calculating on him as the standard bearer of the

Democracy in the national contest just over. Do you think it at all improbable that he might surround himself with decent, moderate and able men of the republican party, and be governed by them and rule as President in conservatism?

To the South this is all important—it is vital. If the latter course is not pursued by him, then history will not afford an example so prostrated, so wicked and so deplorable, as our poor South. This, of course you know, and know it much better than I do. It is all important too that General Grant should determine some time before his inauguration upon his course, so that when he is installed, if his course is conservative, we will be inspired with hope, and our energies for good will begin to display themselves at once. In order then to enable him, or to aid him to determine, it has occurred to me after much long and anxious reflection, that some kind and considerate influences ought to be brought to bear upon him before the 4th of March next, and as soon now as he is rested from his late *heat*, and his sores are healed somewhat. In other words, we should not leave him in the hands of Bingham, Boutwell, Washburne, *ed id omne genus,* for then he will become wedded to his idols. We should look the situation in the face, and accept it gracefully, and study to render it not only bearable, but to deprive it of all its disagreeable and unpleasant consequences as threatened.

As a plan to accomplish this, I have fallen on the following, and I wish you to consider it in all its bearings, and decide on it, viz.: One or two *representative* men of the true *conservatism* in each of ten Southern States should by private agreement meet with General Grant about 1st January next and lay before him the facts as they are in these States, and promise and vouch for the peace and order and obeying of the laws on the part of the people here, if the government is properly conducted. By representative men I mean neither active democrats or republicans in the late contest—but men who have been quiet and have been looking to the peace and quiet of their people, and who have not stirred up strife and bitter feelings among their people. For as you well know, we have been for the last three months ground in between the upper and nether mill-rocks—conservatism proper has been strangled, and bad men on both sides, desiring trouble and commotion have kept the country on fire, just as the late hell-born war was originated in 1860-1. And I do not believe I mistake the facts, when I say, that our people South—I mean those of social, pecuniary and moral responsibility desire peace earnestly and are ready and willing to conform to rules under anyone if they can be protected in their rights as given them even in the general terms of the Constitution; and I believe this assurance full and ample can be made to General G. and strictly within the bounds of truth. These things properly laid before him by men who are able to do. it—who are respected at home, and who are known to be conservative indeed, must make him pause and reflect, and then act as a man of sense and of patriotism, and they will do so, unless he is a fool or a fiend, or both, which I do not believe at all.

And after looking over the whole country, I have concluded of all men, you are the proper person to initiate this and carry it out, if you approve it. Although you were in high position in the Confederacy, yet all men have (and do still regard) regarded you as conservative; and the republicans, north know and acknowledge this; and I know the people north respect your character and judgment, while the South more than respects them. And your quiet and retired course since the war has added largely to your name, and enlarged your powers for usefulness. Now, if you, General Lee, Governor Graham of North Carolina, Orr of South Carolina and others, by concert of action will go to Washington City, as by accident, and meet General Grant and have this kind of a conversation, then all is lost, if good does not come of it. The other names you know better than I. General Joe Johnston would be a good one. I write today myself to Governor Graham and Orr and send them copies of this letter to you. These names would weigh with Grant, and I must think would cause him to pursue a course of administration that would disappoint some of his partizan friends but would bless the land at large. All of you have been quiet and have not wrangled, and what you would preach you have practiced. I might do something myself, but my connection with the *Test-Oath Case* and the Miss. Injunction Case, and being elected by the Legislature of 1866-7 here (which is odious to that party) to the United States Senate, although unasked and unsolicited, would break down any influence I might exert there—although with an assurance of this kind to you gentlemen or others, from General Grant I could quiet **Arkansas** in ten days, I believe, and it would give me the greatest pleasure and joy to do this.

Now I have thought this subject over and over, and have concluded on the foregoing. I make the suggestion to you. Act in it as you think best. I feel well satisfied the gentlemen referred to will aid you, and co-operate in all you do. The object to be attained is worth all the effort. No one, but a friend who copies this letter for me to forward to Governors Graham and Orr, knows I have written it. Something must be done quickly, and we should not hesitate about it. I would do anything on earth to bring about a better state of affairs and can't it be done? Try once more, and then when we have done all we can and fail, let the end come and we are clear of responsibility. Write me in full and see if you can tell me something encouraging or hopeful. See if you can't call back *Tige* by telling him "that d—d varmint is gone." I wish I could see you. Let me know how your health is, and believe me always,

Your friend truly,

A. H. GARLAND.

P. S. When will your second volume on *the war* be out? I read the first with great interest, and look forward, with pleasure, to the reading of the 2d.

Yours,

GARLAND."

The following endorsement appeared on the back of this letter:

A. H. Garland to A. H. Stephens.

"Copy of a letter sent this day to Mr. S. Nov. 9-68. G."

HOMINY HILL.

He bought the home of Major John D. Adams in Little Rock and afterward built the residence on Fourteenth and Scott streets. In 1870 he bought Gibson Springs, a farm of twelve hundred acres in Ellis Township, and changed its name to Hominy Hill. His wife died in the Scott street house, but Garland's summers were spent mostly at Hominy Hill. He was a great deer hunter, being one of the best shots in the country and a great fisherman. Here he developed the farm, read law and history, hunted and fished at pleasure. He had three boys who were accomplished musicians on the violin, flute and piano. Here he was visited by his old-time friends, B. D. Williams, General Fagan, James N. Smithee, John D. Adams, James M. Henry, Captain Rees Pritchard, Zeb Ward, Sr., Judge Compton, Colonel Bob Howard and W. S. Davis, besides many others. Garland, when in the Senate of the United States, made headquarters while in Little Rock at the livery stable of W. S. Davis, whom Garland termed familiarly, William Saltpetre Davis. Davis was an excellent conversationalist and Garland a good listener, especially with a pocketful of peanuts to munch from. Thus passed his life to the beginning of the Brooks-Baxter war.

GARLAND AS GOVERNOR.

The Reconstruction government of Arkansas began with the constitution of 1868 and ended with the Constitutional Convention of 1874. During the last years of this epoch the Republican party split wide open, resulting in two candidates for governor, Baxter and Brooks. The Democrats, after mature deliberation, decided to make no contest and to let the Republicans fight it out among themselves. Thousands of Democrats voted for Baxter and other thousands voted for Brooks. At this day it is easy to say who was elected. There can be no doubt that Joe Brooks, the preacher-politician, was fairly and squarely elected, and there are thousands of democrats today who are willing to die for that proposition. Brooks, however, was not counted in, but Baxter was. The Republicans wanted him and they got him, but after they got him he would not stand hitched. Then the Republicans did not want him and turned to Joe Brooks. Joe Brooks demanded the office after being denied it by all the courts and Baxter let him have it. Then

Arkansas had two governors, Brooks operating from the State house and Baxter from St. John's College.

Here Garland comes in again. He had been practicing law for years and did not consider that there was much difference to the people of Arkansas between an administration by Brooks and administration by Baxter. As a lawyer, however, he decided that the legal forms were on the side of Baxter, although his sympathies ran very largely to the side of Brooks. None of these things, however, disturbed his equilibrium and he went on practicing law, eating three square meals a day and sleeping the sleep of the righteous. Going home one day he heard that Brooks had ousted Baxter, and he said "Good." He kept on, however, to Fourteenth and Scott, when he saluted his wife, ate his supper, read his evening's literature and calmly went to bed. At about midnight a deputation arrived at his door and a knock was heard. Garland was sound asleep, but Mrs. Garland was still at her desk writing, and answered the knock. With a lamp in her hand, she opened the door and her son says was confronted by Judge U. M. Rose, backed up by a deputation of citizens, all armed. Mrs. Garland invited the judge to enter and he asked to see Mr. Garland. Mr. Garland was called out of bed and in due time came downstairs. He was told that a revolution was on hand; that Brooks had ousted Baxter, and that Civil war confronted the citizens of Arkansas. Garland was always a most humorous man, in fact, a genuine wit, and when told that Baxter had gone to St. John's College, said "The Devil. Is he a professor? Is he going to teach school?" He was made to understand finally that a consultation of the leading men of the State was to be had at St. John's College and that his presence was desired. Garland subordinated his comfort to his duty and went.

At St. John's College he found Judge U. M. Rose, Judge Henry Caldwell, Judge Sam W. Williams and Judge Compton, besides several men representing the military arm of government. Garland soon ascertained that Baxter desired to go on to Washington, thinking that by a personal conference with Grant he could control matters. Garland knew better, and besides, knew that if Baxter ever got to Washington he would never come back. Some means would be devised by which Baxter would be held at Washington and the Brooks government perpetuated. Garland decided that it would be better for Arkansas, in the long run for the Baxter government to be perpetuated, and, although his sympathies were with Brooks, he decided to act according to his judgment. He made up his mind at once that under no circumstances should Baxter go out of the State. Baxter in Arkansas was an asset of superlative value to the old Confederates, and to the lasting advantage of good government in the future. He therefore combated Baxter's plan of going to Washington and volunteered to stay with him, and see the thing out, no matter what the outcome might be. The other confreres agreed with Garland, and Baxter decided to stay. He went down to the Anthony House, where he made his headquarters, and Gus Garland went with him, remaining there for six long weeks without returning to his home. With that six weeks of civil war we have little to do—it was brother against brother, Democrat against Democrat, Republican against Republican, a hotch potch impossible to explain.

A Confederate general headed Baxter's troops, and a Confederate general headed Brooks' troops—it was the devil to pay and no pitch hot. Down at the Anthony House, however, Garland's judgment was supreme, and that judgment won out. It gave Arkansas the constitution of 1874, the constitution under which the State has made its grandest strides forward, and under whose operations Arkansas has become a real power in the federal Union. At the first election under that constitution Augustus H. Garland was selected as governor by a vote of seventy-six thousand four hundred and fifty-three out of a total of eighty thousand votes. He served from November 12, 1874, to January 11, 1877. He came in with chaos in the saddle; he went out with law and order on every side. He came in with not a dollar in the Arkansas treasury; he went out with the credit of the State good, and rising every day. He came in without State or county organization; he went out with the most perfect organization that the State has ever known. The name of Garland was a name to conjure with in those days, and that name conjured nothing but law, order and civic righteousness. His Arkansas countrymen decided to send him higher; they had done this once before ineffectually, but this time their efforts were to be crowned with success.

GARLAND AS UNITED STATES SENATOR.

At the close of his term as governor the legislature elected him in January, 1877, to the United States Senate for six years. and in 1883 for a second term of six years. He served one term and a part of the second, being called by his countrymen of the United States to step up higher.

In the Senate he was at once assigned to the Judiciary Committee, where he remained until he left the Senate. His confreres on the committee were Allen G. Thurman, chairman; McDonald, Bayard, Lamar, Davis, Edmunds, Conkling and Carpenter. This was a great aggregation of talent, and the period one which brought the committee in daily contact with questions of the most far-reaching importance. Garland was also made chairman of the Committee on Territories and a member of the Committee on Revolutionary Claims. He was specially selected for work on the committee to investigate the law touching the counting of the votes cast for president and vice president and contributed largely to the making of the present law as to the presidental succession. He was also on the Special Committee on the Freedman's Saving and Trust Company, and drew a bill amending its charter which became a law. He also headed a special committee to investigate the frauds of the late election and was a member of the special committee to provide against the spread of epidemics. He was a hard worker and made more than one hundred reports from the Judiciary Committee. He was not an ornate speaker, but very clear, concise, logical and convincing. He never spoke to the galleries, and never spoke unnecessarily. He made hundreds of short speeches, each of which was full of meat, and.nothing but meat. On the resolution concerning the Thirteenth, Fourteenth and Fifteenth amendments he reached the consciences of men like Edmunds and Conkling and led them to see these amendments in a new light. Garland showed how they were passed in Arkansas and his showing was taken by great Republicans as a truthful showing. He claimed that measures passed as these measures had been passed, by and through the disfranchisement of the enlightened and intelligent voters of a great section, could not be set up as monuments of either moral or legal power.

When the bill to remove the disability from James Monroe Heiskell of Baltimore, a grandson of President Monroe, was up, Garland made a most excellent short speech. Section 1218 of the Revised Statutes of the United States made it unlawful for the president to appoint to a position in the United States army any one who had served in the Confederate army. Garland said that he would vote for the special act relieving Mr. Heiskell from the operation of the law, but that he did not believe in granting amnesty by piecemeal. Either pardon all or keep the disability on all. Believing that universal amnesty was right and that the occasion was ripe, he would test the matter by offering an amendment to the bill repealing section one thousand two hundred and eighteen of the statutes. Senator Edmunds followed, saying: "I am glad that the senator from Arkansas, who is always logical and always brave, has offered the amendment, and I hope that it will pass." It passed almost unanimously in the Senate, but was cut out in the house. Garland kept on, however, until all this class of legislation was removed from the statutes and the way opened for Fitzhugh Lee and Joe Wheeler to become United States brigadiers.

To follow Garland through the wide range of subjects upon which he spoke from 1878 to 1885 would be to fill up several pages of this work, and I must desist. He spoke on many special relief bills for Arkansas citizens and upon every public question that came before the Senate. He was special presiding officer of that body scores of times, and was noted for his courtesy, fairness and judicial bearing. A most instructive book might be written entitled "Garland in the United States Senate."

GARLAND AS ATTORNEY GENERAL.

In 1884 Grover Cleveland was elected president of the United States, and in March, 1885, was inaugurated. In forming his cabinet he chose Augustus Hill Garland of Arkansas as one of its members, assigning him to the office of attorney general. Garland at once resigned his seat in the Senate and was succeeded by James H. Berry. He had barely qualified as attorney general when the vials of scandal were poured upon him. While a senator he had bought three hundred dollars worth of Pan-Electric Telephone stock and was made attorney for the company. The directors of the company were such prominent men as Senator Isham G. Harris of Tennessee, Senator Joseph E. Johnson of Georgia, J. D. C. Atkins and Casey Young. The company was all right, Garland's connection with it was all right, and time has done nothing except to emphasize this righteousness. However, the Bell Telephone Company, with its millions of wealth, decided to throttle the Pan-Electric, and it fought in every way possible every man connected with the new concern. It happened that Garland was a bright and shining light, and the Bell telephone agents selected him as the mark for their most scandalous shafts. Garland had forgotten that he owned stock in the Pan-Electric, but when being apprised of it, said: "What of it?" He then went to President Cleveland and laid the whole matter before him, saying, "I own the stock, and I propose to keep it. It is a mere bagatelle, but it is mine. It is righteously mine and I will hold it. I do not want to hamper the new administration, and if my holding of that stock is to stand in the way, I beg most sincerely to be relieved of my portfolio as attorney general." President Cleveland took the matter under advisement, investigated it and notified Mr. Garland that his holding of that stock was in no way, legally or morally, incompatible with his holding the position of attorney general. The House of Representatives, goaded by Bell Telephone newspapers, ordered an investigation, the result of which was the entire vindication of Senator Garland. What hurt Garland most, however, was not the attacks derivable from the Bell Telephone corporation, but the attacks of men that he had considered his friends at home. These attacks pierced the armor of his soul, wringing anguish therefrom all the more frightful, since the charges were absolutely untrue.

Through all this scandal General Garland became—
   A tower of strength.
   Which stood foursquare to all the winds that blew.

As attorney general he pursued the even tenor of his way and in every case added to the strength of character which had marked his previous career. On the death of Justice Wood in May, 1887, Senator Garland was named as a fit successor. This coming to his ears led him to go at once to President Cleveland and state to him that under no circumstances would he accept the offer and that he desired the president to proceed to the consideration of the question as though he had never heard of Garland. On the 23d of February, 1887, President Cleveland asked Senator Garland to take a place on the Interstate Commerce Commission, which he positively declined.

Senator Garland states that he himself had decided to retire from public life at the close of his term as attorney general, devoting the remainder of his life to the practice of law. He went out of office honored and respected by every great man of the country, irrespective of party and for ten years continued a most honorable practice in that court in which, in 1860, he had been enrolled.

Such is the career of Augustus Hill Garland. By his marriage with Sarah Virginia Sanders he had eight children, four of whom died in infancy. The fifth child, Sanders Garland, was born in 1862, at Arkadelphia, while his father was a member of the Confederate Congress; this son married (1) Annie N. Hening, at Washington, D. C., and had one child, Charles Augustus Garland, now in business in the capital; married (2) Sarah J. Mack of Newark, New Jersey, and had one child, Walter Raleigh Garland, of Washington, D. C.

The sixth child, Rufus Cummings Garland, married Miss Hobson of Virginia, and left two living children, Rufus Cummins Garland and Sarah Virginia Garland.

The seventh child, Daisy Garland, died unmarried in Washington, D. C., October 27, 1893.

The eighth child, William Allen Garland, married Cora McPherson of Benton, Arkansas, and left one surviving child, Rufus M. Garland.

Augustus Hill Garland died in Washington, D. C., on January 26, 1899, in his sixty-seventh year, and was buried at Mount Holly cemetery, Little Rock, by the side of his wife. His remains were taken to Little Rock by his son, Rufus Cummings Garland and James K. Jones, Jr. His mother, Mrs. Hubbard, died in Washington November 17, 1893, and was buried in Rock Creek cemetery, D. C. Thus this magnificent woman, the mother of a most magnificent man, had a pilgrimage worthy of her nobility; born in North Carolina, a transient resident of Tennessee, a longer denizen of Arkansas, and for years a resident of Washington, D. C., she now sleeps in one of the leading cemeteries of the world, awaiting that trumpet which shall recall her to eternal life and unite her to the son she loved.

The glory of any age is its coterie of great men; and every coterie of great men that could have been formed in the United States from 1875 to 1900 would have had as one of its members the commanding presence of Augustus H. Garland. He formed a part, and most commanding part, of the glory of that age.

Mrs. Mary E. Donelson Wilcox has printed a fine little brochure of twelve pages in memory of Mrs. Barbara Hill Hubbard, which abounds in history pertaining to the period 1832-1899.

The Gazette is the oldest and most influential paper of Arkansas. All Arkansans are proud of its career, but it is doubtful whether any act of its long and useful career deserves a greater commendation than the splendid work of the present management in starting and receiving subscriptions for a monument to Senator Garland. Every admirer of Senator Garland as well as every lover of Arkansas can but be thankful for the splendid work of the Arkansas Gazette in this regard.

CHAPTER XXXIX.

THE DESHAS.

One of the fads of modern civilization is an increase of population. This is looked upon as a panacea for almost every ill. The great cry is for more people, and with more people will come a greater development, a greater wealth and a greater happiness. To a large extent the conclusion rests on a sound induction, which accounts for the universal prevalence of the idea.

The demand for a greater influx of population is rational and wise only so far as the population attained is capable of assimilating itself intellectually and economically with the institutions of a people. It is not a question of riches or wealth; a thousand poor, honorable men, no matter how poor they may be, if intelligent and industrious, are as great a boon to a community as a great influx of rich men. Neither is it a question of party; men honestly differ, and honest differences of opinion, political, ecclesiastical and otherwise, are the very life blood of a community. The nearer parties are divided in strength in any community the better will be the administration of the law. The territory of Arkansas wanted a greater population, but it made no such efforts as modern methods seem to demand. Nevertheless, it made all reasonable efforts to secure a wise, temperate and industrious addition to its population, and it succeeded.

INFLUENCE OF A NAME.

It is interesting to note not only the trend of population, but the influence which a single name often bears upon the community to which it attaches. The Huguenots were a wise, temperate, frugal and most accomplished set of people in south France, who contributed most largely to the glory of France, and who attached themselves to the Protestant cause. Catholic France made a great mistake in so prosecuting these Huguenots as to force them to leave their native home for a refuge in the wilds of America. Persecution always reacts upon itself and the Catholics have not been the only persecutors. Protestant New England drove the Baptists from their midst; Protestant Virginia persecuted Quakers, Methodists and Baptists, and so on to the end. One body of these thrifty and cultured Huguenots from France found a home at Manakintown, Virginia, and developed a community from which some of the ablest men and families of the United States have sprung. It gave the Deshas, Duvalls, Jordans and others to Arkansas, families which have at all times been a decided acquisition to territorial and State growth.

Old Ben Desha of Manakintown, was a refined industrious and learned man, descended from an illustrious line of Frenchmen. His sons and daughters became Americans in every sense of the word, and a grandson, Joseph Desha, a general in the United States army and governor of Kentucky. This grand old man sent four sons and daughters into the territory of Arkansas, every one of whom was a tower of strength in the community to which he or she went. His oldest son was named Benjamin, Kentucky born, who in 1812 was made a first lieutenant in the Seventeenth Infantry, which appointment was not confirmed by the United States Senate. In the next year he was confirmed as a third lieutenant in the First Regiment of Light Dragoons; in the next year he was advanced to the grade of captain in the Second Regiment of the United States Rifles. The traditions of Captain Ben Desha are still cherished by Kentuckians, who are descended from soldiers of these regiments. He resigned in 1815 to accept a seat in the legislature of Kentucky, where he won a position almost as distinguished as that of his illustrious father. In 1822 President Monroe offered him the receivership of public moneys of the territory of Arkansas, which position he accepted, and whose duties he performed honorably and well for many years. The thrift of the Huguenots never deserted him, nor did their refinement of manners.

DESHAS OF ARKANSAS.

Old Captain Desha of early Arkansas history was a man of whom all Arkansans were justly proud. He was a Whig of the most pronounced type, but was universally admired by the Democrats. In the unfortunate duel between Crittenden and Conway, Desha acted as second for Mr. Crittenden, and no man exhibited a more genuine grief for the death of his friend than did Captain Desha. He acquired wealth in the territory of his adoption, and died November 21, 1835, universally respected and admired. A county in the State, in whose confines he lived an honored man when it was a territorial part of another division, bears his name today.

Of a second son, Robert Desha, also a captain in the United States army, we have already given a partial account. While stationed at Norfolk, Virginia, with his regiment he became acquainted with Frances Ann Ferebe, a daughter of one of the most aristocratic families of that city. Captain Robert Desha was soon transferred to the Marine Corps, with headquarters alternating between Helena, Arkansas, and New Orleans, Louisiana. His accomplished wife came with him to the territory in 1819, and the thrift of the family was never better exemplified than in the case of Captain Robert Desha. He died November 6, 1822, one of the richest men in the territory. George Ferebe, brother of Mrs. Robert Desha, moved to Helena in 1820, and for many years was one of the leading citizens of that pioneer town. A sister of Captain Desha, coming to Arkansas from Kentucky to visit her brother, was wooed and won by George Ferebe, and one child, Richard Montgomery Ferebe, blessed this union. This boy died in early manhood, and the name Ferebe became extinct in Arkansas, and is almost extinct at its old seating place, Norfolk, Virginia. Such is the fate of individuals and such is the fate of names. They rise, are glorified and then sink into oblivion and decay.

The widow of Captain Robert Desha, within two years after the death of her husband, was married the second time to Captain Hartwell Boswell, one of the most distinguished men of Batesville, Arkansas. Another daughter of Captain Robert Desha of Kentucky, while on a visit to Mrs. Boswell at Batesville, captivated the affections of Joseph Egner, a pioneer of Batesville from 1818. Four children blessed this union, Elvira Fowler Egner, Henry Egner, Virginia Egner and Cornelius Egner. These and their descendants contributed largely to the wealth and refinement of early Independence County, and are now scattered through seven or eight counties of the State.

Captain Robert Desha, who married Frances Ann Ferebe, left two children, Franklin W. Desha and Margaret Frances Desha, whose descendants ramify all eastern Arkansas, and whose life work has contributed largely to the better interests of the State. Franklin W. Desha at Batesville, married Elizabeth Searcy, the sister of Richard Searcy, one of the best lawyers of early days. The children of this marriage were Robert, Benjamin, Stonewall, Mary and Lizzie, all of whom lived to be men and women, doing a great life work, but only one of them, Lizzie, became entangled in matrimony. Robert was sheriff of the county in later days, as was his uncle, Joe Egner, in earlier days. I believe that all these children are dead, except Ben, and the name Desha, so far as Arkansas is concerned, has also become extinct. The blood of Franklin W. Desha, however, is carried down to posterity through Lizzie, who married a prominent citizen of Independence County.

STATE'S MOST BEAUTIFUL WOMAN.

The second child of Robert and Frances Ann Desha was a daughter, Margaret Frances, who married twice, each time to a distinguished citizen of Batesville. Margaret as well as her brother, Franklin W. Desha, was born at the Washington Navy Yard. She was educated at Ellicott City, Maryland, the seat then of the greatest female educational institution of the State. She was a most accomplished woman, as was her classmate, Lucretia Ringgold, the most beautiful woman of early Arkansas history, daughter of the accomplished jurist, Judge Ringgold, and wife of that greatest of early Arkansas writers, Fent Noland, the wandering comet of the literary sky. When Margaret Frances Desha returned to Batesville, the most accomplished woman of the town, she was wooed and won by William French Denton, a distinguished lawyer of Batesville, and a gift of Tennessee to Arkansas growth. Several children followed this marriage, namely, Frances Jane, Franklin Desha, Elvira Fowler and William French. Of one of these children, Franklin Desha, Arkansas may well be proud. For years he was the central figure in the newspaper life of the State, and no one has contributed more to its development than F. D. Denton. He established the Batesville Bee, which had a long and successful existence, and then the Batesville Guard, now controlled by that accomplished gentleman, Edward Givens. Not to have known F. D. Denton from 1870 to 1890 was to acknowledge yourself comparatively unknown. William

French Denton, his brother, dedicated his young life to the Southern cause and was killed at his post.

Margaret Frances (Desha) Denton took for a second husband that distinguished gentleman, Judge Buford H. Neely of Batesville, and had several children. The first child, Mary Euphenia Neely, married Mark Wycough, well known throughout Independence County and the adjacent counties. The second child was Elizabeth Egner Neely, who married J. D. Vance, an accomplished scholar from Tennessee, now engaged in literary work in Washington, D. C. There is no better woman living than Elizabeth Egner Vance, and in her advanced age she remains a distinguished example of the refinement, the courtesy and the intelligence of the old Huguenot Deshas, with the strength which has come through the new lines of blood, the Ferebes and the Neeleys. The third child of Margaret Frances Neely by her last marriage was Esther Ann, who at Batesville made two ventures in matrimony, her first husband being James Ellis, and her second, George Emmert.

Absalom Fowler, a Virginia lawyer, moved to Little Rock in the twenties, and acquired a position second to that of no lawyer of early Arkansas days. He ranked with Chester Ashley, and was a tower of strength to any cause to which he lent his influence. He held legislative positions and was one of the most prominent members of the Arkansas Constitutional Convention. Colonel Boswell, by his first wife, had a daughter named Elvira, who became the wife of Absalom Fowler, but was never the mother of children. In this way the name Fowler, so far as it pertains to this distinguished line, became extinct in Arkansas. Thus three names, the Deshas, the Ferebes and the Fowlers have come into Arkansas life, have entangled themselves with all its stupendous problems, have contributed manfully to their solution, adding dignity and grace to its social institutions, and have passed out without leaving the name as a present inheritance to the State. These names, so far as their relations to these lines are concerned, are extinct, but the blood of the Deshas still runs in the veins of hundreds of Arkansas men and women, and to the last drop, wherever it may be found, carries an assurance of honesty, refinement, energy and intelligence. In these devious ways and by these tortuous methods is the great problems of civilization carried forward to mastery.

A BAD YEAR FOR THE DESHAS.

November 6 will ever be remembered sorrowfully by the Desha family. On that day in 1822 Captain Robert M. Desha of the United States army, and a native of Kentucky, living at Helena, died of yellow fever at New Orleans.

On November 6, 1823, Mrs. Rachel Harriett Boswell, wife of Colonel Hartwell Boswell of Batesville, and daughter of General Joseph Desha of Kentucky, died at her home in Batesville. Robert M. Desha was a most excellent army officer and also a splendid business man. Administration was granted his wife, Frances Ann Desha, and George N. Ferebe, at Helena, in February, 1825. He owned ninety lots in Helena, besides about an equal number in Davidsonville, Batesville and Little Rock. His inventory took a column in the Gazette. He was also the owner of large bodies of land in several counties of the State. Colonel Boswell was the appointee of President Monroe to the Lawrence Land Office, which position he held for many years. He was also a member of the Arkansas legislature and a most capable man. He was for years colonel of the Seventh Arkansas regiment of militia and an honor to the position. On July 1, 1829, Colonel Boswell took a trip to Kentucky and for the second time carried away from the residence of General and ex-Governor Joseph Desha a wife. The first time he took the general's daughter; the second time, his daughter-in-law. He married Mrs. Frances Ann Desha, widow of Captain Robert M. Desha, of the United States Marine Corps, and returned to Batesville, where his wife formed one of the leaders of early Batesville society, at that time the most exclusive society of the State. Colonel Noland had lived there for many years and with his Virginia wife, imported a refinement and courtesy which attracted to Batesville some of the best people of the early days. Colonel Boswell died January 13, 1833.

CHAPTER XL.

Abraham Ruddell.

Before entering upon the meat of this article, a few additions to preceding articles should be made. As early as 1824 there was a Joseph H. Lindsey living in Saline County, who had a daughter named Margaret, born there at that date, who married Philo Howell of Saline County, and died at her father's house in October, 1859. She was a prominent Methodist and her father was the first Lindsey of the name to settle in that part of Pulaski County which is now Saline. On October 9, 1859, B. A. Brown married Sarah Ann Lindsey to William Hill of Pyeatt township. Peter Lindsey entered Arkansas in 1825 and died in Jefferson County in 1839, in his thirty-sixth year, leaving a wife and children.

Isaac Lindsey was a resident of Hempstead County in 1823 and was delinquent $5 for State and county taxes. In 1817 James Lockhart emigrated from Union District, South Carolina, and settled in Pulaski County on the Saline. His wife, Elenor, died in Saline County July 21, 1840, in her sixty-sixth year. On December 25, 1822, his daughter, Elenor, married William Franklin of the same settlement. James Lockhart died a few years before his wife. John Douglas died in January, 1836, at his home, thirteen miles from Little Rock, in his sixtieth year. W. S. Lockhart represented Saline County in the legislature from 1838 to 1840. Louisa S. Hughes, wife of Green B. Hughes of Tennessee, moved with him to Lawrence County in 1819 and to Saline County in 1826. He represented Saline County in 1846. She died in 1859. Elizabeth Martin died in Fourche township, June 28, 1840, in her seventy-sixth year.

An Arkansas Woman of 1800.

Christian Hacker was born at Arkansas Post November 28, 1800, when the entire country was under the nominal rule of Spain. She was baptized at the Post in 1819. She married Thomas H. Tennant at that place and moved to Barren Fork, Washington County, where she died September 28, 1840, leaving seven children, who now, through their descendants, are entitled to admission into the Arkansas Century Society.

REMARKABLE LIFE OF ABRAHAM RUDDELL.

Abraham Ruddell, of Independence County, had a career which the pen of J. Fennimore Cooper might have depicted as it deserved, but which my pen in the space allotted cannot adequately express. He was born as far west as white people at that time had found permanent homes. Far down on the Holstein in Virginia in a log house on August 3, 1774, he first saw the light of day. He never knew much about this home nor his parents, for on June 22, 1780, the Indians fell upon the little settlement and with savage ferocity tomahawked its residents, carrying off as a prisoner the little curley-headed Abraham Ruddell. They carried him over into Kentucky and the same something that prompted his savage captors to spare his life, whatever that may have been, prompted the great Tecumseh to not only further spare him, but to take him into his family as an adopted son. Strange fortune was this! Strange mutation of the little child's life. He grew up under Tecumseh's eye and was trained by that renowned warrior in all the arts of Indian life and Indian warfare. He learned the language of the tribe, played the Indian boyhood games, and took part in all the Indian wars. He was an adept in the use of a tomahawk, though his white blood restrained him from its more barbarous uses. He was skilled with the bow and could contest favorably with all his dusky comrades. In the use of the rifle he had no superior and Tecumseh awarded him many happy encomiums. When the tribe fought other Indian tribes Ruddell fought at Tecumseh's side and fought well. He had no particle of cowardice in his system and was far more venturesome than even his savage friends. He was trained, however, to know that he was white, and Tecumseh always held out to him the fact that at some time he would go back to the whites to live the white man's life. So gentle was Tecumseh to him that he grew to love him and throughout his life had a warm vein of affection for the great warrior. When Tecumseh died there was one white man, at least, that sincerely mourned his death.

Logan, the Mingo, stood alone in his absolute lack of mournful friends; Tecumseh was mourned by his tribe and by Abraham Ruddell. For Tecumseh's brother, the prophet, Ruddell had a supreme contempt, and it was only his love for Tecumseh that kept him from openly showing his dislike.

LIVED SIXTEEN YEARS WITH INDIANS.

After sixteen years of captivity under the provisions of Mad Anthony Wayne's treaty, he returned to the whites. His parting with Tecumseh was grievous, and each shook the hand of the other in proud good faith as they separated. Ruddell went back to his own people, a stranger in their midst. In Kentucky he started a new life, the white man's life with an added Indian education. His counsels were sought by the border woodsmen, and his Indian craft was used to circumvent the craft of the Indians. In 1811 he became a soldier of the United States and with the backwoodsmen of Virginia and Kentucky, with unerring rifles and forest tactics, marched with the brave and gallant Winchester into Canada. He was in the ever memorable fight of the Raisin and with others felt all the mortification of defeat. All day long his eye swept the field of savage faces hunting for the familiar face of Tecumseh. At the risk of his life he would have tried to shake Tecumseh's hand again. He had bullets for the Indians, but none for Tecumseh. But he saw not his friend, nor did he see that other, the Prophet, for whom he had saved a special bullet, and whom he would gladly have shot. Ruddell always attributed the prevalence of the Indian atrocities to the evil eye of the Prophet.

MOVED TO ARKANSAS.

In battle after battle the defeat was retrieved and the war cry "Remember the Raisin," became the rallying cry of all future combats. Ruddell served through the war and went back to his forest home to ever afterwards live a peaceful life. In 1816 the Western fever attacked his neighborhood and with one accord they pulled up stakes and began a journey into the greater and newer West. Crossing the Mississippi below St.

Genevieve they took the old St. Louis and Washita road and turned South. One by one they found their Canaan and blazed their claims. Ruddell found his in the fairest part of what is now Independence County, in that township which will forever carry his name. Grand old Abraham Ruddell! Was there ever a man more respected in the county?

UNIVERSALLY RESPECTED.

Fent Noland, who knew him well, who gleaned the foregoing story from his lips, said, "No. He was a man of his word, honest and clean. He was never asked for a bond, and hated a liar. He was not only respected, but loved, and at his death, February 25, 1841, the whole county grieved. He loved the forest and spent the greater part of his time in its depths. He knew all the trees and communed with them; he knew the habits of all the birds and loved to imitate their music. Every flower of the county was known to him, not by its Latin, but by its loving backwoods name. Such a man had in him all the fire of a poet linked to the soul of a scientist. He never injured any man and all men were his friends. He could lie down in the forest, draw the drapery of a couch around him, and in the presence of the stars sleep that sleep which abounds only in pleasant dreams."

Fent Noland was a clean man—a man of lofty, poetic ideals, and his testimonial to the character of Abraham Ruddell is one of the brightest parts of old Independence County history. He had several children, but at his death had but one son and one daughter living, who with his wife shed genuine tears of regret.

He never sought office, and but one of the name, John Ruddell, is enrolled on the county's official roll. George Ruddell was a citizen of Batesville in 1821. Abraham Ruddell's name marks the township in which Batesville stands, and that is a most signal honor. There on the hallowed ground where James Boswell, Richard Peel, Richard Searcy, Thomas Curran, J. Redmon, Charles H. Pelham, Charles Kelly, J. Egner, John Read, Colonel Miller, J. L. Daniels, Robert Bruce, John and James Trimble, Colonel and Fent Noland, James Denton, Townsend Dickinson, William Moore, and other choice spirits of the earliest times met with him and lived with him—there was he buried amidst the most profound grief of his fellows. No more romantic character ever lived on Arkansas soil, and some rising Arkansas Octave Thanet will do credit to her name by writing a characteristic romance with Abraham Ruddell as its central figure. He was "The Last of the Mohicans," as it were, but his life story ought not to die.

OTHER PIONEERS.

In the same year that Ruddell passed away, in the last days of August another settler who came in with Ruddell in 1816, but who settled in what is now Lawrence County, died and was buried, not with his fathers, but in a new graveyard in the west. His name was Nevill Wayland and he left children to perpetuate his name. In October of 1840, at Spring Hill, Hempstead County, died Aquilla Davis in his sixtieth year, having lived in Arkansas twenty-four years. He left a large family and a most excellent name. His house was headquarters for all the young people and his hospitality knew no bounds. He was said to entertain a poor man equally as lavishly and with the same spirit that he entertained richer people. His cheerfulness was his main characteristic and with this he made troops of friends.

PHILANTHROPIST AND EMANCIPATOR.

John Latta of Vineyard township, Washington County, moved to that neighborhood before it was organized as Washington County. He came from Lexington, Kentucky, and was a man of wealth, as riches were counted in that day. The wiles of lovely women seem never to have ensnared him, either at Lexington or in Arkansas, for he died a bachelor, September 23, 1834, in his forty-fourth year. He had imbibed many of the Henry Clay notions about slavery and was a great believer in the colonization of negroes in Africa. Not to be inconsistent he emancipated his slaves at his death, and not to be inhumane provided for them by a bequest of $2,500 in gold in his will. The hills of northwest Arkansas had no charms for these dusky freedmen and when they got their money they went back to Kentucky to live as freemen in the old haunts where they were born. When men tell me of the horrors of the old time free negro surrounded by slaves, I cannot harmonize it with my own experiences. Although born in Arkansas I was taken back to Kentucky, her nativity, by my widowed mother in my fifth year. My earliest recollections are blended with the slave meetings on Sunday in Anderson County, where many of my white relatives were slaveowners. I remember the white patrols clearly and distinctly, but never saw a disturbance at one of the gatherings and never heard of one, near enough to test it by actual visitation. The stories came from the distance as a rule and in most cases were prepared for a purpose.

FREE NEGROES IN SLAVE TIMES.

Speaking of my own observations I remembered that there were many free negroes in Anderson County, some old and some young. They mingled with the slaves and paid workmen and had their own cabins in some prominent but neglected half-acre on the turnpike. The old free negro women made ginger cakes which they sold to travelers and the sweetest things I ever ate as a boy were these cakes made by the free negro women and sold to my people on county court days as we trooped to the county site to buy and sell the stock of the plantation. All ginger bread is good for a boy, but the best I ever had came from the source I have named, or from other free negroes at their booths on circus days. The free negroes of that day were fixtures and were never maltreated by the people, but on the contrary, when they were decent had the universal respect of all the citizens. When old Horace Witherspoon, the richest man in the county, got on one of his lordly sprees, and from the back of his thoroughbred rode through Lawrenceburg shooting out the lights in the houses, he never deigned to shoot the modest candles of old free negroes. At the first sound of a gun at night every light went out at once except those of the free negro cabins. The whites feared Witherspoon's drunken hilarity, but the free negroes knew that he would never shoot at them. They, too, could approach him when drunk, and do more with "Mars Horace" at such moments, than any of his brothers or friends. The old free "Aunt Sallies" and the "Free Bills" and the "Free Dicks" were numerous and they were as secure as the whites themselves. John Latta as a Kentuckian freed his negroes, provided for them in his will, and left $12,000 besides for his kin. All honor to this old Washington County humanitarian and philanthropist.

RANDOLPH COUNTY.

Randolph County was formed in 1835, but was settled at a date corresponding with the close of the second war with Great Britain, about the time of the creation of Lawrence County in 1815. Much of the interest of the early history of Arkansas clusters around the sombre stillness of Fourche de Mun and Fourche de Thomas. Many of the names which have added glory, interest and power to Arkansas are of those who settled originally in that part of Lawrence which is now Randolph County, and by marriage and removal have become well known in other localities.

One of the earliest Randolph settlers was Ransom Sutherland Bettis, who in February, 1815, settled near where Pocahontas now stands. He was born in North Carolina in 1787 and was twenty-eight years of age when he made his choice of a permanent home in the wilderness watered by the Black. Of a rugged and tempestuous ancestry in the Old North State he was trained to the life which was before him and never flinched from his purposes. He conquered the forest and covered the lands he called his own, and made his holdings productive areas. He was a great marksman and hunted bear, deer and turkeys in the elemental days, when these animals roamed at will throughout all that region. He died at Pocahontas respected and honored by all the community on March 30, 1842, having lived twenty-seven years in that locality.

EARLY LAWRENCE COUNTY BARBECUE.

On July 4, 1821, at Fourche de Thomas, a great patriotic celebration was held. In their enthusiasm they imitated the builders of the Tower of Babel and raised a liberty pole higher than the surrounding trees. This pole stood for several years and was used for kindred purposes. It became one of the landmarks of the times. Jacob Shaler was made grand marshal and upon a Kentucky thorough-bred headed a procession of pioneers and put them through the evolution of infantry tactics. Daniel Ploth read the Declaration of Independence in true ringing style and then invited all the people to his house for a genuine old-time barbecue dinner. Matheas Mock presided, assisted by Dr. P. R. Pitman and William Garrett. Toasts were drunk and the interludes enlivened by martial music and volleys of musketry. A stranger witnessing the scene would have said that patriotism can never die when nurtured by celebrations such as these. Many in the crowd were wild and reckless, ready at all times for a fight or a frolic, but honest, patient and true after their fashion under difficulties that would have dazed the hero of today.

FOUNDER OF BATESVILLE.

It was in Batesville that Hon. J. Woodson Bates settled in 1819, and where he lived for about fifteen years. At a barbecue in 1830 at this town Col. A. S. Walker spoke eloquently to the following toast: "To Judge Bates, the Man of Science —the Man of Hospitality; on the Bench the Guardian of the People's Rights."

John C. Calhoun said of Bates in 1820:

"He was a man of eminent acquirements and naturally of a legislative turn of mind." Judge Ringgold also lived at Batesville. His family was a most estimable one and added much to the charm and graces of Batesville society. Richard Searcy, one of the most eminent of the territorial lawyers, also lived at this ancient town, but was cut off in the midst of his usefulness. He died July 25, 1833, in his sixty-sixth year, having spent twenty of these in Arkansas, beginning as a boy at Davidsonville at its beginning. He came from Tennessee and was a son of a Revolutionary patriot. By personal merit and moral worth he gained the esteem of all who knew him. His name was a household word at the time of his death. William E. Woodruff said of him: "While clerk of Lawrence

County he studied law; was made a judge, and as such had sound judgment, unwavering fidelity and correct decision. He resigned office to practice law and was eminently successful. His life was marked by industry, capability and excellence of character."

James Searcy, his brother, died in Batesville in 1837, leaving his wife and a large family of children.

James Trimble was another Lawrence County pioneer, locating near where Batesville stands, in 1815. His wife, Elizabeth, was born in Culpepper County, Virginia, and died at Batesville in 1836, being forty-seven years of age. Trimble was of an old and distinguished family of Kentuckians.

FIRST ACADEMY AT BATESVILLE.

Through the influence of Col. William Noland, Professor A. W. Lyon of Nassau Hall, New Jersey, was induced to come to Batesville in 1828. He conducted a high-grade academy there for many years, which in 1836, was incorporated as the Batesville Academy. This was the first incorporated institution of learning in the State and had a long and useful career. Its first trustees were: Aaron W. Lyon, Isaac Folsom, Joseph H. Egner, Charles McArthur, Lawson Anderson, Charles H. Pelham and William Moore. The earliest social and educational forces found their best environment in Lawrence and Independence counties from 1815 to 1840.

INDIAN-FIGHTING OLD PIONEER.

The name Magness is inseparably connected with Lawrence and Independence counties. Magness was a Tennesseean and an Indian fighter of the old Davidson district. From 1782 to 1804 Tennessee was bloody ground and the Lindsey, Fletcher, Lafferty and Magness families were always in the thickest of the fight. Three Thomas Fletchers and two Laffertys were scalped in cold blood.

Robert Magness was the Arkansas pioneer of that name, having moved to Lawrence County in 1815, settling in Oil Trough Bottom, now in Independence County. He was not only an Indian fighter, but a feudist, and was mixed up in Tennessee with several of the feuds between Andrew Jackson and Jesse and Thomas Benton. He was lord of all he surveyed in Lawrence County for many years and died June 22, 1837, in his seventy-second year, at the house of his daughter, Mrs. Hardin. The German hunter, Gerstaecker, has left some good stories of the old man and his children, which will forever be of interest to Arkansas readers. Morgan Magness was a member of the territorial legislature of 1831 and 1833 and also of the State legislature in 1838, serving with Fent Noland; member of the Senate 1840-44. Perry G. Magness was one of the commissioners in 1820 to point out a suitable place for the court house for Independence County.

DEATHS IN 1820 AND 1821.

During the years the following persons died in Arkansas after a residence of from three to five years: Hempstead County, 1820, John McClain, John Rowen, George Berry and Benjamin Pool. In 1821, William D. Craig, John Humphries and Andrew Shaddy. In Arkansas County: 1820, John Dortolan and Joseph Cook. At Davidsonville, 1821, Col. Stuart. In Conway County, Miss Nancy Bentley, daughter of George Bentley of Virginia, and Skelton T. De Moss. This gentleman had lived in the State for many years and had large interests at the mouth of the Arkansas and at Cadron. Neal McLane died at Little Rock November 21, 1821, at the age of twenty-nine. He had only been in the State a short time, having come in on the invitation of Robert Crittenden. He was a lawyer of blameless life, and was said to have been appointed circuit judge before he moved to the territory. He undoubtedly acted as judge, but the nature of his appointment is problematical. He was born in New Hampshire, but had lived in Kentucky for three or four years.

On August 1, 1821, a quaint old German citizen died at Little Rock. His name was Christian E. Zoeller, born at Emmendengen in 1758. He was a noted man in his way, having served in the German army and possessing a small estate. He had $1,241 in gold at his death, which was sent to his relatives.

All of the aforementioned people left property and nearly all of them left descendants. Born in various parts of the world, their bodies lie in forgotten graves in different sections of Arkansas. The strenuosity of life is fully equally by the strenuosity of death.

CHAPTER XLI.

THE WILSON FAMILY.

Arkansas history connotes many names of the family, Wilson, and this article must be specially tabbed so as to avoid confusion. It applies directly to the family of Judge Robert B. Wilson of Russellville, Arkansas, but in its entirety may overlap and include much of the history of other Arkansas Wilsons.

To begin with, the word, Wilson, finds its oldest explication in the oldest Norse Sagas, and in the remotest antiquity of the Norsemen connects itself with the gods. Antiquity is a very relative term; in America it cannot mean more than a trifle beyond three hundred years, so far as European-American descendants are concerned; in England, it may mean the Norman Conquest of the eleventh century, or by an easy stretch of the imagination, may mean the conquest of Great Britian by the Angles and Saxons from the sixth to the ninth century. What was the antiquity of Great Britain prior to the sixth century? The Jews show an antiquity four thousand six hundred years greater than this, and the Aryan race certainly had an existence in other parts of the world than Asia-Minor.

The Wilsons have been seated in Scotland from a time whereof the memory of man runneth not to the contrary, and they have been seated in England for almost the same time. Their residence in Ireland cannot go behind the reign of William the 3d, and is of Scottish origin. The kinship of the Scotch and English Wilsons cannot be told with any degree of accuracy. Geographically they are as follows: In Scotland they inhabited the Great Shire of Inverness, the Royal Burgh of Lanark, the Royal Burgh of St. Andrews, the Burgh of Fortrose and the County of Fife of which Dunfermline was their habitat; in England the Wilsons have a most remote residence in the Shires Kent, Suffolk, Westmoreland, Sussex, Northumberland, Herts, Berks, Yorkshire and London. The residence in Scotland antedates the year 1000 A. D., and in England, the year 1200 A. D. They are a prolific and virile race, and the evidence points to a common Norse origin. The English and Scottish coats of arms are numerous and they all agree upon a wolf, or a demi-wolf salient. The crests and mottoes differ slightly, and taken with the arms seem to prove a common origin. The common arms, may be represented by a demi-wolf salient or, holding between the claws a crescent sa. The Scottish arms are simply a wolf salient or, with a motto, Expecta cuncta superne. The Irish arms, derived from the Scottish are a wolf rampant az. on a chief indented of the last three estoilles of the field. The Irish crest is a demi-wolf rampant, per pale indented arg. and az. with a motto, Pollet virtus.

As we are interested in the Scottish line more than the English or Irish, we shall not pursue this investigation further, but bring ourselves more clearly within the lines of sure historic sequence.

Alexander Wilson was the first professor of Astronomy at the University of Glasgow in 1714; Alexander Wilson was a distinguished ornithologist of Paisley of 1766; Andrew Wilson, son of Gabriel and Rachel (Corsar) Wilson was a distinguished physician and author, graduating from the University of Edinburgh in 1749; Arthur Wilson, 1595-1652 was a distinguished historian and dramatist. But to enumerate all the great men of the name Wilson from Scottish soil would take more space than we can allow. It is enough to say that the name is and has been one of luster, fame and renown. In the humble walks of life the Wilsons of Scotland have been above reproach.

In 1692, James Wilson, was a shipmaster in Glasgow; two years prior to that we find John Wilson a bailiff of Dunfermline; in 1684, P. A. Wilson was clerk of the Royal Burgh of St. Andrews; in the same year David Wilson was treasurer of the Royal Burgh of Haddington, and George Wilson, a merchant therein; in 1636, Archibald Wilson was baillee of Queens

Ferry, Burgh of Inverness; in 1692, Alexander Wilson was clerk of the Burgh of Lanark, of which Glasgow was the center; in 1711, John Wilson, Sr., John Wilson, Jr., and Robert Wilson were Councillors of the Burgh of Fortrose; in 1724 John and James Wilson were Councillors of Dunfermline Fifeshire. This John Wilson was a descendant of an ancient John Wilson who migrated to Rashee, Country Antrim, Ireland. This John Wilson of Ireland married Barbara, daughter of Andrew Porter, and died in 1692, leaving children, Frances, Hugh, Robert, Thomas, James, Janet and Susan. With none of these are we concerned save the third child, Robert, who returned to Dunfermline and married Jane Ramsey in 1722, and had children William, John, Hugh and Richard, which last child married Janet Ross in 1752 and moved to Virginia. Richard Wilson cast his fortunes with Scotland in its rebellion against England, and when his cause went down in defeat, suffered severely as to his landed estates. He found refuge in the American colonies, seating himself in the county of King and Queen in the royal province or colony of Virginia. In the sixteenth and seventeenth centuries the Wilson family, although not of the major or minor gentry of Scotland, distinguished itself in war, medicine, law, divinity, science, mechanics, landscape painting, poetry, commerce, manufactures and the drama. The great Christopher North of Blackwood Magazine, was really none other than John Wilson of Scotland, the son of a commoner. The son of a Scottish fisherman Wilson gave the world another Wilson who stood pre-eminent in divinity. They were great soldiers, great lawyers, great preachers, great astronomers, great ornithologists, great poets, great shipmasters and great thinkers. It is remarkable also that these Scottish Wilsons produced a great many women who have come down to the world as equally eminent with the men carrying that name. The Wilsons were men of the "craft" in opposition to the men of the "clan" and added most to the glory of England.

In the new world Richard Wilson and his good wife set about to improve their fortunes as best they could, and through their relations with the Ross family in Scotland, obtained grants to land in the wilds of Virginia. How many children Richard Wilson had is not known but he was certainly the father of James, Elizabeth and Nellie Wilson, whose after fortunes were connected with Fluvanna County, Virginia, and of Hugh Wilson, who was killed and scalped by the Indians, an unmarried man, March 5, 1776, near Harrodsburg, Kentucky. He may have been the father of Robert and Archibald Wilson of Orange County. Richard Wilson afterwards moved to Amherst County where he died. James Wilson was in all probability born in King and Queen County, Virginia, about 1756, and married there Anna Kidd, a daughter of Jesse Kidd, another Jacobite sufferer from the Scottish wars. Jesse Kidd afterwards moved into Fluvanna, where he died leaving a large family. James Wilson grew to manhood in King and Queen and after his marriage removed to Fluvanna. In Deed Book No. 2, page 120 of the Fluvanna land records is a deed from Richard Bennett of Henrico, to James Wilson of Fluvanna, for two hundred and fifteen acres on Ballingers Creek, called Bold Branch, dated April 7, 1786. James Wilson had a residence in Fluvanna prior to this date. The consideration for this property was eighty pounds sterling, and by and through it are we enabled to connect this line of the Wilson family with its ancient forbears.

In the county clerk's office I was introduced by the very polite clerk, Mr. Slaughter, (a man who has held this position since 1875) to Mr. David Wilson, an old man of eighty years. I asked Mr. Wilson if he had ever heard of Mr. Barnett Wilson, and he answered that Barnett Wilson was his uncle, and a brother of his father, John Wilson. I asked him further if he could give me the name of the father of John and Barnett Wilson. He answered that he could not. I then read him the description of the land granted by Bennett to James Wilson in 1786 and he at once brightened up saying: "John and Barnett Wilson were born on that farm, and it remained in our family for nearly a century." This settled the question of James Wilson's relation to John and Barnett Wilson with whom we shall have more to say. It appeared strange to me that a man could live eighty years in a neighborhood, own the ancestral farm on which his grandfather was buried, within five miles always of the county court records, and yet not know the name of his grandfather. David Wilson had all these advantages to his credit and yet could not give me the name of any ancestor behind his father. This is a common experience of mine and shows that family pride, in Virginia and elsewhere is not what it ought to be.

From the minute book of the Fluvanna county court record it appears that James Wilson was a surveyor and a man of considerable parts. His immediate neighbors were John A. Strange, Micajah Bragg, John Ross, John Glass, Archibald Glass, James Glass, Sr., Joshua Bethell, John Fones, Allen Q. Lindsey, Zaccheus Watson, Jesse B. Barnerd and Joseph Pace, nearly all from Scotland. As a surveyor he was frequently selected to collect the tithes of these men, and also to employ their tithables as a surveyor of roads from Lindseys to Broken Back Church. There is a station called Lindsey on the Chesapeake & Ohio railroad in Albermarle County, and it is supposed that this county road ran from that neighborhood to the neighborhood of Kents in Fluvanna. At all events James Wilson surveyed the road from Lindseys to Broken Back Church in April, 1799, more than one hundred and eight years ago. Over the same track or nearly so, the Viriginia Air Line railroad is now building its line from Lindsey in Albermarle to Bremo on the James, thus treating the descendants of these old people to the first screech of the locomotive that region has ever known. James Wilson was frequently chosen to other places of honor and trust by his friends and neighbors between 1782 and 1820, his greatest service to the people being the survey of the old roads, which in all probability are the very county roads now in use today.

In 1782, Joseph Wilson was given a grant of fifteen hundred acres of land on Birds Creek, Fluvanna County, as appears from Book No. 8, page 324 of the Fluvanna land records. Who Joseph Wilson was, I am unable to say, and this appears to have been the opinion of the old residents of Fluvanna County. Certain it is that in 1806, he appeared before the county court and asked for a resurvey of his land, which request was granted. Joseph Wilson then disappeared from Fluvanna County, going back to Scotland or to parts unknown. What became of him history knoweth not. Certain it is that between 1818 and 1823 his lands were regularly forfeited to the State of Virginia over the signature of twelve of its best citizens. These citizens recite that Joseph Wilson was the owner of these lands by grant, that for seven years his whereabouts had been unknown, and that he was without kindred in Fluvanna County. This seems to settle the question that Joseph Wilson was of no kin to James Wilson of Fluvanna, or to Jonathan Wilson of Cumberland.

We are interested to know what became of Elizabeth and Nellie Wilson, daughters of Richard Wilson of King and Queen, and sisters of James Wilson of Fluvanna, and but for the will of James Ross, of Seven Islands, Fluvanna County, dated June 4, 1800, and recorded in Book No. 1, page 192 of Fluvanna wills, we might flounder in the great sea of uncertainty forever. That will, however, enlightens us, not only as to a part of the after history of these girls, but opens up an avenue by which the Wilsons run back to the Earldom of Ross and align themselves with the greater clansmen of Scotland. In this will James Ross recites that he is a brother of Daniel Ross, late of the West Indies, and also a brother of David Ross, one of the greatest landholders of Virginia. James Ross states that during his younger life he managed the interests of his brother, Daniel, in the West Indies, and that later on during the Revolutionary War, he came to Virginia to perform the same office for his brother, David. He seemed to think that his management had a value, and Daniel and David seemed to have agreed with him, for according to his statement they settled an annuity of one hundred and fifty pounds sterling a year on him for life. James must have worked hard for he tells us that he needed a rest and that this annuity was given him in order that he might take this rest in Glasgow, Scotland. He recites that the annuity was paid for a great number of years, until the death of Daniel, who, he says, left money in the hands of David to effectuate it. David, however, seems to have let it lapse, and James, unable to live in

Glasgow without money, came back to Virginia, where David located him upon the Seven Islands in the James, not many miles from the farm which President Roosevelt, or his wife, has purchased in Albemarle County, Virginia. On this farm David seems to have paid part of the annuity and to have used James in many other ways, the principal one being to send him to Great Britain for artificers and helpers for his land schemes in Virginia. In due time James Ross came to his death bed and in view of this made the will from which the preceding historical items are gathered. When he came to dispose of his estate, being a bachelor, he selected those who were his nearest kin, and at the same time nearest in geographical location. He gave Nellie and Elizabeth Wilson all his household goods and each a cow and calf; he gave James Wilson, their brother, a white horse and his wearing apparel, reserving his gold shoe buckles for his nephew, James Colquhoun (pronounced Cowhoon) of Glasgow, Scotland. He then gave all the residue of his estate including the amount due from his brother David on his annuity and the amount due from services connected with the Great Britain promoting expedition to James, Elizabeth and Nellie Wilson. Now James Wilson lived diagonally across the County Fluvanna in its northeastern extremity, and Elizabeth and Nellie lived in the same neighborhood, while the Seven Islands were in the James river at the southwestern end of the line, fully forty miles away. The question arises why should James Ross select James, Elizabeth and Nellie Wilson as his legatees, renouncing all his other relatives, except James Colquhoun, unless they were his nearest of kin in Virginia, with the exception of brother and his children who did not need his help? This deed of gift taken in connection with the fact that the father of James Wilson married Agnes Ross seems to establish the fact, that Agnes Ross was a sister of James, Daniel, David and Peter Ross, and that James, Elizabth and Nellie Wilson were nephew and nieces of the testator, James Ross. In order that there might be no confusion as to Elizabeth and Nellie Wilson, James Ross made a codicil to his will in which he more particularly identified them. He said that Elizabeth Wilson had married Joseph Scott of Fluvanna County, and that Nellie Wilson had married James Farrow of the same county. This great particularity of James Ross further fortifies the conclusion that these women were of the clan Anrias or Ross, his near kinswomen, the ones to whom he was determined his estate should go.

This seems to align the family, Wilson, with the old clan Anrias or Ross of Scotland. Authorities differ as to the origin of this great Scottish clan. A county in Scotland still bears its name and its history as to origin is lost in the very remotest antiquity. The old Norse Sagas contain references to the family Ross, and the better opinion is that the Ross family is of Norse origin; that it conquered a foothold in Northern Scotland in days when the old Celtish clansmen were forming their habitats in that place. Other authorities claim for it a pure Gaelic origin, but they are not well fortified with facts. Whatever its origin may have been the clan Anrias or Ross goes back to the very beginning of the Clans in Scotland, and has equal glory with that of Mackenzie, Macgregor, MacKinnon and the two score or more great clans upon which the glory of ancient Scotland seems to rest. After centuries of clan life the Earls of Ross were accused of treason to the English King and forfeited their political rights. These Earls of Ross were numerous governing with almost unlimited power in what is now Rosshire, Inverness and Nairn, Scotland. A favorite baptismal name of the Rosses was Hugh, a name which as we shall see has clung to the Wilson family to this good day. The Rosses forfeited their estate in the fifteenth century at a time when their retainers numbered about eight hundred fighting men, all kinsmen and part of the clan. With the forfeiture, the Earls of Ross and their nearest of kin became simply great landholders, and parts of the major and minor gentry of Scotland. The commonalty of the Ross family unable to prove its descent by pedigree were enrolled under the banner of the clan MacKenzie, but while carrying a new name, after the advent of surnames, really carried Ross blood. The major and minor gentry, however, had pedigrees, and although without legal right to the title earl or lord, still used it, and were still given it by their immediate friends. In 1692, James Ross was Burgess of Nairn; in 1708 in the Burgh of Fane, fourteen Rosses were connected with the government of the burgh. Their principal citizen was William, otherwise Lord Ross, who at that time was not ashamed to be styled a merchant. Others of the name in the same burgh were Charles, Alexander, Thomas, Robert, Malcomb, David and Andrew. Two Davids appear in this roll of honor, David Ross, late treasurer of Inverchasley, and David Ross of Balingowan, the father of David, James, Daniel, Peter and Agnes heretofore named. The arms of the Earls Ross were: Gules, three lions rampant arg. The Roses as well as the Wilsons seem to have been a sept of the Rosses. Daniel Ross died and was buried in the West Indies; James Ross was buried on the Seven Islands in the James; Agnes Wilson, nee Ross, was buried in Amherst, while David Ross was buried in Henrico. From the Land Books of Fluvanna for 1796 I have calculated more than thirty-two thousand acres of land as the property of David Ross, which property he sold prior to 1830, when but two hundred and fifty acres were assessed to his name. The greatest chancery suit ever known in Fluvanna County was that of Ross vs. McLachlen and Quarles. As early as 1782, David Ross formed a partnership with Allen McLachlen to conduct a trading post in Fluvanna County at the Place of the Fork, now Columbia on the James. Columbia today is a town of possibly a hundred and fifty souls, but in times past was strong enough to secure within one vote of as many votes in the Legislature of Virginia for the location of the capital of the Commonwealth as did Richmond. At Columbia Ross and McLachlen carried on their mercantile busines for more than twenty years, and seemed to have settled it satisfactorily, before the death of McLachlen. When McLachlen died Quarles was made his executor, and he refused to carry out the settlement. A suit ensued which was settled forty years after, when both Ross and Quarles had passed away. David Ross was a member of the House of Delegates from Fluvanna in 1781 and 1783. He was a married man and certainly had one daughter to whom he gave the estate called "Solitude," twenty-five hundred acres just west of Palmyra. He may have had a son David, who married Frances, a daughter of James Wilson, but this is not sure. James Wilson himself carried the Ross blood, but the evidence seems to point to the fact that the David Ross who married his daughter, Frances, was a son of Peter Ross. David Ross, Jr., died in 1857 leaving a son, James Wilson Ross. In the census of 1810 David Ross is enumerated immediately after Peter Ross; Peter being forty-five years of age and over, with twelve slaves, while David was twenty-six and under forty-five, owning one slave.

The descendants of Elizabeth Wilson who married Joseph Scott, and of Nellie Wilson who married James Farrow still ramify Fluvanna County, but I have not busied myself to trace their lines.

James Wilson seems to have died about the year 1820 and his wife, Anna (Kidd) Wilson, about 1821. Their children were Hugh, Barnett, John, Walker, Elizabeth, Frances, Rachel, Joannah and Rebecca. Hugh Wilson died before he reached his maturity but the others were all married and became the heads of families. In Book No. 8, page 372 of the Fluvanna land records, a power of attorney is set out, dated October 27, 1823, from the heirs and children of Anna Wilson, deceased, to Barnett Wilson, one of the children and heirs, authorizing him to proceed to King and Queen County and collect their interests in the estate of a bachelor uncle, Bartholomew Kidd. This instrument recites that the children named are all children of James and Anna (Kidd) Wilson. It shows that Elizabeth was a minor, and on another page in the same book the fact appears, that she had chosen Barnett Wilson, her brother, as her guardian. Walker Wilson was not present, but the instrument recites that he was in the West and had empowered Barnett Wilson to act as his attorney in fact.

Not all of the marriage dates of this family are to be found in the Fluvanna records, but the most of them are. These records show that John Wilson married Nancy W. Johnson on December 18, 1822; that Elizabeth Wilson married Peter R. Johnson on December 16, 1823; that Frances married David

Ross on January 20, 1803; that Joannah married John White on December 22, 1807; that Rebecca married David White on November 20, 1821. The power of attorney shows that Frances, Rachel, Joannah and Rebecca married the men named, and their names, the husbands, are signed to the instrument. When Rachel married William Sadler is not shown in the marriage license record, but the power of attorney shows that William Sadler was the husband of Rachel. The children of Frances, Rachel, Joannah, Rebecca and Elizabeth are widely scattered over Fluvanna County, and many of them have migrated to other States. Walker Wilson married in the West and his descendants are now in Texas. John Wilson who married Nancy Johnson had several children, William, John Mortimer, David, Daniel Sarah Ann, Tranquilla and Betty. David is still alive, residing near Palmyra, Virginia. William left two descendants; John Mortimer married and left two daughters; Daniel married and left three daughters; Sarah Ann Tranquilla married John F. Ohmohundro and Betty married Harvey King, leaving a descendant now in the Senate of Virginia and a promienent lawyer at Clifton Forge.

Why James Wilson selected a habitat in Fluvanna County, Virginia, may never be known. His kinship to David Ross may have a bearing upon the question, and the old coal and gold mines of Fluvanna and Goochland may also have been an influencing cause. It is a well known fact that the earliest mining of coal and gold in the United States was in this region, although the industry, so far as these counties are concerned languishes today. Wilson Town, Carnwath Parish, Lanarkshire, Scotland is a town nearly three centuries old, famous for its iron works and established by the Wilsons. John Wilson was a minister in Lanarkshire in the parish of Crawfordjohn as early as 1647 and had for his patron, Lord Selkirk. Lanarkshire and Renfrewshire have been the seating place of Wilsons for four hundred years, some preachers, and some soldiers, but for the most part merchants, shipmasters and manufacturers of either iron or cloth. John Wilson of Dunfermline invented the fly shuttle and made a new epoch in the art of weaving. The crown invested him with many honors and the burgh looked upon him as one who had contributed most largely to the glory of the town. Wilson's School on New Row, Dunfermline, was created by a Wilson, for the free education of Dunfermline children, specially those bearing the name Wilson. On November 17, 1613, the weavers of Dunfermline met and prescribed the width of table cloths and bed spreads, and among the signatures of those present we find the names of John and Andrew Wilson. Fourteen years before this, this same body met and prohibited the exportation of wool. It will thus be seen that the Wilsons of Scotland have done much for the commerce of England, and this same craft spirit may have led James Wilson into Fluvanna. But the old Wilson spirit was not entirely commercial, for Scotch Wilsons have made great captains, great colonels, and even great generals in the English army. This martial spirit animated James Wilson during the Revolutionary War, leading him to enroll himself in the Virginia line to fight against Great Britain, even as his father had done in Scotland. He was a private in the infantry line and by the Act of Congress of March 18, 1818, was placed upon the pension rolls of the United States, but died within two years after his enrollment. In Document 44 of the Proceedings of the House of Delegates of Virginia for 1834-1835, it is set out that James Wilson was entitled to State land for military services in the War of the Revolution but that he never received it.

Other Wilsons from Scotland settled on the lower James many years before Richard Wilson entered King and Queen, some of whom became distinguished in early colonial history. The great Miles Carey, Rector of William and Marys College, married one of these and became the proprietor of Carey's Ford, Fluvanna County, one of the most noted seating places of the old Virginia landed gentlemen. Descendants of his in 1810 had one hundred and seventy-four slaves, by far the largest number of slaves owned by any family in Fluvanna; next to the Careys stood Joseph Haden with forty-two; then Patrick Woodson with thirty-six; then George Holman with thirty; then James Quarles with twenty-seven. These in their day held themselves as of a higher social stratum than others owning a lesser number of slaves. A very large number owned from fifteen to twenty-five slaves, among whom was James Wilson with seventeen. It is interesting to note that the fewest number of families in the old slave States owned fifteen or more slaves. In Westmoreland County in 1782, there were two hundred eighty-nine slaveholders owning less than ten slaves and but fifty-six who owned ten or more. The average size of slaveholding in most counties was but nine. In fact on most of the slaveholding estates there were more whites than blacks, and an estate having more blacks than whites came to be called a plantation, while an estate having more whites than blacks was but a farm. Every slaveholder who owned fifteen or more negroes was called "Esquire," and "Planter." In addition to this he was in nearly every case a social dignitary. This mingling of the economic and social currents was characteristic of Southern antebellum communities, and James Wilson enjoyed the privileges and immunities of his day. He was an economic success and a man of high social standing.

James Wilson died in 1820 in his sixty-fifth year, honored by all his fellow citizens and lamented by a respectable family of children and relatives. He certainly did his part for country and home and his descendants have every reason to be proud of his memory. The division of his estate among eight or nine children gave each of them a fair beginning in life but not enough to entitle them to the social position of their father.

BARNETT WILSON.

This brings us to Barnett Wilson whose life connects itself more closely with Robert B. Wilson of Arkansas. The marriage license records of Fluvanna do not show the date of his marriage but the traditions are that he married in Goochland County in either 1813 or 1814. His farm was on the line between Goochland and Fluvanna, and in various deeds he is sometimes described as Barnett Wilson of Goochland and at other times as Barnett Wilson of Fluvanna. He married Elizabeth or Polly Parrish, daughter of Anderson Parrish of Fluvanna and Goochland. The Parrishes were an old and respectable family of Virginia, landholders and slaveholders, but I have not been able to trace them back to their landing. The first act of Barnett Wilson after his marriage was to purchase ten acres of land on Bird's Creek in a different part of the county from that in which his father and other relatives were then seated. The land adjoined his father-in-law, Anderson Parrish, and was partly in Goochland and partly in Fluvanna. In 1835, Anderson Parrish deeded to Barnett Wilson of Goochland County one hundred and sixty acres of land in Fluvanna County. In the census of 1830, Barnett Wilson was described as of Fluvanna County with seven children, five males and two females, having a wife, each head of the family being between thirty and forty years of age. In that enumeration he was the owner of four slaves, which seems to prove that he had determined upon an agricultural life. That he had the confidence of his brothers and sisters, their husbands and wives is fully proven by the power of attorney heretofore referred to. This would also seem to indicate that he was a man of good business judgment, with mental parts far above mediocrity. He was reputed to have been a Baptist in good standing with his church and was certainly a Democrat. Both he and his wife died in Virginia on their old home farm where they were buried, leaving the following children: Hugh, Benjamin Franklin, John T., Martha, Judson and Lucy. Hugh emigrated to Shelby County, Tennessee, where he married and lived until the war; he enrolled himself in the Confederate Army and died in that service. John T. Wilson also emigrated to Shelby County, Tennessee, where he married Sally W. Williams. After residing in Shelby County for several years he moved to Arkansas, where he died in 1857 or 1858; his widow is still living at Atkins in Pope County. Judson Wilson married and became the father of one child; he joined the Confederate Army in 1861 and remained with it for nearly four years, being killed in one of the last battles. Before the battle he had a premonition that he would be killed and gave his watch and ring to a fellow officer to give to his wife, which was done. His wife remarried after the war and went to South America.

Martha Wilson married a Richardson, a descendant of one of the gentlemen justices of Fluvanna County, Virginia, and died a few years after the war. Lucy Wilson about the beginning of the war married William Knuckles, and with him made her residence at Richmond, Virginia, where she died in 1887. This leaves Benjamin Franklin Wilson of whose career it is now our purpose to write. This leads us to remark.

Richard Wilson of King and Queen County, and James Wilson of Fluvanna, ancestors in a direct line of Barnett Wilson, were each in their day, far more eminent men in their counties than was Barnett or any of his brothers. James Wilson was easily the equal of any man in Fluvanna in his day, not excepting any of the Careys, who excelled him alone in wealth and education. James Wilson was a man of honor, chivalry, spirit, energy, courage, and of eminent hospitality. His sons had all these characteristics, but fifty years make a remarkable difference in conditions. James Wilson had a county for his field of operation, and in that field he never failed to prove his worth. His children had a narrow field—a neighborhood—and were satisfied with their lot. Self satisfaction not only accounts for differences in condition but also creates new differences. They, these Wilson children, like their father were honorable, slightly less chivalric, immensely less spirited, somewhat less energetic, equally hospitable, but in a different kind. James, the father, entertained his friends throughout Fluvanna, and even entertained his friend William Bolling, whose fine estate on the James was everywhere known as "Bolling Hall," and which through the centuries has cast a glamour of glory around its owner. Barnett Wilson and his brothers entertained their church friends on Sundays with splendid hospitality, but it was only their church friends. You can not separate a true Virginian from hospitality in some one of its forms, and Barnett Wilson, unable to meet the larger demands of the term, limited himself to the church form, that generosity of spirit which invited to his home troops of Baptists after the regular church services of the Lord's Day. Virginia hospitality whether of the older form of the day of James Wilson, or of the younger form of the day of his son, Barnett, cost the man who exercised it far more than it yielded of absolute value. Every great Sunday dinner cost Barnett Wilson more than it yielded him. He could ill afford to give the dinner but as a Virginian he could not escape the law which bound him, nor did he wish to escape it. He must entertain, and be it said to his credit he loved to entertain, and throughout his life he held himself in the ranks of old time Virginians bound by the laws of old time Virginia hospitality. Like a valiant hero, although without ability to do so, he maintained every form of Virginia life, and died a true Virginian, a splendid representative of the old time F. F. Vs. His children, however, went West to escape the calls of hospitality as demanded by the code, and to make for themselves an estate and a name. Some of them, as has been outlined, died on the field of martial glory, fighting for the glorious unfortunate Confederate Cause, leaving names that are immortal. Benjamin Franklin Wilson stuck to his estate, loving it, nursing it and leaving it as a lever by and through which his children might win back the old time credit of their forbears, Richard and James Wilson, splendid representatives of old time first families of Virginia.

BENJAMIN FRANKLIN WILSON.

Benjamin Franklin Wilson was born in Goochland County, April 17, 1823; he was brought up on his father's farm to a life of industry and given the educational opportunities afforded by the Old Field Schools. In his eighteenth year he joined the Baptist church and lived a consistent member thereof throughout his life.

At the age of twenty-one the larger West beckoned him and he answered the call by moving to Shelby County, Tennessee, finding a suitable home near where the old town of Fisherville once stood. There he met Mary Wright Williams, daughter of Robert and ——— (Beasley) Williams, to whom on March 16, 1848, he was married, Elder Askew officiating. Robert Williams was a North Carolinian by birth, emigrating to Tennessee as a boy and settling in Rutherford County. Fortune favored him and he became a moderately wealthy man.

The going security for friends, however, swept away all he had and led him to a second removal into Shelby County, where he died in 1885. Mary Wright Williams was born March 6, 1828, in Rutherford County, Tennessee, and died at the home of her daughter, Martha Luella McReynolds, in Barry County, Missouri, on June 28, 1897, while on a visit to her daughter. She joined the Baptist church in Shelby County, Tennessee, the year she was married and lived a consistent religious life from that time until her death.

In 1853 Benjamin Franklin Wilson moved to Conway County, Arkansas, settling a few miles above Old Lewisburg. Two years later he purchased a farm in the southeast corner of Pope County, on the Arkansas river, where he lived for about twenty years, when failing health, largely induced by exposure as a Confederate soldier, led him to move to Washington County near Cane Hill. He afterwards bought a farm near Springdale in that county, where he lived until the death of his wife in 1897. The remainder of his life was passed among his children in Arkansas and Missouri, dying at the house of his son, Robert B. Wilson, in Russellville, Arkansas, on April 21, 1904, having lived in Arkansas something more than half a century.

From 1853 to 1860 he worked industriously upon his farm, clearing it and preparing it for the raising of stock, a vocation he seemed to love. Arkansas at that time was most sparsely settled; his house was of hewed logs and the floors of the old pioneer puncheon form. In 1861 he voted against secession but when Arkansas seceded, Wilson adhered to the State's decision and joined the Confederate Army. He enilsted twice; first, in a cavalry regiment raised in western Arkansas, in which he served more than a year. During this service he reached his fortieth year and was no longer subject to military duty. He left the regiment and went back home. Later on the necessities of the Confederacy became greater and Wilson decided that his duty was to help his country despite his exemption from service. With him duty was always a law, and he at once enlisted in the First Regiment of Arkansas Cavalry, commanded by Colonel Erastus Stirman, in the company led by that soldierly gentlemen, Captain James W. Russell of Russellville, where he remained until the end of the war. His hardships as a soldier were very great, but at no time equalled those of his wife, a non-combatant, residing in a territory raided and plundered by the irregular troops of the Union army. To the credit of both armies it may be said that the regular soldiers respected the rights of women and children. Armies, however, have troops of camp followers whose only law is revenge, ruin and rapine, and at the hands of these, Mrs. Wilson and her children received the most unsoldierly, and at the same time, the most unmanly treatment. The history of Southern mothers whose husbands were at the front has never been written, but when it shall be, their heroism and self-denial will fairly rival that of their husbands, and their suffering so far transcends that of their husbands, as to make it fairly insignificant. All honor to the mothers who gallantly held their homes in the deadly area between the lines.

Benjamin Franklin Wilson at the beginning of the war had five slaves and a fine lot of cattle and horses. One negro woman came to him from his Virginia father, and was brought by him to Arkansas, where she died shortly after the close of the war. She was always loyal to her master and mistress, and was a great help to Mrs. Wilson during the war. The war destroyed all of the property of Benjamin Franklin Wilson except his farm, to which he returned to recuperate his fortunes by honesty and untiring industry. He was a member of the Galla Creek Baptist Church until he moved to Washington County, where he became a member of the Baptist Church of Springdale. Like his father he was most hospitable, especially to his church friends, and if called on, would not hesitate to entertain a whole Baptist Association. He never held office. When solicited to stand for office in both civil and military life he invariably refused. He was a Democrat and believed the doctrines of that party, loyally supporting it to the end. To Benjamin Franklin and Mary Wright Wilson were born the following children:

1. Mary Elizabeth Wilson who died in infancy; 2. Robert Barnett Wilson of whom we shall have more to say; 3. William Judson Wilson, who died when three years of age; 4.

Martha Luella Wilson, born August 16, 1853; married C. Lee McReynolds and is now living near Purdy, Missouri, the mother of several children; 5. Matilda Mildred Wilson, who died in infancy; 6. Katherine Wright Wilson, born August 14, 1859; married Dr. R. B. Gladden and lives in Purdy, Missouri; 7. Theodosia Wilson, born in 1863, who died in 1883; 8. Benjamin Franklin Wilson, born April 25, 1866; moved to Texas, where he married, and is now living in Oklahoma; 9. James Edward Wilson, born September 18, 1869; married and lives at Lufkin, Texas. The first three were of Tennessee birth, but all the rest were born on Arkansas soil. Such is the eventful history of two splendid Arkansas characters, a history worthy of study and emulation.

ROBERT BARNETT WILSON.

We now come to an Arkansan well and favorably known to Arkansans generally, and to the legal profession particularly. Robert B. Wilson was born in Shelby County, Tennessee, on May 26, 1850. He came with his father to Arkansas in 1853, and is now living in the county in which the greater part of his life has been spent.

There were no schools in his neighborhood and his opportunities to acquire an education were therefore limited. In 1860 his father and neighbors employed a man to teach in the neighborhood, and for ten months he had his first tutelage outside of home. During the war which followed education was a lost occupation and all schools were abandoned. While his father was absent as a soldier and for a long time after his return, the son was compelled to work upon the farm, snatching what learning he could by self help, which after all is the greatest help a man can have. He gathered knowledge as did Lincoln, in the quietude of his mother's log cabin, from such books as he could borrow or buy. At twenty-one years of age he passed an examination for teaching, winning a second grade certificate, upon which he taught a three months school. In March, 1872, he went to Murfreesboro, Tennessee, and attended Union University for about four months. Returning he again taught a three months school in Pope County, Arkansas, but to his dismay found that there was no money in the treasury to pay him after his work was done. The war had been over a long time but reconstruction still held the country in its ruinous grip. This kept him from returning to Union University and led him to take to clerkship in a store at Galla Rock for the fall and winter. In the spring of 1783 he went to Texas and taught a summer school in Tarrant County, preparatory to entrance upon St. John's College at Little Rock. He entered late on account of his teaching work; was interrupted by the sickness of his father and the Brooks-Baxter war of the spring of 1874. For a time he added to his scanty exchequer by acting as janitor for the college. He lived for a while with many of the other students in a frame dormitory attached to the property, but afterwards took a room with one of the professors in the college building, and at the breaking out of the Brooks-Baxter war was the only student occupying a room in that location, and as his professional room-mate had resigned and left, he had these quarters all to himself. This gave him an opportunity to know and see things that otherwise he could not have had. When Brooks ousted Baxter, the latter repaired to St. John's College and placed himself under the protection of the commandant, Major Gray. The students were formed into a body guard for Governor Baxter, and with guns in hand moved with greater alacrity than they had shown when armed with books. The governor was placed in Wilson's room, where he was guarded during one night and until he removed his headquarters to the Anthony House. In this room the portly governor occupied Wilson's bed, but being so much heavier broke it down and slept on the floor. It is claimed that the State of Arkansas owes Wilson for that bedstead to this good hour. The military knowledge gained by Wilson at this broken term was not lost, as he was deputed by Major Gray to aid in disciplining the raw recruits who came in under Baxter's call. For the next year he worked on his father's farm and in a country school house, until in March, 1875, he entered the law office of L. W. Davis of Russellville, where under the scholarly guidance of Judge Frank Thatch he studied law. He was admitted to the bar in May, 1876, and at once opened an office in Russellville to begin the practice of law. For thirty-two years he has been an active practitioner in Arkansas and is still wedded to his profession. He has been a close student during all these years and is thoroughly well grounded in the law. At St. John's College he was a classmate with J. W. Blackwood, George and John Rose, J. E. Williams and others, whose names have since become noted in the law at Little Rock, and where comradeship has been of value through all these years.

Robert Barnett Wilson has never been an office seeker, but at times has held honorable positions under both State and national law. In 1878 he was appointed to fill the unexpired term of the county judgeship and then elected for another term, refusing further preferment. In 1888 he, without his solicitation, was appointed by President Cleveland, Register of the United States land office at Dardanelle, which place he held until by a change of administration he was succeeded by a Republican. For fifteen years he was a member of the Russellville school board, acting as its president for the most part, succeeding Jacob L. Shinn. For many years he has been the local land agent of the Little Rock branch of the St. Louis, Iron Mountain and Southern Railway; is the retained attorney of the Southern Anthracite Coal Company, the Onita Coal and Mining Company and the Peoples Exchange Bank, a leading financial institution in western Arkansas.

He is and always has been a Democrat, responding cheerfully to every call of his party, whether the demand was for work or for contributions; he has served as Chairman of the County Central Committee and has been a member of the State Central Committee.

For years he was a member of the Baptist church at Russellville, but at present affiliates with Methodist Episcopal Church, South, the church to which his wife has always belonged.

On November 21, 1877, he was married at Russellville, to Ann Mary Howell, Rev. W. J. Dodson, of the Methodist Episcopal Church, South, performing the ceremony. His wife was the daughter of Jesse C. and Adalissa C. (Hardaway) Howell, formerly of Hardin County, Kentucky.

It has been said that a good wife is the best fortune a man can have, and in this particular Mrs. Wilson has been a most exemplary woman. She is and always has been her husband's greatest helper. Beginning life poor, she practiced economy and industry as few women do, thus enabling her husband to gain a handsome competency. The children born of this marriage were: 1. Hurley Howell Wilson, born January 6, 1879; graduate of Russellville High School; graduated electrical engineer, University of Arkansas, class of 1901; now and for five years past in the employ of the Pennsylvania Railroad Company, with headquarters at Altoona, Pennsylvania; superintended the electric lighting and power of the new union depot at Washington, D. C.; 2. Mary Wilson, born March 4, 1881; attended Maddox Seminary at Little Rock and Virginia Female Institute at Roanoke, Virginia; married Elbert H. Rankin in May, 1904, and has one child, Robert Wilson Rankin; 3. Frank Connyngham Wilson, born May 31, 1886; graduate of the Russellville High School, and of the Dental department of Vanderbilt University class of 1908; 4. Adalissa Wilson, born October 25, 1893, and 5, Robert Barnett Wilson, Jr., born April 23, 1897.

Judge Robert B. Wilson is a man of firm convictions coupled with a courtesy that wins him friends from all classes of men. No man in the country has achieved a more distinctive success in life than he, another proof of the power of the human will over external circumstances. Without the aid of influential friends,—without that education which comes from the highest college forms and without any antecedent and inherited wealth, he has hammered out of adverse circumstances a position in life second to no one in the county. His word is as good as his bond and his social position that of the best of his fellows. From "Wilsonia," one of the finest houses, if not the finest house in Pope County, he dispenses an elegant hospitality and revives the prestige of the old Virginia name. In years to come men will point with as much pride to the Wilson House in Russellville as in centuries agone they pointed to the famous Bolling Hall on the historic James.

CHAPTER XLII.

The Rector Family.

The Richters are an old family of the German Empire, widely dispersed in locality, of eminent respectability, and far-famed as thinkers and musical composers.

Franz Zavier Richter of Strasburg, first gave musical prominence to the name, 1709-1789, as an author of many productions for instruments of all kinds. He was followed by Karl Gotlieb Richter of Berlin, 1728-1809, who acquired great celebrity as a musician in the service of Princess Amalia of Prussia, as organist of the Cathedral at Konigsburg, and as author of many concertinas for the piano and trios for two flutes and a bass. This fame of the Richters was further enhanced by Ernest Frederick Edward Richter of Leipsic, 1808-1879, Director of Music at the University of Leipsic. His musical works have an immense circulation. Another member of the family of great fame was Ernest Heinrich Leopold Richter, 1805-1876, of the Royal Institute of Berlin. The Catholic Church of the United States boasts a bishop, Henry Joseph Richter, who was born at Oldenburg in 1838. In German history they have also been noted as great soldiers and great merchants. In old German the word, Richter, means a judge, and its Anglicized form, Rector, carries the same idea in part, but is limited to ecclesiastical affairs.

Richter is an old surname in Germany, and has been transplanted to England and the United States. In the latter country the word has been variously spelled, Richtor, Richter, Ricktar, Rechter, but is now almost exclusively spelled Rector. The coat of arms of the family was an eagle displayed sa, in dexter an olive branch, vert. and in sinister a thunderbolt, ppr.

THE MIGRATION TO AMERICA.

The first migration of any of the Richter family to America occurred as follows: About one hundred and ninety-five years ago the inhabitants of the thrifty little German village of Musen, about fifteen miles northeast of the city of Siegen, in the then principality of Nassau-Siegen, the present Prussian province of

Westphalia, were thrown into great excitement by the arrival of agents of Baron D. Graffenreid, seeking skilled workmen to open the iron mines of Virginia for Governor Spottswood.

Siegen is now and was then the center of one of the most noted iron producing and manufacturing districts of Germany, and at Musen is situated one of the most famous iron mines in that country, dating back to 1303. There were, of course, many men, thrifty and honest, who desired to better their condition, and who under the promise of free passage and free lands soon consented to change their habitation. Forty persons agreed with Graffenreid's agent at Musen and Seigen to go to Virginina. This colony did not go as servants as did many of the other German colonies, but as freemen planted a free colony on the Rappahannock in April, 1714. They were received by Governor Spottswood with open arms, placed in a fort on the frontier at a place where Spottswood lived and given twelve hundred acres of land. There were not more than twelve heads of families, who soon provided themselves with log huts forming a nucleus for a new settlement which was called, Germana. Germana is no longer on the map, but in the language of another, is located as follows: "Germana was the famous town of Governor Spottswood; the first county town of Spottsvylvania County; the place where St. George's Parish was organized; where the first iron furnace in America was built; and the first pig iron made as Spottswood claims; the place from which the famous expedition of the Knights of the Golden Horseshoe started; where the first German congregation in America was organized, its first pastor settled, and its first services held."

It is no longer a town but a mere ford in the river, called Germana Ford, in the extreme northeastern corner of Orange County, on a remarkable peninsula of about four hundred acres with the Rappahannock to the north, west, and east of it, about fourteen miles above where the Rapidan debouches into the Rappahannock. The first pastor of this congregation at Old Germana was Henry Hager, and the elders of the congregation in 1714 were Henry Hager, Pastor; John Jost. Merdten (Martin) and John Jacob Rechtor, (Rector), which is attested by the extant credentials signed by them and given to Jacob Christopher Zollicoffer when he was sent by this congregation to Europe to solicit aid to build a church and schoolhouse at Germana. Henry S. Dotterer has given the world a paper containing these facts as taken from the Stadt Bibliothek of Frankfort on the Main, a copy of which in German is in possession of Hon. E. W. Rector of Hot Springs, Arkansas. It is a most valuable addition to the Rector family history. The English Church created St. George's Parish to proselyte these Germans into the Episcopal Church, but Henry Hager was acute enough to hold them to the tenets of the German Reform Church.

The thirteen householders making this German Colony of 1714 were John Kemper, Jacob Holtzclaw, John and Harmon Fishback, John Huffman, Harmon Utterbach, Tillman Weaver, John Joseph Martin, John Jacob Rechtor, Jacob Coon, ——— Wayman, ——— Handback and Peter Hitt. From this handful of Germans, of meager estate but of thrifty and moral habits, have come through two centuries many most prominent men; it gave a great general to the Confederate Army, who was also governor of Virginia; a surveyor general for Illinois, Missouri and Arkansas, William Rector; four governors of the State of Arkansas, James S. Conway, Elias N. Conway, William M. Fishback and Henry M. Rector, besides hundreds of others in somewhat less eminent positions.

In fact, it is doubtful whether any other single group of men of the same size, or of ten times the size, in any part of the world has ever produced through two centuries an equal number of great men. And from John Jacob Rechtor proceeded a greater degree of vigor and power than from any other name of the colony.

In about ten years this colony became dissatisfied at Germana and removed to a point on Licking Run, then in Stafford County, but now in the southern part of Fauquier County, and established a town called Germantown, about eight miles south of the present town of Warrenton. Spottsylvania County is and always has been a very poor county, and these thrifty Germans soon ascertained this truth and moved to a richer part. Fauquier County is a rich county and while Germantown is not located in its cream, the second location was far better than the first. Here these thrifty Germans prospered and laid the foundations for a greater wealth. Old Germantown gave place in time to Fauquier White Sulphur Springs, but in time lost its prestige and is now a mere hamlet in South Fauquier. Thus at Germana and at Germantown began the Virginia family of Rector, the family whose name heads this chapter.

The proof of the date of John Rechtor's migration to Virginia is to be found in Will Book A, pages 3 and 4, of the old Spottsvylvania records, and is recited in Volume 13 of the Virginia Magazine of History and Biography. The recital is as follows:

"At a court held the 2d day of June, 1724, for Spottsylvania County, Jacob Ricktar, (Rector), in order to prove his right to take up lands according to the Royal Charter, made oath that he came into the colony to dwell in the year 1714, and that he brought with him his wife, Elizabeth, and his son, John; and that this is the first time of proving their said importation; whereupon certificate is ordered to be granted them of right to take up one hundred acres of land. The certificates for the land were issued May 30, 1729. Signed, T. A. Harris, Clerk."

John Jacob Rechtor, or as the Spottsylvania clerk anglicized it, Ricktar, must have died between 1724 and 1729, for the certificate for this land was issued to Elizabeth, his wife, reciting the facts. We know from his oath that he was married when he came to Virginia and that he brought with him one child, John Rechtor. So much for this old pioneer. Born in Westphalia and educated as an iron and steel manufacturer; poor yet thrifty; a member and elder in the first German Reform Church ever established in America; one of the guild that manufactured the first pig iron ever made in America, and who died after proving his right to one hundred acres of land, thus becoming a freeholder in America.

We also know from the will of John Rechtor, the 2d, that John Jacob Rechtor, the father, had another son, Harmon, who was given one hundred and sixty acres of land on Licking Run by John, the 2d, who named him as his brother. Harmon Rechtor left descendants around Germantown, where they may be found until this good day, and it may be that some of the descendants of John Rechtor, the 2d, may be found in the same place.

Henry Hager, the pastor at Germana and Germantown, had eleven children, the sixth one born in 1687, being Elizabeth Hager, who in Germany, prior to the migration, was married to John Jacob Rechter between 1707 and 1713. John Jacob Rechter was born about 1680 and died between 1724 and 1729. Henry Hager, the pastor, was the son of Henry Hager of Antshausen, a village of Nassau. The son was well educated, being a teacher of Latin in Siegen before becoming a pastor in the German Reform Church. On December 3, 1678, Henry Hager, the Latin professor, married Anna Catherine Friesenhaugen, daughter of Jacob Friesenhaugen, the Mayor of Freudenburg. This establishes the fact that the Rectors of Virginia descend from German families of the very highest respectability and worth, and evidence is not lacking to show that in more ancient times they had a higher heraldic renown.

JOHN RECTOR, THE SECOND.

That John Jacob Rechtor had a son, John, is proved by his oath in 1724 when he applied for his land. This oath also proves that the son, John, was foreign born, but without fixing the date of his birth. The mother, Elizabeth, was born in 1687, and the son, according to a memorandum of his grandson, Nelson, was born in 1707. We cannot fix the exact date of the son's marriage. In John Fishback's will of date 1733, he mentions a daughter, Catherine Rechter, and John Rechter witnessed his will. John Jacob Rechter was dead at this time, hence the signatory, John Rechter, was the son and the husband of the daughter named Catherine. This daughter was also born in 1707. In John Rector's will of 1773 he names his wife as Catherine Rector. John Rector married Catherine Fishback before the date of John Fishback's will, probably in 1731 or 1732.

John Rector, the 2d, like all of his neighbors, was a farmer and as events prove a very thrifty one. He was an adventurous man, fearless and progressive. His stature was very large, as was that of his children. Fauquier County at that time had no existence as a political division, being a part of Stafford County, and with a few exceptions was a grand primeval forest of the deepest solitude. John Rector plunged through the almost interminable undergrowth of the land and discovered where the better lands lay. He found out that Germantown was in the poorer part of the county, but that in the northern part of the county there were much richer lands, whereon a more abundant living might be made with much less work. As he grew older and wealthier he purchased lands in this locality and upon them made a greater wealth. The Rectors today are located in two distinct parts of Fauquier County, around Germantown and around Rectortown, possibly fifty miles apart. The wealthier Rectors reside around Rectortown, and some of them claim to be of no kin to those around Germantown. The great Rector stature still adheres to each set, which proclaims them of common origin, and there are no other differences which may not be accounted for easily by the differences in the country in which they have lived for more than a century. Those who remained at Germantown are simply Rectors of a poorer neighborhood; while those at Rectortown are pitched in a better natural location. Both sets descend beyond all question from old John Jacob Rechtor of Germana and Germantown.

John Rector, the 2d, lived to be sixty-five years of age and became the head of a large family. We cannot follow his ilfe in detail, but one event deserves special mention as it indicates his progressive spirit and great foresight.

In February, 1772, 12th George III, Henning's Statutes of Virginia, Vol. 8, it appears that the House of Burgesses of Virginia authorized John Rictor (Rector) of the County of Fauquier, the owner and proprietor of lands in that region, to lay off fifty acres of his land into lots and streets for a town, to be called and known by the name of 'Maidstone. This little item of law goes far towards an explication of the passion we shall hereafter discover in the Rectors to lay off and establish towns, a passion which marked their career most strongly in Illinois and Missouri. It may also indicate a point in family history which we may never be able to prove. It is historically certain that the German colony from Musen and Siegen remained in England for some time before making its final trip to Virginia. Who can tell but that John Rector, the son of John Jacob Rechtor and Elizabeth, his wife, was not born during that brief sojourn in England, and possibly at the old English town, Maidstone! It is no wild stretch of the imagination to assume that John Rector, the 2d, in founding the town, Maidstone, and in giving it that name, did so in honor of his own birthplace. Maidstone was in Fauquier County, in its northern part,—in the very cream of the county. After John Rector's death in 1773, the town prospered and held the name, Maidstone, until about 1796, when in honor of its founder, John Rector, it came to be called Rectortown, and by that name is known today.

Maidstone was founded about the beginning of the Revolutionary War, during which struggle John Rector, its founder, died, having sent a grandson, John, and possibly others, into that war. The traditions of the family are clear that his son, Frederick, was a Revolutionary soldier from Virginia, but the condition of the military records of that State makes it impossible to prove this authoritatively. His children asserted it in 1820, and it was doubtless true.

THE WILL OF JOHN RECTOR, THE SECOND.

John Rector's will was dated November 5, 1772, and probated March 22, 1773, and is recorded in Book 1, pages 205-7, of the Fauquier County wills. It names his wife, Catherine, seven sons and two daughters. The will distributed about sixty thousand dollars' worth of property and indicates superior thrift on the part of John Jacob, the immigrant, and of John, the testator. At that time this sum of money marked its possessor as a rich man. He gave his wife, Catherine, his plantation, with all his negroes during her life. He gave his sons, Henry, Daniel, Charles, Jacob, Benjamin and Frederick, and his daughters Catherine and Elizabeth from two hundred to four hundred acres of land each and a number of negroes at the death of his wife. His son, John 3d, was dead, leaving a son, John 4th, who in turn was given land and negroes. The children of John, the 4th, were Elias, Benjamin, Burrell, Blaxton, Eli, Edward, Susannah and Sally. Their descendants, as well as the descendants of Henry, Daniel, Charles, Jacob, and Benjamin, and Catherine and Elizabeth, still ramify Fauquier, Culpepper and Rappahannock counties,—some of them rich, while the greater number are neither rich nor poor, but own their own homes and form a part of that great army of men called, "good livers."

John Rector, the 2d, owned about three thousand acres of land on Cromwell's Run, Licking Run, Goose Creek and in other parts of the county. John Rector, the 2d, was a thoroughgoing man. In June, 1764, he, Isaac Cundiff and John Kincheloe, laid off a road from Ashby's Gap to John Lea's. In May, 1760, he secured the running of a road from Rector's mill on Goose Creek to the main road. On July 23, 1761, Thomas McClanahan and Augusta Jennings, captains, and Jacob Rector, his son, ensign, took the oath to support his majesty's person.

John Rector built mills, bought farms, laid off a town, proved his manhood and worth. He is buried near Maidstone, now Rectortown, and his wife sleeps by his side. Passing the other sons and grandsons, we now come to the third generation of Rectors in America, and shall confine ourselves to Frederick Rector the immediate ancestor of the Missouri and Arkansas Rectors. Catherine Rector died in 1775, two years after the death of her husband.

FREDERICK RECTOR.

Frederick Rector was the seventh and youngest son of John and Catherine Rector and was born July 16, 1750. As a youngest son he was doubtless favored by his parents during their lives, and thus made helpless as to individuality. His father died when he was about twenty-three and his mother died within the next two years.

He had executive ability and was a most honorable man for that, in Will Book No. 1, page 427 of Fauquier County wills, it is set out that he and his brother, Benjamin, were made executors of Henry Rector's will. Henry was a brother, and left sons, William, John and Enoch, and several daughters. His lands lay on Goose Creek. He also witnessed his uncle Harmon's will in September, 1782. From this will it appears that Harmon married a woman named Mary, and left sons, Harmon, Nathaniel, Uriah and Henry. From other documents it is clear that Uriah was a Revolutionary soldier, and died in Tennessee. That Henry had sons and daughters, Polly, Elijah, Caty and Spencer, and that Spencer's children were Edward, John, Henry, Mary and Pency. Nathaniel had children, Anne, Aylette and Joel. Elias Rector, son of John, the 4th, was the father of Franklin, Mary, Annie, Lizzie, Mildred, Charles, Marion, Alvin and William Henry. Frederick Rector grew up among a great mass of Rector kin, both at Germantown and Maidstone. He was evidently a conveyancer and may have been a lawyer. Certain it is that he gave his children, and he had a very large family, superior opportunities for an education, and their careers seem to justify the conclusion that they each and all had receptive minds.

Frederick Rector was given lands by his father on Goose Creek in the richest part of John's possessions, but the education of nine boys and four girls, Virginia fashion, soon ate up the estate. Two negroes, Jeffey and Jackey, came to him at his father's death, before the final division of the residuary estate. The exact date of his marriage was February 7, 1770, and on February 20, 1776, he and his wife, Elizabeth, joined in a deed selling land, which deed recited that the land was given him by his father, John (Fauquier Deeds, Book 6, page 233). Frederick Rector married Elizabeth Conner, daughter of Lewis and Ann (Wharton) Conner, an old Virginia family. Elizabeth Conner was born at Norfolk in 1755. Again, on October 22, 1782, Frederick and Elizabeth sold to John Moffett two hundred acres on Cromwell's Run, reciting that this land came from his father, John, the consideration being $1,500 (Deed Book 7, page 470). Frederick was then living in Maidstone, educating his children and dispensing a hospitality that added to his fame while rapidly diminishing the patrimony given him by his father.

In May, 1782, as shown by the Minute Book of the Fauquier County Court, Frederick Rector memorialized the court that he owned land on one side of Goose Creek and asked the privilege of the court to erect a water mill, which was granted. He was still alive in Fauquier County in 1792, as the minutes of the court show, but after that he drops entirely out of sight on Virginia records. By his marriage he had nine sons and four daughters, each of whom he reared to man's and woman's estate. The names of the sons in order were: Wharton, William, Elias, John, Nelson, Stephen, Thomas C., Samuel and Henry. One daughter was named Ann, or Nancy, and the other three, Sally, Mollie and Lucy. Elizabeth married a Barton, whose descendants are among the wealthiest people of Kansas City. Sallie married a Beale and became the mother of General Wm. K. Beale of the Confederate army. Elizabeth Rector, the mother, died at Oak Hill, seven miles above Kaskaskia, in Illinois Territory, on September 18, 1811, and Frederick died at the same place on October 24, 1811.

4TH GENERATION—THE RECTORS OF ILLINOIS.

In 1806, these nine Rector boys left Fauquier County to seek their fortunes in the West, and their parents soon followed them. All these years we have been hearing about the solid, phlegmatic, philosophical German who reads abstruse speculations on the ultimate theory of matter, and thinks rather than acts. But there is another side to the picture and in following the fortunes of these particular German boys from 1806 to the present we shall be led to see it. Some one has said that no people on earth excel the Berliners in certain aspects of gaiety and pleasure seeking and that they excel all other people in genuine courtesy. The Parisian and American do have much fun and pleasure but they generally get through about midnight—the very time when the German is just getting under good headway. They are not loud in their fun—on the contrary, they are very sedate—but in having it, they fill the cafes of Berlin, Dresden and Munich with their wives and children at four o'clock in the morning, at the very hour that Paris and New York are asleep. They can sit four hours at a table in quiet discussion, all the time eating and drinking, which goes far towards making a really sound mind in a really sound body. They know what they want, and also how to get it. When a German draws near a table partly occupied by others but which the necessities of the case require him to occupy, he draws his heels together and makes a military salute. When his food comes before eating he lifts his glass or stein to all who are at the table. He is trained to respect the rights of others and to do it gracefully. Every one of these Rector boys was stolid, phlegmatic and philosophical but each of them sought and had his pleasures, and each of them retained to the last a most masterful politeness and courtesy.

If there was any difference it was in degree and not in kind. William and Elias were models of courtesy even in the backwoods, but the nine Rector boys as a body made and won friends among all classes of people, the rich and learned and the poor and unlearned. Jared Mansfield was surveyor general of the Northwest Territory from 1803 to 1812 with headquarters at Cincinnati. To him in 1806 William and Elias Rector applied for work and were by him assigned to the Kaskaskia District of Illinois as deputy surveyors. The other brothers were taken as surveyors and helpers. John Rector had been to Kaskaskia in 1804 and had remained there a year, and his brothers in asking for work requested an assignment to that teritory. Montague, in his History of Randolph County, speaks of the work of John Rector as a lawyer in 1804 and then says: "The Rector family consisting of nine brothers, came to Kaskaskia in the year 1806. They were in the United States surveying service and only remained temporarily at Kaskaskia." They remained in the Illinois country until 1816 and in that time surveyed and sectionized almost the whole State. In the letters of the United States Treasurer to the surveyors general these boys are always referred to as the Rectors, and in the main what was said in praise or criticism of one was said of all. They formed a clan of courteous, yet most clannish brothers, and were looked upon by the department at Washington and the surveyors general at Cincinnati as solid and steadfast men.

Each of them was six feet high, straight as an arrow, fearless, yet quiet and courteous. They were law-abiding and honest. Their ancestors gave the Virginias no trouble at Germana and they were true to the teachings of their fathers. They had ideas but they used them for their own edification and not as a means to control others. They also knew their rights and also how to defend them successfully. Under the law they were required not only to survey the government lands but to survey those of private individuals. The private lands were in the main .old French grants and very difficult to outline and the Rectors thought the government should pay an extra compensation therefor. They sent their claims to Congress and in December, 1809, Senator Richard M. Johnson reported that William and Elias Rector had not only surveyed the public lands of the Kaskaskia District, but under compulsion of law had surveyed the claims of private individuals, and that owing to the intricate nature of the work their claim for increased compensation should be allowed, and it was.

Another German characteristic is the love of being governed, not the slavish obedience to all sorts of law, but a philosophic belief that almost any sort of government is better than none, and that the governors are better fitted to devise than the governed, to say nothing of the principle that it is the interest of the governors to devise the best. The letters of the Surveyor General Mansfield to the United States Treasurer abound with the rehearsals of complaints from the deputy surveyors and surveyors against regulations, and in one letter from the Treasurer to the Surveyor General, Mansfield is told that all these complaints have been made direct to the department, but as the Rectors have not complained, the department has concluded that the difficulties grow out of the inherent nature of the work rather than the regulations. The Rectors were not kickers against the regulations and in that they were wise. The correspondence between the Rectors and Mansfield and the department from 1806 to 1812 is voluminous, disclosing not only the difficulties of the survey, but the fact that the Rectors were frequently called to Cincinnati by Jared Mansfield for consultation. William Rector seems to have been the leader and Elias Rector his principal adviser, and in fact the balance wheel of the family, but the interest of one brother was the interest of all. Sometimes William went alone, and sometimes Elias, but not infrequently they all went together. Cincinnati at that time was a mere village but the nine Rectors always made an impression upon that town when they went there together. There they met the distinguished Ohio surveyors, Israel Ludlow, Thomas Worthington and Levi Whipple, forming attachments that were never broken. While at Cincinnati they regularly visited Louisville, and sometimes Frankfort, renewing their friendships with old Virginia friends in their Kentucky homes. How many of the boys were married at this time I am not able to state with exactness. Wharton certainly was, for his sons, Wharton, Elias of Fort Smith, and William V., were all born in Virginia prior to 1806.

These boys were also honest, patriotic and brave. In 1809 Illinois Territory was cut off from Indiana Territory and Ninian Edwards was appointed governor, and Nathaniel Pope, secretary, with power to act as governor during that officer's absence. Nathaniel Pope was a brother of Senator John Pope and was then practicing law at St. Genevieve just over the river from Kaskaskia. He knew the Rectors in Virginia and had renewed his acquaintance in their Illinois habitation. Nathaniel Pope got his Illinois appointment before Edwards and as acting governor set the territorial government to work. His first official act on May 3, 1809, was to appoint Elias Rector, attorney general, John Hay, sheriff, and seventeen justices of the peace. On June 11, 1809, Ninian Edwards arrived and when told what had been done said that he was sorry, as that en route he had written John J. Crittenden offering him the portfolio of the attorney general and would have to stand to his word. Elias Rector said that he had only taken the place temporarily and would be glad to shift it to another. The salary was but one hundred dollars per annum, and he, Rector, was engaged in more lucrative employment. John J. Crittenden declined but recommended his brother, Thomas L. Crittenden who served for a short time. Governor Edwards then appointed Elias Rector, adjutant general of the State militia, but on July 11th of the same year removed him and appointed a man named Morrison. On November 9, 1909, Senator John Pope wrote Edwards a letter in which among other things he said, "I am sorry you removed Rector and appointed Morrison, although you acted correctly. The Rectors are honest men and would have been your firm friends. Morrison I know to be a scoundrel and will not be your friend unless you do the one hundredth good turn." Notwithstanding Pope's harsh judgment, Morrison was a good man and became the ancestor of Hon. William Morrison. On May 10, 1810, Governor Edwards reappointed Elias Rector adjutant general, which position he held to October 25, 1813. Pope thus testifies to the honesty and steadfastness of the Rectors and these virtues do not exist without others. Elias Rector organized the militia of Illinois and had it in readiness for the second war with Great Britain, a struggle in which Illinois Territory suffered severely.

The historian, Moses, recites that in 1812 the Indians on the Illinois above Peoria committed many outrages and Governor Edwards put two regiments of militia in readiness to punish them—Elias Rector being made colonel of the 1st regiment, and B. Stevenson colonel of the 2d regiment. Davidson and Struve say, "The volunteers were divided into two small regiments commanded by Colonels Elias Rector and Benjamin Stephenson respectively." Moses says further: "In these frontier wars of 1812-1814 the names of Samuel Whiteside, James B. Moore, Jacob Short, Nathaniel Journey, Willis Hargrave, Jacob and Samuel Judy, Benjamin Stephenson and William McHenry William, Elias, Nelson and Stephen Rector were conspicuous as commanders of either companies or regiments."

In the roster of the State troops the following attestation occurs:

"Muster roll of general and staff officers of a detachment of Militia of Illinois Territory ordered into the actual service of the United States and commanded by his Excellency Ninian Edwards, Governor and Commander in Chief of the Territory aforesaid:

Ninian Edwards, Commander in Chief.
Elias Rector, Adjutant General.
Benjamin Stephenson, Brigadier Major.
Nathaniel Pope, 1st Aid.
William Rector, 2d Aid.
Nelson Rector, } Volunteer Aids."
Robert Todd,

Endorsed: "Examined, approved, certified and returned by me according to law to the Commander in Chief.

ELIAS RECTOR,

Adjutant General, Illinois Territory, November 23, 1812."

Elliott in the Appendix to Illinois Soldiers in the Black Hawk and Mexican wars, quotes the preceding paper and says: "This paper in an historical point of view is of more interest than that of any small paper connected with the history of the State." I am sure that I agree with him and the Rectors ought to. It is most complimentary to them.

Edwards in his Life and Times of Ninian Edwards places Captain N. Rector in charge of one company in the expedition against Peoria in July, 1811.

Edwards also states that Colonel Elias Rector on August 15, 1812, on his return from a trip to St. Louis brought the first news to Governor Edwards of the fall of Fort Malden. Prior to this Edwards had addressed a letter to W. Eustis, secretary of war, recommending the appointment of William Rector as brigadier general of the Illinois troops but through a mistake at Washington the commission came to Edward's headquarters made out in the name of Elias Rector. By the next mail a letter came from Washington referring to the mistake and asking that the commission be returned for correction. In the meantime the news brought by Colonel Elias Rector made action of some kind necessary and William Rector was recognized as a brigadier general and acted. On August 26, 1812, Ninian Edwards issued the following order:

"Brigadier general Rector is hereby required to take the most prompt and effectual means for calling into active service according to law four classes of the militia from each company in the 1st, 2d and 4th regiments of the militia of the State. The Commander in Chief requests to be notified at the earliest period at which those respective detachments can be prepared to march."

In a short time Rector reported as required and the force took position at Fort Russell, from which Edwards began his correspondence with the war department objecting to General Harrison exercising authority over his troops, ordering them to the Wabash when the Illinois was in greater danger.

In the campaign of 1813 General Howard sent sixty-six of the Illinois Rangers under Captain Stephen Rector up the Mississippi to reinforce the fort at Prairie du Chien, and forty-four regulars in another boat under Lieutenant Campbell. Above Rock Island at the Rapids, Rector's boat got ahead and at a favorable point the Indians attacked Campbell's boat, destroyed nearly all the troops and set the boat afire. Rector seeing Campbell's predicament let his boat drift down the river guiding it alongside the other. Amid the deadly fires from the Indians he lashed his boat to the other, rescued the survivors, carried off every dead soldier and left the burning boat to the Indians. But for the heroism of Rector every one of Campbell's men would have been destroyed. The place afterwards received the name Campbell's Island but Illinios historians aver that it should have been called Rector's Island.

In 1814 another expedition was sent up the river in charge of Major Zachary Taylor. Nelson Rector, Samuel Whitesides and Captain Hempstead were each in command of a boat. They were to penetrate well into the Indian country and returning destroy all the corn on both banks of the river down to Rock Island where they were to establish a fort. They ascended to Rock Island unmolested although the country swarmed with British and Indians. On August 22, 1814, the boats were attacked by a combined force of English and Indians. Taylor anchored his fleet in the river out of reach of the rifles near some willow islands. During the night the British planted a battery of six pieces at the water's edge and landed Indians on the islands. Captain Rector landed on the lower island and drove the Indians off; he then tried to clear the upper island but it was too well protected by the battery on the shore. Taylor withdrew down the river and at a point opposite the present town of Warsaw landed and built a fort, calling it Fort Edwards.

In Reynold's "My Own Times" these further facts are found. In September, 1812, the forces marched to Peoria, the 1st regiment commanded by Colonel Elias Rector and the 2d by Colonel Benjamin Stephenson. John Moredock acted as major; Colonel Desha as a field officer of some kind. Judge Pope, Nelson Rector and Lieutenant McLaughlin as aids to the governor. The governor and brigadier general Rector accompanied the detachment. In another place Reynolds says: "No act of noble daring and bravery surpassed the rescue of Campbell during the war in the West. Rector and his men were governed by high and ennobling principles of chivalry and patriotism." He describes Nelson Rector's dress in the Willow Island fight as follows: "Captain Nelson Rector was elegantly dressed in military costume with a towering feather in his cap, and with his sword drawn led his men to the charge. In this exposed situation with hundreds of guns fired at him he moved on undaunted as if he were in his mess-room with his comrades. The Rector family never knew what fear was."

Parrish in his Historic Illinois gives this spirited account of Stephen Rector's rescue of Campbell and his regulars: "It was at this desperate juncture that Stephen Rector and his gallant crew of Illinoisans, comprehended the horrible situation of their helpless comrades, performed as cool and heroic a deed as ever imperiled the life of man. Deliberately, in the teeth of a howling gale, in full view of hundreds of infuriated savages lining the nearby shores, and within easy reach of their deadly rifles, Rector ordered his frontier heroes to raise their anchor, to lighten their barge by casting overboard nearly all their stock of provisions, and then guided it with the utmost labor and amid tremendous danger down that madly racing current, actually forcing it to the windward of the burning barge and into the very blaze of the Indian guns. Holding it there, in spite of the galling fire fairly scorching their faces, these men coolly rescued the survivors, removing wounded, dying and all to the security of their own vessel, and then swept with them in safety down the river. It was as heroic a deed of daring as was ever performed in war. The island was later named for Campbell, but with Captain Rector and his Illinois rangers remains the true glory of the action."

Reynolds in his Pioneer History of Illinois says: "In 1806, when the United States lands were to be surveyed, the Rector family reached Kaskaskia and remained there for several years. This family in Illinois were numerous and conspicuous in pioneer times. There were nine brothers and four daughters of the family, all born in Fauquier County, Virginia, and many of them raised there. Some of them had emigrated to Ohio and others direct to Illinois. The family were singular in their traits of character. They were ardent, excitable and enthusiastic in their dispositions. They possessed integrity and honesty of purpose in the highest degree. Nature endowed them with strong and active minds, but their passions at times swept over their judgments like a tempest. They were the most fearless and undaunted people I ever knew. Dangers, perils and even death were amusements for them when they were excited. They were impulsive and ungovernable when their passions were enlisted. They were the most devoted and true-hearted friends and the most energetic and impulsive enemies to anyone they thought deserved their hatred. The family in their persons were generally large and formed with perfect manly symmetry. They were noble, commanding and elegant in their bearing and their personal appearance was, for manly beauty, not surpassed in the territory. They possessed an exquisite and high sense of honor and chivalry. An insult was never offered to any one of them that went unpunished."

"William Rector was the oldest brother and a monitor for the balance. He was a deputy surveyor and all were respectable gentlemen. Elias Rector commanded a regiment as colonel in the campaign of 1812. The whole Rector family were patriotic and were always willing and ready to shed their blood in the defense of their country. Nelson Rector while surveying in Gallatin County in March, 1814, was fired on by the Indians and severely wounded; his left arm was broken, a ball entered his left side and another struck his face but he mounted his horse, escaped and recovered."

This account is in the main true. It is wrong in one particular. Nelson Rector was not surveying when attacked but was bearing dispatches as aide to Governor Edwards.

The father of Reynolds settled in Randolph County, Illinois, before the Rectors entered the territory; he was a very rich and influential man; his son, the historian, graduated in 1810 form Knoxville College, East Tennessee, and was for thirty years intimately acquainted with the Rectors.

THE TESTIMONY OF GOVERNMENT RECORDS.

In Volume 2, American State Papers, Public Lands, is a plat of the Common Field of Town Tracts of old Kaskaskia made in 1807, to which the following attestation is made: "We do hereby certify that the above surveys as laid down, were made by us, by the consent, under the superintendence and by the aid of the citizens of Kaskaskia, and that many of the ancient boundaries were found, which governed the surveys, and also that the surveys were correctly executed by us as laid down on this plat. William Rector, D. S., Elias Rector, D. S."

On May 23, 1808, Elias Rector as deputy surveyor, made the same attestation to a survey and map of Prairie du Pont; on January 29, 1810, William Rector, D. S., attested the survey of the village of Prairie du Rocher; on June 2, 1809, that of Fort Chartres and St. Philipps; on May 23, 1808, for Cahokia.

These records show that Elias and William Rector were the first government surveyors to enter Illinois, and the plats of townships surveys in the office of the United States Commissioner of Lands at Washington, which have been examined by the writer, show that these two men did the very largest part of the government work as to township surveys for Southern Illinois from 1806 to 1810. Nelson Rector was recognized as

Pioneers and Makers of Arkansas 389

a deputy surveyor in 1810 and his signature appears to hundreds of township surveys from that on until 1820. Wharton Rector was recognized as a deputy surveyor in 1815 and his name appears to many plats in Illinois, Missouri and Arkansas from that on to 1822. The first surveyor general over Illinois work was Jared Mansfield; the second, Josiah Meigs, from 1812 to 1814; the third, Edward Tiffin, from 1814 to 1816. William and Elias Rector were deputy surveyors under all of them for all the time; Nelson Rector under all of them but for a portion of the time under Mansfield, while Wharton came in under Meigs and lasted throughout Tiffin's connection with Illinois surveys. The names of Thomas C. Rector and Stephen Rector first appear upon the government records in 1818 as deputy surveyors under the surveyor generalship of William Rector, their brother. Their names appear on hundreds of township plats in Illinois, Missouri and Arkansas, and as they always appear together, it is fair to presume that they worked together throughout their lives. Six of the nine boys are thus vouched for by the government as deputy surveyors, qualified to take independent work, and given independent work, four of them by Mansfield, Meigs or Tiffin, and two of them by Rector, their brother. Nowhere upon the records, that I have been able to find, do the names of the three other boys, John, Samuel and Henry appear. John was certainly a lawyer, and although tradition makes him a surveyor, as well as Samuel and Henry, it is certain that they were never recognized as deputy surveyors. I have not been able to find anything concerning the after history of John, Samuel or Henry.

WILLIAM RECTOR AS SURVEYOR GENERAL.

In July, 1815, William Rector submitted a plan to the secretary of the treasury for the survey of Missouri Territory, and with Elias Rector made a trip to Chillicothe, Ohio, to confer with Edward Tiffin. This plan was no doubt worked out by William and Elias, was approved by Tiffin and adopted by the secretary of the treasury. On April 29, 1816, Congress provided for a surveyor general for the Illinois and Missouri Territory; on May 10, 1816, Josiah Meigs, for President Madison, commissioned William Rector as surveyor general for Illinois and Missouri, with headquarters at St. Louis. When William Rector was commissioned he was residing at Kaskaskia, Illinois, but on July 10, 1816, took up his residence at St. Louis, where the rest of the family soon began to assemble. In 1817 William Rector surveyed St. Louis County, and during the same year Elias Rector, Wharton Rector, Nelson Rector, Thomas C., and Stephen Rector, as deputy surveyors, did an immense amount of work in Missouri Territory. William Rector lived upon a farm about three miles west of St. Louis as it was then, and Elias was upon a farm adjoining him. Elias Rector had for years been a lot owner in St. Louis, and the records show that on November 1, 1816, he sold several of these to Colonel Clemson of the United States army. On May 25, 1818, Stephen Rector and twelve others, subscribed an agreement to built a theatre on the south side of Chestnut street. The building was erected according to the plans and became the first theatre of St. Louis. On March 17, 1819, Stephen Rector, Thomas Rector, and William V. Rector, the latter being a son of Wharton Rector, Thompson Baird, Richard Gentry and D. M. Bates laid off the town of Hannibal at the Bear Creek and advertised a sale of lots as proprietors. On the same day Elias Rector, John Miller and Henry Jones laid off the town of Wyaconda at the mouth of the Wyaconda. In May, 1819, William Rector, Thomas Rector, Henry W. Conway and others laid off the town of Osage, Missouri.

On December 8, 1819, William Rector was elected a vestryman of the Episcopal church, soon to be founded in St. Louis. On May 15, 1819, the Independence, Captain John Nelson from Louisville, Kentucky, left St. Louis to go up the Missouri as far as Chariton, being the first steamboat to ascend the Missouri. The passengers were Colonel Elias Rector, Stephen Rector, Captain Desha, and others. They arrived at Franklin, Missouri, on May 28, where a great dinner was spread at which Colonel Elias Rector and Captain Stephen Rector made speeches. They arrived at St. Louis on their return on June 5, 1819.

On June 10, 1819, a great dinner was given at Bennett's hotel in St. Louis presided over by General William Rector, assisted by Colonel Choteau, Major Christy and Colonel Benton. The occasion was in honor of the military expedition then on its way up the Yellowstone, the scientific expedition connected with it and to Captain Nelson of the steamboat Independence as the first navigator to ascend the Missouri river. It was a great occasion and General Rector, as well as Elias Rector made appropriate speeches.

In November, 1819, Captain A. T. Crane died and Colonel Elias Rector was appointed to succeed him as postmaster of St. Louis. He was the fourth postmaster of the city and had for his assistants Lucius T. Thruston and James Sevier Conway. His first act was to move the postoffice to the old mansion of Mrs. Choteau on the corner of Main and Chestnut streets. Colonel Rector held this office until his death in August, 1822.

THE RECTORS IN POLITICS.

Missouri was now ready for Statehood and on April 19, 1820, William Rector announced himself as a condidate for the constitutional convention as a representative from St. Louis on a platform which made the voters sit up and take notice. His platform was short and sweet. It called for the eternal importation of slaves, restricted suffrage and viva voce voting. It took a brave man to announce himself upon a platform like that, but he won, receiving the highest vote of any man on the poll. In the convention he was a valuable member and his influence was felt in the making of the first constitution of Missouri. In 1820, Colonel Elias Rector announced himself as a candidate for the legislature but withdrew before the election. In February, 1821, he announced himself for the State Senate and was elected, dying before his first term had expired. In January, 1821, William V. Rector, son of Wharton, was elected auditor of Missouri, by the State legislature. In July, 1822, Captain Stephen Rector announced himself for the legislature but was defeated. In 1820 the editors, Charles, of the Gazette and Henry, of the Inquirer, got into a difficulty on the street, when Wharton Rector intervened in the interests of peace. He was severely castigated therefor by editor Charles in the next issue of the Gazette and most highly praised in the next issue of the Inquirer. The trouble was Benton and anti-Benton, and as Wharton Rector was a Benton man, Charles accused him of intervening to help Henry and to injure him.

THEIR SURVEYING WORK IN ARKANSAS.

The first goverment surveys of Arkansas were accomplished by William Rector assisted by sixty-two deputy surveyors and an army of surveyors and helpers. General Rector in a document set out in American State Papers, Public Lands, Vol. 4, showed that from 1816 to August 18, 1823, he had employed sixty-two deputy surveyors and gave names of each. Among these we find the names of his brothers, Elias Rector, Wharton Rector, Stephen Rector and Thomas C. Rector; his nephews, William V. Rector, son of Wharton, Henry W. Conway, James Sevier Conway and Frederick Rector Conway, sons of Ann Conway, his sister. This was the beginning of the Rector influence in Arkansas. In May, 1819, prior to the organization of the territorial government in Arkansas, General Rector sent a letter to General Meigs at Washington, accompanied by a sketch of the surveys which had been made and were then making in different parts of the territory. These surveys were made in the neighborhood of the principal settlements and the largest bodies of rich lands, partly on the Arkansas and partly on the Red river. Two million acres were covered by the sketch, which General Rector said were "well adapted to tempt the enterprise of every description of emigrants who may wish to seek their fortunes in new countries." The following extract shows the vigorous character of the man: "In every part of the United States young men are sitting down in idleness, talking of the good times which are passed, when their fathers purchased lands for a trifle which are now worth thousands; they lament that the times are changed, the days of good bargains gone and the field of enterprise exhausted forever. Everywhere these lamentations are heard; yet the fact is that times are as good as ever and better, too; the days of good bargains are more plentiful than they were in the past age; and the theatre of enterprise more wide, rich and magnificent than our fathers had ever seen. The truth is that the fault is not in the times, but in the temper and disposition of those who make the complaint; in their own want of energy; in their womanish desire to hang about their kin and to live and die where they were born, instead of going off to the Mississippi, the Missouri, the Illinois, the Arkansas, or the Red rivers, to set up for themselves and to become the founders of fortunes and families as their fathers did before them."

This letter shows not only the philosophical reasoning of the Rectors but also their courage and independence in breaking away from the East where they were born and founding for themselves names and fortunes, which their ancestors had never known. Thus, before Crittenden, Scott or Bates, were in the territory, five Rector brothers and four Rector relatives were already there laying fast and sure the monuments and boundaries by which the security and happiness of millions who were to follow them were forever to be established, maintained and conserved.

It was the Rector influence that almost elected Stephen Austin, a candidate of the eleventh hour, as the first delegate from Arkansas to the American Congress. It was the same influence that really elected Matthew Lyon as the second delegate, but who was not permitted to enjoy the fruits of his election. The Rector influence was the first to pit itself against the Crittenden influence, and although it was entirely non-resident, it was a superb power. The Rector influence from St. Louis made Henry W. Conway receiver of public moneys at Little Rock in 1820, and postmaster at Little Rock the same year. In the third race for delegate to Congress, the Rector influence elected Henry W. Conway, and again in the fourth and fifth races. It was first the Rector influence alone, exercised from St. Louis through the influence of the surveys; it then took the shape of the Rector-Conway influence with Wharton and Elias, sons of Wharton, Sr., and three of the Conways, Henry W., James S., and Frederick R., residing in Arkansas. The Rector-Conway influence in the sixth race for delegate was transferred to Ambrose H. Sevier, who, while having no Rector blood, was half Conway. With the rise and growth of Sevier the influence of the Rectors diminished, while that of the Conways increased. It was a Sevier influence that brought in the Johnsons and gave rise to that power, the Conway-Sevier-Johnson dynasty, which ruled Arkansas for nearly thirty years, but which was broken up by the indomitable purpose of another Rector, Henry Massey Rector, a son of old Elias of St. Louis. General William and Colonel Elias Rector laid the foundation of the greatest political combination ever known in Arkansas affairs, and Governor Henry Massey Rector smote the idol at the knees and reduced it to nothingness.

MARRIAGES OF THE RECTORS.

Of the marriages of these nine Rector boys I am not fully advised. Certain it is that Wharton was married before leaving the East and that he left three sons and one daughter, and probably, a fourth son. These sons were, Wharton, Jr., Elias of Fort Smith, William V., and possibly Enoch. Wharton, Jr., known as Colonel Wharton Rector, was a 2d lieutenant in the 2d Rifles in 1820, and of the 6th Infantry in June, 1821. He was afterwards made army paymaster, which position he held for a great number of years, dying February 8th, 1842, in his forty-second year. His rank in the army was that of major. His father, Wharton Rector, Sr., was also known as Colonel Wharton Rector but I am unable to state authoritatively where he obtained the title. Wharton Rector, Jr., was a citizen of Little Rock as early as 1825; in September, 1827, he was a second of Ambrose H. Sevier in his duel with Thomas W. Newton, at Point Remove, now in Conway County. In October, 1827, he was also the second of Henry W. Conway in his duel with Robert W. Crittenden. Wharton Rector, Jr., was appointed adjutant general by Governor Fulton in 1835, and he in turn appointed Elias Rector of Fort Smith, his aide. In 1832 Governor Pope appointed Elias Rector of Fort Smith, A. D. C., and upon the death of Colonel Yell appointed William Field, adjutant general with the rank of colonel.

Colonel Wharton Rector, Jr., was married at St. Louis. He was buried at Van Buren, Arkansas, with military honors, the services being conducted by Major Lear of the Army Post at Ft. Smith. He was a director of the Van Buren branch of the Real Estate Bank at the time. The Van Buren Intelligencer said: "Colonel Rector was a Democrat of the most independent character, but his personal friends were by no means confined to members of his party. His uniformly honorable and manly deportment won for him the esteem of all who knew his worth. His rise in the world is another high evidence of what honesty of purpose, industry and application may accomplish."

Another son of Wharton Rector, Sr., was William V. Rector, surveyor under Colonel William and Colonel Elias Rector of St. Louis; auditor of Missouri for many years and a resident of Little Rock in 1829, where he died at the residence of his brother, Wharton, on September 21, 1829, at the age of thirty-three.

The third brother, Colonel Elias Rector of Fort Smith, was born in Fauquier County, Virginia, September 28, 1802; was reared in St. Louis County, Missouri, and educated at Lexington and Bardstown; he came to Arkansas in 1823 as a surveyor under his uncle William; by and through the influence of Senator Benton he was made United States marshal for Arkansas in 1830, which position he held until 1842, when by the death of Harrison and the accession of Tyler, he was superseded by Henry Massey Rector, his cousin, but was re-appointel upon the accession of Polk. The title of Elias Rector of Fort Smith, is indiscriminately that of colonel and major, but that of major clung to him most persistently. Major Elias Rector lived at Little Rock from 1825 to 1837, a period of twelve years, and at Fort Smith forty-one years thereafter. He was the youngest son of the family, served twenty years as United States marshal without the influence of the Arkansas contingent, ten years as United States Indian agent and has been immortalized by Albert Pike as "The Fine Old Arkansas Gentleman close to the Choctaw line." On November 25, 1835, he married Catherine J. DuVal, daughter of William Duval of Fort Smith. He had a daughter, Harriet Amanda who married General William A. Cabell, the idol of Southern soldiers. He had two sons, James B. and Elias.

Colonel Wharton Rector, Sr., had a daughter, Mary A. Rector who married William Walker. He may have had a son, Enoch, as I find an Enoch Rector certified to the Washington department as a surveyor by General William Rector. He was not one of the nine, and I cannot place him unless he was a son of Wharton, Sr.

General William Rector had a sister, Ann or Nancy Rector, born in Fauquier County, Virginia, who married Captain Thomas Conway of Pitts County, Virginia, and moved to Greene County, Tennessee. Captain Thomas Conway was a son of Edward Conway, a revolutionary soldier, and is entitled to that credit. In after time James Sevier Conway, Governor of Arkanass, tried to connect his family line with one of the extinct earldoms of England but failed. Moncure D. Conway after considering the evidence decided it insufficient, but Hayden, the editor of the Conway paper, decided to admit it, not as establishing the claim of Governor Conway, but for its own inherent worth. The Conways have enough to be proud of as the sons of an admitted revolutionary hero, and of their Rector blood, without the flim-flam of English heraldy. The one is absolute and true, the other rests upon the flimsiest of deductions. Thomas Conway in Greene County, Tennessee, would have lived and died a Greene County squire, but for the vigor of Ann Conway, nee Ann Rector, who desired that her husband and her sons should be something more. She knew that her brothers, William and Elias Rector, thought that blood was thicker than water, and when General William Rector was appointed surveyor general, she wrote to Colonel Elias Rector, the mentor of the family, asking if there was any opening in Illinois for her husband and her sons. Colonel Elias Rector at once advised her to induce her husband to pack his grip and move to St. Louis, Missouri. By what methods she succeeded we are not told, but succeed she did. In 1819, Thomas Conway and family were residents of St. Louis and James Sevier Conway, the future first governor of Arkansas was given place by Colonel Elias Rector, postmaster of St. Louis in his office, with a salary fixed by the government at $60 a year and board. In the same year, Henry W. Conway, working with Colonel Elias, his uncle, founded a town named "America," in southern Illinois, and in 1820 opened a store in St. Louis. Through the influence of his uncle, General William Rector, he was sent to Little Rock as receiver of public moneys and through the influence of his uncle, Colonel Elias Rector, was made postmaster of the same city. Both uncles took hold of Frederick Rector Conway and pushed him forward in the work of surveying. Both he and his brother, James Sevier Conway, were afterwards surveyors general of Arkansas. James Sevier Conway was the first governor of Arkansas and Elias Nelson Conway, his brother, the fifth governor of Arkansas. Dr. John Rector Conway also surveyed under his uncles, William and Elias, but devoted the major part of his life to the practice of medicine. William Conway, another son of Ann Conway, was a judge of the Supreme Court of Arkansas, signing himself, William Conway, B. Ann (Rector) Conway counted far better than she knew when she left Greene County, Tennessee; two sons of hers were governors of Arkansas, and two sons surveyors general, while one was a judge of the Supreme Court. Of her other son, Thomas Asbury Conway, and her daughters, Eliza Conway and Sarah Hundley Conway, I am not so well advised. As an indication, however, that the power was Rector rather than Conway, it may be observed that Ann Rector Conway after the death of her husband in Missouri, married a man by the name of Runkle, by whom she had a son, Thomas Sheppard Runkle, a lieutenant in the Confederate army, and Mary A. Runkle, who married William Pelham, United States surveyor general and had a son Thomas Pelham.

Another of the nine brothers, Colonel Elias Rector, born in Fauquier County, about the year 1785; married at Louisville, Kentucky, about 1810, Fannie Bardella Thruston, daughter of John Thruston of Louisville, Kentucky. She was born March 7, 1795, and after the death of her husband, Colonel Elias Rector, in 1882, married General Stephen Trigg of the United States army and a native of Virginia. Her father Cornet John Thruston, was allotted two thousand one hundred and fifty-six acres of land in Clark's grant for his services as cornet in the Illinois regiment in the Revolutionary war, a cavalry office now but rarely used. In passing, it is but right to say that John Rector, a kinsman of these nine boys, was also a member of the Illinois regiment, and the records show that he was entitled to the same quantity of land in the same grant, but for some reason never applied for it. John Thruston was of a distinguished family, being the eldest son of Rev. Charles Mynn Thruston and Mary Buckner, daughter of Colonel Samuel Buckner of Gloucester, Virginia. His brother Buckner Thruston was at one time United States Senator from Kentucky and a distinguished judge of the United States Court. A third brother, Charles Mynn Thruston, Jr., was the second husband of Frances, General George Rogers Clark's youngest sister. Rev. Charles Mynn Thruston, the father of these three boys, was born in Gloucester County, Virginia, in 1738, and died near New Orleans, Louisiana, in 1812; he was educated at William and Marys College, Virginia. At the beginning of the Revolutionary war he raised a company in Clarke County, of which he was made captain; he was wounded at Trenton, New Jersey, and then made colonel of the regiment and was always known as the "War Parson." He was the son of Edward of Gloucester County, Virginia, who in turn was the son of Edward Thruston the immigrant of 1666, who in turn was the son of John Thruston, Chamberlain of the city of Bristol, England. Cornet John Thruston was born August 18, 1761, and after his service with Clark in the Illinois regiment, settled on a beautiful tract of land on Bear Grass Creek, a few miles from Louisville, Kentucky, containing one thousand acres, where he continued to reside until his death, February 19, 1802. He was at that time judge of the court of common pleas and his wife was Elizabeth Whitney. His seventh child, Bardella, married Colonel Elias Rector and General Trigg. By the marriage with Rector, several children were born, one of whom, Henry Massey Rector, born at Louisville, Kentucky, May 1, 1816, will be considered as we proceed.

General William Rector was a married man but without children. His history has been tolerably well set out in what has gone before. It now remains but to give what the records further disclose. Enough has been said to show that his brothers,

Elias, Wharton, Nelson and Stephen were not only surveyors recognized by Jared Mansfield, Josiah Meigs and Edward Tiffin between 1806 and 1816, but that these same men were also soldiers eminent in the defense of Illinois Territory. They were surveyors under Jefferson, Madison and Monroe, and their services were at no time impugned by a living soul. From 1816 to 1823, General William Rector was surveyor general, and when appointed by President Madison, it was well known, that the Rector boys had always clung together, and it is to be supposed that Madison did not object to this. From 1816 to 1824, during two terms General William Rector had charge of the largest surveying force ever given to one man, and surveyed the three large States, Illinois, Missouri and Arkansas. Monroe re-appointed him in 1819 and again in 1823. No complaint as to the surveying was ever made, and no complaint of any character was ever made until 1823, when Senator Barton of Missouri charged General Rector with favoritism in the appointment of his deputy surveyors. He made no charge as to the character of the work but simply asserted that General Rector as a public servant had no right to appoint so many of his relatives and personal friends. General Rector went on to Washington and succeeded in overcoming the charges of Senator Barton. While there, his brother, Thomas C. Rector, by an ill-advised movement undid all that the General had accomplished. In the columns of the St. Louis Gazette in 1822 an article appeared rehearsing all the charges that Senator Barton had made in Washington, over the signature "Philo." When Thomas C. Rector read this, although the charges were what in this day would be considered trivial, he became angry, and at once repaired to the Gazette office and demanded the name of the writer. He was told that Joshua Barton, district attorney of the city of St. Louis, and brother of the Senator, was the author. Without waiting to consult his brothers or friends he at once sent a challenge to Barton which was accepted. They met on Bloody Island where two shots were fired. Reynolds says that Rector was as cool as though he had been hunting rabbits and that his ball went straight to the mark. Barton died on the ground and Rector was uninjured. When General William Rector returned to St. Louis he was very much mortified over the act of his brother but did not condemn him. His life characteristic was to stand by and uphold the Rector blood. Edward Bates took up the quarrel and published a long article upholding the card of "Philo," which in the light of the after reports of General Rector may be considered as first class buncombe. Out of sixty-two deputies but nine were of the Rector blood. Senator Barton also wrote a card. The result was that while Rector had succeeded at Washington, his brother had aroused an opposition at St. Louis which could not be overcome. In February, 1824, President Monroe revoked his appointment of General William Rector for the third term. In this revocation he set out the fact that every act of William Rector had been founded on precedents and that his lifelong character had been fair but that the good of the service demanded a change. The killing of Barton by Thomas C. Rector overcame the good services of General William Rector. He continued his work at St. Louis with his successor, Colonel McRee until the beginning of 1825, when he repaired to his farm to overlook his great landed interests and to commune with his friends. Among his friends were the greatest men of the United States at that time. He died the next year at Edwardsville, Illinois, while on a visit to friends. General William Rector was one of the wealthiest men of his day at St. Louis, and had the estate of Colonel Elias Rector been properly conserved his descendants would today be very rich men. General Rector built a very large house in St. Louis on the northeast corner of Third and Vine in 1816 for a residence and office. It was enlarged in 1819 by him and was known as Bennett's Mansion House Hotel. The first theatrical company to visit St. Louis gave its performance in the dining room and the first constitutional convention met in that house. Senator Bogy of St. Louis said of the Rectors of St. Louis: "They were men of great stature, perfect in symmetrical form; all tall straight and noted for their beautiful hair, which they wore long; they were courtly and cultivated to a marked degree; one of their characteristics was a prompt resentment of any reflection cast upon a woman in their presence, whether of high or low estate; another was their quick resentment of any imputation upon their own character, or an insult offered to one of them, which they never permitted to go unavenged. They were all men of the highest character and always appeared most elegantly attired." No two men had a greater influence on early Arkansas affairs than General William and Colonel Elias Rector, and no two brothers had an equal prominence in the west.

FIFTH GENERATION—GOVERNOR HENRY MASSEY RECTOR.

Henry Massey Rector was born at Louisville, Kentucky, on May 1, 1816, the son of Elias and Fannie Bardella (Thruston) Rector. His father died during his sixth year, and his early boyhood was spent at home with his mother, and in work at the salt works owned by General Trigg in Saline County, Missouri. He attended school in Louisville, Kentucky, in 1834 and 1835; in the last year removed to Arkansas to look after the great landed interests inherited from his father. He was teller of the State Bank of Arkansas in the years 1839 and 1840. During the year 1841 he superintended his farm in Saline County and studied law; in 1842 was appointed United States Marshal for the District of Arkansas by President Tyler, superseding his cousin, Elias Rector of Fort Smith, and served for three years. He then engaged in the practice of law at Little Rock, his specialty being criminal law; served in the State senate in 1848-49, 1850-51, representing Saline and Perry counties; from 1853 to 1857 he served as surveyor general of Arkansas, and in 1855 was elected to the legislature from Pulaski County. In 1858 he was elected as an associate justice of the supreme court which position he resigned in 1859 to make the race for governor of Arkansas. At this time the Conway-Johnson dynasty had full swing and was thought to be in absolute control of the politics of the State. Little attention was given by it to Henry Massey Rector, who for ten years had been building a character among his fellows, which was to make him more than equal to the combined power of the dynasty. At the regular Democratic Convention in 1860, Colonel Richard H. Johnson, a former editor of the Little Rock True Democrat was nominated for governor, and everybody thought that he would surely be elected. The Union party nominated Judge Thomas Hubbard of Hempstead County. Against this array of great men Henry Massey Rector announced himself as an independent Democratic candidate. In the canvass which followed Johnson and Hubbard made great speeches while Rector simply appealed to the sterling common sense of the voters. This statement must be taken cum grano salis. Henry Massey Rector was a natural born orator; his vocabulary was rich in words and richer in suggestive imagery; his natural logic was superb; his appearance commanding; he was conceded by the ablest judges of the times to have been the greatest debater that Arkansas had known, and it is very doubtful to day whether the State has ever furnished a superior. When the votes were counted Rector had a plurality of two thousand four hundred and sixty-one votes. Thus the stone which the builders rejected became the head of the corner. About this time caricature by pictures first entered Arkansas. There was a paper published at Fayetteville called the Independent, edited by William Quesenbury, popularly called "Bill Cush." He made a cartoon after the election which he labeled "Tom, Dick and Harry." Judge Thomas Hubbard was represented as "Old Mother Hubbard" searching the cupboard "to give her poor dog a bone," but the cupboard was bare. Colonel Dick Johnson was mounted on a whisky barrel surrounded by a crowd of his supporters, diligently telling them how it all happened. Colonel Henry M. Rector was represented with a rooster's head, strutting about and crowing lustily. It was certainly a great victory for a man who had been in the State but twenty-five years, and who had opposed to him all the political sagacity of the State. He was elected for a four years' term but did not serve his full time. After being sworn in the Civil War was inaugurated and the secretary of war made a requisition upon Governor Rector for troops to put down what was called "The Rebellion." Governor Rector showed the stuff of which he was made in the answer which he sent to Washington, an answer worthy of the family from which he sprang. That answer was as follows:

"Executive Office, Little Rock, April 22, 1861.

"Hon. Simon Cameron, Secretary of War, Washington, D. C.

"In answer to your requisition for troops from Arkansas to subjugate the Southern States, I have to say, that none will be furnished. The demand is only adding insult to injury. The people of this commonwealth are free men, not slaves, and will defend to the last extremity, their honor, lives and property against Northern mendacity and usurpation. Signed Henry M. Rector, Governor of Arkansas."

No stronger State paper has ever issued from the executive department at Little Rock, nor, for that matter, from any other State department in all the world. That paper alone entitled Henry M. Rector to the honor of being not only a brave man, but a great man. It entitled him to far better treatment than was given him. The regular Democrats smarting under their defeat took an undue advantage of him in the convention of 1861. That body while providing for a new constitution which continued certain offices in force, intentionally or unintentionally omitted to make any provision whatever for the governor's position. Rector's adherents have always claimed that this was done intentionally and from the meager records which have come down to posterity, it is entirely safe to say, that this contention of Rector's friends was true. At all events it was claimed that as the constitution did not provide for the continuance of the Governor, that a vacancy existed, which contention was upheld by the supreme court. Henry M. Rector served as governor from November 16, 1860, to November 4, 1862, when he was succeeded by Acting Governor Thomas Fletcher, who served until November 15th when Harris Flannigan was inaugurated under the new constitution. During this time Governor Rector seized the arsenal at Little Rock and the fort at Fort Smith, together with all the arms, ammunition and stores contained therein. He was a member of the military board which raised and equipped forty regiments for the Confederate army. He is justly entitled to be called "The War Governor of Arkansas." After leaving the office of governor he joined the reserve corps of the Confederate army, refusing a quartermaster's place, and served as a private until the close of the war. For several years after the close of hostilities he was engaged in farming and in 1874 was sent to the Constitutional Convention from Garland County. In this position he was held to be a man of force, brains and power. His whole life had been clean, honorable and conservative, and these influences gave him power in the convention. He had all the fire and courage of the elder Rectors and was known to be a man no man could insult with impunity. He died in Little Rock at the old Rector residence, a landmark of the town, in August, 1899. With him died the last link of antebellum family influence and power.

In October, 1838, he married Jane Elizabeth, daughter of William Field of Little Rock, who died in 1857. William Field was clerk of the old superior court from 1829 to 1836 and of the United States court for many years thereafter. His father, Abner Field, died in Kentucky on April 11, 1831, in his seventy-first year, four years of which were passed in the service of the United States in the war of the Revolution, where he gained the rank of major. In 1859 Governor Rector married a second time, his choice falling on Ernestine Flora, daughter of Albert Linde, of Memphis, Tennessee. The children of the first marriage were:

1. Frank Nelson Rector, who grew to manhood and died unmarried.

2. Ann Baylor Rector, born in Saline County, Arkansas, April 25, 1841; married in 1857 at Little Rock to William M. Matheny, an attorney of Harrodsburg, Kentucky. To them were born four children, three of whom are now living: (1) Mary C. Matheny, who married Walter J. Land in 1879, and had Walter, Rector, Vivian and Leighton. Mary C. was married a second time in 1899 to Eugene H. Starcke of St. Louis; (2) William Ivan Matheny who married Edna Virginia Terry of Washington, Iowa in 1897; (3) Julia Fannie Maud Matheny who in 1905 was married to William Wayne Sutherland of St. Louis and had one child, Junebug Sutherland.

3. William Field Rector, who joined the Confederate army in his 17th year, and at the battle of Helena, was adjutant of Colonel Hart's regiment in General McRae's brigade. In that engagement all the regimental officers were either killed or wounded, and in the charge on Grave Yard Hill, he as adjutant took command; he was but nineteen years of age, immensely handsome and as brave as a lion; he pushed rapidly forward and found himself alone, some fifty yards in advance of the regiment; fearing that his men were about to falter under the excessive heat and the difficulties of the approach, he scaled the breastworks of the enemy, reached the top, within twenty feet of the opposing line, when he stopped, placed his cap upon his sword and held it out with his right hand, cheering his regiment and bidding them to come on; in this position his right arm was broken by a ball from the enemy's guns, and his cap and sword fell to the ground; whereupon with his left hand he picked up his sword, thrust it through his cap, again held it aloft and again cheered his men to action; a second ball from the enemy struck him, passed entirely through his body piercing both lungs and inflicted a mortal wound. The regiment pressed forward and took the fort, but were soon compelled to abandon it by the river flotilla, leaving Rector where he fell. The enemy on discovering who he was had him removed to the home of one of Governor Rector's friends, where he died the following day, leaving a message for his father, that death came to him in the line of duty and that he had no regrets. He was afterward buried in the Rector burial place in Mt. Holly cemetery, where a fitting monument was erected by his father.

4. Julia Sevier Rector, who married Colonel Charles S. Mitchell of the Confederate army; removed to Dallas, Texas, where she died leaving three children, Charles, William and Lilian, the first and last being married.

5. Henry Massey Rector, Jr., who graduated from Missouri Medical College, and practiced medicine at Hot Springs; was in the Confederate army at sixteen years of age, being in the reserve corps; he was a very learned man, but most modest, retiring and reticent; his reading was almost unlimited and he was a master with the pen; member of the Arkansas legislature;

editor Hot Springs Telegraph; member Hot Springs school board; president Hot Springs Valley Bank; universally recognized as a man of great civility and erudition but a man of the supremest courage; married Hebe Gower of Iowa City, and lived in Hot Springs until his death in 1905, leaving one son and three daughters; the son Henry Massie Rector, Jr., married a Miss Mooney of Hot Springs, and had one son, also named Henry M. Rector; the eldest daughter, Grace Greenwood Rector, married William Fry, son of Captain C. B. Fry, of the noted Virginia family of that name, lives in Hot Springs and has one daughter; the second daughter, Ernestine, married Watson Morrison, and lives at Hot Springs; the third daughter, Levison, married Walter Land and lives at St. Louis, Missouri.

6. Elias William Rector was born at Little Rock, June 11, 1849, at the home of his grandfather Field, where his mother was visiting, the father's residence being at Collegeville in Saline County; he was educated at Little Rock and the University of Virginia; admitted to the bar at Hot Springs in 1874; member of the legislature for many terms; during his first service he was chairman of the judiciary committee; in his second term, chairman of the ways and means committee, and in his third term was speaker of the House; he introduced the first bill to become a law, making it unlawful for a State or county officer to ride on a free pass on the railroads of the State; he was also the father of the geological survey bill which has possibly done more for Arkansas than any measure passed since 1875; he was largely instrumental in passing the railroad commission bill; he was also chairman of the house committee appointed to inquire into the expediency of building a new State house, which led to the present law authorizing its erection; he was twice a candidate before the people for the Democratic nomination of governor but was defeated, largely through the opposition of the railroads and other corporations engendered by his activity in passing the commission bill; he is the retained attorney of the Hot Springs Street Railway Company and has been for twenty-five years. E. W. Rector has the hight, symmetry and manly proportions of his ancestry, coupled with their courtliness and courage. I have known him for twenty-four

years as a public man and have always found him in the forefront of the progressive element of the State; his honor is unquestioned and unquestionable, and no person commands the the respect and confidence of his fellows to a greater degree than he; he was fortunate in his marriage, selecting as his life companion Rosebud Alcorn, daughter of United States Senator James Lusk Alcorn and Amelia Walton (Glover) Alcorn, whom he married at Friar's Point, Mississippi, on November 11, 1875, Rev. Mr. White officiating. The wife of the senator was a Glover descended from the wealthy family of that name in South Carolina, and from the Waltons of Virginia, through whom she was lineally descended from Baron Whiteford of Ayrshire, Scotland.

The father of Mrs. Rector, Senator Alcorn, was a most distinguished, as well as a most remarkable man; of Southern birth, he served the South in her struggle for independence, by equipping at his own expense, a brigade for the Southern Confederacy, the command of which his enemies did not permit him to enjoy; despite this he stood by the Confederate cause to the end, and then stood by Mississippi in her after efforts to recuperate her wasted resources. Like Longstreet, he decided that the best way to help the South, was to camp on the enemy's ground, and he became a Republican. Upon his death the Memphis Commercial Appeal said: "Alone, unique, majestic in his dignified aloofness, stands James Lusk Alcorn against whose shield hate has hurled her last arrow in vain. Measured by what he has accomplished for his State he stands without a peer. Misjudged, misunderstood, maligned for a time by those he sought to serve, and bitterly assailed by many in the open, who came to him clandestinely to applaud and commend, he exhibited the courage of a Coriolanus, the splendid contempt of his enemies of an Alcibiades, the wisdom of a sage and the loyalty of a patriot." The editorial from which this was taken was very long, but its cream, its essence, its real strength is quoted above, and is a splendid tribute to the man. The Commercial Appeal exhausted the vocabulary of vituperation against the living Alcorn, but made this glorious reparation to Alcorn dead. The occasion was the selection of a Mississippian for the Hall of Fame, and the Memphis paper, while naming many as worthy of the American Valhalla, gave James Lusk Alcorn double the space of all others combined. A man may be called great from evidence adduced by his admiring friends, but James Lusk Alcorn was pronounced great by his bitterest foes. His title to greatness is therefore without a flaw, and his children and their descendant's may well be proud of their birth.

Rosebud Alcorn, the wife of E. W. Rector, was educated at Mrs. Prince's School in New York City and at the Baldwin Female College of Staunton, Virginia; inheriting the mental strength of her father, as well as his courage, she brought to her married relations a finished and cultivated mind, which has made her an acquisitoin of inestimable value to her husband, to her children, and to her friends.

The children of E. W. and Rosebud Rector were:

1. Alcorn Rector, born December 27, 1876; educated at Hot Springs and Bingham's School, North Carolina; inventor; his inventions being (1) the Rector gas lamp, now owned and operated by the Rector Gas Light Company of New York City; (2) the Rector Help-a-Phone, a device for telephones to aid the hearing, which improvement is manufactured and sold in New York City by two New York corporations, known as the Rector Help-a-Phone Company, and the Inter-National Help-a-Phone Company. Mr. Alcorn Rector is a large stockholder and an officer in each of these corporations and resides in New York City, unmarried.

2. Amelia Walton Rector born April 5, 1878; educated at Searcy Female College, Arkansas, and at Belmont Seminary, Nashville, Tennessee. She is an accomplished vocalist and lives with her father at Hot Springs, unmarried.

3. Henry Field Rector, born April 9, 1880; educated at Hot Springs; large planter in Coahoma County, Mississippi; married Mary Dye, daughter of Rev. Thomas Dye of Mississippi, and has two children, E. W. Rector and Henry Field Rector.

4. James Alcorn Rector, born June 22, 1884; educated at Lawrenceville School, New Jersey, from whence he graduated

in 1906 the valedictorian of his class; entered the University of Virginia in the fall of the same year, and is now in the senior class of the law department; honorary member for life of the New York Athletic Association, and has never been beaten in the United States in a hundred yards running dash; represented the University of Virginia at the Olympic Games in London in 1908, but was beaten by a man from South Africa. He is unmarried.

5. Jane Elizabeth Rector, born March 21, 1886; educated at Hot Springs, Arkansas, and at Springside, Chestnut Hill, Philadelphia, a school presided over by Mrs. Chapman, the daughter of Bishop Polk, the noted Confederate general. She married Middleton Lane Wootten of Hot Springs, Arkansas, a prominent lumberman and became the mother of one child, E. W. Rector Wootten.

6. Sally Phillips Rector, born May 10, 1892; educated under a private governess, and is now at Springside School, Chestnut Hill, Philadelphia.

The seventh child of Governor H. M. Rector was Fannie Thruston Rector, who was born in Saline County, Arkansas, in 1853 and who was married twice: (1) to Roswell W. Foreman of Washington, D. C., and had three children, one of whom is now living, viz.: Helen Foreman, who married Charles E. Ellis of New York, and resides at Yonkers, New York; (2) to Colonel Charles S. Mitchell, whose first wife was her sister; two children were born to this union, Grace and Margaret, who are both married. By this second marriage, Governor Rector had one child, Ernestine Flora Rector, who married (1) McGhee Williams of Memphis, Tennessee, and had three sons, Rector, McGhee and Thruston; (2) Mr. Brunson of Pine Bluff; (3) Mr. Vaughn of Hot Springs, Arkansas. No children by the last marriages.

This ends the history of one branch of the Rector family, lineally descended from the immigrant John Jacob Rechter of 1714. The entire history of this patriarch's descendants could easily be written, but it would far transcend the limits of this work. Other lines abound with great names whose history is worthy of preservation and which in its fulness would illuminate the life of the early German elder with transcendent glory. What is written here is authentic, and although confined to one great and illustrious line, is a lever of power magnifying without injustice or favor, the real dignity of the old German father, and his splendid line of descendants. It is doubtful whether God ever permitted the perpetration of physical stature and attributes for so long a period as has been covered by the Rector regime. E. W. Rector of Hot Springs, carries today every physical property of the Rectors of two hundred years ago. It may be also well doubted whether any family of America through so long a time has maintained its elegant discrimination as to dress or its marked power in the wide realm of courtly civility and almost princely refinements of manners. With all this the courage of the old Germans who combated with Caesar on the banks of the Rhine stands out with pre-eminent force today. Courage in every age of the world has had the highest place in the affections of mankind, and it is worshipped today no less zealously than of old. Homer has deified it and mankind still worship at the altar of the inimitable Greek. The mental powers of the Rectors have in every age kept full pace with their splendid physical parts, making them most powerful factors in the making and keeping of all that goes for the progression, the elevation and the betterment of the world. The Rector influence in Arkansas began before the territory was born; was in full force at the birth of the territory; lasted through every hour of its life; was triumphantly prominent in the formation of the State, giving that formation birth many years ahead of time; and has followed the State through its every vicissitude of fortune, with loving hands. Without disparaging other great Arkansas names, it is but just to say that the name, Rector, shines with a luster equal to that of any other and is undimmed to this good hour.

INDEX.

Adair, Gov.	232
Adam, Matthew	114
Adam and Eve	14
Advocate and Times	126
Adams, Samuel	277
Adams, John D	324
Allen, General William O., 13, 35, 57, 58	
60, 110, 121, 251, 61, 71, 74.	
Allen, James	113
Allen, Mary K	85, 192
Allen, Col. John	85, 192
Allen, Elizabeth	156, 76
Alice of Old Vincennes	23
Alligator Lake	42
Almendras, John F	42
Angel, Lawrence	78, 279
Anderson, Lawson	346
Anti-Gambling Associations	108
Andrews, William	111
Andrews, Henry	144
Alpin, John	160
Archer, Major S. B.	56
Arbuckle, General	91, 141
Architecture, The Two P's	255
Argenta	188, 27
Alcorn, Gov. James Lusk	407, 408
Alcorn, Rosebud	407, 408
Alcorn, Amelia Walton	407
Arkansas P. O.	19
Arkansas Territory	9, 10, 11
20, 21, 22, 29, 30.	
Arkansas, Slavery in	9, 10
Arkansas, See Arkansas Post,	
Arkansas Post, 12, 13, 15, 17, 19, 23, 35,	
58, 61, 76, 80, 83. 20, 148.	
Arkansas, Spelling of	20, 21
Arkansas County	35, 54, 105, 116, 147
Arkansas River Settlements	44, 45
Arkansas Boundaries	45
Arkansas Population	45
Arkansas County Officers	100
Arkansas County, Election	110
Arkansas Cabins	226, 227
Arkansas Baptist Assn	231
Arkopolis	38, 112, 149, 188
Armistead, Col. Geo. F.	61
Armstrong, Henry	87
Arnett, Rev.	219
Ashley, Chester	68, 85
185 to 190, 240, 286, 336.	
Ashley Family	187
Assassination of Major Isaac Watkins.	232
Austin, Stephen	54, 55
Austin, Moses	55
Austin, Jonas	113
Barkman, Jacob	19, 122, 148, 265,
289.	
Barkman, Betsy	289
Barkman, Asa	148
Barkman, John	148
Ballot Box Irregularities	56
Bagley, Archer	78, 161
Bagley, Benjamin	78
Bailey, William	43, 120, 160
Baker, Elijah	160
Bailey, John	161
Baker, Dr. C.	167
Baldwin, Isaac	248
Baldwin, Pamelia	248
Ball, Judge B. B.	221
Banquets	231

Baptist Society	25
Baptist Church, Little Rock	49
Baptist Church of Christ	143
Baptist Church, First	231
Baptist Association, First	231
Bartelmi	25
Barraque, Antoine	26, 74
Bartran, John	44
Bartholomew, Joseph	45
Barbin, D	73
Barraque Township	79
Bartholomew	151
Barber, David	156, 221
Barber, James	221
Bartley, Judge E.	278
Barton, Elizabeth	379
Barnerd, Jesse B	352
Barton	379
Barbecues and Bergus	123, 344
Bassett, William	44
Batesville 47, 75, 104, 114, 115, 148, 346	
Bates & Crittenden	58
Bates James Woodson	54, 58, 82, 134
346, 286, 172, 180, 189, 199, 201.	
Batesville Bee	335
Batesville Guard	335
Bay of White River	43
Bayou, Hunt	44
Bayliss, Mr.	113
Bayou Metou	146
Bayliss, Elinor	76, 156
Bayou Des Arc	148
Baxter	324
Baxter, Gov.	367
Belle Point	43, 149
Berdue, Albert	44, 287
Bean, Robert	114, 87, 156
Bell, M. L.	93
Bell, Capt. John S.	93
Bean, Richard	161
Beddux, Nancy	160
Bewley, Mahlon	144
Bewley, R. S.	144
Belding, L.	160
Bennett, Joseph	165
Bentleys, The	217
Beaver, Lucinda	247
Beaver, Stephen	247
Beaver, Sarah	248
Beaver, Nancy	248
Bertrand, C. P.	248
Benton Academy	264
Bennette, Madame Barbe	287
Bentley, George	218, 347
Berry, Jairus	288
Berry, James H	329
Berry, John	159
Berry, George	347
Beale, Gen. Wm. K	379
Bentley, Joseph	288
Beck, Abraham	288
Bettis, R. S.	344
Beardstown	112, 149
Bethell, Joshua	352
Big Island	42
Big Lake	43
Big Prairie	45
Billingsly, James	87
Biscoe, H. L.	100, 264 to 270
Biscoeville	148, 266
Big Cofoclose	148
Big Piney	142
Bible Society	254

Index

Biscoe Family 268,	269
Biscoe, Capt. Cameron	269
Biscoe, King & Co	269
Billeate, Miss	165
Berkheimer	174
Bill, Cush 266,	402
Black River 43,	104
Blane, Robert	102
Black, Thomas	113
Blakeleytown	76
Blair, W. P. L.	103
Blythe, S. K.	143
Blount, Rueben J 260,	221
Black, Mrs. George	227
Blackwood, J. W	368
Bogy, Lewis	25
Bogie	25
Bonne, Joseph 25,	165
Bonne, Baptiste	25
Bogy, Charles	44
Bogy, Joseph 45,	97
Bonne, Michael	45
Boyd, James	114
Boswell, Col. Hartwell 72, 334,	336
Bonneau, Antoine	76
Bowie, John J	88
Bowie, James	88
Boiling Springs Camp	143
Bollinger, John	143
Boswell, Col. James 341, 336,	161
Bodcaw	148
Bogy, Ignace 286,	25
Boswell, R. H	337
Bryan, William J 32,	33
Bradford, Major 35, 71, 87, 88,	254
Brideoute, Alexander	43
Bright, John	44
Brown, Samuel	44
Brinsbeck, Raphael	44
Brangiere, Louis	47
Bryan, James	111
Bradley, George	113
Brand, George W	68
Brearley, Col. David ... 69, 166, 223,	131
138, 139, 140	
Brierly, Col. Pearson	72
Brinhard, Raphael	76
Bradley, George 76,	156
Brown, Edward	83
Brearley, Dr. J. H.	143
Brown & Bancrofts Map	147
Bruton, John	144
Brooks, Robert	165
Brick Tavern	167
Brumbach, Christian 167,	231
Brick House 167, 168,	231
Breckenridge, Joseph C	205
Breckenridge, John C	205
Breckinridge, Laura	205
Breckinridge, Robert W. J	205
Breckinridge, Benjamin	205
Brown, Nancy	224
Brearly, Jo.	227
Bricelin, Susan	248
Bricelin, Milo	248
Brilhart Family 280,	284
Brilhart, Jacob	280
Brilhart, Rebecca	281
Bradley, John	286
Bradley, Mary	286
Brinsbech, Amelia	287
Bridgman, Nancy	165
Brookfield, Rev. Isaac	166
Brown, Jonathan R	288
Brazenle, J. R	196
Brooks-Baxter War 324,	367
Bruce, Robert	341
Brooks, Gov 367,	324
Brunson, Mr.	409

Bragg, Micajah	352
Burt, J. B.	19
Burnett, Moses 42,	120
Burrell, Peter	44
Bull, John	101
Bullett, Judge George 97,	99
Burton, Mrs. Jesse	160
Burton, Butler M	141
Burr's Collection	150
Buckle	228
Butler, Lillie Dea	248
Burris, Thomas	287
Burris, Polly	287
Buchannan, Widow	287
Buchannan, Rev. A	287
Byrd, Col. Stephen 114,	157
Byrd, Amos	157
Byrne, Capt.	65
Cadron 16, 19, 38, 45, 47, 48,	49
61, 102, 104, 105, 111, 146, 148,	218.
Casatete	45
Catholic Church .... 24' 331,	284
Catholic Fathers	25
Cache River 26, 43,	44
Caney Creek	43
Cassidy, Pat 43, 101,	120
Campbell, James 212,	279
Calais Joseph	43
Catocke Prairie	43
Cathot, John B.	44
Carnahan, Rev. John 48, 49,	251
Camp Ground, First	49
Cavet, Louis	101
Cane Hill	152
Carothers, John 78,	279
Cannan, Matthew	51
Cassidy, Henry 54, 55, 97,	120
Candidate First Legislature	74
Cabeans	150
Caravans of Pioneers	154
Caldwelltown	150
Casey, Mrs. John	100
Caruthers, Mrs. Samuel	160
Carlocks	282
Carden, Mary	287
Carroll, Mary E.	306
Campbell, Nancy	166
Carden, George	220
Carpenter, A. M.	278
Cady, P. J.	286
Carroll, Wiley	306
Caldwell, Henry	325
Carey, Miles	359
Cabell, Gen'l Wm O	396
Cameron, Hon. Simon	403
Chalmette	24
Chassein, Joseph de	25
Chassein, Antoine	25
Chartruce, Enos 42,	120
Cheek, Jesse	14
Chamberlain, John	111
Chactas Prairie	75
Cherokee Treaty	75
Chalmees, Capt.	93
Chamberlain, Jason 113,	289
Cherokee Indian Agents	131
Choctaw Treaty 133, 134,	135
Chicot County	147
Chisholm, Mrs. W	160
Churchill, Gov.	204
Churchill, Abbie	204
Churchill, S. J.	204
Churchill, A. S.	204
Churchill, Juliet J	204
Churchill Emily	204
Churchill, Matilda	204
Cherry, W. C.	248
Colley, John	160

Index

Click, Henry	160
Clarendon	125
Clark, P. O.	19
Clark, David	122
Clanton, Stephen	101
Closseins, The	26
Clover Bend	43
Clark County	56, 76, 101, 105, 116, 147
Clark, Benjamin Sr.	78, 101, 160
Clay, Henry, Speech	82
Clark County Officers	103
Clark, Mrs. Benjamin	160
Clements, Benjamin	167
Clendennin, Judge J. J.	233
Clanton, Priscilla	287
Cotoner, Michael	76
Coulter, Stokely H.	19
Copfot, Francois	25
Copperas Creek	42
Coffman, Christopher	44
Cox, William	113
Conway, James S.	147, 286, 372
Comet, First Steamboat	65
Colonels of Militia	72
Conway, Wm.	78
Covered Wagons	102, 103, 104
Conway Family	106
Columbus	110
Constitutional Journal	126
Collegeville	151
Cornwall	151
Columbia	151
Cotocton	152
Conway County	147, 148, 218, 221
Cox, Mrs. Charles	160
Cox, Charles	160
Copeland, Isaac	165
Conway, Sevier Dynasty	183, 184
Conway Town	218
Cocke, John H., Slaves	239
Collins, Mary	248
Copeland, M.	278
Colville, Joseph	288
Colville, Andrew	288
Colville, Pauline	288
Coffman, Andrew	303
Coffman, C. T.	303
Coffman, Hugh	303
Cook, Capt. R. P.	308
Cook, Robert T.	308
Cook, Garland	308
Cook, Fanny	308
Cook, Laura	308
Compton, Judge	314
Cook, Joseph	347
Colquhoun, James	354
Coon, Jacob	372
Conner, Elizabeth	378
Conner, Lewis	378
Conway, Elias N.	372, 397
Conway, Ann	396
Conway, Capt. Thomas	396
Conway, Edward	396
Conway Moncure D.	396
Conway, Frederick R.	397
Conway, John R.	397
Conway, William B.	397
Conway, Thomas A.	397
Conway, Sarah A.	397
Conway, Henry W.	54, 74, 94, 147, 166, 176, 183, 221
Cocke, Mary W.	205
Crittenden, Robert	16, 30, 32, 35, 37, 54, 58, 73, 79, 82, 87, 88, 99, 102, 118, 168, 172, 176, 178 to 185, 189, 201, 239
Craig, William	19, 83, 110, 112, 121, 122, 128, 169, 170, 189, 347
Crittenden County	42, 118, 147
Crow Creek	44
Crystal Hill	45, 56, 105, 232, 250, 254
Crawford Court House	49, 105
Criswell, Andrew	112, 279
Craig, Nancy	115
Crawford County Heroes	78
Cryer, Morgan	78, 159, 160
Crozier, Francis	85
Crittenden Town	101, 148
Crawford County	105, 147, 194
Crutchfield, J. M.	143
Creus River	146
Crow, Benjamin	160
Crittenden, Conway Duel	176
Crease, John H.	193, 236
Crease, Mary A	194, 233
Cross, Edwards	201, 287
Criswell, Cyrus J	294
Criswells	293
Curran James	13, 288
Curran Thomas	70, 115, 341
Curran Lemuel R.	76
Curran, May F.	205
Current River	104
Cumberland Presbyterian Church	49
Cunningham, Matthew	5, 7, 167
Cummins-Notrebe Wedding	69
Cummins, William	69
Cummins, Mrs. Williams	69
Currenton	111
Cuffmans	304
Cuffman, Thomas	304
Cuffman, Pavatt	304
Cuffman, Josephus	306
Cuffman, Dr. John H.	307
Cuffman, James M.	307
Cummins and Garland	313
Cummins, Ebenezer	313
Cypress Bayou	43
Davidsonville	16, 19, 104, 105, 110, 113, 146, 148
D'Armond, Francis	25
Dardanelle	36, 134, 149, 222
Dardenne, John B.	43, 75
Davis, James	44
Daniel, Wright	49, 77, 87, 260, 288
Davidson, John	54
Davidson, Ephraim C.	75, 97
Dardanelle Rock	76
Daniel, Miss	77
Dardenne, Joseph	98
Davis, Zechariah	101
Dardanelle Settlement	142
Davidson, Robert	143
Davis, Samuel	160
Daugherty, Maria	166
Davis, Clara	263
Davis, Benjamin	280
Davis, Elizabeth	280
Davis Samuel	280
Davis, W. S.	324
Davis, L. W.	367
Davis, James	114
Daniels, J. L.	341
Davis, Aquilla	342
DePlaice, John B.	44
Dernisse, Jean B.	44, 286
DePlasse, Joseph	26
Dernisseau, Mary	44, 286
Dervsier, Peter	45
Delegate to Congress	54
DeChassin, Joseph	74
DeMun, Lewis	112, 279
DePew	108
Delaware Village	148
Descendants, Thomas Fletcher	247
Descendants, Caleb Lindsey	246
Descendants, Frederick Rector	379
Deruseaux, Mary	286

Index

Desha, Joseph	333
Desha, Captain	333
Desha, Robert	333
Desha, Franklin	334
Desha, Margaret	334
Deshas	331 to 338
Desha, Ben	333
Deruseaux, John B.	286
Dean, Sidney	166
Deerman, John	160
Deshler, David	147
Denton, W. F.	335
Desha County	119
Deans	101
Denton, F. D.	335
Denton, James	341
Deaths in 1820	347
Dill, John	43
Diana, John	43
Dinsmoore, Samuel	36
Dinsmoor and Spaulding	84
Dickinson, Townsend	115, 161, 341
Dickson, Mary	160
Dickinson, Thomas	168
Dickinson, Martha A.	300
Dominiques, John	42
Dodge, Mrs. James	71, 115
Dooley, Col. Thomas	72
Dorris, Mr.	93
Dodge, John	99, 165
Dodson, William	129
Dover	143
Dodge, Gen'l Henry	165
Dodge, Dr. R. L.	227
Dodd, C. W.	227
Dodge, Geo. F.	227
Dodd, Mrs.	227
Douglas, John	260, 339
Douglas, Ezekiel	260, 264
Douglas, G	264
Dodd, Thomas	288
Dollarhide, Mrs. John	160
Dodge, Ann	165
Dortolan, John	347
Dotterer, Henry	372
Drope, William	13, 68
Drury, Silas	128
DuVal, George	44
Duel First in Arkansas	65
Dueling Law	65
Duel—Barton and Rector	399
Duel—Scott and Selden	199
Duval, Francois	76
DuVal, Mieranda J.	141
DuVal, Edward	131, 140, 222
DuVals	331
DuVal Catherine	395
DuVal, William	395
Dudley, Catherine	76
Dukes, Sarah	76
Dunn, J. Clark	76
Dunn, Ichabod	76
Dunn, Margaret	76
Duncan, William	160
Dwight's Mission	223
Dye, Mary	408
Dye, Thomas	408
Early Land Grants	40
Early County Administrations	100
Ecore Fabre	151
Edwards, Mary	42, 150
Educational Opportunities	207
Edwards, Gov. William	382
Egner, Joseph	334, 346
Egner, Elvira	334
Egner, Henry	334
Egner, Virginia	334

Egner, Cornelius	334
Elk Lake	42
Eleven Points	113, 147
Eel River	42, 120, 146
Elliott, Mary W.	85, 185
Ellis, Radford	121, 132
Elkins, John	160
Election Practises	167, 168, 169, 170
Ellis, William	221
Ellis, Charles	410
Ellis, James	336
Elliott, Ann Eliza	286
Elliott, Ben	286, 287
Elliott, Laura F	287
Embree, Madame	73, 86
Embrees of Arkansas County	86, 278
Embry, Col. of Atkins	86
Embree, Maria	86
Embree, Jordan	93
Emmert, George	336
Emancipation of Slaves	342, 343
Eno, Miss Clara B	276
English, John	19, 121
Erroneous Notions	254
Erwin, Annanias	114
Escrivieve, John A.	42
Esperanza Camp	41, 118
Eskridge, Judge S. P.	80, 180, 201, 286
Ewel, Charles	165
Farrelly, Terrence	13, 35, 66, 67, 73, 79, 115
Farrelly and Curran	13, 14
Fayac, John	43
Fallen, Archibald	43
Fagot, Anthony	44
Fagot, Andre	97
Fayetteville	152
Fareen, Mrs. David	160
Fareen, David	160
Faulkner County	218
Faulkner, Col. Sanford	221, 226
Far West Academy	224
Family Likenesses	241
Faulkner, Samuel	289
Fagan, Gen'l	324
Fads	331
Farrow, James	354
Featherstonaugh	22, 109, 234
Ferguson, Napoleon B.	76, 113, 156
Ferguson, W. D.	94
Ferguson, James	113, 279
Ferebe, Geo. W.	128, 268, 334, 337
Fentors	101
Fermchea, Caddo	148
Fenton, Betsy	166
Fenner, Dr. R. H.	289
Ferebe, Ann F.	334
First Families	23, 24, 25
First Families of Virginia	39
First Circuit Court	55, 56
First Territorial Legislature	61, 99
First Steamboat	65
First Little Rock Merchants	68
First Town Lot Sale	111
First Judicial Hanging	168
First West Point Cadets	194
First Superior Court	197
First Baptist Church	231
First Baptist Association	231
First Academy at Batesville	346
Field Marshal	14
Fish, Thomas	76, 121
Fish Family	101
Fish, Thomas	101
Finley's Map	149
Fisher, James	160
Finney, Alfred	224
Fishback, John	372, 374

Index

Fishback, Harmon ... 372
Fishback, Gov. Wm M ... 372
Fishback, Catherine ... 374
Field, William ... 404
Field, Jane Elizabeth ... 404
Field, Abner ... 404
Flaery, Isaac ... 114
Flanakin, Patrick ... 161
Flannigan, Gov. Harris ... 403
Fletcher, John Gould ... 114, 242
Fletcher, Acting-Gov. Thomas ... 403
Fletcher Family Slaves ... 238
Fletcher Family ... 240 to 250
Fletcher, Thomas of Little Rock, 241
  245, 247, 248, 272.
Fletcher, Thomas of Pine Bluff ... 241
Fletcher, Henry Lewis, 243, 244, 245
  246.
Fletcher, Richard ... 243
Fletcher, John G ... 245, 249
Fletcher, Jeff ... 245
Fletcher, Thomas M ... 245
Fletcher, Eli ... 245
Fletcher, Capt. Fred ... 246
Fletcher, Martin ... 246
Fletcher, W. L ... 247
Fletcher, Olivia ... 246
Fletcher, John ... 247
Fletcher, T M ... 248
Fletcher, J. R ... 248
Fletcher Lillie Dea ... 248
Fletcher, Ann E ... 248
Fletcher, Mary P ... 249
Fletcher, Maston ... 297
Fooy, Benjamin, 41, 43, 117, 123, 287
Fooy, Isaac ... 118
Fooy's Point ... 117
Fooy, John Henry ... 43
Fooy, Samuel ... 118
Fooy, Charlotte ... 287
Foy, Fannie ... 263
Fort on White River ... 43
Founder of Texas ... 55
Fort Gibson ... 58, 102
Fourche a duMas ... 148
Fommier Creek ... 148
Fourche a Thomas ... 149, 150
Fourche de Mun ... 156
Fourth of July at Batesville ... 161
Folsom, Mary ... 165
Fontaine, Matthew ... 283
Folsom, Isaac ... 346
Fones, John ... 352
Fowler, Absalom ... 336
Foreman, Roswell W ... 409
Foreman, Helen ... 409
French Population ... 13, 23, 24
Francure, Francis ... 43
Frohlick, Jacob ... 91, 92
French Maps ... 149
Free Soil ... 213
Frazier, William ... 220
Franklin ... 254
Francis, Major Henry ... 277
Franklin, William ... 165, 338
Free Negroes in Slave Times ... 343
Friesenhaugen, Anna ... 374
Friesenhaugen, Jacob ... 374
Fry, William ... 406
Friend, Augustas J ... 43
Fry, Capt. C. B ... 406
Ft. Smith ... 105, 148
Furnish, Charles ... 43
Fulton ... 111
Fulton, Robert ... 111
Fugett, Wm ... 113
Fulton, Gov. William S, 215, 216, 217

Gasette, Arkansas, 11, 13, 14, 15, 16, 17
  18, 21, 22, 38, 51, 56, 96, 97, 108, 166
  259, 260.
Gallowhorn, Caty ... 42
Gazzia, Joseph ... 43
Garrett, Jacob ... 113
Galaxy of Grand Old Men ... 113
Galley ... 142, 222, 134
Garrett, W ... 142
Garden, Thomas ... 143
Galbreath, Mrs. Joseph ... 160
Garland, Gov. A. H ... 307 to 331
Garland, Elizabeth J ... 308
Garland, R. K ... 308
Garland, R. K. Sr ... 307
Garland's Letter ... 319
Garland, Sanders ... 330
Garland, R. C ... 330
Garland, Daisy ... 330
Garland, W. A ... 330
Garrett, Wm ... 345
Gerstaecker, Frederick, 22, 155, 156, 347
German Maps ... 149
Germana ... 371
Germantown ... 372
Gerrard, Rose ... 193
Gillet, Aaron ... 162
Gingnolet, Joseph ... 44
Gimblet, Francis ... 44
Gibson, Dr. John ... 80
Gilmore, Daniel ... 143
Girty, Simon ... 228
Givens, Edward ... 335
Gibson, James ... 287
Gladden, Dr. R. B ... 366
Glass, Wm. H ... 43, 277
Glass, Hiram ... 278
Glass, James ... 352
Glover, Amelia W ... 407
Glass, Archibald ... 352
Gonsales, Augustine ... 42
Gossiat, Louis ... 43
Goris, Jacob ... 45
Gossieu, Catherine ... 76
Godin, Adele ... 77
Godin, Achille ... 165
Goceaux, Mary ... 279
Gower, Hebe ... 406
Greely, Horace ... 29
Grace, William ... 41
Grace, John ... 42, 118
Graham, Moses ... 100, 288
Grays ... 49
Gray, Jack ... 49, 78
Gray, Shared ... 49, 78
Gray, Joseph ... 49
Gray, Sampson ... 50, 160, 240
Gray, Harriet ... 77, 197
Gray, Isaac ... 278
Gray, Major ... 367
Graves, Tom ... 266
Gregory, William ... 42, 120
Greenwood, Joseph ... 44
Greenbrier ... 49
Greenoch ... 151
Gregory Township ... 221
Greenwalt, Mary ... 287
Greenwalt, Ann ... 288
Green, Hiram ... 288
Griffith, Mrs ... 288
Griffin Township ... 221
Groson, Francis ... 42
Grues River ... 44

Hardin, Joab ... 121, 217
Hagerstown ... 26
Harrington, John ... 35, 73
Hadsell, John ... 44

Index

Hardin, Joseph, 54, 72, 102, 113, 115, 121
180.
Hamilton, James............69, 194
Harrington, Bartley.......73, 110, 121
Harringtons..............74, 148
Harrington, Alfred.........74, 97
Harrington, Mary............. 75
Harrington Eliza............. 75
Harrington, Allen............ 75
Hardin, Benjamin.........78, 279
Hardin, Jacob............... 113
Hadlock.................... 113
Hanks, Fleetwood............ 130
Haynes, Major.............. 150
Hargrove, John............. 160
Harris, Margry.............. 161
Hayden, Webb E............. 160
Harold, Betsy.............. 165
Harold, Abner..........165, 217
Hardin, G. W............... 194
Harris, Timothy............. 220
Hamlet, Sam R.............. 263
Harris, John............... 284
Harris, Sarah.............. 287
Harrell, John.............. 296
Hairston, Nancy M.......... 296
Hairston, James............ 296
Handy, Thomas B............ 128
Hall, Samuel S............. 115
Hall Family............299, 300
Hall, Wm S................ 299
Hall, David C.............. 300
Hacker, Christain.......... 338
Hardaway, Adalissa C....... 368
Handback.................. 372
Hager, Henry............... 374
Hay, John................. 374
Helena, 43, 108, 118, 125, 129, 148, 265
268.
Hewett, Solomon.......112, 279
Hempstead's History........54, 56
Hempstead County, 56, 101, 104, 116, 147
Hemphill, Emily............. 76
Hemphill, Andrew........... 165
Hempstead Co. Rev. Soldiers... 78
Heredity................80, 82
Henry's Chapel.........112, 284
Hepburn, Col. W. P......... 138
Heads Growing Larger....... 264
Helena Democrat............ 268
Henderson, Mary W.......... 276
Henry, Mr................. 284
Henderson, Joseph.......... 268
Henry, James M............ 324
Hening, Annie N............ 330
Hempstead Court House...... 19
Hix, William Sr........113, 153
Hickland, Abraham........... 43
Hignite, Abner............. 101
Hix, William........112, 153, 279
Hix's Ferry............111, 153
Hibbin, John............... 219
Hibbin, Thomas............. 220
Higgin Township............ 221
Hitchcock, Jacob........t.. 224
Hitchcock, Asa............. 224
Hindman, Gen'l T. C........ 269
Hindman, Blanche..t........ 269
Hindman, T. C. Jr.......... 269
Hindman, Biscoe............ 269
Hill, Barbara.............. 307
Hill, William.............. 338
Hill, Peter................ 372
Hornor, J. J............... 130
Hornor, F. S............... 130
Hornor, J. S............... 130
Hornor, W. B. R, 38, 83, 108, 110, 114
120, 121, 122, 123, 124, 125, 126, 127
128.

Hopefield..............41, 42, 118
Hogan, John................ 42
Hogan, Gen'l, 47, 56, 57, 71, 74, 168, 232
250 to 255.
Hogan, Edward.............. 54
Home of the Brontes........ 58
Holman, John...........78, 160
Hodge, Archibald........... 113
Hogan, W. Russell.......... 87
Honey, Richard W........... 97
Hot Springs........112, 148, 232
Hodges, Willis............. 144
Holaby, Richard............ 161
Homestead Law.........213, 214
Houston, John.............. 221
Hogan, William............. 254
Holt, Sally................ 306
Hominy Hill................ 323
Howard, Col. Bob........... 324
Hobson, Miss............... 330
Howell, Philo.............. 338
Howell, Ann M.............. 368
Howell, Jesse E............ 368
Howell, Adalissa........... 368
Holtzclaw, Jacob........... 372
Huffman, John.............. 372
Hubbard, Judge Thomas...310, 402
Hunt Bayou................. 44
Hunt, Andrew J.........108, 125
Hughes, Isaac.............. 142
Hudgins................... 151
Hubbard...............t... 152
Hubbard, George............ 159
Hunt, John W............... 160
Hudgins, Ambrose........... 160
Hubbard, Archibald......... 287
Hutcheson, Joseph.......... 295
Hughes, Gov. Simon P....... 295
Hunnicutt, Baily........... 306
Huguenots................. 331
Hughes, Louisa S........... 338
Hughes, Green B............ 338
Humphries, John............ 347

Illinois Settlement........ 382
Illinois Bayou............. 142
Imbeau, Francois........... 25
Imbeau, Baptiste........... 25
Imbeau, Judic.............. 165
Imbeau, John B............. 45
Imbeau, Madame............. 288
Imbeau, Monsieur........... 288
Imbeau, Joseph............. 165
Indian Names............... 20
Indian Agents.............. 131
Indian Life............... 339
Intelligencer, Washington.. 22
Independence Co. Heroes.... 78
Independence Co, 105, 114, 115, 147, 180
Infares and Weddings....... 165
Intrigue of 1823.......180, 181
Indictment of Oden......... 196
Indictment of Jouett....... 196
Immigration........104, 106, 107
Izard, Gov., 111, 172 to 178, 182, 222
231.
Izard County............... 147
Izard..................... 152
Irons, Mrs. Jonathan....... 160
Izard, Miss................ 194
Irish Pedigrees............ 290

Jackson, Andrew.......39, 58, 102
Janis, Anthony............. 44
Janis, Nicholas............ 44
Janis, John B.............. 44
Jardelles, Alexis.......44, 97
Jardelles, Jean.........44, 97
Jackson County Heroes...... 78

Index

Jardelow, Peter	101
Jacob's Staff	151
Jackson County Pioneers	276
Jefferson County	79
Jones, Elizabeth	42
Jouett, Charles' 32, 100, 180, 195,	196
Jordales, Peter	44
Johnson, Thomas W.	68, 174
Jones, Mary	73
Jones, William	113
Jones, James K. Jr.	330
Jones, Massack H.	113
Jones, Stephen	114
Johnson, Robert	83, 124
Johnson, Benjamin, 88, 89, 90, 100, 201 to 206.	142
Johnson	152
Johnson, Col. Wm.	161
Johnson Family	202 to 206
Johnson County	200
Johnson, Robert W.	202
Johnson, Juliette E.	204, 211
Johnson, George J.	205
Johnson, Benjamin S.	205
Johnson, Richard H.	205, 401
Johnson, James B.	205
Johnson, Charles E.	205
Johnson, Irene M.	205
Johnson, James V.	205
Johnson, Francis	205
Johnson, Matilda	205
Johnson, Sevier	205
Johnson, Allen N.	205, 248
Johnson, Mary	205
Johnson, James J.	205
Johnson, Sidney	205
Johnson, John A.	205
Johnson, Anna	205
Johnson, Benjamin, Slaves	238
Johnson, Nancy W.	357
Johnson, Peter R.	357
Jordans	331
Jordan, Dr. John A.	205
Jolly	222
Jones, Jacob	288
Judd, Solomon B.	287
Justices Pulaski County	250
Kaufman's Bayou	44, 45, 303
Kaufman, Christopher	44, 303
Kaufmans	300
Kaufman Michael	300
Keplar, George	44
Kepler, C	45
Kepler, Elizabeth	76
Kepler, William	165
Kelley, William	101
Kelly, Isaac	112, 279
Kelly, Charles	98, 114, 162
Kelly and Maddox	189
Kelley, Elizabeth	293
Kellett, Joseph	114
Kellum, Smith	166
Kellum, James	221
Kemble, Asa H.	287
Kemper, John	372
King, Mary	66
King, Wigton	66, 75, 289
King, Sanford	174
King's Mountain Hero	277
King, Elizabeth	289
Kinsall, Jane	305
Kinsall, Moses	305
Kettrell, Lucy H.	300
Killing of Gen'l Hogan	253
Kirkland, Joseph	75
Knuckles, Wm.	362
Kuykendall	38
Kuykendall, Benjamin	75
Kuykendall, Dempsey	75
Kuykendall, James M.	112, 114
Kuykendall, Margaret	160
Lawrence County, 16, 54, 115, 147, 56, 102, 104, 112, 113.	243
Lawrence County Heroes	78
Lawrenceville	125
Lawrence County Barbecue	342
La Louisiane	25
La Farve, Pierre	26
Larquer, John	26
Lacy, Thomas J.	128
Lavergne, John	44
Lavale, Jean	44, 97
Languis, John	44
La Course, Michail	45
La Fargue, Francois	76
Latimer, William	128
Latimer, Gabriel	76, 77
Latimer, Greenwood	127
Latimer, Barradel	77, 167
Langford, Eli	86
Land Fraud Cases	87, 88
Lafferty, Binks	115, 294, 298
Lafferty, Henderson	115, 294, 298
Lafferty, John L.	218, 293, 294
Lafferty, John	279, 290, 291
Lafferty Family	290 to 299
Lafferty, Margaret	293
Lafferty, Sarah	293
Lafferty, Austin	294, 298
Lafferty, Lorenzo B.	294, 298
Lafferty, Widow	294
Lafferty, Vaughn B.	295
Lafferty, Wesley R.	263
Lafferty, George L.	295
Lafferty, John R.	295
Lafferty, Henderson G.	952
Lafferty, Austin D.	295
Lafferty, Alfred W.	295
Lafferty, L. S. H.	296
Lafferty, Dr. J. M.	296
Lafferty, Druzella	296
Lafferty, E. E.	297
Lafferty, Sarah E.	297
Lafferty V. D.	297
Lafferty, M. M.	297
Lafferty, A. B.	297
Land, Walter	404
Langford, Ben	143
Lafayette Court House	151
L'Anguille	151
Lakeport	151
Larrimore, Rev. James	156
Lackey, William	220, 287
Latta, John	342
Lewis, Elijah	13, 19, 65, 67, 76, 77, 100
Lewis, Thomas	114
Lewis and Thomas	13, 14, 18
Lewis, Polly	77
Lewis Family	249
Lewis and Clarke's Expedition	95
Lewis, John Sr., and Jr.	113
Lewis, Rueben	113
Lewis, Gen'l Wm L.	131, 220, 288
Lewis Map	145
Lewis, William Jr.	288
Lewisburg	150, 151
Letcher, Robert P.	31, 100, 180
LeGrande Augustine	41
LeFever, John	43
LeFever, John	43, 120
Leard, George	44
Levy, Louis P.	45
Legislatures Territorial	61
Lemmons, Col. James	72, 239
Leiper, James	78
Lee's Creek	152

Index

Lester, Major Noah............ 288
Little Rock, 12, 37, 38, 87, 108, 112, 148
  150, 188, 189.
Little Rock Times........... 125, 108
Little Rock Settlers............. 45
Little Rock Merchants............ 68
Little Rock Advocate 108
Little Rock & Ft. Smith Ry....... 143
Little Rock & Washington....... 158
Little Rock Speculators.......... 188
Little Rock Tavern............. 230
Little Rock Baptists............ 231
Little Deep River.............. 146
Litchfield 151
Little John................... 160
List of Original Pilgrims....... 186
Lindsey Family Slaves........... 239
Lindsey, Caleb, 245, 246, 269 to 276
Lindsey, Eli........245, 273, 284, 294
Lindseys of Virginia......269, 270, 271
Lindseys Cave School........... 271
Lindsey, John Y............... 272
Lindsey, Col.................. 274
Lindsey, James................ 273
Lindsey, Isaac............275, 338
Lindsey, Peter............275, 338
Lindsey, William H............. 276
Lindsey, Caleb Jr.............. 281
Lindsey, Harrison B............. 282
Lindsey, Rezin W.............. 284
Lindsey, Allen H............... 282
Lindsey, E. W................. 282
Lindsey, Joseph H.............. 338
Lindsey, Sarah A............... 338
Lindsey, Allen Q............... 352
Littlejohn, Mary E.............. 307
Littlejohn, Alex W.............. 307
Linde, Flora.................. 404
Linde, Albert................. 404
Lemoneaux, Francis............ 287
Looney, William............... 113
Lock Creek................... 43
Louisiana Settlers.............. 45
Lockwood, William............. 48
Lovely, John P................. 75
Locke, William B............... 83
Lost Prairie................... 152
Longevity 151, 158, 159
Lorance, Zechariah..........160, 220
Lorance, Betsy................ 220
Lockhart, Elinor............239, 338
Long Prairie.................. 286
Long, Martha D............... 288
Long, Zachariah............... 288
Lockhart, W. S................ 338
Logan, the Mingo.............. 340
Luckie, William................ 112
Luttrell, Nathan............... 114
Lyon, Matthew............131, 122
Lyon, Aaron W........224, 225, 346

Mack, Sarah J.................. 333
Magness, Major David........163, 273
Martin, Allen, 102, 239, 259, 260, 261
Mails Early 16
Magness, Robert 273, 346
Maxwell, John P............... 113
Martin, Joseph................ 114
Martin, Jasto.................. 42
Maloney, Robert............... 128
Magness, Perry G......54, 114, 347
Maxwell 69
Mason, Mr.................... 73
Mason, Polly...............75, 97
Marriages in 1819 76
Martin, Mr.................... 76
Many, Capt. James B........... 97
Mason, Joseph................ 97
Macbeth, John 142

Mason, James W............... 97
Magness, Morgan........98, 160, 347
Martin, B. H.................. 142
Maddox's Bay................. 125
Maps of Territory 144, et seq.
Magnet Cove.................. 151
Marion 151
Marriage Customs, 162, 163, 164, 284, 285
Martin, Joshua................ 160
Mars, Alan & Co............... 167
Mail Routes................... 219
Mathers, Col. Thomas.......217, 219
Martin Family 260, 261, 262
Martin, John Jr............... 262
Martin, Jared C............... 260
Martin, James................ 260
Martin, Matilda............... 260
Martin, Andrew................ 261
Martin, Mahala................ 261
Martin, James A............... 263
Martin, William A.............. 263
Martin, J. C. Jr............... 263
Martin, Mollie D............... 263
Martin, Henry G............... 263
Martin, J. J.................. 263
Martin, Elizabeth.............. 338
Marriages and Deaths........284, 285
  286, 287.
Marriage Posies...........285, 286
Martin, John Joseph........... 372
Martin, John 261
Maidstone.................... 376
Matheny, William M............ 404
Matheny, Mary C.............. 404
Matheny, William I............ 404
Matheny, Julia F. M............ 404
Menifee, Dr. James N, 38, 111, 131, 191
Meredith, Wm................ 113
Methodist Preachers......... 48, 285
Menifee...................... 111
Memphis..................... 111
Methodist Episcopal Church.... 112
Mellick Map.................. 145
Messengill, Thomas............ 161
Medlock, Elizabeth............ 248
Merrick, Col. T. D............. 295
Miller County...........105, 116, 147
Miller, Gov. James, 16, 30, 31, 32, 33, 34
  35, 36, 37, 38, 39, 55, 57, 61, 87, 172, 182
  250.
Migration.................16, 17
Missouri Territory............. 20
Miller, John 113
Michel, Pierre................. 26
Mississippi River Settlements..... 42
Michel, Joseph................ 43
Michel, Francis............43, 286
Michel, Desire................ 286
Michel, Millet................. 76
Minard, John B............... 44
Miller, James of Poke Bayou, 48, 114, 115
  341.
Miller, Mary.................. 48
Militia....................57, 251
Mitchell, W.................. 142
Minyard, John................ 161
Miller, Valentine.............. 161
Mills, Miss................... 233
Milner, John.................. 248
Miles, J. B................... 248
Miller, William................ 258
Millers Creek................. 273
Mitchell, Col. Chas. S.......... 409
Mosely, Samuel..........13, 66, 73
Mount Prairie, 104, 105, 109, 112, 149
  284, 77.
Montgomery Landing.......16, 35
Montgomery, William......25, 35, 64
Monte Carlo.................. 25

Index 419

Moss, James	110
Morse, Pres. James 39,	193
Mooney, Daniel, 43, 48, 50, 65, 67, 76, 123, 124.	72
Morton, Elijah 59, 63, 64, 83, 85,	182
Mosely, Mary	71
Morrison, William 73,	75
Mobley, Isaiah 78,	279
Mobley, Clement 78,	239
Moore, Mores 279,	112
Morris, Ann 85,	184
Moore, William 341,	346
Mount Maria	112
Moore, Col. Ben 115, 161,	286
Monroe County 119,	125
Morrison's Bluff	151
Monroe	151
Montgomery, Margaret	165
Morrison, Joshua	116
Money in Little Rock	176
Monroe, Margaret	193
Mount Holly 227,	229
Mosby, John D	239
Moose, Mary E	248
Moose, John	248
Moore, Rev. J. W	259
Morrison, Wm. P	383
Moses	383
Morrison, William	406
Mooney, J. B	26
Munn, John	110
Murrey, Henry	113
Murphy, Arthur 113,	78
Murch, Clarissa	76
Murry, Thomas	143
McLane, Congressman	9
McLane, Neill 87,	347
McLanes' Store	232
McLain and Badgett	253
McLean, John 42,	120
McLain, John	288
McLain, John	347
McLachlen, Allen	356
McKinney, William	43
McFarlane, B. H 43,	98
McKinney, Elijah	43
McKinzie, James 128,	130
McPherson, Charles	147
McKinney	191
McLaren Township	221
McCaleb, Eritha	295
McCaleb, John	295
McArthur, Charles	346
McCray, Col. Wm	56
McRay, Dr. Robert 69, 110,	121
McKenzie, Clarissa	75
McHenry, Archibald 87,	239
McGregor, Flowers	93
McKinney, David E	100
McIlmurry, John 38, 111,	122
McAdoe, William	113
McCarroll, Mrs Nathaniel	114
McKnight, Wm	114
McDonald, Edward	122
McCarley, John	144
McDowell, Mrs. Benjamin	160
McCall, Samuel	220
McDonald, Wm	288
McDaniel, Eli	308
McPherson, Cora	330
McReynolds, C. Lee	376
National Road	104
Napoleon 108,	146
Nash, Mary W	233
Nash, Dr. John V	233
Nailor, A. T	297
Newton, Thomas W. Sr., 57, 73, 85, 190 to 196, 205.	185
Newton Family 193,	194
Newton, Other	194
Newton, R. C	193
Newton, T. W. Jr	193
Newton, Fenwick	194
Newton, Jane P 194,	233
Newton, John	194
Newton, Basil	194
Newton, Larkin	194
Newton, Jesse	195
Newton, James	195
Newton, Annie	205
Neely, Judge Buford F	336
Neeley, Mary E	336
Neeley, E. E	336
Neely, M. T	336
Neil, Gordon	74
Newman, J. H	142
New Gascony	151
Nichols Township	221
Nicks, Col. John	254
Nine Rector Boys 379,	381
Notrebe, Francis 13, 14, 47, 57, 66, 79.	68
North Carolina	19
Norville, Joshua 81, 82	83
Norville, Maria	84
Non Residents	100
Norristown 134, 142,	223
Norris, Samuel 142,	143
North Carolinians	210
Nuttal, 22, 24, 25, 37, 47, 48, 66, 73, 97, 111, 118, 222, 264.	86
Ouachita	16
Oden, Robert C., 35, 54, 63, 64, 73, 102, 170, 176, 177, 188, 196.	85
Odle, Benjamin F	129
Oden-Conway Race	170
O'Hara, William 111,	287
Oil Trough Bottom	155
Oliver, L. H	93
Old County Officers	100
Old Dwight Mission 142,	223
Oldtown	152
Old men of Lafayette, Izard, Phillips, Hempstead, Conway, Hot Spring, Sevier, Pope, Washington, Clark, Jefferson, Miller, Independence, and Pulaski 159,	160
Old River	168
Old Cherokee Village	254
Old Time Mother Wit	258
Old Time Acumen	259
Old Marriage Poetry 259,	260
Old Pulaski Pioneers	260
Oldest Church Edifices	284
Origin of the Provincial	283
O'Neals	274
Orr, Dr. William	289
Overban, Mrs. George	160
Orr, Mr	224
Owen, E. W	221
Overton, Judge	118
Osborne, Robert W	98
Osage	152
Ookuquahtub	224
Parker, Samuel	101
Palmer, W. M	128
Pattersons	26
Patterson, William 43,	48
Patterson, James	43
Pace, Twitty	142
Paraclifta	151
Paulette, Odelle	286
Palmon, Elisabeth W	286
Paxton, Joseph	289
Pace, Joseph	352

Parrish, Elizabeth	360
Parrish, Anderson	360
Peeler, Richmond...17, 110, 121,	166
Perryman, Montford...41,	118
Pena, Antoine	42
Peel, Col. Richard	161
Peters, Digest	22
Peel, Sam W	161
Perry, Moses...42,	120
Petersel, Michael	44
Pertuis, Michael	44
Pertuis, Peter...44, 45,	95
Perte, Pierre...44,	95
Pertuis, Elizabeth	45
Perry, Leon	45
Pentecost, Darby	128
Peels and Millers	47
Pennington, Col. Jack	72
Peel, Richard	341
Pertuis, Chevalier	97
Pertuis, Nina	97
Pecannerie...105,	220
Pecan Point...112,	149
Petit, Jean...132,	151
Pelham, Charles H...162, 341,	346
Peay, Nick...167, 230,	239
Persecution	331
Pelham, William	397
Pelham, Thomas	397
Phillips, Sylvanus, 26, 30, 43, 48, 77, 289.	120
Phillips County, 26, 105, 115, 123,	147
Pharr, Jonathan	48
Philpot, Warren	78
Pharr, Thomas	250
Phillips, James...277,	289
Phillips, Landing	277
Pike, Albert...108,	126
Piat, J	48
Piat, John	287
Pine Bayou	151
Pierce, John	114
Pinneaux, Agnes	76
Pioneer Coats of Arms	95
Pioneer Habits...95,	96
Pioneer Officers	97
Pine Bluff	112
Pioneers of Lawrence	113
Piats Town	149
Pilgrims	186
Pitman, Nancy	287
Pitman, Samuel	287
Pitman, Dr. P. R.	345
Placide, Baptiste	44
Plum Bayou	97
Pleasant Island	151
Ploth, Daniel	345
Post Offices, Earliest	19
Poetry on Arkansas	23
Porter, William	43
Poke Bayou, 43, 47, 98, 104, 112,	146
Porter, Benjamin A	113
Point Chicot...56, 79,	119
Pope, Gov. John, 57, 69, 90, 205, 239,	268
Point Remu...75, 107,	132
Population...104, 115,	116
Political Intelligencer	125
Politics in Olden Days	134
Pope County...142, 200,	223
Potts, Kirkbride	143
Polet, Clemence	165
Pono, Pierre	287
Pope, Judge...168,	225
Poetry of Senator Spooner	186
Pollard, Sarah	194
Pope, Nathaniel	382
Porterfield, Lavinia	287
Pool, Benjamin	347
Pope, Senator John	382
Polk, Bishop	409
Pocahontas	151
Pryor & Richards...14, 84,	100
Pryor, Capt. Nathaniel	95
Preston, Colonel	24
Presbyterians	49
Proctor, Edward...42,	120
Price, Archibald	101
Pringle, Christian...44, 73,	74
Pringle, John	73
Preston, Isaac	90
Price, J. S.	144
Pre-emption...206,	207
Pre-emption Speeches...211,	215
Pre-emption Laws	213
Prairie Township	225
Pritchard, Captain Rees	320
Pulaski County, 37, 38, 49, 50, 102, 116, 117.	105
Pulaski County Heroes	78
Pulaski Court House	87
Pulaski Commissioners	87
Puritans	185
Pulaski County Slaves	238
Pyeatt, Major John...45, 47, 48,	49
Pyeatt, Jacob...45, 48, 102, 166.	160
Pyeatt, Betsy	47
Pyeatt, Henry P.	49
Pyeatt, Peter...47,	48
Pyeatt, James	49
Pyeatt, Jane	166
Pyeatt, Margaret	48
Quapaw Indians...23, 27,	73
Quapaw Treaty	73
Quarles, William	189
Quisenbery, William...226,	402
Ragan, J. B. O.	16
Ramer, Abraham	43
Racine, Althenas...43,	44
Ramsay, William	162
Rankin, Mary	254
Race Course	254
Randolph County	344
Rankin, Elbert H.	369
Rankin, Robert W.	369
Reed, James...108,	125
Read, John	114
Refeld, Charles...43,	44
Revolutionary Heroes, 49, 50, 77, 78,	113
Rector, Wharton, 57, 133, 141, 147, 394	239
Rector Family, 106, 133, 370 to	410
Rector, Elias	147
Rector, Stephen...147, 383,	390
Rector, Gen'l Wm, 94, 106, 107, 149, 279, 372, 379, 380, 381, 382, 383 to 389	217
Rector, Thomas	94
Rector, Survey...106, 107,	392
Rechter, John Jacob...372,	373
Rector, John...374,	375
Rector, Governor Henry M., 372, 401	409
Rechta,r Jacob	373
Rechtor, John Jacob	373
Rector, E. W. of Hot Springs, 372, 407, 408, 409, 410.	406
Rector, Harmon	374
Rectortown	376
Rector, John's Will	376
Rector Descendants	376
Rector, Frederick...378, 379,	380
Rectors of Illinois	379
Rector Family Names	378
Rector Elias of St. Louis, 379, 380, 382, 383, 384, to 399.	381
Rector, Nelson...383, 384, 388,	390
Rector Influence	393

Index 421

Rector, Elias of Ft. Smith........ 395
Rector, Ann...................... 396
Rector, Thomas C................. 399
Rector, Frank Wilson............. 404
Rector, Ann Baylor............... 404
Rector, W Field.................. 405
Rector, John Sevier.............. 405
Rector, Henry Massey Jr.......... 405
Rector, Grace Greenwood.......... 406
Rector, Ernestine................ 406
Rector, Levison.................. 406
Rector, Alcorn................... 408
Rector, Amelia W................. 408
Rector, Henry F.................. 408
Rector, James A............408, 409
Rector, Jane Elizabeth........... 409
Rector, Sallie F................. 409
Rector, Fannie F................. 409
Rector, Ernestine F.............. 409
Reynolds, Professor.............. 57
Regimental, Colonels............. 72
Reece, William................... 76
Redfield......................... 79
Removal of Indians.........132, 133
Reed, Mrs. Wm.................... 160
Reinhardt, James O............... 297
Reconstruction 324, 325
Redman, J........................ 341
Read, John....................... 341
Riggs, Wm........................ 43
Richland 73, 79
Richie, L.................113, 156
Rightor, N...........124, 128, 147
Riley vs Bradford................ 87
Ridge, John...................... 114
Rival Townsiters................. 188
Ringgold, Lucretia............... 335
Ringgold, Judge.............335, 345
Richardson 362
Roads, Early..........16, 144 to 147
Roosevelt, President............. 20
Roane, Sam C, 26, 68, 73, 80 to 93,
  168, 180, 189, 265.   103
Rodrigues, John.................. 42
Rorer, David 57, 239, 260
Rollin, Mr..................134, 222
Rogers, John................134, 223
Robinson, William................ 112
Robinson, John................... 78
Roane Family..................... 80
Roane, John S................80, 93
Roane, Fannie.................... 93
Roane & Norvelle................. 83
Roane, Hennie.................... 93
Roane, Mary...................... 93
Roane, James..................... 93
Roane, Johanna................... 93
Roane, John Jordan............... 94
Roane, Ida....................... 93
Roane, Samuel C. Jr.............. 94
Roane, Juliet.................... 94
Rose Family...................... 80
Rome.........................83, 111
Roland George.................... 144
Rockfort......................... 151
Royall, John..................... 160
Royall, Mrs. John................ 160
Rogers, Adustin 220, 287
Rowland, Mahala............250, 262
Rowland, Thomas 259, 264
Rowland, Maria S................. 262
Robinson, John................... 278
Robinson, James.................. 278
Robinson, Michael D.............. 288
Rowland, R. N.................... 264
Robinson, William................ 279
Rose, U. M....................... 325
Ross, John....................... 352
Ross, James...................... 353

Ross, Daniel..................... 353
Ross, David...................... 353
Ross, Agnes...................... 354
Rosses......................355, 356
Ross Earls of.................... 355
Rose, George..................... 368
Rose, John....................... 368
Rowen, John...................... 347
Ruddell, George.................. 114
Ruddell, Abraham ......114, 338 to 342
Rutherford, Col. S. M., 57, 100, 265, 268
Russellville.................75, 201
Runkle, Thomas S................. 397
Runkle, Mary A................... 397

St. Louis 12
St. Louis Papers.............22, 104
St. Francis River...........26, 42
St. Francis...................... 125
St. Francis Settlements.......... 44
St. Francis Township............. 38
St. Francis...................... 42
St. Martin....................... 142
St. Helena....................... 146
St. Francisville................. 151
St. Genevieve Road............... 152
St. Francis County............... 254
St. John's College............... 367
St. Louis Republican............. 104
Sampson, George.................. 83
Saline Landing................... 148
Saline Creek..................... 148
Safriet 148
Sanford, Henry................... 165
Safford, Judge W. G.............. 220
Saylors, J. C.................... 278
Sanders, Simon T................. 312
Sanders, Sarah V................. 312
Scarborough 101
Scott, Judge Andrew, 31, 51, 63, 97, 100
  142, 289, 287, 196, 197, 198, 252
  253, 165, 180, 195 to 202.
Scott, John R. H. .., 51, 63, 143, 199, 201
Scott, Geo. W., 63, 64, 165, 231, 239
Scotia 143, 152, 200
Schoolcraft..................149, 155
Schoolcraft and Drummond 155
Scarborough, James 166
Scull, James 13, 194
Scott, Selden Dael............... 199
Scipes, Margaret................. 287
Scott, Joseph 354
Scull, Hewes, 28, 30, 50, 72, 98, 100
Septt, John 20, 51
Searcy, Richard, 19, 30, 88, 102, 112, 114
  189, 341, 345.
Searcy, James 114, 346
Sevier, Joseph...............42, 120
Serrano, Martin.................. 44
Seneca Indian Agent.............. 58
Selden, Joseph,....77, 110, 197, 288
Serville, De Monsieur Le Moir.... 78
Sevier, A. H., 88, 94, 183, 202, 204, 206
  to 215, 239.
Settlements in 1820.............. 109
Sebastian, Wm. R................. 128
Seviers 183
Sevier, Annie M.................. 204
Sevier, Mattie J................. 204
Sevier, Elizabeth................ 204
Sevier, A. H..................... 204
Sevier-Crittenden Race........... 209
Searcy, Elizabeth................ 335
Shirley 120
Shaver, John..................... 114
Shannon, John.................... 115
Shirt Sleeved Millionaires....... 93
Shiloh........................... 143
Shinn, Jacob.................144, 368

Index

Shinn, B. D. R. 144
Shaddy, Andrew 347
Shaler, Jacob 345
Sims, Absalom 144
Siscoe, Henry 160
Simmons, J 221
Sloane, Rev. Robt. 49
Slaughter, R. F 54, 55
Slinkard, Jacob 220
Slavery ...... 235 to 237, 342, 343
Slaveholders 239
Slaveholdings in Virginia 359
Slaveholding Social Currents . 360
Smith, Jefferson 126
Smith, Dr. Geo. W. 205
Smith, Sarah S. 205
Smith, Amelia 205
Smith, Bernard 230
Smith, John 232
Smith, Mary A. 306
Smith, Dr. 124
Smithee, J, N. 324
Socie, Baptiste 25
Spring River 146
Spencer, Capt. 35, 124
Spaulding, Rufus P. 36
Spring Hill 152
Spring River Circuit 112
Spadra Bluff 137, 222
Spanish Land Grants 197
Stephenson, W. 121
Stilwell, Joseph, 17, 27, 28, 42, 50, 69, 77
122.
Stilwell, Harold 27, 110, 121
Strawberry 76, 155, 104
Stephens, Jesse 42, 120
Stenson, Charles 42
Stroud, Adam 101
Stewart, Col. J. M. 101, 110, 195
Stanley, Benjamin 45
Stanley, John 45
Stanley, William 45
Stilwell, John 73
Stuart, Abraham 77, 109, 110
Stuart, Lunetta 110
Stuart, N. E. 110
Stuart, J. L. 110
Stuart, Elijah 110
Stuart, Col. Wm. 110, 288, 347
Stuart, Asenath 288
Stuart, Mrs. Abraham 160
Stewart, Nancy W. 85
Stewart, John W. 160
Stewart, Jane B. 193
Strong, William 94
Steele, John W. 125
Stinnett, H. 142
Strickland, William 168
Stetson, Ella 224
Stevenson, Rev. W. W. 233
Stevenson, Maria 233, 234
Stephenson, John 287
Stephenson, William 288
Stephenson, Mrs. 288
Starr, Moses 286
Strange, John A. 352
Stadt Bibliothek 372
Starcke, Eugene H. 404
Superior Court Salaries 86
Superior Court, 87, 88, 89, 90, 99, 100, 195
Sumpter, S. R. 128
Sulphur Rock 151
Superstitious 285
Surveyors, General 389
Sutherland, William W. 404

Tatum, W. M. 248
Taylor, Congressman 9
Taylor, Polly 113
Taylor, James 113
Taylor, Peter 114
Taylor, Mrs. Joseph 161
Taylor, John 42, 83, 120
Taylor, Archibald 75
Taylor, Creed 165
Taylor, John 165
Tessier, Antoine 26
Texas, Founder of 55
Terry, Edna V 404
Tecumseh 152, 339
Test Oath Cases, 314, 315, 316, 317, 318
Tennesse, Roanes 81
Tennant, Thomas H. 338
Thatch, Frank W. 367
Thruston Family 398, 399
Thruston, Fannie B. 397
Three Brother Theory 255
Thorn, Jacob 278
Thornhill, Joseph 230
Thurston, Paulina 333
Thornton 58
Thompson, Davies 128
Tindall, Thomas H. 19
Titsworth, James 220
Titsworth 237
Town Lot Sales 111, 112
Townships 115, 116
Towns 148, 150
Toncre, Marie 233
Toncray, Rev. Silas T., 231, 261, 263, 286
Toncray, Halda T. 263
Treat, Samuel 43, 44
Trimble, James, 115, 116, 341, 346
Trimble, John 341
Trudean, Joseph 45
Trammell, John 47
Trimble, William, 77, 83, 110, 121, 180
201
Trammel, Nicholas 98
Thomas, Oliver H. 100
Thomas Fort 147
Traveler, The Arkansas ... 221, 226
Trustees Far West Academy 224
Tripletts 274
Trigg, General 401
Turk's Prairie 43
Tucker, Peyton 114

Ultima, Thule 151
Union 152
U. S. Pension Rolls 78
Utica 118
Utterback, Harmon 372

Vaugine, Lewismore 24
Vaugine, Major Francis, 25, 30,45, 68, 73, 86, 97, 165, 286
Vaugines 24, 44
Vaugine, Susette 24
Vaugine Settlement 148
Vaugine, Etienne 26, 74
Vaugine, Walter 165
Vaugine, Francis Jr. 286
Vaugine, Paul 287
Vaugine Township 86
Valliere, Don Joseph 24
Valliere, Francis 25, 44
Valliere, Joseph 25
Valliere, Felicity 165
Varsier, Francis 25, 98
Vasseau, Etienne 44
Vasseau, Francis 44
Vasseur, Victor 97
Varle Map 145
Vann, James 50
Vance, David 78, 161, 229
Van Zandt, James 78, 279
Van Zandt, Martin 114

Index

Van Buren 152
Vaughn, Samuel 160
Vaughn, Mrs. Samuel. 160
Vandegrift, Lina 205
Vance, J. D. 336
Vaughn, Mr. 409
Villemont, Don Carlos 79, 97
Villemont, Matilda. 80
Villemont 148
Vigilance Committee........... 127
Vineyard 152
Votes for Delegate 55

Walter, Congressman 9
Wappenocke...... .... 41, 118
Walter, David 76
Washington........... 108, 110, 148
Watkins, Major Isaac.... 167, 228 to 235
Watkins, George C. . 194, 229, 233, 234
Watkins Family........... 229, 233
Wayland, Mrs. 114
Walker, Col. Alex. S., 47, 51, 61, 79, 101
  232, 252, 346.
Wallis, Perley........... 54, 55
Washington County Heroes 78
Warrell, Stephen 98
Washburn, Rev. Cephas, 141, 222 to 229
  276.
Wallace, George............. 144
Watson's Map................ 145
Washita..................... 148
Walnut Camp 151
War Eagle................... 152
Waters, Mrs. Samuel 161
Watkins Hotel............... 167
Ward, James 221
Washburn, Edward P....... 221, 225
Ward, John 160
Watkins, Dr. R. A............ 233
Watkins, Mary E 234
Walker, James 239
Watauga 243
Walker, vs. Hogan 252
Watkins, Elizabeth M......... 263
Watkins, Dr. Owen 263
Ware, Dr.................... 308
Walker, Isabelle............. 308
Walker, David 308
Ward, Zeb................... 324
Wayne, Mad Anthony 340
Wayland, Nevell 342
Watson, Zaccheus 352
Wayman 372
Walker, William 396
War Governor 403
Wells, Col. Jack 72
Wells, John 113
Wells, Henry C...............
Welden, John.............78, 279
Welch, Mary 114
Welborn, Major 134, 217
Wear, Doctor 144
Webb, Meredith 144
West, D. Porter 144
West, Jonathan.............. 160
Wetmore, Geo. C............. 161
Webb, Eliza 165
Wedding Feasts 162
Welch, Margaret 165
Welch, Robert 165
West Point Cadets 194
Weber, Walter 223
Weaver, J. F................ 226
Westland, Mark 288
Western Land Agency 289
Weaver, Tillman 372
White River P. O..........19, 108
White River 25, 26
White River Settlements 44
Who's Who of Arkansas 29
Wherry, J. A................ 130

White Oak Bayou 47
White, Thomas 219
White, Nancy 248
Whites 274
Whittaker, John 287
White, John 358
Whiteford, Baron 407
Wharton, Ann 378
Winters and Stillwell 26
Winters, Elisha 26, 45, 97
Winters, Gabriel 26, 27
Winter, Stilwell Grant....... 27
Wilson, John 101, 194
Wilson, Mary A.............. 194
Wilson, Dr. John 142, 144
Wilson, Mrs. John 160
Wilson, William 289
Wilson, Family ....348 to 370
Wilson, Richard 350
Wilson, James. 351, 352, 353, 354
Wilson, Joseph 352
Wilson, John 357
Wilson, Elizabeth 357
Wilson's School 359
Wilson, Barnett 361, 362, 363
Wilson, John T 361
Wilson, Benjamin F, 361, 362, 363, 364
  365
Wilson, Martha 361
Wilson, Lucy 362
Wilson, Robert B., 365, 366, 367, 368
  369, 370.
Wilson, Judson 365
Wilson, Martha A............ 366
Wilson, Matilda 366
Wilson, Katherine 366
Wilson, James E 366
Wilson, H. H................ 369
Wilson, Mary 369
Wilson, Frank C 369
Wilsonia 369
Wilson, R. J................ 144
Williams, Thomas 43
Williams, David 114
Wirt, Williams 80, 89, 90
Witter, Judge 84
Williams Camp Ground 143
Williams, Owen 144
Williams, Mrs. Alexander 160
Williams, Matilda........... 204
Williamson, John 277
Williams, B. D.............. 324
Williams, Sam W............. 325
Williams, Sally W........... 361
Williams, J. E.............. 368
Williams, McGhee 409
Woodruff, William E. Sr, 11, 12, 13, 14
  15, 16, 17, 22, 38, 51, 61, 68, 71, 77, 84
  90, 103, 108, 138, 196, 230, 233, 240
  259, 346.
Wolff, Michael 44
Wolf, Anthony............... 45
Wolsey, Cardinal 50, 184
Woodward, William 160
Womack, Larkin 210
Wolff, Jane 287
Woodward, William........... 288
Woodruff, Alden M........... 295
Wootten, Middleton L........ 409
Wright, Claiborne........... 280
Wycough, Mark 336
Wolf, Jacob 100

Yell, Col................70, 103
Yell County 143
Yellville................... 152
Yeomans, William F 126, 208

Zebulon 151
Zoeller, Christian E........ 347
Zollicoffer, Jacob C........ 372

www.ingramcontent.com/pod-product-compliance
Lightning Source LLC
Chambersburg PA
CBHW030104010526
44116CB00005B/88